Commonsense Justice

Commonsense Justice
Jurors' Notions of the Law

Norman J. Finkel

Harvard University Press
Cambridge, Massachusetts
London, England
1995

Library of Congress Cataloging-in-Publication Data

Finkel, Norman J.
    Commonsense justice: jurors' notions of the law / Norman J.
Finkel.
        p.   cm.
    Includes bibliographical references and index.
    ISBN 0-674-14670-0 (acid-free paper)
    1. Law—United States—Public opinion. 2. Juries—United States.
3. Justice. 4. Common sense. I. Title.
KF380.F56 1995
374.73'752—dc20
[347.307752]
    95-10328
      CIP

To my wife, Marilyn,
and in memory of my parents, Max and Dorothy,
for their uncommonly good common sense

Acknowledgments

In writing this book I have been helped along the way by many people, and I am deeply grateful to them all. To begin with, I would like to acknowledge the colleagues and students who have collaborated with me, for their work plays a foundational role here: Steve Sabat, Sol Fulero, Tony Pinizzotto, Chris Slobogin, Marsha Liss, Ginny Moran, Ray Shaw, Susie Bercaw, Juliann Koch, Sharon Handel, Kevin Duff, Kristen Meister, Deirdre Lightfoot, Stephanie Smith, Kevin Hughes, Marie Hurabiell, Steve Maloney, Monique Valbuena, Jen Groscup, Nancy DeCamara, and Janice Weiner. Other colleagues contributed via their own work, their helpful comments, and their general encouragement, which I appreciated more than words can convey: Dave Rosenhan, Ron Roesch, Kirk Heilbrun, Mike Saks, Bruce Sales, John Monahan, Mike Perlin, Irv Horowitz, Valerie Hans, Jim Ogloff, Caton Roberts, Alan Tomkins, Diane Follingstad, Richard Singer, and George Fletcher. To my colleagues here at Georgetown University, whose work and support I drew on, special thanks: Father Dan O'Connell, Rom Harré, Gerry Parrott, Jim Lamiell, Ali Moghaddam, Dan Robinson, Darlene Howard, Sandy Calvert, and Pete Wales. I am grateful to Georgetown University for a summer grant; to Harvard University Press and Angela von der Lippe, in particular, for believing in this book and backing it; and to the anonymous reviewers for providing encouragement, as well as direction that made the substance sounder. Special thanks go to Maria Ascher, who has pruned my purple prose and unmixed my metaphors, bringing greater clarity to the work and the author. Finally, I am indebted to my wife, Marilyn, who listened, reacted, and encouraged me to write about commonsense justice.

Contents

Introduction

At my university, and doubtless at others as well, there is a recurring, seasonal clash involving life and death, order and disorder—and lawn care. When winter suddenly turns to spring, students begin to mix and play on the grassy quad, walking where they will, though seldom on the designated paths. As they create their own paths, however, an annual nightmare starts for the Building and Grounds Department, for "Grounds" sees soil and mud beneath the vanishing grass, haunting and mocking their best efforts. When you work for Grounds, April is the cruelest month.

Alarm sets in among the Grounds crew, for graduation is to take place at the end of May on that very quad, and the arriving parents will no doubt expect to see a well-groomed green in return for the sizable green fees they have been paying. Reseeding efforts are launched, but they fail almost immediately, since the students pay no heed to those little "Keep Off" signs. Panic grows but the grass does not, and eventually Grounds lays new sod over the offending earth.

It is not so much the recurring cycle but its ending that is of greatest relevance here. In the seasonal standoff between students and Grounds, the cycle breaks when Grounds throws in the towel and lays down bricks along the lines the students have worn. The general question was stated by a character in John Barth's novel *The End of the Road*: Should paths be laid where people walk, or should people walk where paths are laid? And the issue of better lawns leads us by analogy to a question about better law: Should the law follow the path laid by community sentiment, or should the community follow the path the law has laid? This is the central question of this book. It involves the law, on the one hand; what

I call "commonsense justice," on the other; and the relationship between the two.

There are two types of "law." There is the type we are most familiar with, namely "black-letter law," the "law on the books." This is the law that legislators enact, the law that was set down by the Founding Fathers in the Constitution, the law that evolves through common-law cases and through appeals decisions. It is the law that law school students study, judges interpret, and jurisprudes analyze. But there is another law—although "law" may be too lofty or lowly a term to describe it: I call it "commonsense justice," and it reflects what ordinary people think is just and fair. It is embedded in the intuitive notions jurors bring with them to the jury box when judging both a defendant and the law. It is what ordinary people think the law ought to be.

These commonsense notions are at once legal, moral, and psychological. They provide the citizen on the street and the juror in the jury box with a theory of why people think, feel, and behave as they do, and why the law should find some defendants guilty and punishable and others not. Black-letter law also has its theories of human nature, culpability, and punishment. But there is mounting and persuasive evidence that the "law on the books" may be at odds with commonsense justice in many areas.

For example, ordinary citizens' views on privacy rights in general, and on the right to die in particular, appear notably discrepant from the law's strictures. Among the laws and rules governing "insanity," there is a hefty literature showing that jurors construe "insanity" in ways that do not conform to legal tests. In self-defense cases, particularly when a battered woman kills her spouse, we again see commonsense justice at odds with black-letter law: differences emerge as to whether a threat is "serious" and "imminent," and as to whether an "objective, reasonable man" or a more subjective perspective should dominate. And in the legal area of why some murders are reduced to manslaughter, we find a complex legal theory of human nature that defines when a provocation is sufficient to ignite emotions and passions to such a degree that reasonable people might not think but strike. Here, too, the psychological theory appears to diverge from jurors' views, which give history, context, and subjectivity a much greater role. All of this, and much more, leads us to an idea of commonsense justice and to problematic discrepancies with the law.

But immediately we can raise an objection to the notion of commonsense justice—one that challenges either the existence of such justice, or the claim that it relates to, affects, and even directs the law. Stated in the form of a question, the objection is: Why study commonsense justice (if it even exists) when the law is *independent* of community sentiment and should remain so? This view claims that the law is different from ordinary views of justice and that legal reasoning ought to remain hermetically sealed from common contaminants. Justice Antonin Scalia twice raised this "independence" objection during the Supreme Court's spring 1992 term. In his dissent in the death penalty case of *Georgia v. McCollum*, he took the Court to task for basing its decision on community sentiment and societal harmony. And in the abortion decision of *Planned Parenthood of Southeastern Pennsylvania v. Casey*, Scalia was "appalled" by the fact that the Court would be "strongly influenced . . . by the substantial and continuing public opposition the decision has generated." Turning from his brethren to the citizens, he stated, "How upsetting it is, that so many of our citizens . . . think that we Justices should properly take into account their views, as though we were engaged not in ascertaining an objective law but in determining some kind of social consensus."

This objection must be answered. In defense of commonsense justice, I offer three counterpoints to the "independence" position, according to which judges should retire from the realm of community to their cloistered chambers, engage in something called "legal reasoning," and derive an objective body of law. First, and most simply, judges cannot do this. We don't have to be Freudians to realize that judges, like ordinary citizens, cannot dissociate and compartmentalize their history and the community's influences merely by closing a door and opening a law book. As the great American jurist Oliver Wendell Holmes Jr. said, "The felt necessities of the time, the prevalent moral and political theories, intuitions of public policy, avowed or unconscious, even the prejudices which judges share with their fellow-men, have had a good deal more to do than the syllogism in determining the rules by which men should be governed."[1] Holmes's point about judges is even more apt for legislators: those who legislate with complete independence are likely to have their tenure abruptly halted on election day. Community sentiment, then, is present in chambers, in Congress, and in the mind, whether it is avowed or unconscious, and the ablest and most experienced judges and legislators use these intuitions and views of public policy—since, as Holmes said, they "know too much to sacrifice good sense to a syllogism."[2]

The second point against the "independence" position notes that there are certain areas of law where the Supreme Court has given "community sentiment" a central if not determinative role. The Eighth Amendment is one such area. Most citizens clearly know the phrase "cruel and unusual punishment," but clarity ends when we ask, "What does it mean?" An illustration may help. On May 5, 1994, an American teenager, Michael Fay, was caned by the authorities in Singapore for vandalism. In the weeks prior to his ordeal, the topic was hot in the United States. Many people called the punishment "cruel and unusual"; the U.S. trade representative, the secretary of state, and even the president weighed in on that side. That different countries and cultures might have different views on whether a punishment is cruel and unusual is interesting, if unsurprising. But the point I wish to make is that the same punishment, had it been inflicted in the United States in the nineteenth century, would not have raised such heat, let alone charges that it was cruel and unusual.

The Supreme Court has understood this and has hinged the meaning of the phrase "cruel and unusual punishment" to the "community's evolving standards of decency," realizing that as society becomes more enlightened, the meaning of the phrase will change. In its efforts to take into account the nonstatic nature of "cruel and unusual punishment," the Court has turned increasingly to objective ways of gauging community sentiment, in order to determine if a certain punishment for a crime is disproportionate *in the eyes of the community*. Ironically, perhaps, Justice Scalia leads the push for a solely objective determination of community sentiment; he would like to see justices refrain from inserting their own views and making "philosopher-king" decisions.[3]

Thus, the first counterpoint notes that community sentiment does affect—consciously or unconsciously—judges' decisionmaking processes, and the second counterpoint notes that certain substantive areas of the law require judges to take community sentiment into account. The third counterpoint brings the community into the law in an even more direct way. The jury—often referred to as the "conscience of the community"—brings the community's judgment to bear on the moral blameworthiness of the defendant. Beyond finding the facts, jurors sometimes reconstrue the law, and at other times even decide on the law. When jurors reconstrue the judge's instructions, whether these are insanity instructions, self-defense instructions, or the definition of "malice" or "provocation," jurors are bringing their own interpretations and sense of justice into play. And when they decide that a law is unfair, or that a punishment is excessive, or that a punishment does not fit a particular defendant, juries have, on occasion, nullified the law. They are, clearly, implementing common-sense justice: registering a "no confidence" vote, refusing to follow the path the law has laid down.

Those who are critical of this practice, which is known as *jury nullification,* see it as a form of anarchy. If juries used their power to nullify with any significant frequency, or reconstrued the law according to their whim, disparate verdicts and unequal justice would result, since laws for all would be applied only to some. Few would find such an outcome comforting. But to ignore or simply condemn jury nullification is to disregard the truth of a prediction made by Roscoe Pound, who asserted that in "all cases of divergence between the standard of the common law and the standard of the public, it goes without saying that the latter will prevail in the end."[4] If we take an inquiring rather than a critical view of jurors, we may see nullification as the jury's desire not to defeat the law but (in George Fletcher's terms) "to perfect and complete the law." If we learn to "read" what jurors are saying about the law, we may come to see that they are showing us a new path—one that, to their minds, is laid on more just grounds.

Commonsense justice and its relation to black-letter law are the subject of this book. In picking the term "commonsense," which is already rife with meanings, I am likely to cause misunderstandings unless I make the ground clear. When I use the noun "common sense," I do not mean folkish knowledge, often propounded in the form of a cliché, which is taken as a truism until it runs smack into another folksy dictum that contradicts it. And when I apply the adjective "commonsense" to justice, I mean something much deeper, more specific, and far less hackneyed.

The words have been used in a variety of ways. Michael Perlin, for instance, writes about "ordinary common sense," by which he means prereflexive, often unconscious thinking, replete with myths, stereotypes, and simplistic heuristics, and quite immune to facts. This unflattering kind of common sense, which Perlin finds among lawmakers and justices in their utterances about insanity, might well be found in the populace as well. But, again, this is not what I mean, for I believe that commonsense justice is more deliberative and conscious, and quite sensitive to facts and to foundational issues of justice.

Still another form of common sense is associated with public opinion poll results. When politicians take the pulse of the community through opinion polls, they are sampling the common sense of the people across specific issues (or so it is said). These results are often interpreted as the "will of the majority." But Ronald Dworkin, in his book *Law's Empire*, makes a useful distinction between majoritarian "fairness" (the will of the majority) and "justice" (which concerns whether decisions "secure a morally defensible outcome"). "Justice," in Dworkin's terms—or "commonsense justice," in my terms—is different from mere majoritarian sentiment as expressed in a poll. Polling questions, which typically are broadly framed and admit restricted responses, are likely to yield answers that are significantly different from the ones jurors would give when confronted by a live defendant, and when given specific facts and actual legal instructions. If we wish to elicit people's deepest, deliberative sense of justice—their "morally defensible outcome"—then we must turn from polls to a different methodology, in which we give people "real life" cases, with specifics, and find out what verdicts and sentences they would render, and why.

Research into juror and jury decisions has progressed and proliferated over the last quarter-century. When Kalven and Zeisel published their seminal work *The American Jury,* readers got an peek into the black box of the jury room. But is was an *indirect* peek, for the bulk of Kalven and Zeisel's data came not from jurors but from judges, who *speculated* about why juries did what they did. Now, more than twenty-five years later, we have better methods and richer findings about juries and jurors, and about the principles of justice they hold dear.

In Search of
Community Sentiment

1

For politicians, the spring of 1992 was a winter of discontent. A record number of representatives and senators were voluntarily giving up the advantages of incumbency and just saying, "No more." What could explain that season's lemming-like rush to retirement? Pundits and "pols" in Washington offered their own interpretations.

A columnist writing in the *Washington Post* put forward one hypothesis.[1] "From outside the Beltway, the complaint is loud, clear and angry: Congress has lost touch with the American people and fallen under the spell of powerful interest groups." This interpretation claims that politicians are failing to read and to follow the community's sentiments. But then the writer offers a second view. "From inside the Beltway, even on Capitol Hill, the complaint is the opposite but just as grave: Congress has become a 'hyper weather vane,' spinning feverishly in response to every poll that comes along, as Sen. Richard G. Lugar (R-Ind.) describes it . . . 'We're too much in touch,' says Sen. Warren B. Rudman (R-N.H.),"[2] one of the voluntary retirees. When we examine these two interpretations, three things stand out. First, when juxtaposed, they appear to contradict each other; second, both cite and centrally situate "community sentiment," the subject of this chapter; and third, each view ultimately fails to answer the riddle.

If the "outside the Beltway" view has some merit, then it raises a puzzling question: In this age of instant communication, in which polling services, networks, and newspapers routinely take "the pulse of community" and broadcast it, how can a politician be out of touch? And if the "inside the Beltway" view has some merit, then the same puzzling question recurs: How is it possible to miss the community's sentiment? To answer this question, and to deepen our understanding of "community sentiment," let's turn to a new set of hypotheses.

One hypothesis readily at hand is that the polls are at fault. Although such a notion easily reconciles outsider and insider explanations, its simplicity just does not fit certain polling facts. We know, for example, that the science of polling has come a long way since the day "Dewey Wins!" was mistakenly proclaimed in the headlines. Methods of sampling (that is, obtaining a representative cross-section of the population) have improved, and margins of error for predictions have generally narrowed. So, on election night, when television networks confidently announce the winners—often, seemingly, within a minute after the voting booths close—they seldom have to offer a retraction. Networks stand by their polls because their polls usually stand up.

This is not to say that there are not bad polls, or even pseudo-polls that masquerade as polls. For example, Ross Perot planned a "national referendum" in which people would be invited to call in or mail in their responses to polling questions. The American Association for Public Opinion Research rightly labeled this "an unreliable and potentially misleading gauge of public opinion, . . . because the people who participate frequently hold very different views from the public as a whole."[3] Putting aside such pseudo-polls, and even granting that a few polls are done badly, the majority are not. Thus, the broad "blame the poll" hypothesis neither covers nor accounts for the fact that congressmen appear to be so off the mark in regard to community sentiment.

A second hypothesis argues that polls may be picking up *transitory* rather than stable sentiment. Transitory sentiment may be the end result of what columnist Ellen Goodman called "instant analysis," a disquieting trend in which "newspapers that once tried to beat each other with stories are now as likely to compete with analysis." This "instant opinion," she points out, is an oxymoron. "You don't get real opinions in an instant. You get reactions. A reaction is something that can come from the knee. Hit it, and it jerks. An opinion is something that best comes from the head. Thinking is—alas—a much slower process."[4]

The confusion between reaction and opinion, between what is transitory and what is stable, is illustrated in polls on the insanity defense. An ABC News poll[5] conducted after John Hinckley Jr. was found not guilty by reason of insanity reported "that three out of every four Americans surveyed felt justice had not been done in the Hinckley case."[6] But the verdict on Hinckley had been rendered June 21, 1982, and the poll had been taken only one day later, when passions were most inflamed. In such a climate, poll results may be seriously inflated. If sentiments, like winds, shift in direction and strength with time and circumstance, weather vane readings may be picking up momentary gusts, having a meaning confined only to the moment.

From other polls on the insanity defense, a third hypothesis emerges. Polls conducted in the mid-1980s indicated widespread animosity to the insanity defense: most respondents believed that the defense was unfair, a loophole greatly in need of revision; they had little confidence in psychiatric testimony proffered at trial.[7] One poll found that 49 percent of respondents favored (or strongly favored) abolishing the insanity defense and 95 percent favored reforming the defense—sentiments that are certainly negative.[8] These beliefs were echoed by senators and representatives during congressional hearings in the wake of the Hinckley case.[9] Many in Congress confidently asserted that their constituency wanted drastic change—wanted either to abolish the defense or to severely restrict it. Although representatives and senators debated which restrictive direction to take, there was general agreement that the community's sentiment was *uniformly negative.*

But consider these results from the poll just cited: 77 percent also agreed (or strongly agreed) that the insanity defense was justified, and 64 percent agreed that the defense was necessary—sentiments that are far more positive. How are we to interpret these conflicting results? The initial, uniformly negative picture dissolves into contradictions and complexities. And this is the third hypothesis: that community sentiment may be both complex and contradictory, such that polls may fail to reveal its depth and crosscurrents. If this is so, politicians, legislators, and Supreme Court justices may be getting superficial and simplistic readings.

The fourth hypothesis, in contrast, claims that the responding public may be *ignorant* about the matters at hand. Public ignorance seems evident in polls on the insanity defense[10]—for example, in cases where researchers have concluded that "the public is badly informed about the insanity defense."[11] This "ignorance hypothesis" was advanced by Justice Thurgood Marshall in connection with opinion on the death penalty. Despite scores of polls showing public support for the death penalty, polls unambiguous enough "to convince even the biggest skeptic,"[12] Justice Marshall remained a doubter. Even the Gallup organization's longest-standing survey on death penalty sentiment—showing that since the early 1970s support for the death penalty has steadily risen, so that "today over three-quarters of the American public say that they favor the use of capital punishment for persons convicted of first degree murder"[13]—did not convince Justice Marshall.

In the face of these seemingly unassailable statistics, the justice put forth what came to be known as "the Marshall hypothesis," which asserts that the public's support for the death penalty is based on lack of knowledge; if Americans were fully informed, they would find the punishment "shocking, unjust and unacceptable" and would conclude that it "is immoral and therefore unconstitutional."[14] But is Marshall merely one of those skeptics and abolitionists who will steadfastly hold to a view in spite of the evidence, or is there some evidence to back up his theory?

First, the Marshall hypothesis is really two separate hypotheses: the first claims that the polling results reflect the community's ignorance; the second asserts that correct information will change attitudes (and subsequent polling results). In a number of studies testing the Marshall hypothesis,[15] researchers have found support for the ignorance claim, but only limited-to-little support for the "attitude-changing effect" of correct information.

Both results are disturbing. If sentiments are resistant to the "reality" of correct information, then "sentiment" may be simply a more refined term for bias or prejudice. If this indeed is the true nature of what we are calling "sentiment," then why should justices assiduously track it, and why should legislators spin like hyper weather vanes in pursuit of it? More important, why should they follow it? Regarding the ignorance hypothesis, for which there is much more support, the question remains the same: Even if sentiment is based on benign ignorance rather than on baser prejudices, why follow it?

The "ignorance hypothesis" attributes the ignorance to the respondents, the community. But a fifth hypothesis inverts the situation, attributing the ignorance to those who read and interpret polls. If we "read" polling results in isolation, apart from a fuller context of attitudes and beliefs, and if we do not seek answers to many relevant and related questions, a spurious picture may emerge. Such "a spuriousness theory of expressed death penalty support" was put forth by William Bowers:

> Consider the possibility that we all, including the Court, have misinterpreted the polls. Perhaps the expressed support they reflect is not a deep-seated or strongly held commitment to capital punishment but actually a reflection of the public's desire for a genuinely harsh but meaningful punishment for convicted murderers. This spuriousness theory is built on three specific hypotheses. The first, and most important, of these is that (1) people will abandon the death penalty when presented with a genuinely harsh and meaningful alternative. This central claim is substantiated by two subordinate hypotheses, which I also seek to confirm: (2) people see funda-

mental shortcomings in the death penalty as a punishment, and (3) they accept the death penalty because they believe the currently available alternatives are insufficiently harsh or meaningful.[16]

In sum, there are at least five possible causes for faulty poll readings: (1) the poll was done poorly; (2) the poll picked up transitory reactions rather than more thoughtful sentiment; (3) the poll failed to pick up complex and contradictory sentiment; (4) the poll picked up sentiment founded on ignorance; and (5) the ignorance lies with us, as we pay insufficient attention to the context and misinterpret the results in some spurious way. But there is a sixth possible cause—namely, that polls, at a very basic level, may be asking the wrong question.

Your telephone rings. The caller is a researcher conducting a poll. Would you be willing to answer a few questions? You decide to play. Question number one: "Are you in favor of capital punishment?" Question number two: "Are you in favor of the insanity defense?" But I believe we should query the underlying effects of this method. What images, examples, pictures, prototypes, or exemplars come into mind for the respondent? Does the respondent think of a Ted Bundy or a John Wayne Gacy, to name two highly publicized serial killers? Does the respondent think of a Charles Manson or Richard Speck or some other highly publicized mass murderer? And does John Hinckley Jr. or Jeffrey Dahmer come to mind in response to the insanity question? The point here is that we do not know what stimulus comes to mind for the subject, and hence what the subject is responding to.

Clearly, this sort of polling question presents an "overly general stimulus,"[17] which, like a Rorschach card, allows the respondent to think of a more definite stimulus that then serves as a basis for his or her response. Subjects are likely to project what is most accessible and salient; this may be some recent, vivid exemplar featured prominently in newspaper headlines and on television.[18] And it is the stimulus that *they* bring to mind— not the objective stimulus the interviewer gives—which is going to determine their answer.

"Analysis of the media's coverage of crime, law, and justice shows that the media mirror does not accurately reflect reality."[19] We know that exemplars featured in the news are not representative of the average murderer or insanity defendant. They do not share the essential or typical features of the category. Although the subject may see them as typical,[20] they are actually extraordinary instances.

What happens when the polling questioner, aware that subjects may easily free associate from "death penalty" to extraordinary exemplars, asks a more precise question instead of a general death penalty query? What happens to death penalty support if the stimulus question delimits the target more precisely? The answer is that death penalty support typically drops; moreover, the support that formerly appeared uniform shows great variability depending on the target. In one study, for example, more than 75 percent of respondents thought the death penalty was appropriate for serial killers of children and for killers of families, but less than 20 percent supported the death penalty for spouse murderers and rapists.[21] If we move from the rare serial killer to the commonplace felony-murderer, support for the death penalty withers dramatically. "Supplementary homicide reports" compiled by the Federal Bureau of Investigation reveal that the "great majority of capital sentences are meted out to those who have committed felony murder, murder committed during the course of another serious felony."[22] Yet in experimental tests of felony-murder scenarios involving a triggerman and accomplices, death penalty support for the triggerman was consistently under 20 percent, and for accomplice felony-murderers (getaway drivers, lookouts, sidekicks), who did not pull the trigger, the figures on average were well under 10 percent, sometimes even approaching zero.[23]

Thus, asking the right question is one way to get a more accurate and specific reading of sentiment. Even a single word in a question can make a significant difference, as a *New York Times*–CBS News poll[24] discovered. The poll asked respondents a question about the level of spending for "assistance to the poor"; 13 percent said it was too high, while 64 percent said it was too low. When the question was asked again with a supposed synonym, "welfare," replacing "assistance to the poor," the results were far from synonymous: 44 percent of the respondents now said the level of spending was too high, whereas only 23 percent said it was too low. Obviously the word "welfare" had far more negative connotations for many of the subjects than did the phrase "assistance to the poor." But this is the point: that between the words of the question and the responses that are given, subjects interpose meaning.

So the wording of a question, and even a particular word, can make a world of difference. But providing better options for responding also affects the results. For example, the standard format for the death penalty question gives respondents a two-way choice: Are they in favor or opposed? When the death penalty question was asked in the standard way to a Georgia sample[25] and a Virginia sample,[26] support for the death penalty was 75 percent and 64 percent, respectively. But when the researchers qualified the question with an alternative (life imprisonment for the defendant, parole impossible for twenty-five years, a restitution program for the victim), support for the death penalty dropped to 48 percent in the Georgia sample and 27 percent in the Virginia sample. When the response set is widened, and when the *strength* of sentiment is gauged (in addition to its direction), we find that "support for the death penalty is not nearly as deep as it is broad."[27]

The above study clearly lends validity to the first hypothesis—that inaccurate readings of sentiment result from poorly conceived polls. A poll whose questions are simplistic, overly broad, and too few in number is likely to produce a faulty reading. It will also be unlikely to register the range, depth, and subtlety of subjects' discriminations, because their responses are restricted. The above study also reveals the outlines of the sixth hypothesis—dubbed the "distortion" hypothesis—which claims that sentiment is distorted because people invoke exemplars, cases that are atypical rather than typical. This is not so much ignorance as it is misperception.

The distortion hypothesis, however, runs into an immediate challenge. We might concede that distortions are likely in rare cases that arouse strong emotion, such as those involving the death penalty or insanity, but argue that distortions would not occur in ordinary cases. Yet in a clever series of studies, Stalans and Diamond found that distortion occurs even in run-of-the-mill burglary cases.[28]

One of their samples consisted of Illinois adults who rode the Joliet-to-Chicago train line. Of these, 67 percent believed that judges were too lenient in their sentencing of burglary offenders. Among the people in their other sample, which was drawn from Illinois residents selected for jury duty, 62 percent believed that judges were too lenient in such burglary cases. However, when all of these subjects were given the chance to "play the judge" and sentence a typical burglary case, they gave sentences that were less severe than the minimum sentence a judge would have had to impose. In explaining this paradoxical finding, the researchers focus on misperception, noting that most laypersons perceive the characteristics of the burglar and the act of burglary as being more threatening than they are in the typical case: "Laypersons often think of burglars as weapon-carrying ransackers of homes rather than the more common unarmed intruders who leave few signs that they entered apart from the absence of a few valuable possessions."[29]

The question then arises: Where do people get their misperceptions? People may recall information reported in the mass media, perhaps about a sensational case, a repeat offender, or an incident in which severe harm was done; they may recall past conversations; or they may draw from direct experience. The tendency to bring to mind what is most easily recalled is known as *accessibility bias.* It is called a "bias" because what is most accessible is not necessarily an accurate reflection of what is. There is also a process in which respondents actually *create* images of criminals and criminal events—a process known as the *simulation heuristic.*[30] Here again, nonrepresentative exemplars intrude. Using either the accessibility bias or the simulation heuristic, or both, subjects may bring to mind an *atypical* offender. In the study just cited, the subjects believed that their images were typical and veridical, but these images turned out to be inconsistent with actual burglary cases that routinely appear before the court.

It is quite clear that most people are not sitting at home reading official statistics on crime. The public is far more likely to be influenced by what it reads in newspapers and what it sees on television news. Crimes are staples in the news. As a general rule, the more outrageous, the more the coverage. Given the coverage that crime receives, it is not surprising that recent surveys show that most Americans believe the crime rate rose during the 1980s, when in fact the statistical rate declined.[31] And the news media per se are not solely responsible for influencing sentiment, since politicians get media time, and when they do, a favorite topic of campaign rhetoric is crime and criminals and the lenient sentences they receive. Perhaps some people assume that everything politicians say is true. To take one illustration, "Dianne Feinstein, former mayor of San Francisco and gubernatorial candidate, made the following unfounded remark in support of the death penalty: 'You can't expect somebody to be deterred from committing murder if they know that they will only serve four or five years.'"[32] Where the alarming but erroneous "four or five years" came from is anyone's guess. What the pols glean from the polls may be in part distorted by their own biases.

Thus, we have a number of hypotheses as to why the pols and the polls are not in sync. Some hypotheses focus primarily on the poll, placing the blame on poor polling questions, inadequate response choices, bad timing of the poll, insufficiently detailed questions, transitory reactions that pass for sentiment, or an inability to tap complex and contradictory sentiment. Other hypotheses focus primarily on the respondents, asserting that their sentiments may be the result of ignorance and distortion. And still another hypothesis centers on the poll readers, who may formulate spurious interpretations because they fail to take context into account.

In searching for community sentiment, we can't help having grave doubts about the methods used in polling. A polling question can be the wrong question, a bad question, or an overly simplistic question. The responses permitted by the question may unduly restrict or distort the readings, because they may not allow for the fullest expression of the nuances and strength of sentiment. Poor timing of a poll may pick up a flow of sentiment that ebbs quickly. In skimming sentiment, we may miss the undercurrents and crosscurrents. And the sentiments we hear may be all noise and nonsense—nothing more than ignorance or the distortion of atypical exemplars.

Why Heed Sentiment at All?

With these hypotheses all pointing to flawed polling results, we are left with two questions, one narrow, the other broad, but both of great consequence. The first and narrower question is dubbed the "Marshall question." Put in blunt form, it is this: If "substantial segments of the public are ill-informed or completely ignorant about some of the most elementary and important political and social questions,"[33] then why should justices or legislators be moved to write law, change law, or declare laws constitutional or unconstitutional based on community sentiment?[34] To phrase it another way, why not reject opinion poll data entirely, if they are inevitably founded on ignorance, distortion, and transitory sentiment? Perhaps legislators and Supreme Court justices should simply cease reading the weather vanes, if the readings have no validity.

This would be faulty logic, I believe. It is one thing to conclude that some polling questions are picking up ignorant, distorted, transient, and shallow sentiments, and quite another to conclude that sentiments lack all substance and should be ignored entirely. That would be like claiming, after examining a defective thermometer, that there is no temperature. It has yet to be proved that all sentiment is mere idiocy, inconsequential babblings of the uninformed. As our discussion has shown, flawed questions may be at least as much to blame as flawed sentiments. And in our review of the possible causes of faulty readings, we've seen ways of asking better questions, and getting better readings. No, the case for sentiment's lacking all substance has not been made, and hence the conclusion that politicians and justices should ignore sentiment does not follow. At this point, we must reject the conclusion implicit in the Marshall question.

But now we come to a second, even broader question, which is dubbed the "Scalia question." Why shouldn't we ignore sentiment entirely even if it *does* have substance? Put another way, why should we care about community sentiment at all? There is a ready answer for legislators, but not so for justices. Legislators who routinely ignore their constituents' sentiments are likely to have their terms shortened on election day. The mournful congressmen now taking their lemming-like leave from Washington do so while clutching the latest polls in their hands. But many judges never face the electorate, and Supreme Court justices, appointed for life, would seem to be immune from the consequences of community sentiment. Why should they take any notice of it?

Oliver Wendell Holmes Jr. wrote in *The Common Law* that the "first requirement of a sound body of law is, that it should correspond with the actual feelings and demands of the community."[35] Why this is so is not yet clear. And while many a justice has echoed Holmes's sentiment, all we know at this point is that justices seem disinclined to drop their weather vanes just yet. But why not?

To answer this question, let's go back to 1992. As spring was turning to summer and things in Washington were heating up, the Supreme Court's term reached its climax. By far the most heated, controversial, and divisive case of the twentieth century has been *Roe v. Wade.*[36] In 1992, nineteen years after the case had been decided, demonstrations in front of abortion clinics and the Supreme Court were still a ritual on the American moral and political landscape, and divisions in the community were as deep as ever. Court watchers on both sides of the issue were anticipating that the new Court, with its recent Reagan and Bush appointees, would overturn *Roe*. But before the justices tackled that issue, they took up their seasonal death penalty cases. In *Georgia v. McCollum*[37] the Scalia question was raised, and an answer was proposed.

The *McCollum* case involved the issue of whether the defense may use its peremptory challenges during jury selection *(voir dire)* to exclude members of a given race based on their race. In a 1986 decision, *Batson v. Kentucky,*[38] the Court had ruled that the State may not engage in purposeful racial discrimination in the exercise of peremptory challenges. Many anticipated that the Court would simply even up the score, so to speak, by placing the same restriction on both defense and prosecution. But in Justice Harry Blackmun's majority opinion, community opinion moved front and center. The Court stated:

> The need for public confidence is especially high in cases involving race-related crimes. In such cases, emotions in the affected community will inevitably be heated and volatile. Public confidence in the integrity of the criminal justice system is essential for preserving community peace in trials involving race-related crimes . . .
>
> Be it at the hands of the State or the defense, if a court allows jurors to be excluded because of group bias, it is a willing participant in a scheme that could only undermine the very foundation of our system of justice [and] our citizens' confidence in it. Just as pub-

lic confidence in criminal justice is undermined by a conviction in a trial where racial discrimination has occurred in jury selection, so is public confidence undermined where a defendant, assisted by racially discriminatory peremptory strikes, obtains an acquittal.

The fact . . . harms . . . jurors and the community.

In the Court's underlying concern, we hear the echoes of Holmes. If citizens lose confidence, if community sentiment turns cynical about justice and fair trials, then the law and the criminal-justice system are threatened.

But in a terse dissent, Justice Scalia found this sort of reasoning and decision to be in error. Making community sentiment and harmony the basis of decisions—"the interest of promoting the supposedly greater good of race relations in the society as a whole (make no mistake that that is what underlies all of this)"—is the wrong way to resolve constitutional issues. It should not matter whether the community is pleased or upset over a decision.

The battle over sentiment's place in Supreme Court decisionmaking intensified when *Planned Parenthood of Southeastern Pennsylvania v. Casey* came to bat.[39] But despite many people's fears, the Court did not overrule *Roe*. And the plurality opinion, coauthored by Justices Sandra Day O'Connor, Anthony Kennedy, and David Souter, hints that community sentiment played a significant part. "Our analysis would not be complete . . . without explaining why overruling *Roe*'s central holding would not only reach an unjustifiable result under principles of stare decisis, but would seriously weaken the Court's capacity to exercise the judicial power and to function as the Supreme Court of a Nation dedicated to the rule of law." Something beyond the principle of letting past decisions stand was at play, and they gave a Holmesian hint that a decision inconsistent with community sentiment would undermine the Court's capacity and power. If such undermining were to take place, the Court might no longer be perceived as representing the nation or upholding the rule of law. In the following quotation from the plurality, the justices spell out their concern even more clearly: "Whether or not a new social consensus is developing on that issue, its divisiveness is no less today than in 1973, and pressure to overrule the decision, like pressure to retain it, has grown only more intense. A decision to overrule *Roe*'s essential holding under the existing circumstances would address error, if error there was, at the cost of both profound and unnecessary damage to the Court's legitimacy, and to the Nation's commitment to the rule of law." Here the justices not only make the link explicit, but endorse community sentiment's vital role.

For a decision at odds with sentiment would profoundly damage the Court's legitimacy, and if the Court's "rule of law" departs from the people's sense of what the law ought to be, Law itself is undermined. To get the opposite opinion—that the link ought to be severed and that decisions should not be based on public opinion at all—let's look at Justice Scalia's stinging dissent.

> I cannot agree with, indeed I am appalled by, the Court's suggestion that the decision whether to stand by an erroneous constitutional decision must be strongly influenced—*against* overruling, no less—by the substantial and continuing public opposition the decision has generated. The Court's judgment that any other course would "subvert the Court's legitimacy" must be another consequence of reading the error-filled history book that described the deeply divided country brought together by *Roe* . . .
>
> But whether it would "subvert the Court's legitimacy" or not, the notion that we would decide a case differently from the way we otherwise would have in order to show that we can stand firm against public disapproval is frightening . . .
>
> In truth, I am as distressed as the Court is . . . about the "political pressure" directed to the Court: the marches, the mail, the protests aimed at inducing us to change our opinions. How upsetting it is, that so many of our citizens . . . think that we Justices should properly take into account their views, as though we were engaged not in ascertaining an objective law but in determining some kind of social consensus.

Scalia's rejection of community sentiment and of the practice of reading weather vanes appears unequivocal. Presumably, it would not matter to Scalia that the day after the decision in *Planned Parenthood*, newspapers reported that public opinion poll results seemed to support the Court's decision. As one writer put it, "The Supreme Court, in theory the government's least political branch, closely mirrored public opinion polls in its decision on abortion."[40] Although plurality justices might note those polls with satisfaction, Scalia would find them irrelevant, for on this playing field he leaves no place for such public sentiment. But how he would go about "ascertaining an objective law" is not yet clear. In Chapter 5 we will take up the matter of "objective law," and of whether that "entity" is real or chimeric. But in the face of Scalia's challenge—a challenge to the claim that sentiment has a role *at all*—we must offer a reply.

The search for sentiment must continue, I believe, because acknowledging sentiment, in its deepest sense, is *foundational* for the continued functioning of government and for a society in which its laws are respected and obeyed. This, I believe, underlies what the plurality in *Planned Parenthood* was trying to articulate. It is essential, then, that legislators and judges understand public sentiment, so that they can govern and adjudicate fairly and justly. Sentiment serves to justify and support the law of the land, and when the law follows the path laid down by community sentiment, it is both grounded and supported. As Holmes recognized, the law "draws its vivifying juices" in part from the community's moral, social, and psychological sense of what is fair and just,[41] and if the law were not grounded in, and consistent with, community sentiment, people might well perceive that law to be unsound, and unworthy of respect.

Citizens can express their discontent in a more ominous way than through poll responses: the jury—"the conscience of the community," as it has been called—may *nullify* the law by reaching a verdict of not guilty, despite persuasive evidence of guilt. Nullification may produce a "wildcat operation"[42] in the jury room and "wild justice"[43] in the streets. Thus, for positive and negative reasons, continuing to take the pulse of the community reflects a faith that there is a pulse worth taking, and a conviction that law's life and legitimacy are tied to it.

The sentiment we are after is more enduring than a momentary feeling and more consequential than a surface opinion. It is deeper than what columnist Michael Kinsley calls "today's fashionable pseudo-populism, which holds that all wisdom lies with ordinary citizens, who are rightly outraged at all those out-of-touch, inside-the-Beltway cultural elitists etc. etc."[44] Rooted in substantive stuff, this deeper sentiment conveys commonsense justice—what ordinary people believe is right, fair, and just.

Law's Empire

In *Law's Empire,* Ronald Dworkin identifies three virtues of a political and legal system: fairness, justice, and procedural due process. "Fairness" refers to a "fair political structure."[45] When we elect representatives by majority rule, and when we enact laws by majority vote, we may speak of the system's being fair, or majoritarian. The phrase "the rule of the majority" conveys the sense that, all other things being equal, the will of the majority should prevail.

"Justice" refers to a "just distribution of resources and opportunities."[46] The focus here is on decisions reached and on whether those decisions "secure a morally defensible outcome."[47] When judges rule on the constitutionality of laws, they are often deciding whether or not such laws are just.

The third virtue, which Dworkin calls "procedural due process," refers to another type of fairness—one that involves "an equitable process of enforcing . . . rules and regulations."[48] This is what most adults refer to when they say "I'm an American citizen; I've got rights!"[49] And this is what children may "act out" when they angrily stomp off to their room after being punished by a parent for some infraction. They may react angrily not because they deny guilt, which would be a "justice" claim, but because they did not get their "day in court"—that is, because the procedures of adjudication and punishment were not fair. This is a claim of procedural due process.

Dworkin's three virtues help us assess the nature and contours of commonsense justice, and the difficulties in determining its sources. To avoid confusion between his two types of fairness, let's call his three virtues "majoritarianism," "justice," and "fairness," where the last term stands for the fairness of procedural due process. Commonsense justice is rooted in all three virtues, though all the roots do not run equally deep. Moreover, commonsense justice sometimes manifests itself in contradictory ways, and determining the deepest root will take a Herculean effort.

Take, for example, a situation in which majoritarianism, expressed in a statute enacted by the majority's elected representatives, appears to conflict with justice, as expressed in the Constitution. Put another way, the conflict here is between two differing expressions of community sentiment, or two roots of commonsense justice. Alexander Hamilton took up this issue in *The Federalist Papers*,[50] arguing that no legislative act contrary to the Constitution could be valid, because that would make "the representatives of the people . . . superior to the people themselves."[51] Note his two uses of "people," one linked to majoritarianism and the other to justice; and note which of them he gives priority. To Hamilton, the Constitution of "we the people" reflects our embodiment of justice more directly than a statute that is an indirect reflection of the people's "agents." Hamilton was quite aware that shallower sentiments—"a momentary inclination [that] happens to lay hold of a majority,"[52] or sentiments that lay hold of a judge—may conflict with the deeper sentiments embodied in the Constitution. For Hamilton, the Constitution stands superior to either judicial or legislative sentiment.

For a second example of how the roots of justice may conflict, let's go back to Justice Scalia's challenge to some of his brethren over the place of community sentiment in Supreme Court decisionmaking. The argument appears to focus on whether the Court ought to follow the path laid by community sentiment. Yet the issue may be not whether the Court should follow sentiment but *which* type of sentiment it should follow. If Scalia's "ascertaining an objective law" means something like determining what the Framers of the Constitution meant by "we the people," or what the current "we the people" means, then the conflict may be between majoritarian and justice sentiments, or between two differing "readings" of sentiments—poll results and street demonstrations, on the one hand, and some yet unspecified "objective" gauge, on the other.

Dworkin's three strands of justice may not only conflict, but may support one another in ways that are not always obvious. Take, for example, Justice Blackmun's concern in *McCollum* and the plurality's concern in *Planned Parenthood*. Blackmun believed that "public confidence . . . is essential for preserving community peace."[53] He was concerned that people should accept and comply with the Court's decision, for if they do not, law and justice are threatened. The plurality in *Planned Parenthood* also worried that a decision not grounded in community sentiment would "weaken the Court's capacity to function as the Supreme Court" and would cause "profound and unnecessary damage to the Court's legitimacy."[54]

But were these justices worrying too much about loss of legitimacy and lack of acceptance? After all, many a Court decision in the past two hundred years has gone against public opinion, yet there has been no successful attempt to write the Court out of the Constitution; and although there certainly have been demonstrations on the steps of the Court, as Scalia noted, people generally obey the law even when they disagree with it. Why is this so? It may mean that the Court's "legitimacy" is stronger and more firmly established in people's minds than some of the justices believe. If legitimacy is not eroded with one unpopular decision or even a string of unpopular decisions, then what factors operate to bolster legitimacy in the face of perceived unjust decisions?

Social scientist Tom Tyler has looked at why people obey the law.[55] Tyler's work stresses "procedural fairness," or what some call "due process." People are more likely to accept a decision that goes against them when they believe that they have had a fair hearing. When they have had their day in court and feel that the procedures have been fair, they are more likely to accept a decision that they consider wrong and unjust, and accept the court's legitimacy as well. Tyler and Rasinski have extended the work to the Supreme Court.[56] They claim that when people perceive the Supreme Court as following fair procedures in deciding cases, people develop a higher regard for the Court as a "more legitimate institution," and this greater respect increases their acceptance of decisions.

In contrast, J. L. Gibson believes there is no conclusive evidence that procedural justice enhances legitimacy.[57] In his view, it is more likely that legitimacy is maintained by "diffuse support" deriving from people's socialization, political values, and satisfaction or dissatisfaction with the Court's decisions. Although "socialized beliefs" (in Gibson's phrase) may give legitimacy older, deeper, and broader supports, a series of "bad decisions" may erode it relatively quickly. Tyler and Rasinski's notion that perceptions of fairness strengthen legitimacy means that the Court can retain public support through a string of unpopular decisions. But Gibson, Tyler, and Rasinski use just the sort of opinion poll survey questions that we found suspect earlier. Here is one of the five propositions that Tyler and Rasinski presented to respondents, in their effort to measure legitimacy: "If the United States Supreme Court continually makes decisions that the people disagree with, it might be better to do away with the Court altogether." What decisions? We don't know. Which people disagree? We don't know. How long does "continually" run? We don't know. This vague, abstract, general item is not likely to reveal the deeper sentiment we seek.

Finding "the people"—and the people's deepest sentiments, their notions of commonsense justice—may be more difficult than we imagined it would be. Sentiments may lie deeper than our detecting instruments, and may run in conflicting directions. When Dworkin sets a heroic task for his imaginary judge Hercules—to interpret law in a way that best reconciles conflicting virtues—Hercules and Dworkin reach for a superordinate concept: *law as integrity*. But at this point in our discussion, we're still not sure that commonsense justice contains any *integrity*, any *common* denominator, or even any *common sense*. We shall see.

Understanding Nullification

2

Talk about having a bad day. Consider Oedipus.[1] The man simultaneously discovers that he was orphaned and adopted; that he has a real father and mother; that he has killed the former, and wedded and bedded the latter. After his self-inflicted blinding (a rather pricey penance, in modern currency, for a few honest mistakes) and subsequent death, the gods still aren't through with him, for centuries later Freud will come along and mutilate his myth. But this story is not about Oedipus; it's about his daughter Antigone.

Antigone seeks to bury one of her slain brothers. But the king, her "uncle" Creon, has issued a decree forbidding the burial. In other words, there is a law that makes burying that body a punishable crime. Unlike Oedipus' story, this one entails no possibility of a mistake: Antigone knows the law and its penalty, yet chooses to break the law. Just as "mistake" will not exculpate, neither will negligence or recklessness mitigate; for in legal language, her act is willful, intentional, purposeful, deliberate, knowing, premeditated. Were this case a civil one, which it isn't, it could be called *Creon v. Antigone*—just a case of two individuals disputing. But the case is a criminal one, *Rex v. Antigone,* and she is up against the power of the State, for she has broken a "legally sanctioned law."

Antigone's defense, a natural-law defense, is that she is acting in accordance with a much deeper and higher authority—an ancient, perhaps timeless law transcending any that earthly kings or legislatures might enact.

> Nor did I think your orders were so strong
> that you, a mortal man, could over-run

> the gods' unwritten and unfailing laws.
> Not now, nor yesterday's, they always live,
> and no one knows their origin in time.[2]

And when a human law, such as Creon's, conflicts with a higher law, her duty is to the latter, not the former. Unfortunately for Antigone, the issue is to be decided not on Olympus but on earth, within the precincts of the State, and here her case is weak. A modern attorney might counsel her to plea bargain or throw herself on the mercy of the court, for in regard to the elements of the crime—whether she committed the act *(actus reus)* and whether she had the requisite intent *(mens rea)*—there is no question of her guilt.

If the case were to go to a jury—and the audience that witnesses the play is just that—Antigone's argument would be directed neither to the factual elements nor to the jury *as factfinders;* rather, she would address the jurors as *judges of law as well as fact,* and she would ask them to nullify the law. In concrete terms, she would ask them to bring in a "not guilty" verdict, even though all elements of the crime were proved beyond a reasonable doubt. In terms her father would understand, she would be asking jurors to turn a blind eye to the law and see the true Law instead.

Judges of Law as well as Fact

The Interregnum began in 1649 with the capture, trial, and public execution of Charles I. Although the king and monarchy were dead, the issue of nullification was very much alive, brought to the fore by John Lilburne, a radical opponent of Cromwell and a leader of the rebel group known as the Levellers. Lilburne himself would face trial in 1649 for high treason, and his case would cause far more headaches for Cromwell's regime than did that of Charles I. Lilburne is famous for a celebrated phrase, an aphorism that was repeated at his trial and again in 1670, when a Quaker stood in the docket: he appealed to jurors "as judges of law as well as fact."[3] This phrase came "to stand for the sanctity of the community's judgment regarding the substance of the 'true law.'"[4]

But what gives jurors the right to pass judgment on the law? What was Lilburne's defense for "extracting" from judges the responsibility for law's interpretation and transferring this responsibility to jurors? One argument was the Puritan belief that just as the people have the right to interpret Scripture, so, too, do they have the right to interpret the law. Since many people accepted that Scripture was the "principal basis"[5] of the law, as the Levellers did, then this claim was likely to strike a responsive chord in a sizable segment of the populace. It seems but a variant of the natural-law claim advanced by Antigone.

A second argument was "historical"—a mixture of facts, romantic license, and myth that came to be known as the "Norman Yoke" theory. In this account, the Norman invasion was alleged to have severed England's connection to its Anglo-Saxon past. "The Leveller 'myth' of Anglo-Saxon liberties argued that in that almost forgotten age all men were 'free,' held their land freely, met in free popular assemblies, declared the law, and judged one another in their free, local, and popular courts."[6] The post-Conquest laws, claimed the Levellers, were "Norman feudal perversions of the 'true' law."[7]

This Norman Yoke theory of law appeared to be a radical departure from the establishment view, which had been best formulated by the great jurist Sir Edward Coke. Yet in some ways Coke had paved the way for the Levellers' arguments. Coke had successfully refuted the Stuart king's claim that he had a divine right to interpret the common law. Coke's argument was that the common law, which had evolved in case upon case over centuries, was an expression of reason; it was accessible to and interpretable by men of reason, especially (as one might guess) by those men who spent their lives studying the law—lawyers and judges. And since the law was based upon reason rather than revelation, the king lost special standing. The lawmakers in Parliament, who believed themselves to be knowledgeable men of law, joined the judges and lawyers in supporting Coke's position.

> Coke's view was attractive to the parliamentarians who beheaded the king in the name of the law. For if the common law was as old as English society and had never been supplanted by monarchical force—in 1066 William had confirmed and assented to the liberties of the common law—then law preceded kingship. Thus kingship and prerogative were part of and must conform to the rules of the common law, and the assembly of the kingdom was responsible for defense of the fabric of the common law.[8]

Coke's position was a *superiority* claim. It maintained that those who have studied the law possess superior ability when it comes to interpreting that law. Grounding the law in reason, however, was a great leveler: not only did it give judges, jurists, and parliamentarians power that was equal (or superior) to that of the king, but it also enabled the common man, with his common sense, to claim a right to interpret the law.

Invoking common law is different from invoking natural law (as Antigone did), though there is a similarity. Both common law and natural law base their claims to legitimacy on something deeper, truer, more commanding of respect. Antigone looks to a transcendent, timeless law; Lilburne and Coke look to a law that evolved from "time long ago." Yet Coke's notion of the law is clearly different from Lilburne's. Coke's is "evolutional": the "true law" emerges over time from the judicious application of reason, as each century's jurists refine and improve upon the law that went before. Lilburne's is more "archeological," in that recent layers of dross must be cleared away before the true law can be revealed.

What makes the Levellers' claim radical is that it goes beyond asserting that the common man is *equal* to the common-law judge in interpreting the law: it proclaims that the common man is *superior* to the judge. The origins of this claim lie in the early history of the jury—a history that, the Levellers believed, gave juries the power to interpret the law. Most historians, however, find the origins of the English jury far more obscure than they are in the Levellers' clear-cut account,[9] and the right to interpret the law seems far more equivocal than Lilburne was willing to admit. On Lilburne's side is factual evidence showing that early juries had great power, often acting as prosecutor and defense attorney (these did not become separate dramatis personae until later) and often interpreting the law. That early juries had such power was enough for Lilburne's "history"; that jurors had lost this power to judges over the ages only strengthened his call for a return to the "natural order"—in which judges "*ought* to be 'mere ciphers'" and in which jurors should be "judges of law and fact."[10] Thus, according to Lilburne's revisionist history, he was not "extracting" a right but merely redressing a wrongful usurpation and returning the right to its proper owner.

At his trial for high treason, Lilburne was denied the assistance of counsel. He asked to speak to the jury himself:

> *Lilburne:* . . . that I may speak in my own behalf unto the jury, my countrymen, upon whose consciences, integrity, and honesty, my life, and the lives and liberties of the honest men of this nation, now lies; who are in law judges of law as well as fact, and you [the court] only the pronouncers of their sentence, will, and mind . . .
>
> *Lord Keble:* Master Lilburne, quietly express yourself, and you do well; the jury are judges of matter of fact altogether, and Judge Coke says so: But I tell you the opinion of the Court, they are not judges of matter of law.
>
> *Lilburne:* The jury by law are not only judges of fact, but of law also: and you that call yourselves judges of the law, are no more but Norman intruders; and in deed and in truth, if the jury please, are no more but ciphers, to pronounce their verdict.

To the "ciphers" on the bench, Lilburne's legal claim lacked validity. When Lilburne tried to bolster his argument by citing Coke—that jurors could render a verdict "upon the whole matter"[11]—the judges were quite aware that Lilburne's legal scholarship was faulty. Coke had simply acknowledged that there were some questions in which fact and law mixed, and in those situations the jury could "apply the law to the facts as it found them."[12] The judges also knew that Lilburne had carefully omitted Coke's appended dictum: "Judges, not juries, are to respond to questions of law; juries, not judges, are to rule on questions of fact."[13]

If the judges scoffed, the jurors did not, for in less than an hour they returned a "not guilty" verdict. From one vantage point, this verdict can be seen as an instance of jury nullification. But is it? Perhaps the jurors simply rendered a "not guilty" verdict because the government's case was weak. Put another way, when is a "not guilty" simply a "not guilty," and when is it nullification? If it was nullification, why would the jurors nullify? Unlike the case of Antigone, where she was appealing against a "bad" law that contradicted Divine Law, Lilburne's case revealed no discernible sentiment that Englishmen were against the crime of high treason. Perhaps the jurors were nullifying not the law but the penalty that attached, for by bringing in a "not guilty" verdict they spared the defendant the death penalty. Or maybe they were exercising individualized justice—stating that the law or the punishment did not fit this case and defendant. Then again, perhaps Lilburne's jurors were nullifying not on substantive grounds but on procedural grounds, because they considered the procedures unfair (for example, the fact that Lilburne was denied counsel).

Raising these possibilities serves to highlight two basic questions regarding the topic of nullification. First, how can we be sure that a "not guilty" verdict is an instance of nullification? And second, even if we suspect nullification, how can we determine why it is occurring?

A Quaker Acquitted, a Juror Condemned

Lilburne's legacy, the Leveller theory of the law, endured. "The Levellers insisted that law was not inherently complex; in criminal trials it was just a matter of right and wrong. Law came to the mind and conscience of the simplest man. The very nature of law presumed judgment by peers in accordance with standards comprehensible to the defendant. Jury trial was not to be formed in the image of enacted laws; rather, enacted laws were to conform to the logic and purpose of trial by jury."[14] When Levellers spoke of "conscience," they meant the "community's sense of justice."[15] The Interregnum ended in 1660 with the restoration of Charles II, but the issues of jury nullification and the role, power, and rights of the jury were far from settled when two Quakers named William Penn and William Mead were brought to trial in 1670.

The persecution of the Quakers during the Restoration was evident in the Quaker Act of 1662, the Conventicles Act of 1664, and the renewed Conventicles Act of 1670. The latter two acts were aimed at suppressing seditious meetings ("conventicles") that were held, according to the 1664 act, "under pretence or colour of religion."[16] In modern terms these "sedition" laws are problematic, because they equated meetings and preaching with sedition: proof of the former became proof of the latter. Penn and Mead were arrested for "preaching seditiously and causing a great tumult of people . . . to be gathered together riotously and routously."[17] The government "charged them with causing an unlawful assembly and a disturbance of the peace, charges that came close to an indictment for insurrection."[18]

During the trial, both defendants "admitted with pride that they had assembled to preach and to pray. Neither defendant believed that the Crown's evidence, even if true, amounted to the breaking of any law."[19] At one point, Penn dramatically asked that they be shown the law: "Produce the law . . . you say I have broken." The Crown responded that "the indictment was based upon 'the common law' and that he could not 'run up so many years, and over so many adjudged cases, which we call common law.' This drew Penn's famous retort: 'If [the law] be common, it should not be so hard to produce.'"[20]

It becomes quite clear that Penn was playing to the jury, asking them to exercise their power to nullify. Like Antigone and Lilburne before him, he invoked a higher, deeper, more fundamental law than the one he was charged with violating. Like Lilburne, he appealed to the jurors as judges of both law and fact. And in addition to his substantive appeal—that the Conventicles Act was an attack on basic freedoms under the mask of law—he made a fairness claim: that the court's refusal to read the indictment for the jury amounted to railroading the defendant. Looked at in this light, Penn's statement below appears to give the jurors two bases for nullifying—namely, justice (substantive) and fairness (procedural).

Shall I plead to an indictment that has no foundation in law? If it contain that law, you say I have broken, why should you decline to produce that law, since it will be impossible for the jury to determine, or agree to bring in their verdict, who have not the law produced, by which they should measure the truth of the indictment, and the guilt, or contrary of my fact? . . . The question is not, whether I am guilty of this indictment, but whether this indictment be legal.[21]

When the jury's deliberations began, *Penn's Case* merged with *Bushell's Case*. Initially, the twelve jurors were split, with eight ready to return a "guilty" verdict. The eight came downstairs, but the four dissenters remained upstairs. When the dissenters were led down, one of them, Bushell, seems to have been singled out: "Sir, You are the cause of this disturbance, and manifestly show yourself an abettor of faction; I shall set a mark upon you sir!"[22] All twelve jurors were sent upstairs to reconsider their decision.

> When the jury returned, the foreman reported that they had found Penn "guilty of speaking in Gracechurch Street," to which the Recorder replied that they "had as good say nothing." The mayor questioned the jury: "Was it not an unlawful assembly? You mean [Penn] was speaking to a tumult there?" But further questioning availed the bench nothing; the jury was not prepared to answer to the core of the indictment . . . Bushel and the others who would not bring in a guilty verdict stood upon their "conscience," as Penn had exhorted them to do. It was, or so Penn contended, the juryman's "right."[23]

In the end, all twelve jurors found Penn not guilty, but the court fined the jurors "forty marks a man," and marched all twelve off to Newgate prison for contempt of court. Bushell appealed his imprisonment, and won, in a landmark case that helped bring to an end the court's practice of "attaint"—punishing jurors for verdicts that displeased the judges. Whereas *Penn's Case* reasserted jurors' right to judge the law, and hence nullify the law, which they may have done, *Bushell's Case* gave to the jury, or gave back to the jury, its independence. A jury's "not guilty" verdict was the final word, free from judicial coercion. But whether the jury should have the last word, and more particularly the *right* to nullify, is still the subject of controversy.

Divided Sentiments about Nullification

When the Philadelphia lawyer Alexander Hamilton took up the defense of the "hapless publisher" John Peter Zenger,[24] he began at a double disadvantage. First, Zenger was charged with the crime of seditious libel, a crime that required the jury to render only a special verdict—a determination of whether Zenger had in fact published his newspaper—rather than a general verdict of guilty or not guilty. Showing that *what had been published was true* was no defense against seditious libel, so it did not matter if the published allegations against William Cosby (the governor of New York, appointed by the king) were true or not. Second, on factual grounds, there was no question that Zenger was the publisher. Thus, neither the law nor the facts favored Hamilton's client.

Some historians claim that when Hamilton addressed the New York jury in 1735, he was introducing a novel argument, a "'law of the future' rather than the law of the day."[25] But Hamilton followed the strategy used in the cases we examined above. His argument for nullification, subtle and smooth, echoed the past invocations of the strident Lilburne and the calm Quaker Penn. Hamilton claimed that the crime of libel involved an entwining of law and fact, and that the jury needed to consider both to make their factual determination; in other words, constraining the jury to a special verdict instead of a general verdict was a usurpation of the jury's rights. He argued that the jury had the right to scrutinize the governor's abuse of power and "that they were not obliged by the law to support a governor who goes about to destroy a province or colony."[26] In his words we hear echoes of the statement that the jury is the "conscience of the community," the final bulwark against tyranny imposed by overzealous courts, parliaments, or rulers. And jurors, according to Hamilton, are free "to see with their own eyes, to hear with their own ears, and to make use of their own consciences and understandings, in judging of the lives, liberties or estates of their fellow subjects."[27] Thus, they may bring into their deliberations factors that today we might consider "extralegal."

Hamilton was not alone in his advocacy of the jury's right to determine both fact and law. Among the Founding Fathers, John Adams, Thomas Jefferson, Elbridge Gerry, and others believed that the jury ought to decide law as well as fact. When Chief Justice John Jay presided over *Georgia v. Brailsford*,[28] he noted that whereas juries determine facts and the courts are the best judges of the law, it was nonetheless the jurors' "right to take upon . . . [themselves] to judge of both, and to determine the law as well as the fact in controversy."[29] The "ascendancy of the jury" seemed to be a generally accepted fact from colonial times through the Jacksonian era.[30]

But the debate over letting juries decide the law had begun, and the jury would soon yield power to the judge. To understand this shift, we must recognize that nullification can run in two directions. In the cases of Lilburne, Penn, and Zenger, the juries' "not guilty" verdicts indicate a merciful direction. But it can also take a vengeful direction: jurors can disregard the law and bring in a "guilty" verdict when, for example, they find a defendant unsympathetic. Nullification of this sort reflects prejudicial sentiments and majoritarian vengeance—a tyranny of the twelve, so to speak.[31] But this tyranny, in contrast to merciful nullification, is not final, for the innocent defendant who is found guilty can appeal the decision. No such corrective exists for the "not guilty" merciful nullification, for that decision is final.

Some opponents of the jury's right to nullify feared not just vengeful nullifications but all nullifications, whether merciful or vengeful. They feared *anarchy*. If jurors have the "right" to do whatever they want with the law, then a rational system of laws based on general principles will collapse. Blind and equal justice will give way to individualized sympathy and idiosyncratic discretion. Instead of similar cases producing similar verdicts, the system will produce varying verdicts that depend on the vagaries and whims of a particular jury. Although some juries might compliantly follow the law, "runaway juries" will do what they like. To the opponents of nullification, who were gathering strength, such anarchy was anathema.

In practice, juries still nullified periodically, as in trials that stemmed from the 1850 Fugitive Slave Act. Northern juries often refused to bring in guilty verdicts for abolitionists who were caught helping slaves escape. This, however, shows only that the jury has the *power* to nullify. Opponents of nullification were contesting the jury's *right* to nullify, and they were gaining the upper hand in legal decisions. For instance, in *United States v. Morris*,[32] a case involving the Fugitive Slave Act, the judge refused to let the defense counsel make the nullification argument to the jury, noting that "power is not the right."[33]

The apparent nail in the coffin for the jury's right to nullify was driven home in 1895, when the Supreme Court decided the case of *Sparf and Hansen v. United States*.[34] In *Sparf*, two sailors were charged with murder, and the defense "argued that the jury ought to be allowed to consider the lesser charge of manslaughter."[35] The trial judge refused, and the Supreme Court affirmed the trial judge's ruling, thereby explicitly limiting the jury's right to consider the law. The Court reasoned that "if the jury cannot be permitted to increase the penalty, they cannot be allowed to reduce the penalty either."[36] This ruling undercut the right to render either merciful or "partial" nullification (that is, to render a "guilty" verdict under a lesser charge and thus reduce the punishment). Though *Sparf* appeared to remove the *right* to nullify, the *power* to do so still remained with the jury—a discrepancy that led to the "institutionalization of conflict." As M. R. Kadish and S. H. Kadish put it, "Such a system extends discretion to deviate from the rules, discretion not simply a violation (since it is legitimated), but not therefore a compliance. By the counterposition of duty to comply and privilege to depart, the legal system has generated freedom in a very fundamental respect: the freedom of people not simply subject to the law, but, always within limits, independent of the law and capable of using that law for the ultimate ends of the legal system."[37]

In 1968, in *Duncan v. Louisiana,*[38] the Supreme Court appeared to reopen the apparently dead issue. The Court noted that "one function of the jury is to guard against official departures from the rules, but an equally important function is, on proper occasions, to depart from unjust rules or their unjust application."[39] The Court's meaning is ambiguous. Is "depart from unjust rules or their unjust application" just another way of saying "nullify"? If it is, is the Court sanctioning the *right,* or only saying, in a fashion, that jurors have the *power?*

In 1972, in a more direct way, the United States Court of Appeals for the D.C. Circuit debated the jury's nullification power, and the right of the jury to be informed of that power. In *United States v. Dougherty,*[40] a case that grew out of protests against the Vietnam War, Judge Harold Leventhal, writing for the two-to-one majority, acknowledged that nullification had been a recognized right during colonial times but ruled that explicitly informing the jury of this power would "lead to anarchy in the courts."[41] Judge David Bazelon, dissenting, felt that candor was the best policy. Let jurors know what they can do, and inform them of the power they indeed have. As to what would happen, Bazelon predicted the opposite: anarchy would not follow if the nullification power were spelled out, and "juries would not set free dangerous defendants."[42]

In this short history of the nullification debate, sentiments are clearly divided. Horowitz and Willging refer to our attitudes about nullification as "bipolar,"[43] meaning that proponents and opponents not only occupy distinct ends of a spectrum, but, like the affective disorder (bipolar) they allude to, their arguments have a strong emotional tinge. Some people favor and other people oppose the *right* to nullify; some are thankful for and others are fearful of the *power* to nullify. About the very term "nullification" and its meaning, there is division. G. P. Fletcher finds the label "unfortunate and misleading, because it suggests that when the jury votes its conscience, it is always engaged in an act of disrespect toward the law."[44] A careful reading of history will show that the jury uses its power "not to defeat the law, but to perfect the law, to realize the law's inherent values."[45]

There are divisions not only *about* the phenomenon but *within* the phenomenon. T. A. Green believes that the generic term "nullification" masks important distinctions among types of nullification.[46] In Antigone's case it is clear that the appeal is to nullify a bad law, but in Lilburne's case it is far from clear why the jurors nullified, if indeed they did. We have already seen one division—that between merciful nullification and vengeful nullification (the latter being "the less sanguine face of nullification").[47] There are other types as well.

Jurors may nullify because they judge the law to be bad, as in seditious libel or the Fugitive Slave Act cases. Jurors may nullify not because they disagree with the law but because they deem the penalty too severe. For example, early nineteenth-century England was ruled according to the "Bloody Code," which made some two hundred offenses punishable by death. "In 1819 English bankers requested that the death penalty for forgery be eliminated, since juries refused to convict forgers because of the severity of the penalty."[48] Jurors were not refusing to classify forgery as a crime, but they were refusing to consider forgery a crime that warranted the death penalty.

Still another type of nullification accepts both the crime and the punishment that attaches to it, but maintains that neither the crime nor the punishment fits the particular defendant. In a case of euthanasia, a "mercy killing" in which a husband kills his long-suffering, terminally ill wife, a jury may nullify because they feel the defendant has suffered (that is, been punished) enough. The jurors may believe in the legitimacy of the crime, and may believe that it warrants punishment generally—but not here.

In instances of "partial" nullification, juries bring in a "guilty" verdict to a lesser offense than the one originally charged, thereby sparing the defendant a harsh punishment. An 1815 South Carolina case of "pious perjury" is an example.[49] A defendant was charged with grand larceny, defined as stealing goods worth more than ten cents. There was sufficient evidence that the goods taken were worth more than ten cents, yet the jury rejected the charge of grand larceny in favor of that of petty larceny. The crucial factor seems to be that grand larceny was punishable by hanging, but petty larceny was not. Partial nullification was also the issue in *Sparf.*

Judge Not, Lest Ye Be Judged

While the likes of Lilburne, Penn, and Hamilton applauded and defended the jury's right to nullify, critics still claim that if jurors have the right to jettison the law and steer by sentiment, it is justice that runs aground. Even when this right is limited or proscribed, many critics still judge jurors harshly for merely exercising the power, quite apart from the result. The debate over nullification tends to focus on jurors. One way of widening the scope is to ask: Do judges nullify as well? Although documenting judicial nullification is at least as difficult as documenting jury nullification, we do have a few suspects.

Consider case that was tried in Miami.[50] Ramiro de Jesus Rodriguez was driving a car in the company of his wife and his three-year-old daughter, Veronica, who was sitting on her mother's lap. The car was involved in an accident. The child was thrown into the windshield, and she died four hours later. But long before his grief ebbed, Mr. Rodriguez was charged with homicide. "The 31-year-old Nicaraguan immigrant is believed to be the first parent in the nation prosecuted for the death of a child because of failure to use a child-safety seat in the car. Rodriguez was charged with vehicular homicide, which carries a maximum penalty of five years in prison."[51]

The fear of nullification was in the air. Jury selection "took much longer than expected because many potential jurors said they could not vote to convict a man who had suffered the death of his child."[52] As one potential juror put it, "For the father to have a child die, and then to be put on trial for it, is a horrible thing."[53] That potential juror was excused. Another potential juror said, "I know he's Nicaraguan, and my feeling is he's being crucified and being made an example to prove the law."[54] That potential juror was also excused. But the fear of jury nullification was premature: the judge handed down a directed verdict of not guilty, so the case never got to the jury. Was this a judicial nullification of a bad law? The past president of the Florida Criminal Lawyers Association seemed to think so, believing that the judge was sending a strong message—namely, that the State should end such prosecutions because they were "ill-founded, and the community at large is not in favor of these prosecutions."[55]

In a drug-selling case in the shadow of Thomas Jefferson's University of Virginia, a judge apparently wanted to nullify but restrained himself.[56] A nineteen-year-old student pled guilty "to selling three-quarters of an ounce of marijuana and a bag full of hallucinogenic mushrooms near a school."[57] Federal law dictated a minimum sentence and allowed no parole in cases where drug sales occurred within one thousand feet of a school. The sale was alleged to have occurred in a fraternity house just within the thousand-foot designation. "It tears up the court's conscience in a case like this," the judge said. "But if I am to be true to my oath, I have no choice but to follow federal directives."[58] In this case, the judge did not want to nullify the *law,* as in the babyseat case, but wanted to nullify the mandatory punishment so that the student could continue his studies.

Whereas the first judge may have followed his (and the community's) sentiments to strike at an unpopular law, the second judge reined in his sentiments by holding to his oath. Following is a third case, in which a judge partially nullified a first-degree murder charge by manufacturing a new defense.

Bobby Ray Stanbery, seventeen years old, was described by two psychologists as borderline retarded.[59] He entered his parents' bedroom one morning and fired three shotgun blasts into the body of his sleeping father, killing him; he was charged with first-degree murder. The teenager claimed that "his father gave him $20 to help pay for a hunting and fishing license, but he lost the money playing cards. Hoping to win it back, he stole about $120 from his father's wallet and returned to the game. He said he lost most of that money too."[60] There was a history of violence: Stanbery "said he had been regularly beaten, kicked, whipped, degraded and threatened with death by his father, Dennis Stanbery, since childhood."[61] But at the time of the killing, there was no threat, as the father was asleep.

Yet Judge Darlene Perry, in a nonjury trial, found that the killing was done in "partial self-defense," a term she seemed to fashion on the spot. But "partial self-defense" in law is as problematic as "partial pregnancy" in life. Noting that "the circumstances of the killing did not 'neatly fit' Maryland's legal definition of self-defense,"[62] the judge's creative concoction led to a manslaughter verdict, which saved the defendant from the weightier conviction of murder. Offering a justification for this partial nullification, the assistant state's attorney said, "Sometimes the court will bend the law to achieve a practical, just and fair result . . . Certainly it's her job to do so."[63]

But is it the judge's job to bend the law? Or, as the judge in the drug-selling case put it, should the judge obey the oath and follow the law? When Judge Perry bent the law, she was applauded. Yet when jurors do likewise, many critics are less forgiving. Whether nullification emanates from the jury room or the judge's chambers, it may reflect a desire to insert *discretion* into the process of deciding guilt or setting a sentence. But the discretionary urge runs smack into a legal response that demands greater control of impulses. The trend since the Jacksonian era has been to curb jurors' discretion and limit nullifications. When we look at judges' discretion in light of recent history, the same trend is discernible: both federal sentencing guidelines and congressional enactment of mandatory sentencing laws leave judges with far less discretion.[64] Although sentencing variability may have been reduced, a number of judges have become more vociferous in deploring their lack of discretion, claiming that unjust and indefensible outcomes are resulting.[65] And at least one judge is refusing to follow federal sentencing guidelines,[66] claiming that they violate "both the due process clause of the Fifth Amendment and the Eighth Amendment protection against cruel and unusual punishment."[67]

These examples of possible judicial nullification highlight the fact that nullification is not something only jurors do. Judges, too, sometimes bend or even discard the law. And although governors and the president have the power to grant executive clemency, a power that makes it "legal" rather than extralegal, the very use of clemency—whether in the form of pardons, amnesty, reprieves, or commutation of sentence—may be symptomatic of a *failure* of the law to produce justice, necessitating executive discretion to make things right.[68]

The use of discretion remains problematic even on the part of an executive who has the right to do so. When "President Gerald Ford fully pardoned forever all of Richard Nixon's crimes, known or hidden," he said "he was responding to his conscience."[69] When Pontius Pilate pardoned Barabbas on the Passover feast, he was responding to the crowd.[70] And when it came to "the oldest crime in history, Cain's murder of his brother," God commuted Cain's sentence of banishment, "allowing him to live in the land of Nod."[71] God's discretionary leniency is founded on mercy, yet such leniency can also be motivated by error or whim, producing freakish and capricious outcomes. In all cases, however, clemency bears a similarity to jury nullification, for discretion is used to bend if not defeat the law, in order to achieve a different outcome.

A Verdict Sparks a Riot

On April 29, 1992, the jury in the trial of Rodney King returned its verdict on four Los Angeles police officers. The officers were on trial for assault with a deadly weapon and for use of force that exceeded their authority; two of the four were also charged with filing a false police report, and one was also charged with accessory after the fact. The jury brought in a "not guilty" verdict on ten of the eleven counts, and was unable to reach a consensus on the final count. Los Angeles erupted. Over the next few days, rioting spread throughout the city and many people were killed or injured; National Guard troops and, by presidential directive, U.S. Army troops were sent in. Citizens, political leaders, the news media, and talk shows all weighed in with stories and opinions. Riots often have numerous causes, but they are rarely sparked by a courtroom verdict. The situation was highly unusual.

Under ordinary circumstances there may never have been a trial, let alone a verdict that incensed so many or created a national furor. What was extraordinary about this case was that on the night of March 3, 1991, an amateur cameraman had been awakened by the altercation between King and the police and had filmed the incident from a distance of only 175 feet. "His tape showed more than 50 baton blows and kicks directed at King as he lay on the ground after being stopped for traffic violations."[72] It was played over and over again on television news programs, and turned almost everyone who saw it into an eyewitness "juror." In a way, then, when this case finally came to trial, it had two sets of jurors. The first comprised the official twelve, drawn from the city of Simi Valley, California; the second consisted of virtually everyone else in the country. And as comments and opinion polls after the verdict would reveal, the two groups of jurors seemed to hold irreconcilable views.

As a member of the Los Angeles City Council put it, "The jury is trying to tell us we didn't see what we saw."[73] The mayor of Los Angeles also criticized the jurors: "[They] asked us to accept the senseless and brutal beating of a helpless man"[74] and to believe that "what we all saw with our own eyes wasn't a crime."[75] Said one incredulous citizen, "I can't understand how you can watch the tape and not see it."[76] Then came the polls. A *Washington Post*–ABC News Poll revealed that 64 percent of whites and 92 percent of blacks believed the police officers were guilty.[77] In a poll conducted by *USA Today,* 86 percent of white respondents and 100 percent of black respondents thought the verdict was wrong; in a *Newsweek* poll, the proportions were 73 percent and 92 percent, respectively. And a poll conducted by *Time* magazine, which asked respondents how they would have voted if they had been on the jury, found that 62 percent of whites and 92 percent of blacks would have voted to convict the officers.[78]

Given that public figures called the verdict a "travesty and a miscarriage of justice," that editorialists claimed the jury had blundered in spectacular fashion, and that public opinion poll results solidly supported these views, we ask: Did the twelve official jurors nullify the law? In trying to answer this question, we run into some formidable obstacles. In real life, which is nothing like Hollywood movies, we are forbidden to observe the jury's deliberations; and after the jurors reach a verdict, we cannot compel them to reveal what was said, or tell us why they did what they did. This guarantee of privacy and secrecy, in part a legacy of Bushell, means that we do not know, and in all likelihood will never know, what went on in the jury room at the Rodney King trial. Since this fact has not stopped others from speculating, let's join the fray for a moment and hypothesize that the jurors were nullifying, bringing in a "not guilty" verdict despite persuasive evidence of guilt. While this hypothesized nullification appears merciful rather than vengeful (because it is a "not guilty" verdict), the case differs in important ways from Lilburne's, Penn's, and Zenger's. In those cases, the "not guilty" verdicts appeared to accord with the views of a sizable segment of the population; in the King case, the verdict was overwhelmingly at odds with broad community sentiment. Moreover, there was no appeal to "higher justice" in the King case; on the contrary, some critics alleged that the jurors gave in to baser standards of justice.

If we can hypothesize nullification in the first Rodney King trial, we can do so as well in the second, where two of the four police officers from the first trial faced federal charges stemming from the beating caught on tape. After all, there was talk in the press and on network news, and by the mayor and the police chief, that if the second jury also brought in a "not guilty" verdict a second riot might erupt. Perhaps the second jury nullified in the vengeful-direction, bringing in a "guilty" verdict despite reasonable doubt, to stave off a riot and soothe the citizenry.

These speculations reveal that nullification is easy to assert but difficult to document. Not all merciful nullifications accord with broad community sentiment or with the community's higher sense of justice. The jury's power to nullify may produce an injustice that is both vengeful and merciful. Our sense of justice can be shaken and our belief in the fairness and integrity of the criminal-justice system can be undermined when the innocent are punished, when the guilty are punished too severely, and when those perceived as guilty are found not guilty. Jurors' discretionary power, if used wrongly or too often, can "seriously weaken the courts' capacity to exercise power and function according to the rule of law," as the majority in *Planned Parenthood* affirmed.[79] Yet the jury's discretionary power to nullify in the merciful direction can produce higher justice and greater confidence in the system, when the law seems ill-conceived or the punishment discordant, or when neither fits the defendant.

From Nullification to Commonsense Justice

Nullification can be viewed from a purely normative perspective. Regarding the *right* to nullify, jurists and jurisprudes can offer arguments about what an ideal legal system ought to be, and whether the right to nullify is consistent with the ideal; philosophers (moral, social, political) and others can weigh in with their arguments. But such a debate remains sterile, in a way, if it fails to connect the normative realm with what jurors do *in fact*.

For example, if the argument against the *right* to nullify is based on the fear of anarchy, then empirical findings showing that the fear is groundless—that jurors apparently do not abuse the right in the three states that inform jurors they have the right[80]—may undermine the argument. At this point, I believe that the empirical questions are the more interesting and compelling, and potentially the most informative. And the most interesting question of all, I suggest, is: Why do nullifications occur? For if we knew jurors' reasons for nullifying, we could answer the question concerning *type* of nullification: Are jurors nullifying the law, or the punishment, or appropriateness of the law and the punishment to the defendant? We could also remove the guesswork regarding the *direction* of the nullification—merciful or vengeful—and be in a position to see if the jury's reasons comport with community sentiment or reflect some higher or baser sense of justice. In sum, by determining the reasons for nullifying, we learn whether jurors are disrespecting or perfecting the law.

The answers to these questions, and the confidence we have in those answers, depend on the methods used to reach them. We've seen that this is true of opinion polling, and it is likewise true of research on nullification. The historical-archival method, which we used to generate the examples of Lilburne, Penn, and Zenger, produced speculation without confirmation: as historians viewing those cases from the outside, and at great distance, we suspected that nullification may have occurred, but we could not know for sure what really happened inside the "black box" of the jury room.

Yet if we could enter that black box and penetrate jurors' minds—unearthing their declared reasons for doing what they do—we would acquire knowledge of great value. If jury decisions are one of the accepted "objective indicia" of community sentiment, as the Supreme Court has confirmed in its Eighth Amendment jurisprudence,[81] then jury verdicts may tell us more about sentiment than opinion polls do. Unlike polling questions, which are often general and hypothetical, a jury trial is specific and real. Jurors confront a real, live defendant and real-life consequences, whereas polling respondents do not. It's one thing to tell a poll taker you're in favor of the death penalty, but it's quite another to actually give a death sentence.

Thus, if jury verdicts give us a different and perhaps more powerful gauge of sentiment, then jury nullifications, if they can be instantiated and substantiated, become a means for discerning commonsense justice—a finding that goes beyond signifying disrespect for the law, or a desire to perfect the law. When nullifications depart from black-letter law, and when we know why this is happening, we can illuminate the true sense of commonsense justice. If commonsense justice is flawed, then the law's task is to correct, restrain, or abolish it. But if commonsense justice is sound—if it draws on the power of "the gods' unwritten and unfailing laws" (as Antigone says) or just manifests good earthly common sense—then it offers blind Justice a new vision, whereby the Law may be enhanced by and harmonized with the sentiments of the community.

Revealing Jurors' Sentiments

3

In order to use nullification as a means of studying commonsense justice, we must first verify that nullification *is in fact* occurring, and, second, determine *why* it is occurring. These are sizable hurdles. A nullification claim rests on two tenuous assumptions: that we know what the "true" verdict should have been, and that the jury likewise knew it but consciously chose to reject it. The first assumption is theoretically problematic; the second is pragmatically so. If we knew a priori what the correct verdict should be, the trial would be purposeless, for the jurors would serve not as finders of truth but merely as window dressing. Since we cannot obtain the metaphysical "true" verdict, we settle for less, using common sense, or consensus, or the opinions of learned jurists on what the *right* verdict should be. How much less this turns out to be is an open question.

In Chapter 2 we looked at a number of suspected nullification cases, where the historical-archival method was our focusing lens. Although this method of going back in time to past cases provides hunches and hypotheses, it is short on confirmation: there was considerable ambiguity in a number of those cases about what the right verdict should have been, and there was significant doubt as to whether jurors were consciously rejecting the legally correct verdict. In Zenger's case, we may be fairly confident that he should have been found guilty on the special verdict, since the evidence was uncontroverted that he published the paper; but our confidence of the right verdict wanes in Penn's case, and wanes even more in Lilburne's. As to whether the jury consciously rejected the right verdict: even when we view the Penn case in light of Bushell, we are still in the dark about what went on upstairs in the jury room before the eight-to-four vote for "guilty" became known, or in the ensuing interval that ended with the jury's final vote for acquittal. Just when we want to see into the black box, the scene goes dark.

The historical method has other disadvantages as well. The further back in time we go, the greater the likelihood that we will misunderstand the historical context surrounding the case, and the greater the likelihood that the facts of the case will be incomplete. Beyond these problems is the even more troublesome difficulty of *perspective:* when we use the historical approach, we are *outsiders* trying to get an *insider's* view of the jury room and of jurors' thinking. Yet always on the outside and often from afar, we ultimately can do no more than speculate about how jurors were seeing the case and interpreting the law. This is hazardous. Our empathetic intuition ("If I'd been a juror, here's how I would have seen it"), or our knowledge of how that society viewed such matters in general, may not fit at all with what that particular jury perceived, thought, and did.

The Insider's View

When jurors speak out, or agree to be interviewed by social scientists about their deliberations in a case, we in retrospect enter the black box and get the privileged insider's view. But before we take the jurors' utterances as gospel, we need to understand the limits of this method as well. First and foremost, most jurors do not speak about their deliberations, and cannot be compelled to speak; we may hear silence when we most want explication. Second, if a few jurors do talk, we may be getting only self-selected perspectives instead of the whole picture. Third, when interviews occur months after the trial, there are the usual problems of forgetting and memory distortion. Fourth, even when interviews follow immediately upon the trial, jurors' statements may still be suspect, particularly after controversial trials in which nullification might have occurred and in which the public may have been critical of the verdict. This concern arises in both of the Rodney King trials. Are we hearing what really happened, or are jurors' selected statements self-serving, aimed at justifying what happened? Are they making their statements in the service of truth, or out of guilt and in the hope that confession will be followed by forgiveness? We cannot know for sure.

When we examine the statements made by some of the jurors following the first Rodney King trial, the insider and outsider accounts contrast. One outsider hypothesis blamed the jury's composition. "The makeup of the jury, many observers believe, made the defense task easier. It included no blacks, largely because the trial was moved from Los Angeles to the overwhelmingly white, still partly rural, community of Simi Valley."[1] It was also noted that Simi Valley was "long known as a bedroom community for retired police and firefighters."[2] This hypothesis alleges that the jurors were biased against the black victim and/or biased in favor of the white police officers, and thus predisposed to see things the police officers' way. According to this outsider hypothesis, sentiments that had been formed before the beginning of the trial determined the verdict in the end.

One juror, who said she held out for a "guilty" verdict before yielding to group pressure, claimed that most jurors had made up their minds before deliberations began: "The people's [jurors] eyes weren't open."[3] This insider statement, however, does not confirm the bias hypothesis, for we know from jury research that it is quite common for jurors to have a verdict in mind before the deliberations, and that the first round of balloting usually correlates closely with the final verdict. Perhaps the other jurors were convinced based on *evidence* rather than bias.

Still, the bias hypothesis, and several offshoots, got a lot of play in the analyses after the trial. If some commentators blamed the jury, others cited the prosecuting attorney and the judge. Did the prosecuting attorney do enough to try to prevent the radical change of venue, or prevent a change of venue at all? Why did the judge take the case out of Los Angeles and place it in Simi Valley? If prospective jurors favored the defense, as the demographics suggest, did the prosecuting attorney fail during *voir dire* to eliminate prospective jurors who were biased? These offshoot hypotheses, putting the blame further back in the chain of events, distract us from the outsider's prime suspect: a biased jury.

But when we return to the prime suspect, we have no case. Beyond circumstantial evidence, we have nothing substantive to go on, other than our own convictions. And if we followed them, we'd be doing what we're accusing the jury of doing: using predilections in the absence of evidence. A problem with validating this hypothesis is that the sort of evidence we would need—a public admission by most of the jurors that they were biased—is something we'd never get in reality. Since we can neither confirm nor disconfirm this hypothesis, we turn back to an insider's view.

As defense attorney Michael Stone put it, the goal of the defense was to get the jurors to view what was happening "not through the eye of the camera but through the eyes of the police officers who were at the scene."[4] And from the comments of some of the jurors who spoke out after the trial, it appears that the jurors took the *subjective* view of the police officers rather than the *objective* view of the disinterested, reasonable person. One juror said, "They [the police] were afraid he was going to run or even attack them. He had not been searched, so they didn't know if he had a weapon. He kept going for his pants, so they thought he might be reaching for a gun."[5]

The *subjective perspective* matters, and it is one that jurors embrace beyond the particular set of circumstances surrounding a trial. This is the first important element to take into account when studying jurors' verdicts, and it will come up time and again in our search for commonsense justice. We will see that jurors readily take the subjective perspective over the objective perspective in insanity cases, self-defense cases, felony-murder cases, euthanasia cases, and more. Although jurisprudes have spent much time discussing the nature of "objective" criminal law and the place of the subjective in the law,[6] ordinary individuals who sit on juries have little trouble entering the subjective and adopting its view.

But what happens when the subjective view is distorted, as it was in the King case? The police believed that King was intoxicated on the drug PCP and that they were confronting a man who had superhuman strength, yet that belief turned out to be false. Do jurors then shift to the objective reality of what is true in fact, or do they stay within the subjective, albeit distorted view? Let's make an analogy to a situation in which an individual mistakenly claims self-defense— "mistakenly" because there was actually no serious threat to his life. Does his claim fail because in external reality there was no real threat, or does the claim succeed because in his interior reality he believed there was a threat? If "belief" is all that matters—if false and true beliefs are one, just because the individual believes they are—doesn't this case move closer to insanity cases, since mistaken, distorted, or delusional beliefs are at the heart of each? These questions will recur in subsequent chapters.

Context is likewise an essential element in jury deliberations, as the King trials illustrate. "The videotape was just a small portion of the information we had," said a juror.[7] But the countrywide "jury" that criticized the verdict had nothing but the tape, and that was all the evidence it needed, for the tape portrayed "the moment of the act." But the context of the act for the official jurors was apparently far broader, extending backward and forward in time.

It extended backward in time to when the police first stopped the car. As one juror said, "Had Rodney King gotten out of his vehicle, as he was ordered to do, and complied with the policeman's orders, nothing would have happened to him. The other two gentlemen that were with him in the vehicle got out quietly and were searched for weapons and were handcuffed. That's all it was. But Rodney King chose to do otherwise."[8] In this context, in which King was compared to the two other passengers, King was considered responsible for what happened because it did not happen to the others, who obeyed instructions. Thus, "but for" his behavior, "nothing would have happened to him."

The context also extended forward to include medical reports and photos. As one juror put it, "I wish they could [see] all the medical reports. I wish they could all see that King only had a small broken bone in his leg; how the facial damage came about; could see the photos of him two days after the incident with only a little swelling in his face. A lot of those blows could not have possibly connected with his body. We had to look at the evidence before us. He just was not as damaged as you'd expect after seeing that small clip of video on television."[9] This may be an instance of what psychologists call *hindsight bias*.[10] If individuals have knowledge of the outcome—if, for example, one group of subjects is told that the trunk of a car contained illegal drugs, whereas another group is told that it contained no drugs—subjects may change their judgments of whether or not a warrantless search of the car's trunk by the police was legal. With such hindsight bias, the jury in the King case may have reasoned that if the physical damage to King's face and body appeared minimal, then the blows seen on the video couldn't all have struck home. The police must have "pulled their punches," so to speak, and thus the claim of "excessive force" had to be false.

A knowledge of context is also vitally important for understanding where and how commonsense justice departs from black-letter law. Where the law tends to take a narrow view of context, asking jurors to focus on the moment of the act (as in insanity and self-defense law), jurors may often take a wider view. In the first King trial, the jurors apparently widened the context under consideration and arrived at a different view of the events caught on tape.

A third important element in jury deliberations is *construing*. For example, one juror in the King case said that King was a person "who was out of control," whereas a second juror said that "he never lost control . . . Rodney King was directing the action."[11] Assessments about who is in control, out of control, or causing the action are judgments. The action per se doesn't tell us; rather, we *construe* and *interpret* what is happening, attributing causality and its direction to one of the actors. These jurors were saying that King's "resistant behavior" was causing the police officers' "reactions"—that is, causing the officers to use their batons; thus, King's actions were the cause, controlling and producing the effect (the violent actions of the police). But most television viewers favored an alternative construction in which cause and effect were reversed: the police "beatings" were the cause, and King was merely "reacting" to the blows. According to this construal, the police were in control of the situation.

That one person's "beating" is another person's "reaction" tells us that "fact finding"—the jury's sanctioned role, which no one seriously disputes—is itself fraught with construing. Finding the facts, even when the action is captured on videotape, is anything but certain, as the King case makes clear.

Even if jurors agree that an alleged "criminal act" did occur, they've done only half the fact finding. They must also agree on intent. Whereas acts can be captured on videotape, intentions must be inferred. Members of the jury in the second Rodney King trial had an important advantage over the jury in the previous trial: the crucial but blurry tape had been sharpened by enhancement techniques developed by the Federal Bureau of Investigation.[12] The second set of jurors, or at least enough of them, now "saw" a blow to the head—and this, said the foreman, was enough for them to infer intent and find guilt. Moreover, once we see the blow to the head, followed by King falling, cause and effect seem clear. If we take these statements at face value, the claim is that certain actions, if seen, provide a potent if not determinative clue as to the defendant's intent and who is causing and controlling the action. But do they? The foreman in the second King trial thought so, saying, "When you look at the video, you can tell what happened first and what happened second . . . And no one that testified had the sequence correctly."[13] Yet philosophers would take issue with this statement, claiming that we not only do not "see" causality but *cannot* see it: since "causality" is metaphysical, rather than physical, we infer it rather than see it. Mere sequence does not imply causality. Tape or no tape, regular tape or enhanced tape, determining who caused what and what intentions were in the mind of the actor-defendant involves *construing*.

Some intentions lie close to the surface—are worn on the proverbial sleeve. Other intentions lie far below, in the depths of the mind. In general, the further down we plunge, the greater the inferential leap and the less sure we are of our landing.

A Case Study

George Fletcher's book on the trial of Bernhard Goetz, the "subway vigilante" who shot four black youths, illustrates the virtues of the case study method.[14] In this method, the observer, though still an outsider, gets much closer to the action than the archivist, and is often present at the trial itself. Unlike a historical survey, which presents a panoramic view of many possible nullification cases, the case study focuses on a single trial, narrowing the focus to yield fine-grained resolution and detail. In doing such a study, closeness to the action is the key, and Fletcher may have had the best seat in the house.

The presiding justice, Stephen Crane, allowed him to sit in as an academic observer and to speak privately with prospective jurors about their knowledge and biases. Fletcher had conversations with the attorneys for the prosecution and the defense. He was privy to strategies on both sides, and knew of motions and decisions that occurred out of the jurors' earshot, including a Court of Appeals ruling that was handed down even before a jury was picked. He had research assistants in court, and he had transcripts. His work turned out to be even more than a case study, for his outsider perceptions were supplemented by the insider views of two jurors, who agreed to be interviewed after the trial. If ever the anatomy of a case and a jury's decision could be understood, these could.

At the time of the shooting, a few facts were clear. On December 22, 1984, a Saturday, at about 1:00 P.M. Bernhard Goetz entered an IRT subway car at Fourteenth Street in Manhattan. As Fletcher describes the incident:

> [Goetz] sits down close to four black youths. The youths, seeming drifters on the landscape of the city, are noisy and boisterous, and the 15 to 20 other passengers have moved to the other end of the car. Goetz is white, 37 years old, slightly built, and dressed in dungarees and a windbreaker. Something about his appearance beckons. One of the four, Troy Canty, lying nearly prone on the long bench next to the door, asks Goetz as he enters, "How are ya?" Canty and possibly a second youth, Barry Allen, then approach Goetz, and Canty asks him for five dollars. Goetz asks him what he wants. Canty repeats: "Give me five dollars." Suddenly, the moving car resounds with gunshots, one aimed at each of the young blacks.

Although much was unclear in the factual testimony, let's stop here, *at the moment of the act,* and ask: How can this be an act of self-defense, as the defense claimed? From the objective, outsider's view, the criteria that need to be satisfied for a successful claim of self-defense do not appear to have been met—not even minimally. It would strain reasonableness to hear "How are ya?" as a threat, let alone a serious threat to cause bodily injury or harm. Even if the second and repeated utterance, "Give me five dollars," were viewed as a shakedown or an intimidating threat, how could this be a serious threat to cause bodily injury when no weapon was brandished? And if it was a serious threat, the threat had to be imminent in order to justify a claim of self-defense. To the outsider, this does not appear to have been the case.

If it was a serious and imminent threat, Goetz's response had to be necessary, and proportional to the threat. But didn't he have a number of other options? Couldn't he have warned the youths to back off? Or just brandished the pistol as a warning? Or even fired a warning shot? Or, as a last resort, shot at the legs of the youths? From the objective, outsider's view, Goetz's firing shots into the midsections of all four seems excessive and unnecessary.

To present the other side, we must make use of the three elements discussed above: *subjectivity, context,* and *construing.* We must see the action from the perspective of Goetz. We must widen the context to include the fact that three years earlier, Goetz had been mugged by three men, and afterward had twice foiled muggings by flashing a pistol. Though the words "How are ya?" sound innocent or ambiguous, not having (in Fletcher's words) "the crisp, hard edge of 'Okay, motherfucker, give it up,'"[15] Goetz claimed to have heard this as "the standard opening line"[16] of a mugging in progress. Add to this context the fact that the doorman at Goetz's apartment building had been brutally mugged and that his mugging had begun "with an innocent-sounding 'How are you doing?'"[17] From Goetz's subjective vantage point, with his contextual history, he construed that the mugging ritual had begun. And when two youths got up, advanced, and stood over this slightly built man in an enclosed subway car, entombed underground far from the light of day, and repeated "Give me five dollars," Goetz saw this as a "kill or be killed" moment.

The trial involved issues on a number of levels. On the legal level, one question was whether the objective or the subjective standard of self-defense would apply, within the judicial context of New York State. Which instruction and what wording would the justice give to the jurors? Obviously, a subjective standard would favor the defense, whereas an objective standard would favor the prosecution. This battle was fought in the Court of Appeals in Albany, New York, prior to the start of the trial.

But the issue was even more complex. Supposing that Goetz had misread the youths' intentions, we could see his act not as "ordinary" self-defense but as putative or mistaken self-defense. If we take a purely subjective view, as the defense urged, then mistaken self-defense should be treated as equivalent to true self-defense, since the defendant believed that the threat was real. Or do we insist, as the prosecution argued, that the mistake must be *reasonable* as measured by an objective, community standard of reasonableness? But the defense countered with the subjective again, claiming that reasonableness ought to be judged by what appeared reasonable to the defendant. The objectivist would reply that if the standard of reasonableness can be defined only by the defendant, then there is no standard. These issues, fascinating to the jurist, turned out to be almost irrelevant to the jury.

At yet another level, never far from center stage, was the issue of nullification. There was much speculation that the defense would try to argue in favor of jury nullification. During jury selection, one of the defense attorneys tried "to sound out the jury's willingness to vote their feelings in the face of strict legal instructions to convict. Justice Crane clamped down hard on any suggestion that the jury had the discretion to 'nullify' the law. He made it clear that if they found Goetz guilty on the law as applied to the facts, they must convict."[18] It will soon become clear that the jurors did not nullify, at least not in the sense that the defense had hoped.

During the trial, the jurors heard two conflicting stories. In the language and imagery of the prosecution's story, Goetz was mentally unbalanced but not insane; he was not a reasonable person but a vigilante hunting for victims. In the language and imagery of the defense's story, the victims were villains, referred to repeatedly as the "gang of four." In the defense's story, Goetz was the victim, the "everyman" who in self-defense finally struck back, on behalf of all law-abiding citizens. The latter story had all the makings of a complex and classic self-defense case—except to the jury.

The defense "never seriously challenged whether, as a matter of fact, Goetz intended to cause death by shooting the four youths,"[19] thus conceding that Goetz had attempted murder. Instead of refuting the act or the intention, the defense's strategy was to claim that the shooting was justified, on grounds of self-defense. But the jury saw it quite differently, conceded nothing, and never even got around to considering the self-defense claim per se.

The jury brought in a "not guilty" verdict for twelve of the thirteen counts; the exception was the minor charge of criminal possession of a weapon in the third degree. On the main charges, the four counts of attempted murder, the verdict was "not guilty." Here is how the jury reasoned, and how that reasoning departed from legal reasoning. One juror asked, "Where have they [the prosecution] proved the intent to murder?"[20] Instead of viewing "intent" in the legal sense—where the criterion is a "cold factual judgment that an actor sought to bring about a particular result"[21]—the jurors were "mixing the issues of motive and intent"[22] and moving "closer to a moral conception of intent."[23] When the jurors tried to determine Goetz's *motive* to murder, they couldn't find one. The prosecution offered revenge as a motive, but the jury didn't buy that.

In their analysis of intent, the jurors brought in self-defense motives: if Goetz's motive "was to ward off the attack,"[24] then he never had "a malicious motive to kill."[25] Whereas the law looked at "intent" in intellect terms (Did Goetz *know* that he was firing a deadly weapon at four human beings?—a question that focuses on what Goetz knew and thought), the jurors' concept of intent added a motivational component that included desire, passion, feeling, sentiments, and more. This made the jurors' view "closer to a moral conception of intent";[26] and "if the motive for the killing is not heinous, there is no intent worthy of moral censure."[27]

Fletcher makes it clear in his commentary that the jurors rendered neither a merciful nullification grounded in sympathy for Goetz nor a nullification reflecting a rejection of the law. Rather, they "brought their common sense and their moral sensibilities to the instructions that Justice Crane gave them, and as a result they fashioned a mode of analysis that no one expected."[28] The jurors' "mode of analysis," although it departed from the accepted legal analysis, was not necessarily inferior to the latter; though their bearing was not on the legally sanctioned navigational charts, this does not imply that they were too dumb to understand or too willful to comply, or that their course had run aground.

Looking to the thoughts, feelings, and motives of a defendant widens the narrow legal context, yet fits with how ordinary people try to understand the actions of other ordinary people. This is what we do when we read detective fiction and try to figure out whodunnit, or when we speculate on the actions and inactions of Hamlet. Jurors' commonsense understanding of defendants reflects a "psychology of human nature" that appears broader than "legal psychology." Commonsense justice, as exercised by the Goetz jury, employs that wider psychology, according to which acts are not neatly partitioned into behaviors and thoughts but are integrated with emotions, motives, and morals in complex and often messy ways. In "law's empire,"[29] intentions may be neatly and clearly fashioned into lofty legal structures using the building blocks of centuries of jurisprudence. Yet, in Fletcher's words, sometimes "the most carefully constructed legal edifices crumble at the touch of the jury's common sense."[30]

Call the Goetz verdict a nullification, if you like, although it is a nullification of a different stripe. In widening the context for defining intention, in taking the subjective perspective, and in employing a commonsense psychology, jurors were able to construe—or, more aptly, *recon-*

strue—the judge's instructions. In the Goetz case such a course produced a "not guilty" verdict, although it does not always end up that way. Fletcher's case study method, augmented as it was by juror interviews, yielded high-resolution detail of what happened during the trial and why. But its virtue is also its drawback: we cannot generalize from this one case to other self-defense cases or other cases where intent to kill crops up. It just may be that the results in the Goetz case are unique. To get beyond the Goetz case, to reach conclusions that are general rather than particular, we must turn to other methods.

A Jury Study

When a study is done well, it offers insights across cases and between cases. If certain data are available and sufficient, we may be able to reconstruct how jurors were construing the facts and the law, what sentiments they had, and why they did what they did. A prime example of such a revealing study is the seminal work of the University of Chicago Law School Jury Project, which was described by Kalven and Zeisel in their book *The American Jury*.[31]

The project gathered data on more than 3,500 cases covering some fifteen crime categories, from 555 judges who cooperated in the study by responding to a questionnaire. Three responses were at the heart of the study: the judges indicated (1) how the jury had voted ("not guilty," "guilty," or hung) in each case; (2) "how they would have decided it [the case], had it been tried before them without a jury";[32] and (3) why they thought the real jury had disagreed (if it had disagreed) with the verdict they themselves would have rendered. Thus, the researchers had two perspectives on each case—the "judicial perspective," as reflected in the judge's verdict, and the "commonsense perspective," as reflected in the jury's decision.

While the design of this study is elegant and ingenious, it still yields an outsider's perspective, since our "knowledge" about why the jury rendered a verdict different from that of the judge comes solely from the judge's speculation. In this research, the jury "speaks" only through its verdict—and verdicts, as we have seen, are difficult to decipher. But as in the case study method, when an outsider has a ringside seat (and isn't the judge's seat precisely that?) his or her speculations will tend to carry weight with us. Moreover, the judge has more contact with the jury than does the case study observer, and his or her speculations are thus more firmly grounded than those of the researcher. When the jury has questions about the law, or wants instructions repeated or clarified, or wants exhibits brought into the jury room, the judge can make inferences about what factors the jurors may be weighing. All in all, then, judges' speculations are worth considering.

If we eliminate the 5.5 percent of cases in which the jury failed to reach a verdict (since judges do not deliver hung verdicts), the results across all cases show 78 percent agreement between judge and jury verdicts: in 64 percent of the cases both judge and jury convicted, and in 14 percent of the cases both judge and jury acquitted.[33] The most interesting findings emerge from the 22 percent of the cases where judge and jury disagreed, for the disagreement did not split down the middle: in 19 percent of the cases the judge convicted but the jury acquitted, whereas in only 3 percent of the cases did the judge acquit while the jury convicted.[34] What these results show is a *leniency* effect on the part of the jury. The jury was more lenient in 19 percent of the cases, whereas the judge was more lenient in only 3 percent of the cases. Thus, there is a 16 percent net leniency effect for the jury. Why?

Kalven and Zeisel offer three hypothesis. To make sense of these, we must first examine how the researchers categorized the judges' speculations for the disagreement. They used three categories: judge and jury disagreed about the facts alone; judge and jury disagreed about both values and facts; and judge and jury disagreed about values alone. The cases were distributed among the three categories as follows: 34 percent (facts alone), 42 percent (values and facts), and 24 percent (values alone).

In the 34 percent of the cases where judge and jury disagreed over facts alone, the researchers put forth two hypotheses, the "credibility hypothesis" and the "reasonable-doubt hypothesis," to explain the discrepancy. According to the credibility hypothesis, some of the disagreement resulted from the fact that judge and jury gave different weight to certain pieces of evidence, or believed the evidence to different degrees. The jury may have accepted some evidence as proof, whereas the judge rejected it as not credible; or the jury may have given great weight to one witness's testimony, whereas the judge found it insubstantial. According to the reasonable-doubt hypothesis, the disagreement arose not because judge and jury assessed the credibility of the evidence differently or weighed it any differently, but "because the jury will tolerate less doubt in convicting than will the judge."[35]

Kalven and Zeisel's third hypothesis, the "liberation hypothesis," is more central to our concerns, for it relates partly to the disagreements over values alone, and centrally to the disagreements over values and facts. In the latter situation, we find cases where "there is evidentiary difficulty to which the jury may be responding and there is also a sentiment or value to which it may be responding."[36] According to the hypothesis,

> Sentiment gives direction to the resolution of the evidentiary doubt; the evidentiary doubt provides a favorable condition for a response to the sentiment. The closeness of the evidence makes it possible for the jury to respond to sentiment *by liberating* it from the discipline of the evidence . . .
>
> The point here is fundamental to the understanding of jury psychology and jury process. We know, from other parts of our jury study, that the jury does not often consciously and explicitly yield to sentiment in the teeth of the law. Rather it yields to sentiment in the apparent process of resolving doubts as to evidence. The jury, therefore, is able to conduct its revolt from the law within the etiquette of resolving issues of fact.[37]

Finally, there is the realm of values alone, where the jurors' sense of justice—their sentiments *concerning the law*—may lead them to hold standards that are different from those of black-letter law. In self-defense cases, for example, juries take a broader view of the "imminence" requirement, an interactive view regarding who provoked the incident, and a wider historical view (which might lead them to consider, say, the past abuse that a man inflicted on his wife when she is on trial for killing him). When we extend the time frame beyond the moment of the act; when we judge not just one person, the defendant, but two people interacting; when we consider the historical context, which may have arisen long before the moment of the act, and consider how that context may affect the defendant subjectively and psychologically—then we come to see why jurors see the situation the way they do, and why they are more forgiving than judges. Kalven and Zeisel state that "in many ways the jury is the law's most interesting critic."[38] And they are critical of "the nicety of the law's boundaries hedging the privilege of self-defense. We are reminded of a familiar epigram of Justice Holmes in a self-defense case, which captures in large part the sense of the jury's realism: 'Detached reflection cannot be demanded in the presence of an uplifted knife.'"[39]

In our discussion of Antigone, we noted that had her case been civil it might have been called *Creon v. Antigone,* a dispute between two parties; but the case was criminal, and so the State replaced Creon. Although "it took centuries for the law to come to the position that the state is the other party in a criminal case," this is a view that "the jury does not entirely embrace."[40] Jurors seem to invoke civil-law concepts, such as contributory negligence or the assumption of risk, and inject them into criminal cases ranging from rape to fraud to negligent homicide to drunken brawls. "There are two sides to every story," goes the adage; and jurors accordingly will consider the victim's actions, motives, and intentions when a judge might not. In effect, the jurors are saying that we can neither understand the drama *Hamlet*, nor judge Hamlet's guilt, without also judging Claudius.

Another sentiment emerges from *de minimis* cases—that is, cases which seem to the jury to involve trifles. When the social harm seems minimal, when the defendant's actions just miss being legal, or when the legal line seems quite arbitrary (say, the line between petty and grand larceny), the "jury will exercise its de facto powers to write these equities into the criminal law."[41]

Is there evidence that juries nullify the law? Yes, but by and large juries nullify sumptuary laws, so-called blue laws. These unpopular laws "attempt to regulate personal expenditures or activities on social or moral grounds,"[42] and reflect paternalism on the part of the State. Laws against gaming, gambling, and liquor sales and to a lesser extent laws against drunk driving are examples. If we view nullifying the *law* as the strongest and most serious form of nullification, as many do,[43] then the jury's "war with the law"[44] is actually quite modest.

The study by Kalven and Zeisel may seriously underestimate nullifications of all types because they never heard directly from the jurors. When we rely on judges' interpretations of what went on inside the black box, we face the outsider's problem once again. But there's another reason the jury's war with the law may be hotter than we detect here: we may not be seeing the full force of the jurors' *desire* to nullify, because judges' instructions serve to keep it in check. What if this check were removed and jurors were given permission to nullify? Would they go wild, or wilder than we've seen in Kalven and Zeisel's study? Here we reach the limits of the study. To answer this question, we need a method that will enable us to control the key variables.

Nullification Experiments

Suppose we conducted a field study in which all the criminal verdicts handed down in a single year in Maryland (a state in which juries are routinely instructed about their right to nullify) were compared with all the verdicts rendered that same year in Virginia (a state with no nullification instruction). Suppose our hypothetical results show that Maryland has a substantially higher percentage of "not guilty" verdicts. Although these results might be statistically significant, they may be of little significance overall, for they could have been the product of "confounds." Can we really say that the nullification instruction caused the difference, or did some other, uncontrolled variable (a confound) produce the effect?

Perhaps the two groups of cases were not equivalent to begin with. If Maryland prosecutors turn out to be more willing to go to court with a weak hand, whereas prosecutorial discretion in Virginia ensures that only sure bets will be brought to court, the results may have nothing to do with nullification instruction. Then again, even if the two groups of cases were equivalent, perhaps the two groups of juries were not. If jurors in Virginia tend to be more conservative (oriented more toward crime control than due process, for example) and if juries in Virginia comprise fewer women and minority members, then differences in juror characteristics may be producing the effect. Field studies have drawbacks. We cannot precisely control the independent variable; we cannot be sure the two groups are equivalent; and we lack control over extraneous variables. In contrast, *experiments* enable us to control variables and to establish parity between groups.

The work of I. A. Horowitz is an excellent example here. In his first experiment, Horowitz tested three types of instruction pertaining to jury nullification.[45] The first type, called the Standard Pattern Instruction, made no reference to nullification. Subjects who received this instruction may have known on a *sotto voce* level that they had the *power* to nullify, but this instruction clearly conferred no *right*. The second type was a nullification instruction based on the key phrases of the one used in Maryland: "So that whatever I tell you about the law, while it is intended to be helpful to you in reaching a just and proper verdict in the case, it is not binding upon you as members of the jury and you may accept or reject it. And you may apply the law as you apprehend it to be in the case."[46] Some proponents of nullification find the Maryland instruction too vague, and others question whether jurors will comprehend what the instruction is implying. So Horowitz also tested a more forceful version, called the Radical Nullification Instruction, which told jurors the following:

1. Although they were "a public body bound to give respectful attention to the laws," they had "the final authority to decide whether or not to apply a given law to the acts of the defendant on trial before them";

2. They represented the community, and therefore it would be "ap-

propriate to bring into their deliberations the feelings of the community and their own feelings based on conscience";
3. "Nothing would bar them from acquitting the defendant," despite their respect for the law, if they felt that "the law, as applied to the fact situation before them, would produce an inequitable or unjust result."[47]

Horowitz manipulated not only the instructions but also the case. He had subjects apply the Standard, the Maryland, or the Radical instruction to one of the following three cases: a murder case, in which the evidence pointed strongly to guilt; a drunk-driving case involving vehicular homicide; or a euthanasia case involving a nurse accused of the mercy killing of a terminally ill cancer patient. Horowitz hypothesized that if the nullification instructions made any difference, they would have a greater effect on the second and third cases than on the first.

Since the experiment combined three instructions and three cases, there were nine possible combinations (three times three). The subjects consisted of 170 people drawn from the juror rolls in Ohio. They were randomly assigned to one of the nine groups, and further divided up into six-person juries.

The differences in the cases had, as one might expect, a significant effect on the verdicts: the juries were more inclined to vote "guilty" in the murder case than in the drunk-driving and euthanasia cases. But surprisingly, the differences in the instructions had no overall effect, though instructions and cases often acted *together* (an interaction effect) to influence verdicts. What does this mean? It means that the subjects who received the Maryland nullification instruction and those who received the Standard instruction rendered verdicts that were quite similar. The interaction effect was apparent only when the drunk-driving and euthanasia cases were decided in light of the Radical instruction. Compared with the other two instruction groups, the "jurors" who received the Radical instruction rendered significantly more "guilty" verdicts in the drunk-driving case and significantly more "not guilty" verdicts in the euthanasia case.

We must remember that no state uses this Radical nullification instruction. When we look at the experimental results obtained with the type of nullification instruction that is actually used—the Maryland instruction—we find that jurors did not "go wild" or become anarchic; in fact, the verdicts were not significantly different from those rendered under the Standard instruction. As for predictions that anarchy would result if jurors were given the right to nullify, Horowitz's results show that Judge

Leventhal was wrong and Judge Bazelon was right. But when Horowitz gave the instruction in Radical form, there was an effect, albeit confined to the drunk-driving and euthanasia cases. Here, Leventhal might find grounds for his fear of anarchy, if "anarchy" merely means different verdicts. Bazelon might well claim that the difference revealed by the study was small, indicating that the jury's war with the law (if it is a war) is indeed modest. And if instructions liberated sentiments in Horowitz's experiment, as evidentiary doubt did in Kalven and Zeisel's work,[48] they seemed to liberate punitive sentiments in the drunk-driving case and merciful sentiments in the euthanasia case.

The Radical instructions affected not only the verdict but the jury's deliberations, causing the jurors to spend more time on certain topics. From the tape recordings of the jury deliberations, Horowitz found that, compared with the other two groups, the group given the Radical instruction spent less time discussing evidence and more time discussing instructions and "telling stories" based on their personal experience.

In a second experiment, Horowitz manipulated four variables.[49] The first was the type of case. He used the drunk-driving and euthanasia cases from his first experiment, but replaced the case of murder with one involving illegal possession of a weapon—a case that had already proved to be one in which jurors might nullify. He again manipulated the instructions, but this time used only the Standard and Radical versions. The third variable consisted of the lawyers' arguments: the defense attorney either made reference to a nullification argument in both the opening and the closing statements, or made no reference to nullification at all. The fourth variable involved challenges to nullification: the prosecutor either reminded the jurors, in both the opening and the closing statements, of their obligation to follow the law regardless of their sentiments, or made no reference to this obligation at all.

As in the first experiment, variations in the type of case had a significant effect on the verdict: subjects voted for conviction most often in the drunk-driving case and least often in the case involving illegal possession of a weapon. The type of instruction likewise had a significant effect: the Radical instruction produced harsher verdicts in the drunk-driving case and more lenient verdicts in the cases involving euthanasia and illegal possession. Differences in the lawyers' arguments also affected the verdict, much the way changes in the instructions did. Challenges by the prosecution to nullification did dampen jurors' tendency to act according to either their harsher or their more lenient sentiments.

Horowitz then performed three path analyses, one for each case, to see which variables best predicted the verdict. Surprising, perhaps, was his finding that the independent variables had only modest effects. More surprising was his finding that the "evidence" variable (that is, jurors discussing evidence during the postdeliberation sessions), which had a .40 total effect in the drunk-driving case, had only a -.05 and a -.18 effect, respectively, in the cases involving euthanasia and illegal possession of a weapon. Interestingly, a variable he called "justice notions," involving the stories that jurors tell during deliberations and that reflect their sense of justice, had an effect of approximately .22 across cases.

These findings reveal a few things. First, even when manipulating certain variables produces significant results, the manipulations may account for only a small portion of the variance. Put another way, jurors' verdicts are determined in large part by unknown factors. Those factors may be objective variables that the experimenter does not manipulate in a particular experiment. Or the factors determining a verdict may be subjective. This implies that, between the time the objective variables are first manipulated and the time the verdict is rendered, there is an intervening process in which jurors construe, interpret, and fashion stories—and these stories play a significant role in determining the verdict. Knowing only the first step, the objective variables the experimenter manipulates, does not tell us all we want to know about the last step, the verdict. Thus, our methodology for getting at commonsense justice must somehow take us further inside the black box—to the jurors' reasons for their verdict.

Strengths and Weaknesses of the Experimental Method

Of all the methods we've looked at for understanding why jurors do what they do—opinion polls, archival analyses, case studies, aggregate jury studies—the experimental method affords researchers the greatest control over the variables that may affect verdicts, and is the only method that can yield causal conclusions. These are major advantages. Hunches become hypotheses, and speculation can be confirmed. And whenever we have two different explanations for an outcome, a well-designed experiment can rule one out. A major advantage indeed. Yet, as with other methods we have examined, the experimental method also has drawbacks.

When we increase our control, we often sacrifice reality. For example, let's assume a researcher wishes to test whether jurors will nullify the law in a case of accessory to felony-murder. The researcher gives written scenarios of a case to two groups of subjects (mock jurors). The fact pattern of the case is the same for both groups, except that in the first scenario the defendant is the felony-murder triggerman, whereas in the second scenario the defendant is the felony-murder accessory (the getaway driver). It is clear that both triggerman and getaway driver conspired to commit the underlying felony (armed robbery), and it is also clear that a death occurred in the course of committing the felony. Under the law, then, both should be found guilty of felony-murder, but the researcher believes that the subjects will nullify and bring in more "not guilty" verdicts for the accessory. And this is indeed what happens. Since the only difference between the scenarios is the type of felony-murder defendant—triggerman versus getaway driver—the researcher concludes that type of defendant caused the difference in the verdicts.

But a litigator looking at this experiment might say, "Providing subjects with a brief, written scenario of a case is not the same as allowing jurors to hear a real-life case. Moreover, giving this case to a bunch of college students is not the same as allowing adult jurors to hear all the evidence and then deliberate. And providing people with brief written instructions on the law is quite different from letting them hear instructions from a judge. In short, the experimental situation is artificial." This litigator, inclining strongly toward realism, is unsure, in social science terms, of the "ecological validity" of the experiment. The litigator asks, "Can we generalize these results from an artificial task to the real world of jurors, courts, and cases?" Many people share these doubts.

The litigator would say, "If it ain't real, it ain't real." And the more the experiment departs from realism, the louder the criticism, in general. When the experimenter uses college sophomores, critics may loudly question whether the results can be generalized to real-life jurors, even though experimental tests of students versus real-life adult jurors have often shown little or no difference in the verdicts of the two groups.[50] The experimenter may counter by using adult subjects, but if that still doesn't meet realists' objections, the experimenter may obtain adults from jury rolls. When the realists still object, because these jurors are not engaged in actual deliberations, the experimenter may counter by having them deliberate.

But the objections do not end. "The choice of subjects is not the only issue," says the realist. "The written scenario remains artificial." Trying to respond to this type of objection, experimenters have videotaped mock trials in which actors play the key roles. "Still not the real thing," says the critic. "In real life the juror's eye is free to roam about the courtroom and is not restricted to just what the camera shows." Researchers have even gone so far as to create "shadow juries," made up of jury-eligible subjects who are paid to sit in the courtroom throughout a trial and who then go off to deliberate. But the absolute realist again cries "Artificial!" for if the shadow jurors were excused from trial during *voir dire,* they are already different from real jurors. And even if the experimenter got jurors who were not excused but were just alternate jurors, they would be rendering a verdict that did not count—and this is not the same as what real jurors do.

The experimenter must concede the truth of this absolute-realism argument. No matter how closely experiments may approximate the real, they will always remain not quite real. But now the experimenter takes a new tack and says to the realist, "Sacrificing some realism for precision and control may be worth it. To illustrate, let's take the paper-and-pencil experiment you objected to—the one concerning accessory felony-murder. Let's imagine we could do a natural field experiment in which a felony-murder triggerman and his getaway driver had separate trials. The fact pattern and the alleged crimes would be the same in both cases. Now we have the real thing, and the jury for the triggerman finds him guilty of felony-murder but the jury for the accessory finds him not guilty. Can we conclude, as we did before, that variations in the type of defendant produced the difference in the verdicts?"

"No," says the experimenter, "because this highly realistic setting is—like real life—messy and confounded. The cases have different attorneys. One attorney may be more attractive than the other, or more competent. One may be male, the other female. One may wear ill-fitting suits, while the other is highly tailored. One wears a power tie, the other a bow tie. One is a scratchy tenor, the other a rich baritone. Perhaps uncontrolled 'attorney variables' are responsible for the difference. What's more, the two juries now see a 'real' defendant before them. Maybe one looks sympathetic or likable, while the other looks seedy and repugnant. One sneers while the other looks earnest; one laughs inappropriately while the other weeps. Perhaps it's some uncontrolled 'defendant variable' that's causing the difference in the verdicts. Furthermore, the cases are probably tried by two different judges, and the instructions to the jury probably differ in some ways. Perhaps the difference in the verdicts is the result of some uncontrolled 'judge variable' or 'instruction variable.' The reality of realism is that it is a messy nightmare, replete with uncontrolled and potentially confounding variables."

So now we understand that there is an *advantage* to artificiality, and no small one at that. A written scenario removes characteristics of defendants, attorneys, and judges that may act as uncontrolled variables. A picture may be worth a thousand words, but it may produce a thousand confounds—which the written word does much to eliminate. Ensuring that defendants, witnesses, attorneys, and judges are faceless removes possible confounds, and limiting their words to the essence of the matter creates a cleaner test of things. Although this type of basic research simplifies the real-life complex drama in order to isolate particular variables that may affect jurors' construals, judgments, and verdicts, it has the virtue of enabling us to *know* what causes what.

This does not mean that the researcher dismisses all concern for reality. To the contrary, the question of whether findings based on the artificially simplified can be generalized to the messy and real is an important one. But the social scientist's "faith" in the findings does not hinge on a single experiment, for the perfect experiment is an ideal. Rather, faith builds as findings accumulate, from a variety of experiments and from a variety of methodologies. When results from archival work, case study analyses, aggregate jury studies, and experiments all point in the same direction, findings take on "convergent validity" and faith in them grows.

Our discussion of various research methods and their findings begins to reveal some truths about jury sentiments. Kalven and Zeisel's work showed that evidentiary doubt can liberate jurors' sentiments—and even without evidentiary doubt, jurors' sentiments about the law may yet determine their verdict. The Goetz case taught us that jurors can reconstrue the instructions regarding one element of a crime—intent—so as to produce a commonsense verdict which may surprise the legal purist. We've looked at different types of nullification, and seen that juries may nullify for various reasons. And Horowitz's experiments showed that when jurors are given mild permission to nullify, normality rather than anarchy reigns. The jury's war with the law (if it is indeed a war) seems a modest one. Yet even though we've learned a great deal, much in the black box still eludes us.

There are a few directional signs that deserve our attention. The stories that jurors tell about their personal experience—stories that Horowitz says reveal "nonevidentiary factors, such as the jurors' concepts of what was just rather than lawful in these instances"[51]—are one signpost. Still another signpost comes from Kalven and Zeisel, who at the end of their book wonder whether they mightn't have been studying the wrong thing. "Have we not been working in just one corner of the world of the jury and ignoring a substantial part of the total phenomenon? Have we not, that is, let the real quarry, the nature of jury decision-making, escape?"[52]

Let's pursue the quarry further—into the black box, into the very mind of the jurors. We place a great burden on jurors: from the case of police on a Los Angeles street to that of Bernhard Goetz on a New York subway, we ask jurors to comprehend the act, infer the intent, and reach a judgment about culpability and blameworthiness. Particularly in terms of fathoming *intent,* jurors must plunge from often hazy facts into a defendant's mind, where a darkness that eludes even videotapes reigns. We ask jurors to emerge with the truth. Just as jurors pursue the mind of a defendant, we will pursue the very mind of the jurors—to uncover the reasons, stories, and interpretations that are central to their decisionmaking.

How Jurors Construct Reality

4

Imagine three things. First, imagine Hamlet in better shape—less "scant of breath"[1]—than Shakespeare portrayed him, so that when he dueled with Laertes, touché became parry and Hamlet evaded the poisonous rapier. Thus, with Hamlet toned and buffed, he survived at the drama's end, but the fates of the king (his uncle), the queen (his mother), and Laertes remained the same: all three died. Second, imagine that there were no witnesses to the carnage, no "mutes or audience to this act,"[2] save Hamlet. And third, imagine that the State is bringing first-degree murder charges against Hamlet for the deaths of the king and queen.

There is one other point to keep in mind: the jurors who will hear this case have neither seen nor read *Hamlet*. Not having one of the privileged perspectives—the audience's, the author's, or God's—they do not know the *true story* of what happened in the external reality (that is, in the context of the play). Their method, then, comes to resemble the one that readers of detective novels follow: in trying to discover whodunnit, they attempt to construct a story that makes the best sense of the facts, a story that is both plausible and sound. In other words, they do not so much *find* reality as *construct* it.

They construct the story from more than just facts, since jurors never come to the jury box as blank slates. They may even come with information about this particular case: in our imaginary scenario, there's plenty of pretrial publicity concerning *State v. Hamlet*, with the tabloids and the nightly news shouting headlines about the assassination of the king. The jurors also have in mind certain stereotypes (typical notions about specific offenses, such as murder) and images (prototypes) about certain offenders, such as assassins. They have their own memories, beliefs, and sentiments as well. After the process of jury selection *(voir dire)*, the jurors who are finally seated have, ideally, little or no prior knowledge of the case (but this is unlikely here, given Hamlet's high-profile situation—and would be unlikely in any case). Or they have sworn that they can put aside their knowledge and hear the facts with an open and unbiased mind (an arguable legal assumption and a testable empirical claim). Let's imagine that they can indeed do this. Jurors thus may catch glimmers of the defense's and prosecution's strategies from questions tossed at them during *voir dire,* but not until they hear the opening statements can they first put those inklings together into a story.

The story the prosecution plans to tell is a story of consuming ambition, malevolent hatred, and conniving deception: Hamlet would do anything and eliminate anyone in order to get the crown, including murder his uncle and mother and maybe even kill his father. Yes, says the prosecution, "he was more than kin, but far less than kind!" He is corrupt enough to throw suspicion on innocents and drive honest folk to their graves. He even feigns madness, all to hide his premeditated treachery.

And what story would Hamlet tell? His attorneys float the insanity defense. They remind Hamlet that the jury is likely to be thinking of insanity, since assassins of monarchs, ministers, and presidents have often been madmen. "The press has already speculated in that direction, and we can trot out a number of witnesses to reinforce the claim, witnesses who will recount your eccentricities and peculiarities. A couple of shrinks will then testify, turning your oddities into symptoms, your symptoms into a psychiatric disorder, and there you have it: Hamlet not guilty by reason of insanity!"

But Hamlet won't hear of this. He wants to tell his story.

"What *is* your story?" asks counsel.

"Why, it's revenge," says Hamlet.

The attorneys patiently explain the legal facts of life, one of them being that taking the law into your own hands is not justifiable. "And where's your proof that your uncle killed your father?" they ask. "Even if we exhume the body, and even if the autopsy shows death by poison as you claim it will, the State is ready to charge you with the poisoning. And don't repeat that story about 'The ghost told me'—not unless you want to play the insanity card. You see, hallucinations don't make convincing witnesses, unless you choose to claim 'not guilty by reason of insanity.'"

"But what about self-defense?" says Hamlet. "My uncle was trying to kill me!"

"Ah, but where's your proof? You were the one found with the deadly weapon in your hand. The State claims that you tried to kill him and that you succeeded: you figured that if you didn't get him with the poison you planted in the cup of wine, then your poison-tipped rapier would certainly do the job. Your so-called accidental killing of Polonius further belies your claim, since again you appear to be the aggressor and he the victim. Now, as for getting the jury to buy the self-defense claim, it's a tough sell. The king was sitting on the throne, no visible weapon at the ready, presenting no serious threat, no imminent threat; and even if he was, you had the option to retreat, which you didn't take. So you see, my good Dane, the self-defense angle just won't work. You might try for *putative* self-defense and claim that you mistakenly believed the king was out to get you . . ."

"That sounds like insanity!" Hamlet is becoming more exasperated by the moment.

"So it does. Our best strategy, in my opinion. Delusions led you to believe that the king was out to get you, but it was all in your mind. After all, you were still grieving for your dad when your mother jumped into another man's bed, dad's body barely lukewarm. Why, the Oedipal possibilities abound! Surely there were enough to have unhinged a son's mind. Plenty of mitigating circumstances here, if you ask me."

"It wasn't all in my mind that he sent me to England with a Bellerophontic letter that said, 'Kill the bearer of this letter'!"

"But your proof, dear Hamlet? Rosencrantz and Guildenstern, along with the letter, are dead and gone. And if you take the stand and tell the jury that you discovered the letter, and that you premeditatively doctored it knowing Rosencrantz and Guildenstern would die as a result, then by your own testimony you add two more counts of first-degree murder to the indictment."

The Story

We are left to wonder which tale the defense will tell. And we are left to ponder whether the story the jurors finally construct will look anything like *Hamlet,* given these few but significant emendations. But what we do not have to wonder about, if the social scientists are correct, is the fact that the jury will construct a story.

In their book *Reconstructing Reality in the Courtroom,*[3] W. L. Bennett and M. S. Feldman show that jurors transform evidence into stories. Why stories? First, a story is a handy analytic device for organizing large amounts of information. It serves as a *filter,* a device for reducing a vast array of facts to manageable proportions. Second, it functions as a *framework* for organizing, situating, and interrelating facts. If jurors did not have such a framework, even a crude one, they might find it quite difficult to understand the evidence.

Take, for example, the prosecution's case in *State v. Hamlet*. In all likelihood, the prosecution is going to present its case out of sequence, perhaps even backward, or in some piecemeal fashion. The prosecutors may begin by calling the policeman who first discovered the bodies. Then a parade of medical experts may testify—toxicologist, pathologist, coroner, and so on—showing that the deaths were unnatural, and what caused them. The jurors, impatient to get on with it, have to sit through complex and disjointed testimony in order for the prosecution to present its case in a legally sound way. But this way of storytelling is unlike that of the journalist (a straightforward "who, what, when, where" approach), the Bible ("In the beginning . . ."), or the fairy tale ("Once upon a time . . ."). Without the prosecution's opening statement—which is a story of what happened and why—the jurors may not be able either to follow the prosecution's fragmented tale or to situate the disjointed trail of testimony.

And there's a third reason for creating a story. As Bennett and Feldman put it,

> If trials make sense to untrained participants, there must be some implicit framework of social judgment that people bring into the courtroom from everyday life. Such a framework would have to be shared by citizen participants and legal professionals alike. Even lawyers and judges who receive formal legal training must rely on some commonsense means of presenting legal issues and cases in ways that make sense to jurors, witnesses, defendants, and spectators.
>
> Our search for the underlying basis of justice and judgment in American trials has produced an interesting conclusion: the criminal trial is organized around storytelling.[4]

It's the story we're after; and of the many stories spun at a trial, it's the *jurors'* story we're most interested in. In the Goetz case, for example,, the jurors' story (in which Goetz acted without malice) was quite different from the prosecution's vigilante story, and different as well from Goetz's self-defense story. Although jurors are presented with stories—often two competing stories—they may nonetheless fashion their own account, which is likely to determine their verdict.

Are there reasons for constructing a story that go beyond the need to condense great quantities of facts or organize those facts into a framework? Is the story merely a mnemonic, an aid to the memory? Or, like an outline, does it simply provide a schematic map of the trial's twists and turns?

Bennett and Feldman propose a deeper reason for constructing stories. They note that "in isolation . . . behaviors or actions are ambiguous."[5] We saw this in the Rodney King case, where even though jurors could view a videotape of the beating, they found it difficult to decide what had happened and who had caused what. In our example from *Hamlet,* the alleged criminal act—putting poison in a glass of wine—can be construed in many different ways when extracted from the social context, including ways that do not impute any criminal intent at all. We could construe the poisoning as murder, suicide, accident, or mistake—and these do not exhaust the possibilities. It is only when we set the act within a social context that meaning emerges. As Bennett and Feldman state, "Much of the meaning and, therefore, the interest and importance of social activity depend on who does it, for what reasons, through what means, in what context, and with what sort of prologue and denouement."[6] Social context and social activity are essential, and "stories are everyday communication devices that create interpretive contexts for social action."[7]

How do we construct a story, and what elements go into it? Bennett and Feldman say that first we "locate the central action,"[8] which, in *State v. Hamlet,* would be the deaths of the king, queen, and Laertes. Next we "construct inferences about the relationships among the surrounding elements in the story that impinge on the central action."[9] This social frame includes the scene, the act, the alleged agent, the agency, and the purpose.[10] It will provide background (prologue), tell who did it, by what means and for what reasons, and in what context. In the prosecution's version of Hamlet's actions, the surrounding elements include Hamlet's moodiness, his surliness, and his disrespect for the new king. When we add to these the fact that he killed Polonius—mistaking him for the king, claims the prosecution—the social context becomes one of festering hatred, in which Hamlet moved craftily toward a premeditated killing.

Does this story work? According to Bennett and Feldman, interpreters test a story in essentially two ways. First, they ask whether the story hangs together as a plausible and unequivocal account of what happened. We can call this a test for internal consistency. Do the elements of the story cohere, or do they contradict one another? In other words, could the events have happened this way? But one could devise any number of versions that make good stories and appear internally consistent. The prosecution's case in *State v. Hamlet* weaves the facts into a plausible, even convincing tale. Yet the tale may be false, even if well told. And this leads us to the second way in which interpreters test a story: they assess its match with reality, asking, "Is the story valid?"

Reality acts as a check and constraint on the storyteller, since the storyteller does not "have complete freedom to create reality."[11] Consider Hamlet's story in light of reality. Hamlet first claims that a ghost—the ghost of his dead father—told him that his uncle murdered his father. Since it's difficult to call a ghost to the witness stand, this conversation is hard to verify. Moreover, the prosecution would probably object to any testimony about such a conversation, labeling it hearsay concerning the hereafter. And the claim that the new king's "reaction" to the play-within-the-play is factual proof of guilt (Hamlet stages his version of his father's murder, using a troupe of actors) is rather easy to dispute. Though Hamlet hoped to "catch the conscience" of the king, a conscience is neither catchable nor visible in the external reality. The "reaction" Hamlet saw may have resulted from the king's eating a burrito before the play. Of the two criteria, validity and internal consistency, Bennett and Feldman give far greater weight to consistency:

> On the one hand, courtroom stories must be built on definitions of the material evidence that comes from the incident in question. In this sense "the facts" do exercise some constraint over the possible stories that can emerge in a case. However, this constraint is considerably less binding than the conventional mythology of justice shared by most legal professionals and ordinary citizens would indicate. Each fact introduced in evidence is subject to a whole range of definition and placement tactics, the selection of which affects the contextual relations between the fact and all the other evidence that has been defined in story form. Each fact in a case, then, is subject to the permutation of meanings determined by its possible definitions, its possible connection to other story elements, and the variety of meaning that comes from altering definition and connection in relation to all the other definitions and connections in the ongoing story. In the final analysis, it is less the role played by evidence in the natural event than the degree to which the evidence can be redefined and relocated within stories and about the event that determines the outcome of a case.[12]

The Story of the Story

The dominant epistemological position in psychology in the first half of the twentieth century was logical positivism-empiricism. Although this position had been attacked previously, the shelling started in earnest with Thomas Kuhn's influential work *The Structure of Scientific Revolu-*

tions.[13] Thereafter, philosophers of science began scoring direct hits.[14] Over the past few decades, "the drubbing that logical empiricism . . . received from philosophers of science"[15] has taken its toll and has had a predictable effect: new perspectives and approaches have been developed. Currently, the field of psychology remains an epistemological battleground, on which a retreating-but-not-yet-dead empiricism is being challenged by social constructionism[16] and scientific realism.[17] And it is the latter two "isms" that supply the underpinnings of the story—the story of the story.

Rom Harré,[18] writing about the ontology of the science of psychology, proposes "that there are at most two human realities. One of these comprehends our biological nature as relatively closed systems of molecular interactions. The other comprehends our social nature as elements of a network of symbolically mediated interactions."[19] Harré, with homage to Ludwig Wittgenstein[20] and L. S. Vygotsky,[21] sees social reality as arising from conversational exchanges—from language and discourse. Such psychological phenomena as remembering, learning, "emotional talk," norms, and imperatives arise from the conversational world. According to this view, story construction (as well as thinking in storylike fashion) lies much closer to the essence of social being than it does to mere devices. Our norms, imperatives, and moral rules may take the form of "social representations."[22]

Psychologists have been taking a new look at stories in such diverse areas as cognition, memory, moral development, social psychology, and psychotherapy.[23] For example, Jerome Bruner has proposed that there are two distinctly different modes of thought, *propositional thinking* and *narrative thinking.*[24] These two modes each provide "distinctive ways of ordering experience, of constructing reality."[25] Whereas propositional thinking is logical, abstract, context-independent, theoretical, and formal, narrative thinking is concrete, interpersonal, situational, and descriptive of reality. If jurors think along narrative rather than propositional lines—a sensible assumption given that a case is about particulars (a particular defendant, act, and set of facts, and a moral decision about the blameworthiness of that particular defendant)—then stories may be the jurors' *natural mode* of both understanding the case and communicating their understanding to one another.

The fact that, in the vast majority of jurisdictions, jurors are prohibited from taking notes during trial places an added premium on memory.[26] And according to researchers in the field of memory research, the narrative mode may be one of the ways we remember. Endel Tulving has proposed that there are two distinct kinds of human memory: *semantic* and *episodic.*[27] Semantic memory, similar to Bruner's propositional thinking, is "independent of a person's identity and past," whereas episodic memory is the "recording and subsequent retrieval of memories of personal happenings and doings."[28] If episodic memory is indeed activated during trial and deliberations, this may explain a phenomenon observed in a good many mock-trial experiments—namely, that a substantial part of the deliberations is taken up with jurors' telling stories! Now, however, we see that such stories could be something other than time-wasting irrelevancies. Jurors may engage in storytelling because that is how they remember, think, and communicate; moreover, stories are relevant to the drama they are witnessing, and to the moral decision they must make regarding the defendant's blameworthiness.

In the world of morality and moral education, the child is more likely to be taught through stories and parables than through maxims and precepts. Martin Hoffman,[29] who studies empathy in children, and Robert Coles,[30] who has written extensively on children's moral lives, cite numerous such stories and parables—in contrast to Lawrence Kohlberg, who emphasizes abstract principles in children's thinking.[31] Yet the controversy is not just about the way in which children think, but also about the way in which adults think. Carol Gilligan[32] has argued that women, more so than men, focus on the interpersonal rather than the abstract aspect of morality, and reconstruct moral dilemmas in a narrative mode.

But although women may have a proclivity for the story, as Gilligan believes, men engage in storytelling, too. Ask a man or a woman to tell you about his or her life, and you are likely to get a story—not just a bunch of facts, but facts given structure and shape. The social psychologist Theodore Sarbin[33] sees the story as a "general metaphor for understanding human conduct . . . The story or narrative model allows psychology to make contact with the historical context of individuals and with the insights into human social behavior found in stories, drama, literature, and history."[34] Although "metaphor" would seem to imply a device for conceptualizing about people, Sarbin sees the story as more fundamental: it is not just something scientists make up—it is a tool people use to interpret their own lives. They interpret their lives as stories. As Sarbin puts it, "Our plannings, our rememberings, even our loving and hating, are guided by narrative plots."[35] K. Scheibe[36] makes a similar point, stating that individuals interpret their lives as adventure stories.

George Howard,[37] writing about psychotherapy, asks: "Have you noticed that therapy usually begins with an invitation to the client to tell his or her story? Therapists have favored ways of phrasing their readiness to hear the client's tale, such as 'Can you tell me what brings you here?' . . .

Clients understand that their task is to tell the part of their life story that appears most relevant to their presenting problem."[38] Alfred Adler, who developed a subjectivist psychology and who was the heir presumptive to Freud until their ways parted, placed great emphasis on "fictions."[39] Borrowing from the philosopher Hans Vaihinger,[40] Adler saw the mind as inventive, weaving fictions out of thought itself. The "self," then, may be just a construction, an "as if" story. This suggests a notion which George Kelly[41] would develop more fully—namely, that all our constructs are subject to revision or replacement. According to this "constructive alternativism," life becomes "the stories we live by," psychopathology becomes "stories gone mad," and psychotherapy becomes "exercises in story repair."[42]

In thinking, memory, moral development, social psychology, and psychotherapy we see the ubiquity of stories, and strong evidence supporting the hypothesis that jurors create and use stories in their deliberative process. Howard speaks of the human being as "*Homo fabulans* (man the storyteller)."[43] Whether storytelling is bred in the bone or born of a culture whose commerce is stories is an issue that takes us beyond the scope of this inquiry. But if the nature-versus-nurture question need not concern us, the realism-versus-relativity question does; for whether a story is "true" or merely an interesting "story" has a bearing on issues of justice and fairness.

As John Barth states in an early novel, "The same life lends itself to any number of stories—parallel, concentric, mutually habitant, or what you will."[44] And some forms of social constructionism espouse just this sort of relativism, claiming that truth is unobtainable, for there are only stories and more stories. In one of his essays, Barth speaks of the novelist as "a mere storyteller. Which is to say, a professional liar."[45] A professional liar may be treasured as a storyteller but is unlikely to be valued as a juror. Upon jurors we impose a heavier weight and a solemn oath. By placing this burden and obligation upon them, we demand far more than a tale, however cleverly constructed. We want not *a* story but *the* story—the truth—even as we know that the *true* story transcends the jurors' perceptual capacities.

Neither sensory experience nor revelation provides *the* story. Nonetheless, even as jurors construct a story, the law's expectation is clear: the jurors' story must pay homage to the truth, rather than merely winking at it *en passant* or ignoring it entirely. The law is not demanding metaphysical certainty—something that cannot be obtained. In asking jurors to be "fact finders," it is asking them to find those facts *as best they can;* and "best" means that they should take reality into account, rather than create *ex nihilo*.

Story Ingredients

What are the raw ingredients that give the jurors' story its shape and substance? The obvious ingredient, which the law hopes will be the only ingredient, is the *evidence* brought out at trial. But in reaching their decision, jurors may also use *extralegal factors*[46]—that is, legally irrelevant
information, such as the race[47] or physical attractiveness of the defendant
and victim.[48] During the trial, prejudicial statements and legally inadmissible material, even after the judge has admonished the jurors to disregard
these, may still wend their way into the jurors' deliberations and influence
their decisions.[49] Many such extralegal factors arise in the course of a
trial; but there is another ingredient that is present long before the trial
commences. We shall call this ingredient *prior knowledge,* which recognizes the obvious fact that the jurors' slates have already been written on
long before the first word of testimony is uttered.

Jurors come to the court with memories, images, beliefs, attitudes, expectations, and sentiments—all of which is known as prior knowledge.
For example, prospective jurors are likely to have in their memories representations of crimes, actors, and outcomes: images of what certain
crimes look like,[50] the types of people who commit such crimes,[51] and the
types of harm that ensue.[52] These representations may take the form of a
general composite—that is, a stereotype or prototype of the typical burglar, the typical burglary, or the typical harms that result in a burglary.
But what people think is typical turns out, in most cases, to be far from
typical. To understand why this is so, we must consider the likely sources
of these general composites.

The most likely source is the mass media. As Valerie Hans[53] notes, "because a relatively small proportion of the public has direct experience
with the justice system, public knowledge and views of law and the legal
system are largely dependent on media representations."[54] Much of local
news,[55] whether reported on television, on the radio, in newspapers, or in
weekly magazines, is taken up with stories involving crime, harm, law,
and justice. In addition, these topics are staples in Hollywood movies, on
call-in radio shows, and on television talk shows, weekly series, and
docudramas. Actual courtroom dramas appear on cable television channels, and fictional courtroom dramas can be found on all channels. In
short, the media saturate us with information and images relating to
crime, criminals, and harm.

This saturation "does not reflect reality," since "violent and sensational crimes . . . dominate media coverage of both fictional and factual
crime."[56] The media's portrayal of crimes and criminals, of the harms

they do and the sentences they receive, accents the extreme, the atypical, and the extraordinary, rather than the representative; in this sense, the media actively construct a "crime reality" which is a distorted and more violent version of the actual world. For example, D. A. Graber[57] analyzed the content of news reports and found that murder was represented in 25 percent of the stories, although murder figured in less than 1 percent of all crimes reported. Similarly, when researchers analyzed the content of stories concerning sentencings, they found that the sentences reported by newspapers were "equally atypical of actual practice."[58] Opinion poll studies in the United States, Canada, Great Britain, Australia, and elsewhere show that people underestimate the severity of sentences, the severity of maximum penalties, and the amount of time offenders spend in prison before parole; in contrast, they overestimate the leniency of sentencing, the number of people released on parole, and the numbers of those who go on to commit new offenses.[59] Many people have a consistent set of views about criminal justice matters which turns out to be incorrect. And when they enter the jury box, their prior knowledge enters with them.

Media reports shape our general composites, and these composites are fairly stable; they tend to change slowly, and tend to be linked to attitudes and to religious and political values.[60] But the media provide another source of information that affects our prior knowledge, and this source turns out to be specific and unstable: it consists of specific crime stories, usually high-profile, atypical, and sensational cases, that recently dominate the news. When people are asked to recall information about crimes, criminals, harms, and punishments, they typically recall these recent cases. In accordance with what social scientists call the "availability heuristic" (what is most recently stored in the memory is what is most readily used),[61] people's recall is biased by these atypical and sensational cases—biased because what is most recent is not necessarily representative. The availability heuristic and the more general stereotypes and prototypes are likely to be activated when jurors begin to hear the evidence, construct their stories, and ultimately decide which verdict category best fits the story.

Not only may jurors be affected by recent cases, but they are likely to be affected by pretrial publicity concerning the particular case they are to hear. Research has shown that pretrial publicity can bias jurors' judgments, and very recent studies reveal that judicial remedies—whether these take the form of judicial admonitions, more extensive *voir dire* questioning, or leaving it to jury deliberations to steer discussion from proscribed to prescribed topics—generally fail to correct the bias.[62]

Prior knowledge also includes mental representations that derive not from media sources but from interpersonal and personal accounts of crimes. A prospective juror, for example, may have heard a story concerning his Aunt Sadie being mugged, his neighbor's house being burgled, his employer's car being stolen. These interpersonal accounts of crimes, according to Loretta Stalans,[63] tend to be more representative of actual crime scenarios than are media portrayals, and may act as a as a counterweight to the media's influence.

Although interpersonal sources may offset media portrayals, we see little evidence of realism in subjects' portrayals when we look at Vicki Smith's data.[64] She asked subjects to write down all the attributes they could think of in connection with the crimes of assault, burglary, kidnapping, murder, and robbery. The typical features they listed for each crime differed significantly from the defining criteria that are specified by the law. For example, "subjects tend to use the terms *robbery* and *murder* as general labels for deliberate takings and intentional killings, respectively. Under the law, many deliberate takings are not robbery, but theft, and many intentional killings are not murder, but manslaughter."[65] The typical features her subjects ascribed to burglary, kidnapping, and assault were also different from those defined by the law.

Smith then devised two sets of scenarios—typical and atypical—for assault, burglary, kidnapping, murder, and robbery cases. Even though the typical scenarios contained many of the features that subjects attributed to crimes and the atypical scenarios lacked such features, both sets met the legal definition of the crime. But when subjects were asked whether the defendant was guilty of a crime, they said yes significantly more often in the typical scenarios than in the atypical ones, given the assault, burglary, and kidnapping cases. Based on experimental data rather than supposition, Smith's conclusion stands on solid footing: there is, she says, "strong evidence that laypeople are not blank slates with regard to the law; their prototypes of crime categories can influence both their perceptions of fact situations and their categorization decisions."[66]

Story Construction

The most detailed and well-researched model of story construction is Nancy Pennington and Reid Hastie's "story model" of juror decision-making.[67] These researchers propose, as did Bennett and Feldman,[68] that jurors construct narrative story structures to organize and interpret evidence, and that this process is *explanation-based*: jurors seek to account for the facts by inferring causal and intentional links among particular facts. This process begins *during* the trial. Clearly, the law's assumptions and injunctions—that jurors suspend judgment, hear all the evidence, and then weigh the evidence and decide—is at odds with what jurors actually do.[69]

In this constructive process, three types of ingredients are coordinated and combined:

> (a) case-specific information acquired during the trial (e.g., statements made by witnesses about past events relevant to the decision); (b) knowledge about events similar in content to those that are the topic of dispute (e.g., knowledge about a similar crime in the juror's community); and (c) generic expectations about what makes a complete story (e.g., knowledge that human actions are usually motivated by goals). This constructive mental activity results in one or more *interpretations* of the evidence that have a narrative story form.[70]

With ingredients (b) and (c), we see how prior knowledge enters the mix and provides the contextual ground. That ground, which may differ substantially from what is actually typical, is nonetheless the source of both sentiments and inferences. According to Kalven and Zeisel,[71] sentiments are most likely to be "liberated" when evidentiary doubt is greatest; inferences, on the other hand, are liberated all the time, since inferences are necessary to fill out the story. If, as Pennington and Hastie believe, the jurors' task is *fundamentally interpretive* (as opposed to logical-deductive, mathematical, or actuarial), then subjectivity not only enters but *must* enter; and in the three-part blend of ingredients, subjective prior knowledge accounts for two-thirds of the mix.

We thus see that story construction is both subjective and interpretive, and arrive once again at the relativist's and novelist's position: the same set of facts can spawn more than one story. Yet as Pennington and Hastie state, "one story will usually be viewed as more acceptable than the others."[72] On what grounds is one story selected over the others as *the* story? Pennington and Hastie cite three principles: coverage and coherence (which determine the acceptability of a story), and uniqueness (which contributes to our confidence in that story).[73] *Coverage* "refers to the extent to which the story accounts for evidence presented at trial . . . The greater the story's coverage, the more acceptable is the story."[74] *Coherence* consists of three parts: consistency, plausibility, and completeness. "Consistency concerns the extent to which the story does not contain internal contradictions. Plausibility concerns the extent to which the story is consistent with knowledge of real or imagined events in the real world.

Completeness refers to the extent to which a story has all of its parts. These three components combine to yield the coherence of a story."[75] If there is one story among several that appears more coherent, then it will have *uniqueness,* and jurors will be more confident in accepting this story as the story.

Coverage, consistency, completeness, and to some extent uniqueness all refer to what Bennett and Feldman called "internal consistency," or what the novelist means when asking, "Is it a good yarn?" But where is validity? That enters with the element of *plausibility.* Like Bennett and Feldman, Pennington and Hastie give greater weight to internal consistency than to external validity: they stress the subjective note, as opposed to the objective note. But Pennington and Hastie go beyond Bennett and Feldman by empirically demonstrating that the story model provides a better fit with jury decisionmaking than do traditional models—be they legal or mathematical—of the way in which jurors integrate and weigh information and reach a decision.[76]

One might argue, to the contrary, that the facts in most cases are so clear-cut and indisputable that only one story is really possible; that, moreover, if the facts are so self-evident, then the story is more likely to follow from (be deduced from) the facts than be constructed in the mind. But consider this argument in the light of a tort claim for emotional injuries. Physical injuries are visible and medically documentable, but where are the clear-cut and indisputable facts of emotional injuries? How are the jurors to determine if some minimal level of emotional harm has been sustained? How are they to determine if the harm is severe? And how are they to determine whether the claim is "genuine or fictitious"?[77] These "factual determinations" need to be made before legal liability can be assigned. But instead of leading us out of the subjective, inferential woods, such questions take us deeper still. For deciding if the defendant "intended to inflict the emotional injury upon the plaintiff"[78] clearly involves an inference, not a deduction. And when jurors conclude that the conduct of the defendant was "extreme and outrageous,"[79] they have made a "social judgment, rather than a factual determination based on objective criteria."[80]

Inference and subjectivity are paramount during the story-evaluation process in certain cases—namely in criminal trials, where jurors are asked to judge not only the facts of what happened *(actus reus)* but why the events happened, the mental state and motivation *(mens rea)* of the defendant. In insanity cases, for example, the question "Who did it?" does not arise. We know the defendant did it; but we do not know whether that defendant was responsible for his or her actions, or whether the defendant knew what he or she was doing, or whether he or she knew that the actions were wrong. In cases of alleged rape where the defense claims the plaintiff consented to the sex, and in murder cases where the defense claims self-defense, the issue turns not on the *who* of "Who did it?" but on the *it*, and here the jurors must leap from the objective into the subjective, deciphering thoughts, feelings, and motives that are impossible to perceive directly. These are the inferences that flesh out and fill in the story. In social psychology, this is the realm of attribution theory.[81]

One type of attribution that jurors are often asked to make involves *causation:* Who or what caused the alleged criminal act to happen? In a social world whose cause-and-effect relations are often extremely messy and in which there may be many apparent causes for an event, jurors have to select the prepotent cause. A related type of attribution involves *intentionality:* Did the actor intend that act or harm to happen? Did he or she do it purposefully, knowingly, recklessly, negligently, . . . or none of the above? In legal and sequential thinking, if *cause* and *intention* are attributed, then a judgment regarding *culpability* can follow. But recent work by M. D. Alicke[82] shows that jurors may not work that way, for "causal judgments are conflated with ascriptions of blameworthiness."[83]

Imagine two different scenarios in which John is driving over the speed limit, hits another driver, and causes a variety of injuries to the other driver. In both scenarios there is a clear causative factor (an oil spill on the road, a tree branch blocking a stop sign, a moment's negligence or inattention on the part of the other driver), and the causative principles of necessity, sufficiency, and proximity are held constant. But in one scenario John is speeding home for a socially desirable reason: he wants to hide an anniversary gift from his parents. In the other scenario, his motive is socially undesirable: he's speeding home to hide a vial of cocaine. In the latter case, jurors would hold John both more responsible and *more the cause* of the harm. It would seem, then, that a judgment of greater culpability leads jurors to ascribe greater causal influence to the actor. And here is where prototypes, stereotypes, biases, and sentiments again may color the causative attributions that bind the story together.

A Fitting Story

Once a story has inferences and attributions in place, and meets the principles of coverage, coherence, and uniqueness, it must be situated in a legal context of verdicts. The verdict possibilities are given by the judge when he instructs the jury on the law; it is the jurors, however, who "must make a category membership decision,"[84] deciding and choosing which verdict best fits the story. Again, jurors' prototypes and stereotypes regarding the nature of certain crimes interact with the judge's formal instructions and, as Smith shows, sometimes override instructions. Rather than deciding if the legally necessary and sufficient conditions are met, as the law would have it, jurors assess whether the story contains enough of the *typical* features of their crime category prototypes for inclusion.

From beginning to end, the jurors' process is replete with construing, constructing, interpreting. Objectivity and facts play a part—but the smaller part, as it seems. The jurors' subjective faculty, where sentiments and prototypes abound, is largely responsible for shaping the facts into a story. The stories they construct reveal their sentiments and their commonsense notions of justice, which thereby come fully, determinatively, and dispositively into play.

The subjective methods of jurors apparently form a sharp contrast with the decisionmaking practices of judges, who seem impelled by *stare decisis* and legal training toward more objective judgments. Although jurors' judgments are infused with sentiment and subjectivity, we envision judges differently, imagining Solomon, Socrates, and the syllogism as their guiding lights. But is the contrast between jurors and judges real or illusory? In Chapter 2 we saw some instances in which judges may have nullified the law, and others in which judges chafed under sentencing guidelines and mandatory sentencing schemes that limited or removed their discretionary power. Judges are certainly not immune to the influence of community sentiment. Mightn't they, too, be pulled and influenced by sentiments and subjective attitudes, even to the point of yielding to them? Or do they decide law in some more objective manner—by deduction rather than construction, perhaps—using syllogisms instead of stories to reach their verdicts? Let's continue our discussion of objectivity and subjectivity, but turn our focus from jurors to judges.

Objectivity versus Subjectivity in the Law

5

Oliver Wendell Holmes Jr., who has been called "the greatest jurist and legal scholar in the history of the English-speaking world,"[1] was clearly no average man. In *The Common Law*,[2] "widely considered the best book on law ever written by an American,"[3] he tackled uncommonly difficult questions about the nature, shape, and coherence of the law. Though few would agree with every jurisprudential answer he gave, none would deny that he left an enduring mark. And his jurisprudence, cast in the terms of this chapter's title, comes down forcefully on the side of objectivity.

Holmes believed that "the standards of the law are external standards."[4] Since the "law only works within the sphere of the senses . . . it is wholly indifferent to the internal phenomena of conscience."[5] Yet we've seen that jurors, far from being indifferent to the internal, are quite ready to venture deep into the subjective in order to discover the motives, intentions, and culpability of actors. If the law is to be grounded in objectivity rather than in jurors' subjective predilections, then how does Holmes propose to prevent us from plunging into the dark interior, a plunge we seem naturally inclined to take? The restraining force he offers is "the conception of the average man, the man of ordinary intelligence and reasonable prudence."[6] It is this Promethean man with a pedestrian name who will keep us rockbound, anchored to terra firma and out in the light of day.

In addition, this average man has a best friend—a discerning dog that figures in a well-known aphorism of Holmes's: "Even a dog distinguishes between being stumbled over and being kicked."[7] But the dog's discernment unleashes a problem for Holmes's objective theory. For if a man seems to be able to tell what's in a dog's mind, and a dog seems to be able to tell what's in a man's mind, and if such knowledge is so easy to acquire, what's so difficult about discerning intent? If even a dog can distinguish accident from intent, can't a human being go a bit further? Do people have the ability to distinguish intent from mistake? Can they distinguish, as the Model Penal Code prescribes,[8] actions that are done purposely from those that are done knowingly, recklessly, or negligently? Can they tell a blameworthy killing from a justifiable or excusable one?

Such legal questions require discriminations, sometimes very fine ones, and to make these the fact finder will have to turn from external reality to the mind and motives of the actor. But there are two other possible choices. The "strict-liability" advocate argues that making such discriminations is a mistake: the question is not whether people *can* make the discriminations, but whether the law *should*. Holmes, in contrast, believes that the law should make discriminations but without subjectivizing or psychologizing. Holmes's average man must not only keep us grounded in the external but help us make those necessary discriminations without veering into subjectivity. This exemplar must carry considerable freight, then, and whether it is up to the challenge remains to be seen. But first let's imagine a legal world in which neither man nor dog chooses to discern—a world that does not need any restraining influences because subjectivity and the mental life are simply out of bounds.

Strict Liability

A strict-liability world is one in which only the outer conduct of the accused is of concern. Here, harm is hinged directly to the actions of the accused, without consideration of intent. Such a world once existed in pre-Norman England: the Saxon legal system was based on strict liability. Any person who harmed another was held responsible and was expected to compensate the victim. Whether he shot an arrow at what he thought was a deer but hit a man, or whether his arrow ricocheted off a tree and hit a man, or whether he deliberately shot at a man and hit him, he was held equally responsible. And if the harm was the same in all cases, so was the "crime," since distinctions among mistake, accident, and murder were irrelevant.

After responsibility was assigned, compensation was assessed, and the assessment was backed up by the threat of retaliation. The operative maxim was "Buy off the spear or bear it."[9] The amount of compensation depended on the harm done and the status of the victim. There were three possible types of compensation: a *bot*, a *wer*, and a *wite*. The *bot* went to the victim for the harm. The *wer* went to the deceased's relatives. And the *wite,* the last to evolve, was a fine that went to the Crown for disturbing the king's peace.

This system was more "civilly" than "criminally" oriented: the *bot* and the *wer* addressed and redistributed resources *between individuals.* With the later addition of the *wite,* the State entered as a player, and the civil drama began to take on a criminal cast. Such a strict-liability system, with its admixture of civil and criminal law, meets the test of externality and objectivity. But it fails as a workable and coherent system of criminal law for three main reasons: because it does mix and confound civil and criminal law; because there are "*bot*less" crimes for which there is no adequate compensation; and, most of all, because strict liability fails to accord with the community's sense that punishment should be hinged to the actor's intentions.

If the prevailing system were one based on strict liability—a system in which a death is a death is a death—the legal outcome would be the same regardless of how the death was caused. Various types of homicide would merit the same punishment, along with deaths resulting from accident, mistake, self-defense, insanity, negligence, or recklessness. To this form of "equal justice" we are apt to cry foul. We want our laws to take into account what we intend when we commit an act. Young children often say, "I didn't mean it," when they spill something. Not only do these young "lawyers" already know the difference between premeditation and negligence or accident, but as defendants before parental judges they know that negligence should not be punished to the same extent as pre-meditative acts. We want the law's sanctions to be applied not strictly but justly—a course that requires assessing the blameworthiness of the act and the actor. And this, it seems, leads us back inward.

Reasoning Subjectivity Away

With regard to the law, the problem of trying to fathom thoughts, intentions, and motives has been recognized for centuries. In 1477 a chief justice of England said, "The thought of man is not triable; the devil alone knoweth the thought of man."[10] A modern jurist, Lady Wootton,[11] made a similar point, with a dissimilar attribution. In referring to an issue relevant to insanity, she argued "that a man's capacity to resist temptation is 'buried in (his) consciousness, into which no human being can enter,' known if at all only to him and to God: it is not something which other men may even know; and since 'it is not possible to get inside another man's skin' it is not something of which they can ever form even a reasonable estimate as a matter of probability."[12] Whether God alone, the devil alone, or the man alone knows his innermost thoughts, the problem is that judges and jurors, alone or together, cannot know them for certain.

What Holmes proposes and develops is a way of assessing the act and the actor without giving way to subjectivity. He first clears away some shibboleths, noting that there are laws that sanction punishment where we do not find violations of any moral standard, laws that allow society to treat the individual as a means rather than as some Kantian end. Here, we may think of laws based on custom, economic schemes, or strict-liability offenses. For example, a driver of a car may be punished for driving on the left side of the road in the United States, but punished for driving on the right side of the road in England; custom, rather than moral violation, seems to be operating. Laws and punishments for monopolies vary depending on time, country, and economic system, and do not seem tied to a moral issue. And barbering without a license, driving a motorcycle without a helmet, selling liquor to a minor who presents (fake) proof of being over the legal age may all lead to punishment, though the underlying moral basis may be tenuous. Thus, for Holmes, the Hegelian "mystic bond between wrong and punishment"[13] is a fiction: this theory of retribution, which "is instinctively recognized by unperverted minds," is, on closer inspection, "absolute and unconditional only in the case of our neighbors."[14]

Yet Holmes is not endorsing strict liability, for he recognizes that criminal and civil liability "is founded on blameworthiness"; to deny the connection "would shock the moral sense of any civilized community . . . [and] would be too severe for that community to bear."[15] He not only intends to keep blameworthiness in the picture, but he intends to keep community sentiment centrally situated, since the "first requirement of a sound body of law is, that it should correspond with the actual feelings and demands of the community, whether right or wrong."[16]

Holmes begins his analysis of murder with the element of "malice," which, "in common speech, includes intent, and something more."[17] The something more is a "wish for the harm," the feeling of pleasure in causing suffering. This latter feeling, a *motive,* is irrelevant for murder, in which only intent matters. Holmes then resolves "intent" into two components: "foresight that certain consequences will follow from an act, and the wish for those consequences working as a motive which induces the act."[18] Where foresight involves cognition, the motive involves feelings, passions, wishes, and more. Holmes argues that these are irrelevant. If the actor knows that the act "will very certainly cause death,"[19] he is guilty of murder. But now comes the final step: Holmes tells us we do not need to know what the actor knows. "The test of foresight is not what this very criminal foresaw, but what a man of reasonable prudence would have foreseen."[20]

First, Holmes's position is a *comparative* position, measuring the accused against the average man. In making the comparison, we need not fathom what the accused knew, for it is enough to presume what the average man would have known. Second, Holmes's psychology is *behavioral* and *cognitive:* we first focus on the actor's act, and then we focus on what the average man would reasonably have known. Whether we speak about knowledge, foresight, or thinking, the accent is clearly on the cognition rather than on the feelings, motives, and will of the actor. But does this "legal psychology" work? Does the comparative standard hold up?

When the Reasonable Man Isn't Home

An intentional killing is murder rather than manslaughter if the act entailed no provocation or heat of passion.[21] A defendant is considered to have been "provoked" if he "was substantially impaired in his self-control at the time of the killing."[22] As G. P. Fletcher notes, "The issue is plainly normative in the sense that the homicide is not mitigated to manslaughter by a mere factual showing that the slayer was provoked. He must be provoked under circumstances and to such a degree that he is not expected completely to control himself. The standard of adequate provocation is obviously shaped by social convention."[23]

A major problem with the reasonable-person standard, in the context of provocation, is that "the reasonable person is hardly at home . . . since the reasonable person does not kill at all, even under provocation."[24] A second problem for this cognitively based legal psychology involves explaining how passions can get the best of us at times, overturning the cognitive governor of reason. If the law assumes that reasonableness holds sway, and further assumes that breaching the standard indicates culpability, then why mitigate the punishment in such circumstances? Why not punish fully? A third problem arises from the fact that people can be "substantially impaired in their self-control" by mental or physical disorder. If the only question is whether the reasonable person could control himself, we end up convicting those who might deserve mitigation.

Take, for example, the case of *Bedder v. Director of Public Prosecutions* (1954).[25] As Fletcher tells the story, Bedder

killed a prostitute who was allegedly taunting and hitting him in a fracas about his inability to perform the negotiated sexual act. The claim was that the accused was impotent and particularly sensitive about his incapacity. Nonetheless, the House of Lords affirmed the instructions to the jury not to consider the impact of the accused's impotence on his reaction to the prostitute's taunting. It may be that the accused should have controlled himself whether he was impotent or not, yet this is a fact that should have been decided by the jury with full appreciation of all the pressures bearing on the event. One can hardly say that the jury passed judgment on Mr. Bedder if they did not even consider the most significant facts that influenced his loss of control.[26]

Before we deal with Bedder, what of the reasonable man? The reasonable man is not likely to be found with a prostitute, but if he should commit this indiscretion, the reasonable man does not typically happen to be impotent. So if a prostitute taunts the nonimpotent, reasonable man for failure to perform when in fact he has performed, the taunt becomes a non sequitur and the situation becomes ludicrous and surreal. This is not the situation Bedder faced, and the mythical standard is thus irrelevant to his circumstances. If we ignore Bedder's facts and perspective, then our reasonable-man comparison becomes inapt, and the legal doctrine becomes "totally alienated from the moral sentiments that give rise to it."[27]

Let's look at a second example, this time a case in which the defendant claimed insanity. Rita James Simon tape recorded the jury's deliberations during an experimental trial of this type and revealed that, once again, the reasonable man was nowhere to be found.[28] Jurors who found the defendant not guilty by reason of insanity and those who found him guilty both pointed to the same determinative facts, but construed those facts differently. The jurors who voted "not guilty by reason of insanity" said, in effect: Who but a crazy person would break into a home in broad daylight, risking five to ten years in jail, in order to steal a cheap pair of cufflinks and a cigarette lighter worth less than fifty dollars, and be caught crouching in the middle of a room with a newspaper over his head? The jurors who voted "guilty" answered, in effect: A smart criminal would. Broad daylight is a good time for breaking and entering, because most people are away from home; small goods are easily carried away without arousing suspicion, and are easy to fence; and when you know you're about to be caught, crouching like a duck might be a clever way to set up an insanity defense.

Note the two exemplars that are present, and the one that isn't: the insane individual and the smart criminal battle it out, while the reasonable person is AWOL. And he's not just absent—he's irrelevant: the reasonable person neither breaks into houses nor crouches with a newspaper on his head. If we wish to settle legal questions of insanity, provocation, and more, we must seek to understand what's in the accused's head, along with his motives, impulses, and controls. If the reasonable-person exemplar is inapt or simply fails to keep us on objective ground, then we must inevitably turn inward, to the subjective.

Objective and Subjective Liability

By the tenth century, the Saxon legal system of strict liability was undergoing "subjective" modification. Under King Æthelred, new laws were drafted which emphasized *inner facts* as the criteria for determining culpability.

> And if it happens that a man commits a misdeed involuntarily, or unintentionally, the case is different from that of one who offends of his own free will, voluntarily and intentionally.
> . . . Likewise he who is an involuntary agent of his misdeeds should always be entitled to clemency and better terms owing to the fact that he acted as an involuntary agent.
> Careful discrimination shall be made in judging every deed, and the judgement shall be ordered with justice, according to the nature of the deed.[29]

In subjective liability, the "nature of the deed" is distinct from the manifest act; the "crime" resides far more in the intent *(mens rea)* than in the subsidiary act *(actus reus),* which merely demonstrates "the firmness rather than the content of the actor's intent."[30] Almost the reverse is true for objective liability, which begins with a discernible criminal act. From this perspective, intent is a subsidiary appendage "linked conceptually to the commission of certain acts"; it is not "some mysterious inner dimension of experience that exists independently from acting in the external world."[31] In objective liability, "nonintent" functions as "a challenge to the authenticity of appearances, rather than as a basis for inculpating the actor."[32]

The topic of "attempts" accentuates the differences between objective and subjective perspectives. Take the question, "When has an attempted bank robbery begun?" The answer is more important for objective liability, since that position requires, first and foremost, that the crime consist of an overt act. Salmond, a justice in New Zealand, defined a criminal attempt "an act that shows criminal intent on the face of it."[33] If that is so, then the attempt cannot start when the robber first has the idea, since we cannot see the thought. Nor can it start when he first sketches plans or obtains the necessary equipment, for these acts may be indistinguishable from legal acts, not having "criminal intent on the face of it." Even going into the bank and approaching the teller is indistinguishable from what ordinary law-abiding citizens do all the time. So under objective liability the criminal act begins at the moment the robber draws his gun and says, "This is a stickup." The community would probably prefer interdiction at an earlier point.

From the viewpoint of subjective liability, the crime begins when the criminal intent takes shape. But what if the robber procrastinates, or obsesses, or fantasizes, such that his intent leads to no action? Are we to find this person guilty of attempted robbery? Such an outcome would appear odd, if not unjust, precisely because no act has occurred. We need some sort of act, although it need not be as specific as the sort required by objective liability—that is, it need not "demonstrate the actor's commitment to carry out his criminal plan."[34]

Now let's consider "impossible attempts." Consider these five.[35] A man aims and fires a gun at a tree stump, believing he is shooting at a person. A woman trying to kill a man fires shots into his body as he lies sleeping—but he died in his sleep hours ago. A husband drives his wife to a secluded spot, pulls out a gun, and fires at her head, realizing only then that he forgot to load the gun. A wife tries to poison her husband by dropping arsenic-laced sugar cubes in his tea, but mistakenly drops in ordinary, unadulterated sugar cubes. A woman tries to kill another woman by sticking pins in the heart of an effigy. For all five cases, is it attempted murder?

The advocate of objective liability would say no: shooting a tree stump or a dead body, pulling the trigger of an unloaded weapon, dropping sugar cubes into tea, and putting pins into dolls are not criminal acts. But for the advocate of subjective liability, the answer is yes, since the intent in all cases is to do evil—to do something that is morally blameworthy and legally forbidden. Yet partisans on both sides may feel uncomfortable with some of these outcomes.

The advocate of objective liability might have trouble with the unloaded weapon and the sugar cube examples, feeling that the perpetrators in these cases are guilty of an attempt. But on what basis, once you rule out the act? Advocates of this position have tried to rescue such cases from a "not guilty" outcome by invoking, as Holmes did, the concept of the "degree of apprehension felt"[36] that is, the degree to which the conduct is unnerving to the community. However, "degree of apprehension" is a subjective concept. One person's apprehension is not necessarily another's. This point comes clear in two Alabama cases, one antebellum, one twentieth century.

> Yet the standard of community apprehension also bears a serious flaw, which derives from grounding liability in a case-by-case assessment of public apprehension. This flaw is suggested by Holmes' discussion of an antebellum conviction for attempted rape in Alabama; a slave had "run after a white woman, but desisted before he caught her." In a more recent case, the Alabama Supreme Court sustained a conviction for attempted assault with an intent to rape in a case in which a black man followed a white woman down the street and said something "unintelligible," but never came within "two or three feet" of her.[37]

The irony here is that the objective-liability position is smuggling in a subjective concept to impute guilt, yet this concept opens the door to just what the objective-liability advocate most fears: a total surrender to subjective sentiments.[38]

Advocates of subjective liability have problems, too, perhaps feeling that a person should not be convicted for superstitiously sticking pins in a doll. But why not, when her intent was to kill? We could rescue this defendant in one of two ways. We could go further into the subjective, into her beliefs, finding them ludicrous or delusional, a course that would push the case toward a verdict of not guilty by reason of insanity. Or we could go toward the surface, to the objective act, and argue that in the external realm of cause and effect her actions could never produce death. But this is an objective-liability position, focusing on whether or not an act is criminal. The objective and subjective positions are thus beginning to move toward each other.

The subjectivist and the objectivist would of course take different views of the case in which a woman tried to kill a man who was already dead. For the advocate of objective liability, the problem is this: if the woman happened to shoot one second after natural death occurred, then there is no crime; but if she shot one second before natural death occurred and the bullet proved fatal, then she is guilty of murder. The difference turns on fortuity. The objectivist can say, "Well, that's the breaks." But the subjectivist will be quick to respond, "Are you telling me that one of those two acts is less blameworthy than the other?" For the subjectivist, the moral judgment on both acts is the same and cannot be lost or obscured by happenstance.

But can't it? Let's bring the dead body to life. In one case the woman shoots and kills the victim, but in another case the victim ducks and is merely wounded. The question for the subjectivist is: Why should we punish murder more harshly than attempted murder, when the intent is the same in both cases? The subjectivist might say we shouldn't, yet that position doesn't seem to fit with either community sentiment or our criminal codes. If subjective liability needs amending, we should do this not by invoking the act (for the act of shooting is the same in both scenarios) but by invoking another concept—that of harm.

Thus, criminal law in the United States mixes harm, act, and intent, in ways and proportions that stubbornly defy coherence. Objectivity and subjectivity commingle, but not always cordially, as each pulls the other toward the surface or the depths. The chief danger of swinging all the way to objectivity is that the law can lose its normative, moral basis: concepts such as malice and intent become solely intellectual, denuded of their motivational and emotional force, divorced from ordinary modes of understanding. According to this view, the actor's blameworthiness is either in the act, and unrelated to the inner dimension, or derived in a comparative way from the mythical reasonable man, who, if he'd been home, might have done otherwise. The chief danger of swinging all the way to subjectivity is that the law can lose its norms and its bearings: we may end up judging and punishing for thoughts and motives hidden from external view, and may undermine the law's validity and objectivity. With dangers on both sides, how can judges find their way?

"The Life of the Law"

Holmes, an objectivist, viewed the law as grounded in external reality and in the concept of the average, reasonable person. But when it came to the question of *how judges decide the law,* his position, expressed in what is perhaps his most famous aphorism, has a decidedly subjective flavor: "The life of the law has not been logic: it has been experience."[39] He takes a pragmatic swipe at those who view the law as derivative, as if it were mathematics or an exercise in logic. The "law is administered by able and experienced men, who know too much to sacrifice good sense to a syllogism."[40] If judges do not logically deduce the law through syllogisms, then how do they decide the law? Holmes's answer is pragmatic, messy, and psychological—and no doubt true. A judge brings to his or her decisionmaking the "felt necessities of the time, the prevalent moral and political theories, intuitions of public policy, avowed or unconscious, even the prejudices which judges share with their fellow-men"; and these factors, says Holmes, have "a good deal more to do than the syllogism in determining the rules by which men should be governed."[41]

Before we dispense with the syllogism merely on Holmes's say-so, we must answer the question: Why can't law be decided logically, in cases where major and minor premises lead to a syllogistic conclusion? To do so, let's draw on the works of Ronald Dworkin and Richard Posner, jurisprudes who are on different ends of the spectrum but who nonetheless reach some similar conclusions.

Dworkin highlights what can be called the major-premise problem.[42] Unlike the major premise "All men are mortal," which is taught in every introductory philosophy course and which we have no trouble understanding or accepting, the law's major premise in a given case is often unclear. The "plain-fact" view of the law—that the law consists of nothing but words and texts, and that "interpreting" is little more than mechanical and literal jurisprudence—quickly proves an illusion. As any reader of dense prose, airy poetry, congressional legislation, or Supreme Court opinions understands, words do not automatically or mechanically serve up their meaning. Many laws are written abstractly, tersely, or even cryptically; we can read phrases such as "due process," "equal protection," or "cruel and unusual punishment" and still not know their meaning and import. If words do not clearly convey a meaning, or if words refract, yielding several meanings, then a judge may have to go behind the words to the intentions of the legislators. Then the judge, as if interpreting a poem, must engage in construction rather than deduction—fashioning a deeper understanding that illuminates the meaning of those statutory words.

Justice Antonin Scalia has opposed using legislative history to decipher intentions and meanings, stating that "we are governed by laws, not by the intentions of legislators."[43] He has urged his colleagues to ignore intentions and "look only to the actual words in the statute,"[44] calling legislative history "the last hope of lost interpretive causes, that St. Jude of the hagiology of statutory construction."[45]

Scalia's position was put to the test in *John Angus Smith v. United States*. According to commentator Nat Hentoff,[46] the facts and issue were these: "Smith, approaching an undercover agent, offered to trade his firearm, an automatic, for two ounces of cocaine that he planned to sell at a profit. Upon being apprehended, Smith was charged with a number of offenses—most seriously with 'using' a firearm 'during and in relation to . . . a drug trafficking crime.' . . . There was no doubt that John Angus Smith had offered to trade the weapon for cocaine, but is the meaning of 'trading' the same as 'using' a gun?" In the Court debate, Justice Sandra Day O'Connor, writing for the majority which upheld the penalty against Smith, "turned to standard dictionary definitions to interpret what Congress meant when it increased the penalties for a defendant who 'uses or carries a firearm.'"[47] On the other side of the debate was Scalia, who took the word "use" in its ordinary sense. "The court does not appear to grasp the distinction between how a word *can be* used and how it *ordinarily is* used," Scalia wrote. "The word 'use' in the 'crime of violence' context has the unmistakable import of use as a weapon, and the import carries over" to drug trafficking crimes.[48] Hentoff sides with Scalia, likening O'Connor's position to that of Humpty Dumpty in *Through the Looking Glass:* Humpty Dumpty declares that when he uses a word, he makes it mean "just what I choose it to mean." In his analogy, then, Scalia becomes Alice, "a textualist in a strange land,"[49] who questions "whether you *can* make words mean different things."[50] But in Hentoff's disenchantment with the result, he somewhat misses the point. Scalia is not the textualist here, any more than O'Connor, since the word "use" in the statute remains *ambiguous.* The very "fact" that these learned justices are divided six to three is prima facie evidence that the textual word does not yield one sacred, biblical meaning. No, what we have here is a battle between *two* interpretive positions in which Scalia tries to ground his view in *commonsense* interpretation—what ordinary people mean by "use"— and then to claim that this is what the statute writers probably meant. Hentoff may prefer that side, but it is a *constructive, interpretive* position, not a textualist position, and not the plain-fact view of law. If anything, this case illustrates the failure of the plain-fact view, showing, even at the level of a simple verb, that judges must interpret and must be more creative and constructive than literal and mechanical.

The view that the law consists of nothing but logic and syllogisms is not one favored by Richard Posner,[51] who finds that in law "the truth of the major and minor premises is often contestable." A minor premise, such as "Socrates is a man," involves a factual assertion. But in law, "finding the facts . . . is often difficult; and finding facts is not a process of logic."[52] Recall the cases of Bernhard Goetz and William Penn. Even if the major premises of the laws regarding self-defense and unlawful assembly had been clear, which they were not, the minor premises in these cases were likewise unclear. What Goetz thought about before and during the act, and what Penn did and intended, were ambiguous. The fact finder must *construe* the facts, or construct the best story that fits the data; but such construing is not a process of logic.

Holmes's dissenting opinion in the case of *Lochner v. New York,*[53] which Posner calls "merely the greatest judicial opinion of the last hundred years,"[54] contains the following statement: "General propositions do not decide concrete cases. The decision will depend on a judgment or intuition more subtle than any articulate major premise." Yet if we do not have major premises to fall back on, and if minor premises are contestable as well, and if the syllogistic exercise is really inapt, then what sort of judgment are we making? Is Holmes's reference to "judgment or intuition more subtle" just his subtle way of confessing to subjectivity? If so, doesn't this lead to the legal realist's claim that there is no such thing as law, or that "law is only a matter of what the judge had for breakfast"?[55] But if this is the case, then the law's consistency is likely to suffer.

Constructing the Story of the Law

If we asked judges about the factors that influence their decisions, few would probably cite their breakfast cereal. Most judges would honestly claim that they are acting on a *principled* basis, even if they could not cite the principles involved. If the basis for judges' decisions is not logic, and Holmes, Dworkin, and Posner all agree that it is not, then what is it? In the seventeenth century, Lord Coke claimed that judges use a form of "artificial reason" which "only a person trained and experienced in law could exercise."[56] But today we see that it is Coke's claim which is artificial and contrived, since "there is no such thing as 'legal reasoning.'"[57] So how *do* judges decide the law?

Dworkin suggests we think of the law as a chain novel—an ongoing novel with multiple authors in which each author writes one chapter. There are constraints on the authors (that is, the judges and lawmakers): they are not allowed to change the story at will, but must write their chapter to fit with the continuing plot—must "make the novel being constructed the best it can be."[58] Not all chapters are equal. For example, the first chapter, in which the Constitution is written, has a "foundational"[59] power that is greater than the power of the other chapters, although this is not a canonical power. Moreover, since the slate is clean before the first chapter is written, that author has the greatest degree of freedom to write. But once this chapter has been completed, the next author who must write a chapter is constrained by what went before; the next author is further constrained; and so on. What principles guide each author/judge in deciding a case and thus writing a new chapter? Clearly, the past is important. The current author must look back at what has been said and decided, but this is not quite *stare decisis*, and certainly not in accordance with historicist claims that we must limit "eligible interpretations of the Constitution to principles that express the historical intentions of the framers."[60] Such a view gives unwarranted canonical authority to the first author. Moreover, it freezes time and context, both of which need to be taken into account. Last but not least, it freezes principles, which "cannot be seen as stopping where some historical statesman's time, imagination, and interest stopped."[61]

The framers' Constitution is not some static icon but an organism still developing and still in need of interpretation. Holmes said,

> We must realize that they [the framers] have called into life a being the development of which could not have been foreseen completely by the most gifted of its begetters. It was enough for them to realize or to hope that they had created an organism; it has taken a century and has cost their successors much sweat and blood to prove that they created a nation. The case before us must be considered in the light of our whole experience and not merely in that of what was said a hundred years ago.[62]

Dworkin proposes three principles that ought to guide the judge. The first is majoritarian fairness: all things being equal, laws and cases ought to be decided in accordance with the will of the majority. This "fairness in politics"[63] principle holds that when legislators elected by the majority pass legislation, presumably representing community sentiment, that will ought to carry great weight. The second virtue for Dworkin is justice, which concerns whether our laws that "distribute material resources and protect civil liberties . . . secure a morally defensible outcome."[64] All things being equal, the judge ought to promote just outcomes. Third is fairness in the procedural, due process sense. All things being equal, the principled decision ought to promote fair procedures.

But things are seldom equal. In tough cases, principles are likely to conflict. A majoritarian law requiring the death penalty for the crime of rape will conflict with the principle of justice, which holds that such punishment would be cruel and unusual. A majoritarian law denying bail to those charged with crimes involving guns will conflict with the principle of due process fairness. So the judge needs a superordinate principle, and Dworkin supplies it: the principle of integrity.

Assume, says Dworkin, that all our laws and rights and duties were created "by a single author—the community personified—expressing a coherent conception of justice and fairness."[65] Integrity seeks to find the common thread—the interpretation that best fits with the deeper coherence of the ongoing story. Integrity is more than just another name for internal consistency, for the consistency sought is not just vertical, meaning in terms of the past, but horizontal, meaning "across the range of the legal standards the community now enforces."[66] Integrity is more than an expedient solution for reconciling conflicting virtues, but is itself a distinct virtue. It is a political integrity that embodies the "community's conception of justice"[67] and the underlying moral justifying principles, woven into "a single, coherent scheme of justice and fairness in the right relation."[68]

Dworkin has proposed an ideal way for judges to interpret law and decide cases. His scheme treats law and the process of deciding law not as objective, given, or logically deducible but as subjective, constructive, and thoroughly interpretive. They contain antinomies, being textual and atextual, contextual and acontextual, backward looking and forward moving. But what unifies the opposites in a *mysterium coniunctionis* is community, its moral threads coherently woven by each judge—each weaver—personifying the community, into the best possible tapestry. It is not a slave to the past, as the historicist would have it, although the past clearly serves as a guide. It is forward looking, but not with the freedom the legal realist would sanction, a freedom contingent on tomorrow's breakfast. The subjectivity, here, leads to neither chaos nor incoherence, for it is principally guided by commonsense justice and morality, which supply the law and the judge with a common thread.

Dworkin's scheme has been criticized by Judge Posner, who finds his "offbeat suggestion"[69] of a chain-novel analogy "misleading"[70] and his overly broad view of the law "unconvincing."[71] Yet when we parse Posner's criticisms, his own proposal ends up quite close to Dworkin's. Posner is critical of the chain-novel analogy because "it places the judges who interpret the Constitution on the same plane as the framers of the Constitution: the framers just get the ball rolling."[72] But Posner ignores the fact that Dworkin does grant the first chapter a special place, not only for its constitutional content but also for its power to limit the freedom of subsequent writers, who must compose their interpretations and contributions with that chapter in mind. Moreover, both Holmes and Dworkin might point out that, in some ways, subsequent authors *are* on the same plane as the framers, or even on a higher plane, if the Constitution is to be interpreted horizontally as well as vertically. For example, Holmes's interpretation of the "cruel and unusual punishment" clause would, in his own day, be accorded primacy over the framers' interpretation, and interpretations by current justices would supersede those by Holmes and the framers in our own day. Posner, who advocates interpretation in light of the present, seems suddenly historicist and text-bound in his criticism.

Yet Posner finds the chain-novel analogy misleading on still other counts. In contrast to Dworkin, he believes that (1) interpretations would be "highly tentative" in the first chapter of the novel, (2) subsequent chapters would be freer to deviate if experience showed that the first chapter "took the wrong direction," and (3) subsequent chapters would be freer to change as the "background conditions" changed.[73] "The final oddity about Dworkin's analogy," Posner concludes, "is that there are no good chain novels. There might be no good constitutional law if it were constructed on the chain-novel analogy."[74]

This sort of criticism seems pettish and peevish, making the analogy overly concrete. If anything, Dworkin's proposal is more vulnerable to criticism on grounds that his hypothetical judge Hercules is a wanderer and philanderer, roaming too widely from, and wedded too lightly to, the first chapter's vows. Posner is more convincing when he focuses on Dworkin's decidedly mixed bag of principles—a blend of morals, ethics, political norms, and policy preferences. Given that our society is "morally heterogeneous,"[75] Posner believes that Dworkin's correct or "right" interpretation becomes illusory.

> Without social, cultural, and political homogeneity, a legal system is not able to generate demonstrably right, or even professionally compelling, answers to difficult legal questions, whether from within the legal culture or by reference to moral or other extralegal norms—the traditional province of natural law. For without either nature or a political, social, and moral community so monolithic that the prevailing legal norms are "natural" in the sense of taken for granted, natural law can be but a shadow of its former self—can be but a name for the considerations that influence law even though not prescribed by a legislature or other official body.[76]

In short, for Posner, "Dworkin has created a rich vocabulary for masking discretionary, political decision making by judges."[77]

Posner's own view, like Dworkin's, rejects formalism in either its natural-law or positivist forms, for either "approach spares the lawyer or judge from a messy encounter with empirical reality."[78] Not only does the syllogism fail, but so too do artificial reasoning, legal reasoning, and legal rules, which mask —but "do not eliminate and may not even reduce—the role of the subjective and the political in the formation of legal rights and duties."[79] What, then, remains?

Posner cites intuition, "tacit knowing," the unconscious, reliance on authority, reasoning by analogy, and even rhetoric—all of which are aspects of practical reasoning. Summoning those aspects, the judge tries "to reach the most reasonable result in the circumstances."[80] Public confidence in legal decisions may have little to do with how scrupulously "courts confine themselves to fair interpretations of commands laid down

in the texts—about which the public knows little—as distinct from notions of justice or fairness that are independent of fidelity to texts."[81]

Commonsense Justice as Subtext

In Constantin Stanislavski's *Building a Character*,[82] the main character,
Tortsov, describes for his young acting students the type of actor who is
meticulously wedded to the spoken words and who recites them with precision, but who completely ignores the subtext, which contains "the inner
rhythm of living and feeling."[83] In a way, commonsense justice is a form
of subtext. When the law chooses to ignore the subtext, as in strict liability, or attempts to bypass the inner dimension through the artifice of the
reasonable person, it becomes lifeless; it is out of human and humane
character. This is perhaps what Roscoe Pound meant when he said,
"Legal monks who pass their lives in an atmosphere of pure law, from
which every worldly and human element is excluded, cannot shape practical principles to be applied to a restless world of flesh and blood."[84]

Apart from those who, like Antigone, acknowledge only the gods' unwritten and unfailing laws,[85] most see the law as a distinctly human creation pertaining to human actions, thoughts, feelings, and motives. Expressed in the law's penumbra or subtext is a psychology of human
nature. When that human nature stops being human, or ceases to have
anything but a cardboard similarity to the real thing, it fails the community test. As Pound put it, "In all cases of divergence between the standard
of the common law and the standard of the public, it goes without saying
that the latter will prevail in the end."[86]

Even Holmes, while swiping at Hegel, could not get far from the community and the community's sense of justice, which connects blameworthiness to liability and which would not tolerate liability where blame
could not be imposed. The law's legal dramas, fought out in criminal-
court cases or appellate-court decisions, can never be mere conceptual
dramas, bloodless affairs turning on the nuances and niceties of mere
words; nor can ordinary words be denuded of human shadings, intellec-
tualized into airy legal forms that make little contact with the
community's ground, if we expect them to command respect. These dramas, then, are moral, psychological, and political, replete with human
passions, played out in messy empirical reality.

Judges, who decide law, have no immunity from community. They are
affected consciously and unconsciously by the subjective subtext, even as
those principles that cannot be named tacitly affect, and vivify, their decisions. Whether we term them principles or virtues or commonsense jus-

tice, they are called upon even where the summoning is beyond conscious intention. Once the pretenses of logic, syllogism, artificial reasoning, and legal reasoning have been unmasked and stripped away, reaching a decision involves construing and interpreting—processes that are subjective and complex, yet quite ordinary. Ordinary people, who sit on juries, do their own construing and interpreting, as we saw in Chapter 4.

The judge's *interpretive process*, then, once brought down from the dais, may not be fundamentally different from the ways in which ordinary people make decisions, although this is not to say that the methods are identical. According to practical reasoning and along vertical lines, judges will no doubt weigh past decisions more heavily than the ordinary citizen does, since *stare decisis* weighs more heavily on them. Yet along that same vertical line, ordinary citizens, as well as Holmes, Dworkin, and Posner, will hear the community's sense of justice, and those deeper and more enduring strains are likely to resound in their decisions and interpretations.

For Dworkin's judge, a correct interpretation may be possible; for Judge Posner, there is only the best fit possible. Nonetheless, the process for both appears to be fundamentally interpretive and constructive. Ultimately, the judge constructs the best story, as the jury does. The word "story" is not meant to denigrate the interpretive endeavor. Rather, it signals that decisions are not given in or found in or deduced from the objective, external reality, but constructed in the judge's and jurors' subjective reality.

The Sacred Precinct of the Bedroom

6

In 1965, in *Griswold v. Connecticut*,[1] Justice Potter Stewart referred to a Connecticut law that had been on the books since 1879 and that made it a criminal offense for anyone to use contraceptives. He called it "an uncommonly silly law." Griswold, the executive director of the Planned Parenthood League of Connecticut, and Buxton, a physician, professor, and director of the league's center in New Haven, were arrested for giving "information, instruction, and medical advice to *married persons* as to the means of preventing conception."[2] Today, of course, the situation is vastly different: abortion battles have been raging for twenty years, the AIDS epidemic has taken an increasingly deadly toll, unwanted pregnancies among teenagers have become alarmingly frequent, and condoms are being distributed in high schools. The Connecticut law now seems ludicrous.

But *Griswold* was no joke. Though inspired by a silly law, it was an extremely serious debate regarding privacy. The argument concerned the law and its limits, for in *Griswold* the law's reach was curtailed by a privacy claim, a claim that the law may not cross a certain boundary line: on the other side of the line is a zone that is private and off limits. Putting forth this claim was easy; justifying it proved far more difficult.

The majority in *Griswold* struck down the law as "an unconstitutional invasion of the right of privacy of married persons"[3] and declared that certain "zones of privacy" did indeed exist. However, the justices had great trouble finding solid support for the right, since six justices wrote separate opinions, and those who found such a right found it in diverse places. Like UFO sightings, amendment citings were frequent, varied, and unconvincing: the First, Third, Fourth, Fifth, Ninth, Tenth, and Fourteenth amendments were cited, but the very number suggests a cumulative strategy of desperation, where a collection of amendments encircle the target when no one amendment hits the mark. Justice William O. Douglas defended the right to privacy with the celestial metaphor of penumbras: writing for the majority, Douglas stated "that specific guarantees in the Bill of Rights have penumbras, formed by emanations from those guarantees that help give them life and substance."[4]

Betwixt shadow and light, but more than just gray, these penumbras contain meanings that could not be crammed into the specific words of amendments. The common-law origins of this "sacred right"[5] of privacy, a right which is "older than the Bill of Rights—older than our political parties, older than our school system"[6]—lie in the penumbras. Having reached to the heavens, Douglas returns to the bedroom: "Would we allow the police to search the sacred precincts of marital bedrooms for telltale signs of the use of contraceptives? The very idea is repulsive to the notions of privacy surrounding the marriage relationship."[7]

In his concurring opinion, Justice Arthur Goldberg displays his agility, bounding nimbly across the constitutional landscape, landing lightly on the Fourteenth, trumpeting the silent Ninth, and then touching down in the ethos. First he claims that the Fourteenth Amendment's "concept of liberty protects those personal rights that are fundamental, and is not confined to the specific terms of the Bill of Rights."[8] When Justice Stewart protests that "I can find no such general right to privacy in the Bill of Rights, in any other part of the Constitution, or in any case ever decided by this Court,"[9] Goldberg counters with the Ninth Amendment: "The enumeration in the Constitution, of certain rights, shall not be construed to deny or disparage others retained by the people."[10] The Ninth, silent on specifics, is the source, says Goldberg, and he cites the author of the Ninth, James Madison, who feared enumerated rights because they could not "cover all essential rights"[11] and because "no language is so copious as to supply words and phrases for every complex idea."[12] So Goldberg's claim is that the right to privacy originates in the unmentioned rights of the Ninth. To literalists on the Court or in the community, such rights sound like UFO sightings once again: even when you can't see them, they're still there, only invisible. And that is where Goldberg finally takes us, to an unspecifiable ethos, finding "the right of privacy . . . emanating 'from the totality of the constitutional scheme under which we live.'"[13]

Trying for a bit more "solidity," Justices Byron White and John Harlan, in separate concurring opinions, both ground the right to privacy in the due-process clause of the Fourteenth Amendment, which, in Harlan's words, stands "on its own bottom."[14] Due-process words may have a solidity that vague emanations lack, but as Justice Hugo Black's dissent makes clear, the bottom still falls out whether one invokes the First, Fourth, Ninth, or Fourteenth Amendment; for one has to "stretch the Amendment,"[15] or "substitute for the crucial word or words of a constitutional guarantee another word or words more or less flexible,"[16] in order to find the "right to privacy." Justice Stewart, in his dissent, also ridicules this "play on words."[17] While Black acknowledges that the Supreme Court must engage in interpretation, and not just "niggardly" interpretation,[18] Black finds that the majority stretches its constructions too far.

Black saves his toughest language for the airy argument referring to emanations. This argument, he says, boils down to ideas of natural law and natural justice, concepts that are "mysterious," "uncertain," and, more important, "subjective."[19] Invoking such concepts is to apply "no fixed standard,"[20] since "the ablest and the purest men have differed upon the subject."[21] If justices relied on these methods, they would leave the sanctioned safety of constitutional boundaries to "roam at will in the limitless area of their own beliefs."[22] Black concludes by quoting Judge Learned Hand: "For myself it would be most irksome to be ruled by a bevy of Platonic Guardians, even if I knew how to choose them, which I assuredly do not."[23]

In the *Griswold* debate, some earlier themes resound. The plain-fact view of law,[24] where judges adhere to the law's objective words, apparently goes head-to-head with an interpretive, constructive view of law as story fashioning. But this clear-cut opposition is incorrect, for Justice Black, who is clearly on the plain-fact side, acknowledges that justices must interpret, and not just in a "niggardly" fashion. So in reality the justices are disagreeing over two types of interpretation, or differing degrees of interpretation. On the side favoring the plain-fact view, the law is constrained by words strictly construed and is confined to the past—to an age in which the framers' foresight, good though it was, could foresee neither contraceptives in Connecticut nor the need to declare a right to privacy. On the side invoking emanations, there is subjectivism: stories are imaginatively fashioned out of ethos instead of sacred text. Here, unelected Platonic Guardians use personal predilections disguised as "natural law" to decide the law; and the law then becomes, as the legal realists have claimed, what the judge had for breakfast.

What is missing from this legal, conceptual, interpretive debate is any solidity—any firm ground to stand on. The words per se do not provide such ground: some justices clearly perceive the right to privacy in some words, although they differ on which words; other justices see nothing there. Each side puts forth its arguments, but those arguments fail to move the other side. In the end, some believe there is a right to privacy, while others do not.

Absent from this argument are the sentiments of the community. Justice Goldberg does wonder whether privacy is rooted in the "traditions and [collective] conscience of our people,"[25] but he neither explicates this point, nor, more important, undertakes an empirical analysis. The possibility of an empirical analysis was not lost on Justice Black, who quickly excluded it: "Our Court certainly has no machinery with which to take a Gallup Poll."[26] But what if the Court had had the machinery, or if such a poll had already been conducted? If 60 percent or 70 percent or even 80 percent of respondents had agreed with Justice Stewart's sentiments that the law against contraceptives was an "uncommonly silly law," would Justice Stewart, for one, have shifted his belief about the right to privacy? Would anyone have shifted? We do not know. What we do know is that community sentiment was not gauged. Instead, the Court moved to a new case, in which the justices confronted a package of Emko Vaginal Foam, and, in the process, altered the zone of privacy and the limits of the law.

Multiple Zones and Erogenous Zones

The zone of privacy which in *Griswold* was restricted to married persons was extended to single persons in *Eisenstadt v. Baird* (1971).[27] Professor Baird, speaking to students and faculty at Boston University on the topic of contraception, personally handed one woman a package of Emko Vaginal Foam at the end of his lecture. He was arrested under a Massachusetts law designed in part to regulate "the private sexual lives of single persons."[28] *Griswold*'s privacy right "inhered in the marital relationship"; in *Baird* the Court claimed that a "marital couple" was not "an independent entity . . . but an association of two individuals each with a separate intellectual and emotional makeup."[29] Since there was no "marital couple entity," only individuals, the Court held that "if the right of privacy means anything, it is the right of the *individual,* married or single, to be free from unwarranted governmental intrusion into matters so fundamentally affecting a person as the decision whether to bear or beget a child."[30]

Baird produced little of the heat of *Griswold*. Chief Justice Warren Burger, the only dissenter, did note that by relying on *Griswold* "the Court has passed beyond the penumbras of the specific guarantees into the uncircumscribed area of personal predilections."[31] Although the phrase "uncircumscribed area" connoted an unbounded, ever-expanding constitutional zone and a still-vague justification for the privacy right, the issue in *Baird* nonetheless seemed clear-cut: it required an expanded zone, or a new zone, or a rezoning of privacy, such that individual persons have the right to decide whether or not to bear or beget a child.

One year later, the question before the Court was whether this right to bear and beget included the right to abort. *Roe v. Wade,*[32] the "abortion case" that would divide the United States longer and more deeply than any other case in the twentieth century, was, at the time, decided with only two dissents and little of the passion that marked *Griswold.* Citing the Fourteenth, and the Ninth as a minor chord, Justice Harry Blackmun defended a woman's "qualified right to terminate her pregnancy."[33] In this tripartite ruling, based on trimesters, the rights of the woman, the State, and the unborn assumed varying importance. During the first trimester of pregnancy, the right to decide whether or not to bear a child seemed to reside with the woman; during the second trimester, the State's right increased while the woman's decreased; during the last trimester, the interests of the State and the unborn predominated, except in cases where the life or health of the mother was in jeopardy.

This decision did relate to empirics—that is, to the biological and medical facts of fetal development. The decision, however, remained loudly silent on another empirical concern: community sentiment. Though the majority opinion began by acknowledging that strong sentiments and "vigorous opposing views"[34] exist, it nonetheless added that "our task, of course, is to resolve the issue by constitutional measurement, free of emotion and of predilection."[35] The majority intended to set sentiments aside, yet just how this compartmentalization was supposed to be achieved, Blackmun does not say. Moreover, Blackmun does not specify what "constitutional measurement" means, a phrase redolent with objectivity but one that may mask the subjective sentiments of Platonic Guardians.

Engaging in his own brand of "constitutional measurement," Blackmun cites the historical context, observing that abortifacients were known in biblical and Bill of Rights times, and that abortion laws are of "relatively recent vintage . . . not of ancient or even of common-law origin."[36] Justice William Rehnquist, in contrast, cites the current context and brings community sentiment into the equation.

> The fact that a majority of the States, reflecting, after all, the majority sentiment in those States, have had restrictions on abortions for at least a century is a strong indication, it seems to me, that the asserted right to an abortion is not "so rooted in the traditions and conscience of our people as to be ranked as fundamental" . . . Even

today, when society's views on abortion are changing, the very existence of the debate is evidence that the "right" to an abortion is not so universally accepted as the appellant would have us believe.[37]

Although Rehnquist notes in his dissent that some thirty-six states had abortion laws in 1868 (when the Fourteenth Amendment was ratified) and some twenty-one states had abortion laws in 1970 (roughly the time of *Roe*), he does not comment on whether the downward trend from thirty-six (97 percent) to twenty-one (42 percent) signifies a shift in sentiment toward favoring abortion, as it appears if we look only at the percentages. As for Blackmun, he steers clear of this sort of empirics altogether, quoting with approval[38] Justice Holmes's admonition in *Lochner v. New York*:[39] the Constitution "is made for people of fundamentally differing views, and the accident of our finding certain opinions natural and familiar or novel and even shocking ought not to conclude our judgment upon the question whether statutes embodying them conflict with the Constitution of the United States."[40] This quote bolsters Blackmun's point that even if laws seem "natural and familiar" and appear to reflect majority sentiment, that sentiment does not bar the Court from striking down such laws if they conflict with the justices' reading of the Constitution. Put another way, empirical findings are not only not determinative, but may be no bar at all to a repeal based on constitutional principles. Rehnquist, too, cites Holmes's quote,[41] claiming that the majority opinion distorted its meaning, since Holmes was neither advocating that justices be superlegislators nor finding "a right that was apparently completely unknown to the drafters of the [Fourteenth] Amendment."[42] Thus, in a *stare decisis* tug-of-war over Holmes, each side gives the same phrase its own interpretive spin: Rehnquist's spin is toward the plain-fact view, and Blackmun's spin is toward the interpretive. Yet when this battle over quotes has ended, neither side has won, for each has failed to persuade the other of the soundness of its interpretation.

With *Baird*, the zone of privacy regarding contraceptives expanded from married to single persons; in *Roe*, the Court constitutionally recognized a new zone regarding abortion, a zone that has been shifting and shrinking with time. But as the zones expand and multiply, the constitutional basis of the right to privacy still remains as incontestable to some as a UFO sighting. As conservative columnist George Will put it, the Court seems to be saying, "You say the Ninth Amendment, I say the Fourteenth. You say 'tomato,' I say 'tomahto,'" leaving the Supreme Court "most prolix when least principled."[43] Yet Will may be quite wrong here: prolixity need not reflect a position lacking in principles.

Rather, it may reflect the belief, expressed by Madison, that copious words are needed to formulate complex and essential rights that were intended but not specified.

If the added and expanded zones have anything in common, it might be found in Justice Douglas' quote in *Griswold,* where he expressed revulsion for the idea of police searching the "sacred precincts of marital bedrooms for telltale signs of the use of contraceptives."[44] But privacy grounded in the sanctity of the bedroom turns out to be illusory, as the 1986 case of *Bowers v. Hardwick* made clear.[45] Here the Court sanctioned a Georgia law that would allow the police to search the sacred precincts of bedrooms when consensual sodomy was taking place.

In this five-to-four decision, the majority framed the issue in terms of whether the Constitution conferred a fundamental right upon homosexuals to engage in sodomy. The majority thus easily distinguished *Bowers* from *Griswold, Baird,* and *Roe*—cases that involved family relationships, marriage, and procreation—declaring that there was no connection between those areas and homosexual activity. The majority dismissed the defendant's claim that such conduct was "deeply rooted in this Nation's history and tradition"; they disparaged that claim as "at best, facetious,"[46] and countered with quotes alluding to "the infamous *crime against nature,*" "*a crime not fit to be named.*"[47] The Court heaped on the historical facts—for example, that sodomy was a criminal offense in all of the original thirteen states when they ratified the Bill of Rights, and in thirty-two of thirty-seven states in 1868, when the Fourteenth Amendment was ratified.[48] It then added recent facts, such as that sodomy was outlawed in all fifty states until 1961, and that in 1985 twenty-five jurisdictions outlawed the practice.

Once the Court had defined this as "a case of sodomy," a crime proscribed in biblical times, Bill of Rights times, and even today, it could declare this alleged zone different and insupportable. Lumping sodomy with other prosecuted sexual crimes, such as adultery and incest, crimes that exposed the individual to prosecution even when committed in the home, the justices declared that "we are unwilling to start down that road."[49]

In his vigorous dissent, supported by Justices William Brennan, Thurgood Marshall, and John Stevens, Justice Blackmun found the majority going down the wrong road, distorting, in its haste and obsession, what the case was about: "This case is no more about 'a fundamental right to engage in homosexual sodomy,' as the Court purports to declare . . . than *Stanley*[50] . . . was about a fundamental right to watch obscene movies, or *Katz*[51] . . . was about a fundamental right to place interstate bets from a telephone booth. Rather, this case is about 'the most comprehensive of rights and the right most valued by civilized men,' namely 'the right to be let alone.'"[52] To back up his point, Blackmun here focuses on the wording of Georgia's "sodomy" statute (section 16-6-2), which the majority in its haste either ignored, or distorted with its "almost obsessive focus on homosexual activity."[53] For the statute reads that "a person commits the offense of sodomy when he performs or submits to any sexual act involving the sex organs of one person and the mouth or anus of another." Note that this is not "sodomy" in the classic sense of homosexual buggery; in fact, the statute is neutral in terms of sexual orientation, gender, and marital status. In short, it could apply to any two people—a husband and wife, for example—who place the specified organs and erogenous zones in configurations that sex researchers tell us are common among couples.

Justices need not be Freudians to recognize the obvious. Yet the obvious is just what the majority missed, according to Blackmun: only "the most willful blindness could obscure the fact that sexual intimacy"[54] is a powerful part of human relationships, of the way "individuals define themselves,"[55] and that "much of the richness of a relationship will come from the freedom an individual has to *choose* the form and nature of these intensely personal bonds."[56] Blackmun is not just arguing for yet another zone, but arguing for a basic rezoning of privacy itself. He would like to conflate or fuse different zones into one privacy right, and bring together "two somewhat distinct, albeit complementary, lines"[57] of privacy cases, so as to allow individuals the freedom to choose and control how they will live. The freedom to choose is key, whether this involves choices about intimate associations, sexual preferences, contraceptives, or abortion.

In addition, the fact that in *Bowers* the controversial actions took place in the home brings in the Fourth Amendment, which Blackmun gives a broad reading. He states that the essence of this privacy protection is more than just a guarantee that one's door will not be broken down, or one's closets will not be rummaged, or one's phone tapped, or one's mail read. This right is not just an aggregation of individual zones of privacy but an "indefeasible right of personal security, personal liberty, and private property."[58]

The majority tried to distinguish *Bowers* from *Stanley v. Georgia* (1969),[59] claiming that the latter was really a First Amendment case. The majority in *Bowers* interpreted *Stanley* as holding that Georgia's undoubted power to punish someone for public distribution of obscene material did not permit Georgia to punish for the private possession of such material; the majority relied on the First Amendment, claiming that "a State has no business telling a man, sitting alone in his house, what books he may read or what films he may watch." But Blackmun finds this interpretation "entirely unconvincing."[60] In *Stanley*, the State of Georgia did have the "undoubted power" to punish anyone who publicly distributed obscene material.[61] But the defendant Stanley had been reading the material in his home. It was not the "reading" or the "obscene material" (First Amendment concerns) but the "home" (a Fourth Amendment concern) that was determinative in the case, and Blackmun reminds the majority that if they reread *Stanley* they will find the citings to Brandeis' now vindicated dissent in *Olmstead v. United States*[62] regarding the right to be secure in one's home, to have one's spiritual nature, feelings, beliefs, thoughts, emotions, and sensations protected from governmental intrusion. This is what *Stanley* was about, says Blackmun, and this is precisely what *Bowers* is about.

In Blackmun's efforts to justify the right to privacy, he lands on the Fourth Amendment, "perhaps the most 'textual' of the various constitutional provisions that inform our understanding of the right to privacy"—a provision which reaffirms that "a man's home is his castle."[63] However "textual" Blackmun's argument may be, its threads are woven with neither syllogistic certainty nor empirical solidity. Rather, it remains an interpretive tale, weaving man, home, and castle into an earthier story than the ones that feature penumbras, emanations, and ethos. But when we examine Blackmun's threads more closely, when we see beyond the references to man, home, and castle which create the illusion of substance, these threads are but airy notions of rights—every bit as gossamer thin as the threadbare tales of *Griswold*. However well told, his argument remains, at bottom, just a story, and the minority story at that.

A different approach is illustrated by the decision in *Commonwealth v. Jeffrey Wasson et al.*, in which the Supreme Court of Kentucky struck down Kentucky's seventeen-year-old sodomy law banning oral and anal sex between homosexuals but not heterosexuals.[64] Although this case raises an equal-protection as well as a privacy claim, it differs from *Bowers* in that its decision rests on a great deal of empirical evidence. The supporting data come largely from "an American Psychological Association brief on gay and lesbian sexuality and the effects of discrimination on homosexuals."[65] For example, in regard to the privacy argument, "the opinion notes that there is overwhelming scientific and social-science evidence supporting the fact that the sexual behavior of gay men and women doesn't harm anyone and that homosexuals are harmed psychologically if they are legally prohibited from having a normal sex life. No such data were cited to support the constitutionality of the state's statute banning sodomy, the opinion emphasized."[66] Whereas the *Bowers* majority opines that sodomy is an "infamous crime against nature," the Kentucky court notes the *fact* that this consensual behavior harms no one. When Blackmun's minority opinion asserts that sexual intimacy is a powerful way "individuals define themselves," this assertion is, by itself, unsupported, except for a footnote citing another assertion that mental health professionals no longer regard homosexuality as a "disease" or disorder. Yet when the Kentucky court asserts that prohibiting and criminalizing sodomy do harm the homosexual, this assertion is grounded in evidence. In addition to using data to support its argument, the Kentucky court uses the empirical data to refute, as "simply outrageous," the claims made by the commonwealth "that gay males are more promiscuous than heterosexuals, are pedophiles and are more prone to engage in sex acts in public than heterosexuals."[67] Empirical facts can bolster one argument and effectively undermine another.

The Collective Conscience and Reasonable Expectations

Blackmun locates the sources of the right to privacy beneath specific privacy zones, rezoning privacy itself according to more fundamental, secure, and textual principles. But in bringing together "two distinct, albeit complementary, lines" of privacy cases,[68] he opens an empirical door, for the second line all but demands an assessment of people's expectations. This second line of privacy cases involves situations in which the police stop a suspect, conduct a search, and seize evidence without a warrant. The question here is: Does the right to privacy constitutionally bar such intrusions, thereby making it necessary to exclude seized evidence from the trial? In the landmark case of *Katz v. United States*,[69] Justice Harlan proposed a two-part test: "There is a twofold requirement, first that a person have exhibited an actual (subjective) expectation of privacy, and, second, that the expectation be one that society is prepared to recognize as reasonable."[70]

To determine empirically if the individual satisfies the first part of the test, all we need do is ask him. Although the empirical criteria are minimal, this subjective part, by itself, is problematic: all a person need claim is an expectation that his or her person, car, or suitcase full of cocaine was private and off limits. More absurdly, a burglar caught in the act of escaping with "the goods" could simply claim that he had a reasonable expectation he would not be caught. That is why the objective, second part of the test is necessary: the expectation has to be a reasonable one.

But reasonable to whom? The court says "society," the community of ordinary people.[71] Thus, if it is commonly held that a certain type of search violates privacy, then the search would violate the second part of the test. The decision in *Katz,* then, grounds the right to privacy in empirical evidence and community sentiment, rather than in a vague area between amendments and penumbras. In *Rakas v. Illinois,*[72] the U.S. Supreme Court affirmed that legitimation of expectations of privacy must have a source outside the Fourth Amendment, either in concepts of real or personal property law or in understandings that are recognized and permitted by society. It acknowledged that the legitimating source for expectations is found not in an amendment's words or in an ethos but in commonsense justice—in what the community believes is legitimate and reasonable. This is what legitimates the right to privacy.

Although Justice Blackmun brought the two lines of privacy cases together *conceptually,* he did not *empirically* link community sentiment to the sexual behavior at issue in *Bowers.*[73] Had he demonstrated, with empirical evidence, that community sentiment supported the privacy claim in *Bowers,* it is uncertain what effect, if any, such evidence would have had on the other justices and on the decision. To assume that Blackmun's minority opinion would have become the majority opinion is to assume too much, for this question is itself empirical. Yet privacy and community sentiment were linked. Community sentiment, existing outside the bounds of the Fourth Amendment, can inform the privacy issue: the collective conscience of the community provides an empirical way of legitimating and validating expectations.

In an interesting test of court claims about privacy rights and the intrusiveness of various types of search and seizure, Christopher Slobogin and Joseph Schumacher[74] asked more than two hundred subjects to rate the "intrusiveness" of "50 different types of law enforcement investigative techniques, taken primarily from U.S. Supreme Court cases."[75] Based on subjects' ratings, the various types of searches were rank-ordered, so that $R = 1$ represented the least intrusive and $R = 50$ the most intrusive. The researchers found that the Supreme Court and community sentiment had very different views as to whether a type of search is or is not intrusive.

For instance, ranked as very intrusive are use of a hypodermic needle ($R = 46$) and urine samples ($R = 39$) to test for drug usage among employees, findings that tend to contradict the Court's assertion that minimal expectations of privacy are associated with these actions (*National Treas. Emp. Union v. Von Raab,* 1989; *Skinner v. Railway Labor Exec.'s Ass.,* 1989). Similarly, various types of undercover activity are ranked as intrusive, including covert use of a chauffeur ($R = 31$), a secretary ($R = 34$), and a bank ($R = 38$), again in contrast to Court decisions holding or suggesting that little or no expectation of privacy is associated with these actions (*Hoffa v. United States,* 1966; *United States v. Baldwin,* 1981; *United States v. Miller,* 1976).

Additionally, whereas the Court has found that both dog sniffs ($R = 23$) and entry onto privately owned "open fields" ($R = 21$) are not searches for purposes of the Fourth Amendment (*California v. Greenwood,* 1988; *United States v. Place,* 1983), the survey participants ranked these investigative techniques at roughly the same level of intrusiveness as a frisk ($R = 19$), which the Court has clearly indicated is a search (*Terry v. Ohio,* 1968). Finally, and perhaps most dramatically, just last term the Court strongly suggested that boarding a bus and asking passengers to consent to a search of their luggage is not a seizure (*Florida v. Bostick,* 1991), yet subjects in this study ranked this scenario as very intrusive ($R = 44$).[76]

If the Court opens the door to empirical evidence, and that evidence suggests that the Court's assumptions about community sentiment are off the mark, what is to be done? As Slobogin and Schumacher see it, the Court has three options.

If the Court finds that the path laid by community sentiment differs from the law's path, the law can simply ignore the data and continue on its own course. This "denial" option isolates the law from all but itself. Such a course ignores Roscoe Pound's prediction that "in all cases of divergence between the standard of the common law and the standard of the public, it goes without saying that the latter will prevail in the end."[77] If commonsense justice is to prevail despite the law's denial, then it may do so by means of nullification, when jurors simultaneously disrespect and perfect the law.

Second, the Court can admit that much of its jurisprudence in this area is "based on flawed assumptions about society's perspective on privacy and autonomy values and change its case law accordingly."[78] The law's path is thus brought into line with the path laid by the community. In following this "acceptance" option, the Court agrees with Pound's claim: "Sooner or later what public opinion demands will be recognized and enforced by the courts."[79]

Third, the Court could compromise: it could "redefine the expectation of privacy . . . independently of societal understandings."[80] Thus, after acknowledging the need and opening the door for empirical evidence of the community's legitimate expectations, the Court could immediately shut the door when the evidence presented did not conform to the justices' expectations. We do not yet know which option the law will choose—denial, acceptance, or hypocrisy. At this point, empirical evidence *does* inform the privacy question, most directly in terms of reasonable expectations.

There is additional evidence concerning reasonable expectations of privacy in cases where there are searches with third-party consent.[81] Consider a college student who lives with three or four other students in a house. Each student has her own bedroom, except for two, who share a room. There are also common areas in the house, such as a living room. One afternoon, the police knock at the front door, and only one student is home—one of the two women who share a bedroom. The police, who do not have a warrant, ask if they might come in and search—they are looking for evidence of drugs in connection with her roommate. She says yes. But is it all right for a third party to give consent? The police say they want to search the bedroom that the two women share, as well as common areas such as the bathroom, kitchen, and living room. In the living room is a chest belonging to the roommate—a chest that doubles as a coffee table; the police want to search that, too. The student says fine. But, again, is third-party consent sufficient for such a search?

In *United States v. Matlock* (1974),[82] the Supreme Court held "that it is reasonable to recognize that any of the co-inhabitants has the right to permit the inspection in his own right and that the others have assumed the right that one of their number might permit the common area to be searched."[83] The Court assumed that common areas give rise to common authority, and that people who live with people assume the risk, understanding that another co-occupant may give permission. But was the Court correct in these assumptions? Does an individual who shares a bedroom really believe that her personal things, located in her drawers or in her closet, are really in a common area merely because another shares the room? Do we believe that the living-room chest, which makes a good coffee table, can be searched because it is in a common area? And do we assume that a roommate can give permission for a search? Or, on the contrary, do we believe that only the individual can grant permission for a search of her own possessions? And what if the person in question is at home—in the shower, let's say—when the roommate gives permission? If the police now begin their search with third-party consent, and the individual emerges from the shower and demands that they stop, can the police ignore this demand?

Empirical research has shown that in a few areas legal assumptions and lay beliefs part company.[84] Most people believe that when police want to search an individual's things and that individual is home, his or her consent must be obtained. People place far more emphasis on the specific item to be searched than on the law's definition of "shared or common space." If the item to be searched is a container of personal effects, it does not matter whether it is located in the living room, for the right to privacy is not limited to the bedroom.

The Sacred Precinct of Privacy

In *Griswold,* Justice Douglas coined the phrase "the sacred precincts of marital bedrooms."[85] What goes on in the privacy of the bedroom, and how it is viewed by the law, has been the central focus of this chapter. Whether the issue has been the contraceptive decisions of married persons (as in *Griswold*) or of single persons (as in *Baird*), or the abortion decisions of single or married persons (as in *Roe*), or the sexual practices of single, married, heterosexual, or homosexual individuals (as in *Bowers*), the private precinct of the bedroom has been the battleground. Although most have argued that the bedroom ought to be private—a domain free from State intervention and legal judgment—the arguments in this direction have suffered precisely because of their private nature. They have taken place within the private precincts of the law, divorced from community sentiment and located not in the bedroom but in outer space, where penumbras, emanations, and ethos, along with disputable interpretations of airy amendments, engage in conceptual battle.

Far removed from the justices are the people back on earth, who are grounded by their own views and beliefs and who certainly have views about privacy—strong views, we suspect, at least insofar as these relate to their own lives. We are not even close to a complete understanding of people's sentiments on these zones of privacy, and we do not know whether these sentiments are shared by a large enough segment of the population to make them "reasonable" and "legitimate" expectations. But although we may not know enough to satisfy the social scientist, we are far from ignorant, particularly about sentiments concerning abortion, since yearly opinion polls on this topic have become routine, despite the limitations of such gauges (see Chapter 1). Still, the Supreme Court, following Justice Black's view that the Court is not equipped to do a Gallup poll, has seemed unwilling to either do empirical research or to comb the literature for research findings, whether in the area of contraception, abortion, or sodomy.

But just because you don't take the pulse of the community doesn't mean there is no pulse. If the Court rules that there is no privacy in the bedroom for certain common sexual acts between consenting partners, and the community feels otherwise, then the law and the community part company. But the law will lose, as Pound predicted. It will lose not only because people have no respect for the decision, but because people may express their disrespect in noncompliance. We can only guess how many residents of the State of Georgia have been happily violating the Supreme Court's holding in *Bowers,* for example. Moreover, as we saw in Chapters 2 and 3, jurors sometimes do not restrict themselves to judging the facts, but may judge and nullify the law when they perceive it to be unfair and out of tune with community sentiment. Thus, the law can lose for another reason: namely because citizens themselves function as jurors, as the conscience of the community.

The Right to Die

7

As we have seen, the legal principles underlying the right to privacy are hard to locate. In the 1960s and 1970s the zones of privacy changed their boundaries, but the Supreme Court's decisions on privacy matters—especially those concerning the sacred precincts of the bedroom—still rested on shaky legal ground, sometimes on nothing more than the beliefs of individual justices. These Platonic Guardian decisions failed to hit bedrock. Though in cases involving search and seizure, justification for the right to privacy had a firmer basis—namely, the legitimate and reasonable expectations of ordinary people. In this chapter we'll look more closely at this sort of justification. What beliefs do people hold about privacy matters? And to what extent do those beliefs accord with the law?

Many of us fear Big Brother's intrusion into parts of our lives we deem private. And it's not just government we're wary of, but business, the mass media, and other citizens; not just government wiretaps on our phone conversations, but unsolicited "nuisance calls" that disrupt our peace and quiet, intrude on our privacy. When government workers violate the privacy of people's tax returns, perusing private records for their own voyeuristic pleasure, there is considerable alarm.[1] And personal information is often accessed by businesses—a practice that some people likewise consider an invasion of privacy, though how many share this opinion is unclear.

The right to privacy is not absolute, since successful challenges to that right have come from many quarters. The individual's claim to privacy and the press's right to report the news is one such conflict zone. When a reporter resolved to publicize the fact that former tennis star Arthur Ashe had AIDS, Ashe was deprived of the right to decide when he would tell his young daughter that he was dying. The loss of privacy was a loss of control. This is also the case when private citizens "out" someone who is gay—that is, inform the world of an individual's homosexuality without that individual's permission. Under some circumstances, as in trials involving juveniles, the courts may bar the press from releasing the juvenile's name and may impose punishments if the press fails to comply. Once, when the *Wall Street Journal* published the name of a young alleged offender, the judge excluded the *Journal's* reporter from the legal proceedings, while granting access to other media that had not revealed the name.[2]

The individual's right to privacy, the right of a free press to publish trial facts, and the defendant's right to present the best defense all come into conflict in cases of alleged rape, particularly when the defense claims consent on the part of the plaintiff. The highly publicized case of William Kennedy Smith in 1991 is an example. "Rape shield" laws, and the Privacy Protection for Rape Victims Act of 1978,[3] often keep the plaintiff's name and sexual history out of the trial. In the Smith trial, which was broadcast on television, the alleged victim appeared on camera with an electronically generated blue dot obscuring her face, and although most newspapers and news organizations honored the anonymity, NBC broadcast her name.[4] NBC's action generated considerable controversy, which nearly overwhelmed discussion of the defendant's right to privacy. It may be a legally naïve question, or just a question of balance—but why wasn't the defendant given a blue dot as well? After all, he was only an *alleged* rapist and was innocent until proven guilty. As it turned out, Smith was acquitted, but one could argue that his life has been affected negatively by having his face and identity exposed daily during the trial.

As these incidents and cases reveal, there are times when we want our facts, faces, and history to stay off the front pages. More than just wanting privacy, many of us clearly believe it is our right; we do not want to lose control over a zone we consider ours. But as these incidents and cases also reveal, we are not sure how many people would allege a privacy *right* in these circumstances. In which situations would the claim to privacy garner the greatest support? With conflicts rife between one citizen and another, between the press and the citizen, between business and the citizen, and, of course, between government and the citizen, how does community sentiment delimit the zone of privacy in such various instances? The questions may change from conceptual and constitutional to empirical, but we still await answers.

One area in which there are strong and unmistakable expectations of privacy concerns our own health. We expect that when we see a doctor our health records will remain private, and the Hippocratic Oath has long affirmed the doctor's duty to protect our right to confidentiality. That was certainly the expectation of a twenty-four-year-old man who, in 1991, lay in the intensive care unit of a hospital in Rockville, Maryland; but when the fact that he had AIDS became generally known, he "filed a $4.5 million lawsuit against Shady Grove Adventist Hospital and two respiratory therapists who worked there, saying one of the therapists—a high school acquaintance not involved in his care—obtained his hospital record from the other and called his friends and relatives, telling them that he had AIDS."[5] This case seems straightforward: the patient's right to privacy had been violated. Yet other sides to the issue are a good deal more complex, as the next two cases reveal.

"The D.C. Court of Appeals . . . refused to block a test to determine the presence of HIV antibodies in the blood of a rape suspect who allegedly told his victim during the assault that he was infected with the AIDS virus."[6] Although the suspect's lawyer said it was an "extraordinary invasion of Mr. Brown's most valued and important rights," the government prosecutors countered that Brown had given up his privacy rights, since he had "placed the issue of his infection with the AIDS virus in the public domain when he made that frightening statement" during the rape.[7] The judge overruled the defendant's privacy claim and came down on the side of the alleged victim: "There are some things which to me are so right, just so absolutely right and humane, . . . that it really just strikes me as absolutely appropriate to order that it be done."[8] Yet few things seem "absolutely right" and "absolutely appropriate" when it comes to privacy.

Unlike the accused rapist Brown, who may have forfeited his privacy rights, Dr. David Acer, a dentist, committed no crime. Acer, too, wanted his AIDS condition kept private, and it was kept private by the Florida health officials who regulate health workers. Yet his patient Kimberly Bergalis—who had never had sexual relations with anyone, had never used intravenous drugs, and had never had a blood transfusion (three facts quite germane to her case)—nonetheless became infected with the AIDS virus. And she had become infected, as it turned out, during dental treatments by Dr. Acer. Kimberly Bergalis died, but before she did she raised the issue of her right to know in a letter to Florida health officials— officials she blamed for knowing about the risk Dr. Acer posed and doing not "a damn thing about it."[9]

Bergalis' case is heartrending. But if her right to know were regarded as taking precedence over Dr. Acer's right to privacy, then wouldn't all patients have a similar right to see the private records of their doctors and dentists? Do students have the right to see the medical records of their teachers, or teachers the right to see the medical records of their students? After all, exam papers and blue books, along with who knows what viruses, are continually being passed back and forth. Employers and employees are in a similar situation. The question of how far one can go in obtaining the private health records of individuals came up in a 1992 Texas Court of Appeals case, *Cheatham v. Rogers,*[10] in which a divorced father sought a subpoena for the personal mental health records of a court-appointed psychologist who had recommended that the father's right to visit his child be restricted. The psychologist argued that the subpoena should be denied because her records were private, privileged, and confidential. The court rejected her argument, claiming in part that her right to privacy was outweighed by a "compelling state interest" in the welfare of the child.

Therapists have known since the *Tarasoff* case of 1974 that "the protective privilege ends where the public peril begins."[11] A patient's right to confidentiality, and the therapist's duty to protect that privacy, must yield when the lives of third parties are in danger. According to state laws, privacy must also yield when the welfare of a child is at issue, as in suspected cases of physical or sexual abuse. But according to the appeals court in *Cheatham,* it was the therapist's own privacy, not just the patient's, that had to give way.

In cases such as these, the right to privacy is challenged by a competing claim, a claim that some other party has a right to know because an individual's welfare or life hangs in the balance and should take precedence over privacy. These are tough cases because the arguments on both sides seem strong. But this does not appear to be true for cases involving the right to die. Here, the privacy of one individual is not pitted against the life or welfare of another individual, yet the individual's claim to the right of privacy faces a stiff challenge nonetheless. In this area we have some empirical evidence with which to evaluate the claim and counterclaim—evidence about where community sentiment stands.

The Right to Die

As the twentieth century comes to a close, Americans are living approximately twenty-five years longer than their ancestors of 1900,[12] and much of the credit goes to medical advances. But for some people, living longer does not necessarily mean living better.[13] For these individuals, the scientific question "Can medicine prolong life?" is superseded by the normative question "Should it?" Challenging the claim that "preservation of life at all costs is the highest good," they counter with a new zone of privacy, claiming the "right to die."[14] Believing that they should be the ones to decide when "enough is enough," they want the right and power to determine their final exit, to "pull the plug" without interference from the medical profession or the State.

The courts have been not only listening to but affirming these arguments.[15] From *Quinlan* in 1976[16] to *Cruzan* in 1990,[17] with a spate of lower-court decisions in between,[18] the right to die, at least in vague, abstract form, seems to have won a place in the legal landscape.[19] But what does the amorphous phrase "right to die" convey? If it turns out that the "right" is short on specifics but long qualifiers, entailing many technical, legal, and medical requisites, then the right may be minimal when all the requisites have been met.

But our question is: Where does community sentiment stand on the right to die? Case law, the collection of individual decisions in specific cases, tells us little about community sentiment, since these cases are typically decided by a judge, not a jury. To assess community sentiment, then, we must look elsewhere.

In Chapter 1 we assessed public opinion polls as a gauge of community sentiment, and found problems: polls may pick up transitory, shallow, or uninformed sentiments; polls may fail to register complex and contradictory sentiments; polls may ask the wrong questions, or overly general questions; response options may be artificially limited; and subjects may invoke atypical exemplars that distort true sentiment. In Chapters 2 and 3 we looked at the jury as the conscience of the community, and although we suspected that jurors were nullifying the law in some cases, we could not be sure. Now let's turn to more controlled gauges of community sentiment.

Assessing Sentiment under the Toughest Condition

Imagine an experiment in which the subjects are given the written account of a case. It's a detailed text, running five single-spaced pages, including the facts (who did what), the testimony of key witnesses, and a full discussion of the issues. Unlike an opinion poll question, this text provides a concrete and specific stimulus: it has seemingly "real" characters, a patient, a defendant, doctors, and lawyers, all involved in a life-and-death drama. The account of the case is accompanied by eight pages of "jury instructions" admonishing subjects to follow the law as it is written (that is, cautioning them against nullifying). The subjects render a verdict, write out the reasons for their decision, and provide some ratings on the case.

In studies of actual jury decisions, many different cases are aggregated to get a general sense of sentiment; but in an experiment a researcher controls the case, introducing systematic variations to test whether certain variables produce an effect. One such variable, called a within-subject variable, is *case*. Subjects may get, in random order, a number of cases in which the right to die has been asserted either by the patient or by the spouse acting on the patient's behalf. If the researcher uses only one case—for example, a disguised version of *Cruzan*—there's a risk that the case might generate great sympathy or antipathy, which would distort the reading of sentiment. For example, that Nancy Cruzan was young, that her condition seemed hopeless, that her parents seemed caring, and that friends were supporting her right to die are all facts that pull toward support of the right; but in a different case, with a different fact pattern, the right may have much less support. Moreover, presenting several cases enables the experimenter to vary the *competence* of the patient, since competence is often a central concern in such right-to-die cases, as it was in *Cruzan*.

Let's say we do indeed set up an experiment, and that the experiment makes use of four cases. The most competent of the patients involved, who are all fifty-eight-year-old women, has amyotrophic lateral sclerosis, which doctors say affects primarily motor abilities and not the mind; the next most competent is a patient with lymph cancer, but here the disease is exacerbated by emotional and mental symptoms, including periods of delirium and depression; the third most competent is an Alzheimer's patient who is paralyzed and whose mental state is extremely disordered; the least competent is a comatose patient. In all of the cases, the doctors and hospital challenge the patient's competence to make a right-to-die decision. Will the subjects' judgments of the patients' competence differ from those of the medical professionals? If subjects are willing to sustain the right-to-die claim *only* when they are sure the person is competent, then support for the right to die should decrease as the patient's competence decreases and becomes more doubtful.

A second variable, known as a between-subject variable, is *intent*: How clearly did the patient express her wish to die, to whom, and in what form? Let's say our four cases present three levels of *intent*. At the middle level, the patient expresses her wish to die to two people: in the cases of sclerosis, cancer, and Alzheimer's, this means her doctor and her husband; in the case of the comatose patient, her husband and sister reveal that she expressed such a wish before lapsing into coma. At the highest level of intent, the patient has not only expressed her wish to two people but has also made a living will (though it is nine or ten years old) that affirms her wish to die if she were in similar circumstances; with this condition, we can see if the fact that a patient has made a living will affects people's views of the case. At the lowest level, the patient has not expressed such a wish to anyone, but her husband claims that she wanted to die and that a husband just knows these things after living with his wife for thirty years. Each subject gets all four cases at one of these three levels of intent. If intent is the key variable—the simple fact that the patient made her wish known—then we should see differences between the lowest level and the middle and highest levels. But if subjects require more than just an oral statement and want to see long-standing intent legally documented in a living will, then we should see differences between the highest level and the middle and lowest levels.

Let's assume, furthermore, that this test of the community's support for the right to die is being conducted *under the least favorable condition*—that is, under circumstances that involve *active euthanasia*. Although the World Medical Organization views active euthanasia as a crime,[20] the courts and the medical community are aware that the line between passive and active euthanasia is often blurry. So let's make the situation more clear-cut by looking at a much less sympathetic case: an alleged criminal act. In each of the four cases the husband enters the hospital room and shoots and kills his wife. The means of death is clearly active and violent; the evidence presented unquestionably confirms that the husband did the shooting; and the manner and timing of the act strongly suggest "malice aforethought," "deliberation," and "premeditation." Thus, in all four cases the defendant is facing first-degree murder charges, in cases set up such that all the conditions of first-degree murder appear to be satisfied.

By deliberately testing the right to die under its weakest case—active euthanasia—we will no doubt suppress the true level of public support for the right. There will probably be subjects who would support the right to die under more typical or ideal conditions but who could not support it in a case where murder had been committed. Still, the question here is this: Given a presumed unsympathetic scenario (active euthanasia) in which conditions are unfavorable for the defendant (all elements of first-degree murder are satisfied), what percentage of subjects will nullify the law and render a "not guilty" verdict, or partially nullify and render a verdict for a lesser offense?

Our last variable (also a between-subject variable) concerns legality—

that is, whether the defendant first attempts to seek hospital and court approval to disconnect the machines, or simply acts on his own. Even though subjects might support the right to die, they may nonetheless feel little sympathy for a man who takes the law into his own hands and who (negligently) failed to pursue available legal options after being rebuffed by the hospital. In the other scenario, after being rebuffed by the hospital he turns to the court for permission to disconnect the machines, but is turned down because the judge also has questions about the patient's depression and competence; following the court's rejection, the defendant takes matters into his own hands. In this scenario, where the defendant attempts to work through legal channels, subjects might feel greater sympathy for him. In both scenarios, the defendant shoots his wife one week after the hospital or court refuses his request, and the delay strengthens the view that his act was deliberate and premeditated, since he conceivably had ample time to calm himself.

Nullifications and Their Causes

The experiment we've been imagining was conducted in 1993 by me and two former students, now law students, Marie Hurabiell and Kevin Hughes.[21] The results were interesting, but not what the law might have predicted. Table 7.1 presents the verdicts across cases and conditions, then for each of the three intent conditions, for the "court–no court" conditions, and for the four cases. "Lesser offenses" include second-degree murder, voluntary manslaughter, and involuntary manslaughter; the vast majority of verdicts in this category were for voluntary manslaughter. Even though all of the cases were unfavorable for the defendant, only 35.9 percent of the verdicts were for first-degree murder. The large percentage of lesser-offense verdicts (38.8 percent) and the sizable number of "not guilty" verdicts (25.3 percent) suggest that partial and complete nullifications were occurring, but unless we examine the subjects' reasons, this finding cannot be confirmed.

The intent variable produced significant verdict differences, largely as a result of the living will, which induced more subjects to vote "not guilty." Thus, it was not sufficient for the patient to have simply announced her intention, for the fact that there was legal documentation of her wish in the form of a living will significantly increased the number of "not guilty" verdicts. Regarding the court variable, subjects' ratings differed significantly on the issue of whether the defendant had tried every option available. Subjects recognized that the defendant in the no-court condition had not tried every option, but this large difference in ratings

Table 7.1. Verdicts in the case of a husband who shoots his seriously ill wife, claiming her wish for the right to die.

Variable	Verdict: First-degree murder: Number of subjects	Percent	Lesser offense: Number of subjects	Percent	Not guilty: Number of subjects	Percent
Patient's intent:						
Expressed in living will	17	32.1	17	32.1	19	35.9
Expressed to two persons	19	33.9	25	44.6	12	21.4
Expressed to no one	25	41.0	24	39.3	12	19.7
Attempts at court resolution:						
No court	34	39.1	35	40.2	18	20.7
Court	27	32.5	31	37.4	25	30.1
Case:						
Amyotrophic lateral sclerosis	61	35.9	66	38.8	43	25.3
Lymph cancer	60	35.3	72	42.3	38	22.4
Alzheimer's	61	35.9	68	40.0	41	24.1
Comatose	62	36.5	57	33.5	51	30.0
Overall	244	35.9	263	38.7	173	25.4

did not translate into a large difference in verdicts. Whereas the court condition does show more "not guilty" verdicts, the difference just fails to reach significance. And the case variable did not significantly affect the verdict. Although ratings again reveal that subjects registered differences among the cases as to the patient's competence and the clarity of her wish, these significant rating differences did not translate into significant verdict differences. Thus, the patient's competence was not alone sufficient to influence the verdict, just as the fact of whether or not the defendant went to court was not in itself sufficient.

Once the subjects' reasons for their verdicts were reliably categorized and cluster analyzed, the results showed conclusively that nullifications had occurred and revealed a complex variety of nullifications. At one extreme, some subjects considered the death not a legal matter at all but a private matter, involving a zone of privacy into which the law should not intrude; as expected, these subjects rendered "not guilty" verdicts. Some subjects expressed a slightly less extreme view: privately, they endorsed this zone of privacy and saw the act as not unlawful in a higher moral sense; but in their public role as jurors, they chose to follow the "disagreeable law," even going so far as to convict the defendant for first-degree murder. This finding—that subjects in the public role of juror may suppress their private sentiments—indicates that sentiments will not always run wild if jurors are apprised of their right to nullify. As Kalven and Zeisel[22] noted, the jurors' "war" with the law may be modest.

Other subjects expressed even less extreme views: they recognized the law's place but viewed the law's position as wrong. Some nullified with a "not guilty" verdict. Others convicted the defendant of first-degree murder but made a plea to the judge for mercy, in effect hoping that the judge would do the nullifying and render justice. Here again subjects appear to have followed a law they considered bad, despite their private convictions. Although they held their sentiments in check when it came to the verdict, these sentiments nonetheless leaked out indirectly when they asked the judge to do what they wanted to do but didn't.

In addition, one view was expressed by many of the subjects no matter what verdict they rendered: these subjects saw the defendant not as an actor in his own right but as an extension of the patient, merely implementing her wishes. According to this view, he became her arms and legs, making it possible for her to commit suicide. Some subjects found this lawful and voted to acquit the husband; others considered it a mitigating factor and found him guilty of a lesser offense.

Finally, some subjects nullified either completely or partially by using a commonsense definition of "malice" or "malice aforethought" rather than a legal one. Even though the jury instructions told them that malice aforethought "does not necessarily imply any ill will, spite or hatred towards the individual killed,"[23] subjects invoked the commonsense, dictionary meaning, which does stress those qualities. This is reminiscent of what the jury did in the *Goetz* case.[24] When subjects found no malevolence on the part of the defendant, their verdict was reduced to manslaughter or even to "not guilty."

Assessing Sentiment Directly

In the experiment described above, we did not *directly* test sentiment concerning the right to die: it was "underneath," so to speak, since the charge of active euthanasia made the case a criminal matter, an issue of first-degree murder. Moreover, by combining a deliberate, violent death with the right-to-die claim, we could not evaluate support for the right under clean, fair, optimal conditions. Nevertheless, even though the situation was manipulated, many subjects rendered complete or partial nullifications, despite fact patterns that pressed them to convict the defendant for first-degree murder, and despite jury instructions that reminded them of their oath to follow instructions. If we removed the active-euthanasia condition and left only the right-to-die cases, community sentiment in favor of the right would probably increase greatly, since many subjects in our earlier experiment privately endorsed the right to die but were clearly disturbed that the defendant had taken the law into his own hands. A second experiment was designed to test this hypothesis.[25]

Subjects received three cases, in random order, and were asked to play the part of the judge. The patient (or the spouse on behalf of the patient) was asking the court to remove life-sustaining mechanisms (feeding tube, respirator, kidney dialysis machine). The mock judges thus had to decide whether or not the mechanisms should be removed, and then give the reasons for their decision. As in the earlier experiment, a reliable method of categorizing those reasons was developed.

Three cases were selected, each involving a woman of thirty-four or thirty-five who was being treated in a hospital and who was hooked up to life-support systems. In this experiment the age of the patient was chosen so as to put her somewhere near the midpoint of life, since, if the patient were older, subjects may have been more inclined to grant the right to die, and the experiment might have given an inflated reading of sentiment in favor of the right. Subjects were asked to consider three cases: a woman who had cancer, a woman who was comatose, and a woman who was a quadriplegic. The cases varied along a number of dimensions. For example, the quadriplegic was presented as the most competent to claim the right to die; the comatose patient was the least competent; and the cancer patient was in between. If competence were the major determining variable in right-to-die decisions, then the percent of "remove" decisions should have varied directly with the competence of the patient. But there were other dimensions and possibilities. The cases also varied as to whether or not the patient was terminally ill. The cancer patient arguably was, but the other two, from the medical testimony in the cases, clearly were not. Other dimensions concerned whether or not the patient was aware of her condition (only the comatose patient was not) and whether the patient was in pain (the woman with cancer was in great pain, whereas the other two women were not).

The second independent variable (a between-subject variable) involved the presence or absence of a living will. In cases where there was such a will, it was nine or ten years old.

Table 7.2 shows the number and percent of subjects who voted to

Table 7.2. Subjects who voted to allow the removal of life-support systems from three seriously ill patients.

	Case					
	Cancer patient		Comatose patient		Quadriplegic	
Variable	Number of subjects	Percent	Number of subjects	Percent	Number of subjects	Percent
Patient has a living will	41	65.1	49	77.8	27	42.9
Patient has no living will	46	71.9	48	76.2	26	40.6
Total for all conditions	87	68.5	97	77.0	53	41.7

allow the removal of life-support mechanisms. The numbers were broken down according to case, and according to whether the patient had drawn up a living will. The results varied significantly by case, but the differences were the opposite of those that would have been predicted strictly on the basis of the patient's competence. The case in which the patient was judged least competent had the highest percent of "remove" decisions (the comatose woman: 77 percent), whereas the case in which the patient was judged most competent had the lowest percent (the quadriplegic: 41.7 percent). Although there appears to have been significant overall support for the right to die, that support was not uniform across cases: the percents in the cases of the comatose and cancer patients (77 and 68.5, respectively) were quite high, but only a minority of subjects favored removal in the case of the quadriplegic (41.7 percent). Some uniform decisionmaking was apparent among the mock judges: 9.5 percent rendered "do not remove" decisions in all three cases, while 28.6 percent rendered "remove" decisions in all three cases. But the majority of mock judges (61.9 percent) rendered discriminating decisions across the cases. This finding suggests that the determinative reasons for either the "remove" or the "do not remove" decision were probably situated in the specific fact patterns and not in some general attitude. A general attitude may have been the key dispositive suspect for the 9.5 percent who rendered uniform "do not remove" decisions and for the 28.6 percent who rendered uniform "remove" decisions; but for the 61.9 percent who switched decisions, case factors clearly outweighed whatever general attitude they may have brought to their decisionmaking.

The presence or absence of a living will was nonsignificant across cases. Although it was anticipated that the living will might not matter in the cases of the cancer patient and the quadriplegic, since these patients could testify to their wishes, it was surprising that the absence of a living will did not matter in the case of the comatose patient. Thus, whereas the living will produced more "not guilty" verdicts in our earlier experiment and played a significant role in *Cruzan,* it did not do so here.

Table 7.3 shows ratings for general attitude on seven different variables, broken down by case. Subjects generally support the view that the right to die is a private matter (R1) and the view that the law should yield to the wishes of the patient (R2); these strongly supported attitudes do not vary by case. On ratings regarding the clarity of the patient's wish (R3), the patient's competence (R4), whether the disorder is terminal (R5), whether the disorder is irreversible (R6), and whether the patient is in pain (R7), we do see significant differences among cases, as well as clear indications that subjects are *construing* the patient's illness differently from doctors and perhaps from the courts.

To illustrate, in the scenario concerning the comatose patient, doctors testified that her condition was not terminal and that she could live another thirty-five or forty-five years. Most of the subjects, however, re-

Table 7.3. Mean ratings for seven variables in the cases of three seriously ill patients.

	Case[a]		
Variable	Cancer patient	Comatose patient	Quadriplegic
A private matter (R1)	6.89	6.92	6.58
Law should yield (R2)	7.03	7.47	6.76
Clear wish (R3)	8.95[b]	5.06[c]	9.04b
Competent (R4)	7.68[b]	5.52[c]	7.11b
Terminal (R5)	8.05[b]	7.08[b]	3.97c
Irreversible (R6)	8.23[b]	9.13[c]	8.86b
In pain (R7)	8.22[c]	4.29[b]	4.91b

Note: These ratings were made on a 1-to-11 scale, where 11 represents the greatest support for that view of privacy or that judgment of the patients's condition, and 1 represents the least support. A rating of 5.5 would fall halfway between the extremes.

a. The Wilks Lambda for the MANOVA, testing for an overall case effect, was (7,352) = 230.9, $p<.0001$.

b. The ANOVA was significant for this variable at $p<.05$.

c. The ANOVA was significant for this variable at $p<.05$. The variables marked "c" are significantly different from those marked "b."

garded this patient not as a living, sentient person but merely as a body being kept alive. According to their construal, she was a "terminal" case not in the narrow medical sense but in the sense of *what constitutes a person.*

As another example of disparity, doctors acknowledged that the cancer patient was in considerable pain but claimed that the comatose patient and the quadriplegic were not in any physical pain. Yet subjects' ratings indicated they believed that the latter two patients were experiencing moderate levels of pain. Subjects construed "pain" as encompassing more than merely physical pain: they brought psychological pain and emotional anguish into the construct.

The most important difference occurred in the way in which doctors and subjects construed the reversibility of the patient's condition (R6). For example, doctors said that people can come out of coma and thus that the condition is reversible. Most subjects, however, regarded the comatose state as irreversible: even if the patient were to emerge from the coma, they did not see that she had any chance of living a *meaningful life.*

Of all the reasons that subjects offered for their decisions, three reasons for the "remove" decision and three for the "do not remove" decision were the strongest predictors of their decisions. For the "remove" decision, subjects cited a general belief in privacy and in the right to die; in their construal of the facts, they saw the case as irreversible; and they believed that the patient had expressed a clear wish to die. For the "do not remove" decision, subjects cited a general belief in the right to life; they construed the case as reversible; and they believed that depression was affecting the patient's competence when she expressed her wish to die.

At one extreme, there were some subjects (among the 28.6 percent making uniform "remove" decisions) who viewed the decision to die as not a legal matter at all but a private matter, existing outside the bounds of law. For those subjects, this generalized belief was dominant and determinative; fact pattern nuances counted for little.

A larger group of subjects endorsed this "zone of privacy" view but wanted to make sure that the wish to die was clear, and untainted by depression. But when those provisos were added, the zone of privacy was opened—just wide enough to allow the State a role in assessing the patient's competence. And whenever the zone is widened in this way, the question becomes factual and empirical, not just a matter of a generalized belief. In essence, then, this "remove" group favored rational decisionmaking. Whenever the patient appeared rational and competent, they were willing to let her make the decision; but when the patient was comatose, they preferred to let the spouse or surrogate, rather than the State, make the decision.

At the other extreme was a small minority (among the 9.5 percent making uniform "do not remove" decisions) who endorsed the views that the right to life is paramount, that it cannot be waived by the individual, and that the State's duty is to protect life. For this group, as for the group at the opposite end of the spectrum, belief became determinative as fact pattern nuances receded in importance.

Occupying a less extreme position was a larger group that endorsed a qualified right to life, with provisos regarding irreversibility, terminal illnesses, and depression. This group was willing to "pull the plug" if the person's condition was irreversible (as broadly construed), if the disease was terminal (also broadly construed), and if depression did not impair competence. This group tended to be suspicious of spouses and family surrogates, to question their motives, and to believe that the State should control the decision. Thus, although this group set a greater number of preconditions that had to be met, these obstacles were not insurmountable. Whereas the State began as the controller, the State had to yield its control if the patient claiming the right to die could make her case.

From these results, we can see that community sentiment regarding the right to die is certainly not uniform. This finding is no surprise, given the strong and polar divisions among the populace on life-and-death issues in general. But division and complexity do not mean that the picture is incoherent. A fair reading of the two experiments shows a sizable sentiment for the right to die, although those who would go so far as to tell the law to "keep out" represent only a minority. Still, when we add to this minority a group that finds the law "wrong" and another group that believes the law ought to "yield" to the individual's right to privacy claim, we've compiled a sizable majority.

For most people, the belief in privacy and in the right to die, although strong, is tempered by the facts of the case. But "facts" do not influence people's decisions independently of their theories and beliefs; rather, people construe and interpret the facts, and their beliefs play a part in determining just how they will view those facts. This process of construing is certainly not unique to citizens, since we have seen justices construe facts differently and have seen how their views on privacy can shape their framing of a case. As for the way in which the community assesses the facts, we have ample evidence that subjects construe the patient's condition not from a strictly medical or legal perspective but in different and wider ways. In raising questions about what constitutes a person, a meaningful life, and psychological anguish, the community brings a full and rich set of concerns to the decision of when to terminate life. The issue is over who has control over life and death; it is about autonomy[26] and liberty. And at "the heart of liberty is the right to define one's own concept of existence, of meaning, of the universe, and of the mystery of human life."[27]

"Dr. Death" versus the Law

"For four years, Jack Kevorkian has been the director and leading actor in a macabre drama of his own creation, casting himself as 'Dr. Death.'"[28] By 1994 Dr. Kevorkian had helped some twenty people to end their lives, taking advantage of the fact that Michigan had no law that prohibited assisting in a suicide. But the Michigan legislature responded to Kevorkian's acts and passed such a law. Kevorkian promptly tested the law—and public sentiment—by openly assisting in yet another suicide, betting that the jury would nullify and acquit. He was right.

Kevorkian's attorney, Geoffrey Fieger, claimed that the verdict "'drives a stake into the heart' of the state's law banning assisted suicide."[29] To put this in less macabre language, Fieger was claiming that the jurors had nullified the law. Why had they done so? Fieger had predicted "that no jury ever would convict his client"; the jury's verdict "could buttress the arguments of those who contend prosecution of Kevorkian is futile and that physician-assisted suicide should be legalized but tightly regulated."[30] In other words, the Kevorkian camp was claiming that the jury nullified because the law was out of tune with community sentiment. Howard Simon, executive director of the Michigan branch of the American Civil Liberties Union, seconded this thesis. The Michigan law, he said, "is dead because juries are not going to implement it . . . The legislature is seriously out of touch with the general public" on the issue.[31]

But when we turn to the jurors' comments, a more complex and ambiguous picture emerges. First, many of the jurors said they were deeply moved by the videotape of thirty-year-old Thomas Hyde, who, suffering from amyotrophic lateral sclerosis, tearfully pleaded for an end to his pain and suffering. Clearly they construed "pain" as including not just physical pain but psychological anguish as well. Second, the tape made the matter real, for it inserted into this abstract legal drama a flesh-and-blood victim with evident pain and a moving plea. As assistant prosecutor Timothy Kenny noted, "We needed the jury to look at what may seem to be more abstract notions of the need to follow the law, while before them there was a very poignant case."[32] In this case the abstract confronted the concrete and poignant, and legal notions confronted the intuitive and emotional. The specific facts of the case did seem to matter. We do not know whether the jury would have reached the same verdict without such evidence of pain and without the tape.

Rather than forthrightly rejecting the law, the jurors split legal hairs, finding a phrase in the law to justify an acquittal. The jurors said they believed that Kevorkian was trying "to relieve this man's pain and suffering"[33] rather than intending to help Hyde commit suicide. But the prosecutors found this argument insulting: physicians who use pain killers such as morphine are easing suffering, they said, yet Kevorkian well knew that putting a mask over Hyde's face so that carbon monoxide could be administered would end his life. The jurors doubtless knew this as well. Their reasoning may have seemed illogical or evasive to the prosecution, but it may have been their way of justifying an acquittal *in this case*. Had they been operating according to a general belief that banning assisted suicides is wrong per se, then they could have said so. They could have brought in a "not guilty" verdict, announced that the law was asinine, and not bothered with hair-splitting reasons or rationalizations. But the fact that they did seek reasons suggests that their verdict was not extreme but located in a middle area where case-specific factors dominate and where jurors "craft" answers.

This case had the virtue of making the matter real for the jurors—of bringing Thomas Hyde to life, so to speak. But unfortunately, it was only a single case: we do not know what this Michigan jury would have done when confronted with other situations and different conditions. A likely interpretation, based on research findings, is that these jurors were saying that a complete prohibition on assisted suicides is not right; but this is a far cry from granting physicians a blanket right to end life. When this case and the research findings are put together, case-specific factors seem to have a greater determinative effect than does a generalized and extreme attitude. In the area of community sentiment on life-and-death decisions, there is a limit relating to assisted suicides, but it is not where the Michigan legislature drew it; nor is it likely to be at "terminal—dead in six months," as some propose, for such a limit would have denied Thomas Hyde the right to die; nor is the limit likely to be at "great physical pain," for if psychological anguish is left out, Hyde again would have been disqualified.

Making smaller headlines, but having greater import, was a 1994 ruling by chief U.S. district court judge Barbara Rothstein in a case involving the State of Washington's law banning assisted suicide. Rothstein, citing privacy rights, ruled the law unconstitutional, a ruling that came one day after Kevorkian's acquittal.[34] Columnist Charles Krauthammer wrote that Judge Rothstein "has discovered buried deep in the Constitution what no one had heretofore been able to find: the right to assisted suicide."[35] Whether Rothstein's legal analysis turns out to be incisive or merely "chutzpah," as Krauthammer believes, it brings up the old problem of judges' trying to find the root of privacy in some airy amendment, this time the Fourteenth. Although Krauthammer is no fan of assisted suicides, he is even less inclined to favor the imposition of a judicial solution: "I have no great expectation that over the long run the people and their legislatures will firmly hold the line against physician-assisted suicide. But I would rather see the ban overturned by popular will after vigorous debate than by judicial fiat."[36]

In the Matter of Privacy

We began with *Griswold,* which was about the beginnings of life and whether married couples could control their fertility from a zone of privacy, free from government intrusion. In answer to this question, the majority on the Supreme Court said that they could. We concluded with the Kevorkian case, which was about the right to end life and whether death is to be viewed as a part of life still under the autonomous control of the individual. In answer to this question, the majority of subjects said yes, with only a few provisos, indicating rather broad support for the right to die, even when the right is tested under the most unfavorable conditions.

Between the life decision and the death decision are a host of privacy matters that we have left unexamined. Many of them have come before the courts; many more will no doubt do so. On some of these matters, we remain in the empirical dark, not yet knowing where commonsense justice stands. We have incidents and headlines, even some cases, but in the absence of some experimental rigor, these tidbits remain speculative. We may surmise that people value privacy and autonomy as deeply as our Founding Fathers did,[37] even if the latter failed to codify constitutionally what seemed obvious; but others might surmise in the opposite direction. Cryptic constitutional phrases and single cases leave too much room for Rorschach-like interpretation, making it impossible to read sentiments accurately. Given such stimuli, we are more likely to see projections than answers.

Yet for some of these privacy matters, we do have empirical data to show where sentiment stands and what expectations seem reasonable and legitimate to the community. We have such an empirical foundation in right-to-die cases, and in search-and-seizure cases as well. And when the data are examined, we find that the law's path and the path laid by community sentiment do not always accord; in fact, they show notable divergence. If Roscoe Pound's prediction holds, the best guess is that common-sense justice will prevail in the end, with the law moving closer to the path laid by community sentiment.

But the law cannot absent itself, even when a sizable number of subjects believe that the law does not belong in certain zones. The law must nonetheless decide such privacy cases. How is the law to decide? We have seen decisions based on the way in which justices interpret constitutional amendments—a particularly shaky undertaking when the Constitution falls silent on privacy. As an example, Justice Blackmun thought that the essence of privacy was to be found in Justice Brandeis' "right to be left alone" and in his own "right to choose." But these *ideas* of privacy's essence, like ethereal penumbras, failed to persuade Blackmun's earth-bound colleagues that this is indeed the root that warrants constitutional endorsement, and the Court was thus split. And in the opinion of some people, Judge Rothstein's verdict on assisted suicide removes the decision from the people and their legal representatives, the first branch of government—and this creates a different sort of split, also unwholesome.

When justices, as Platonic Guardians, construe meanings, they place their interpretations before their brethren. If these interpretations contained some compelling logic, we would assume that the other justices would see it, and yield. But we discarded the view of law-as-logic a few chapters ago, as most justices have. The Blackmun-Brandeis view might yet carry the day, since the composition of the Court changes. In this version of "musical chairs and justices," a new majority, confronting a new case, might accept those phrases as the root of privacy. But community sentiment itself would have to change in that very small and unelected community of nine. The right to privacy would thus be established by shifts in sentiment, not necessarily by the intellectual force or logic of the ideas.

The relationship between ideas and empirics in validating the right to privacy can be sharpened with this question: Why is Brandeis' phrase so often quoted, and why do people say that his dissenting position has been vindicated? Not because his dictum displays masterly rhetoric:[38] it contains no poetic turn of phrase, no pleasant alliteration, no clever allusion. Still, it must have some power, and an enduring power at that. Moreover, in the process of being vindicated, the view must "strike a chord," "hit home," or have the "ring of truth." We reach for analogies and quotation marks to indicate that we sense some truth. In our individual ways we validate those ideas in the ethos that "seem to us valid," leaving the others as flotsam in space.

"Individual validation," however, is an unreliable basis for the right to privacy, since what one person may validate another may not. But by aggregating individual validations to piece together the collective conscience of the community, the sentiment of the community, a more substantive and representative picture emerges. This community picture is likely to be more representative than the sentiments of Platonic Guardians, even if those guardians serve on the Supreme Court. The right to die, involving the right to choose and the right to be left alone, "hits home" for the majority, and this sentiment adds a new element beyond texts, penumbras, and emanations. When syllogisms are empty, empirics can provide substance, founding the airy right of privacy not in words but in the community itself. Sentiments may not and need not be dispositive, but they do provide a ground. To some, this is neither solace nor surety. Yet in the matter of privacy, where the alternative is peering at penumbras, it may be the best we can do.

Cruel and Unusual Punishment

8

Privacy's claim is that there is a zone into which the law may not enter, a zone outside law itself. Punishment appears different, seeming to fall well within the limits of the law. Whereas many may question the State's right to intrude into the privacy of the bedroom, few would seriously question the State's right to punish.[1] Yet as soon as we ask the question "When may the State punish?" we see that the unquestioned right is nonetheless bound, restrained by certain limitations.

In answer to this question, which concerns the *distribution* of punishment,[2] ordinary citizens are likely to say something like, "When a harm is done, the State may punish." Justifying punishment in terms of the *harm* individuals have caused has a certain plausibility to it. When we think about crimes and punishments, we often think of exemplars that involved grave harm; and when such harms are done and the perpetrator is convicted, punishment usually follows. But not always. Even the most severe harm, namely death, is generally not punished if it has been caused by accident.[3] And harms that result from mistake, be the mistake reasonable or unreasonable, often lead to exoneration as well.[4]

Accidents occur, says George Fletcher, "in the realm of causation," whereas mistakes occur "in the realm of perception."[5] A wildly ricocheting bullet that kills an innocent bystander is an accident; in contrast, "it was no accident that Oedipus killed his father and slept with his mother, but it was a tragic mistake."[6] We exonerate accidents because the causative and purposive link between the defendant's action (say, firing a bullet) and the fatal outcome has been broken: chance, something unforeseen (the ricochet), has intervened. Whereas accidents "happen," "mistakes . . . are 'made'";[7] Oedipus set out his own erroneous course *before* he slew dad and jumped into bed with mom. Concerning the question, "When may the State punish?" it is enough to note that both accident and mistake are exceptions to the answer, "Whenever harm has been caused." These exceptions tell us that something more than just harm is needed to justify punishment, for these exceptions are some of the restraints on the State's unquestioned right to punish.

No Harm, No Foul?

Before looking at what that something more is, we must look at something less, for the State may legitimately punish an individual when no harm has been done. "Attempt crimes" are paradigmatic. If someone attempts to kill another person but fails, we still feel that punishment should follow. Here we generally discard the criterion of "harm" in favor of the broader notion of "criminal act," and amend our answer to say that "punishment may follow when a criminal act has occurred."

The concept of the *criminal act*—which focuses on the manifest behavior of the individual rather than on the harmful consequence that results—while appearing more inclusive than the notion of *harm,* nonetheless has some troubling oddities and exceptions of its own. The oddities are those impossible situations in which the act appears criminal but in which circumstances show that a crime (or harm) cannot have occurred. In Chapter 5 we encountered a good example: a man aims and fires a gun at a tree stump, believing he is shooting a person. From the vantage point of the outside observer, shooting a tree stump is not a criminal act. We also looked at the case of a woman who tries to kill a man and fires shots into his body as he lies sleeping, only to find out that he died in his sleep hours ago. Although this act appears murderous on its face, the discovery that the man died a natural death indicates otherwise: one cannot murder someone who is already dead, and the fortuity of the victim's natural death appears to undercut the claim that the woman committed a criminal act.

We looked at two other cases as well. A husband and wife try to kill each other: the husband attempts to shoot his wife, but forgets to load the gun and fires an empty gun at her head; the wife, wishing to give her husband his lumps, attempts to poison him with arsenic-laced sugar cubes but mistakenly drops normal sugar cubes in his tea. Here, the "crimes" appear to be precluded by ineptness. The couple's mistakes turn their gestures into impossible acts: you cannot kill someone by firing an empty gun at him or by feeding him plain sugar cubes. And we looked at a fifth case, in which a woman tries to kill another woman by sticking pins in the heart of an effigy. From our "modern" point of view, we see a causal impossibility here: we do not believe that "murdering" an effigy can cause the death of a human being.

Thus, when considered within a legal system based on manifest liability, none of the abovementioned cases involves a criminal act. And this is precisely the difficulty when we try to justify punishment as a response to a criminal act, for such a justification does not fit with the commonsense judgments of ordinary people.

In an experiment that my associates and I conducted,[8] subjects were given one of the five cases described above and were asked two questions: Had a crime occurred? If so, was the defendant guilty or not guilty? Subjects were also asked to give their reasons for their answers. The two questions yielded nearly identical results, but the results were neither identical across cases nor anywhere near what the manifest-liability advocate would predict (see Table 8.1). In cases 2, 3, and 4, the percents of subjects voting "guilty" were 86, 100, and 100, respectively; and the reasons the subjects gave were, overwhelmingly and consistently, "The defendant intended to commit a crime," "The defendant planned the act," "The act was premeditated." These subjects clearly invoked a subjective factor, namely *intent*, and when they found evil intent they found guilt, despite the absence of a manifest criminal act or a harm. Put another way, subjects were not willing to let these defendants profit from fortuitous or inept mistakes.

In the case of the man who shot at the tree stump, however, subjects divided fairly evenly: 53 percent found the defendant guilty, whereas 47 percent did not. Their reasons differed along subjective-objective lines: the subjects who voted "guilty" cited the defendant's intent to kill, and

Table 8.1. Judgments of criminality and guilt in the cases of five "impossible" crimes.

	Percent of subjects answering yes in each case				
Question	Firing at tree stump (1)	Shooting a dead man (2)	Attempted murder with empty gun (3)	Attempted murder with plain sugar (4)	Attempted murder with effigy (5)
Was the action a crime?	53	90	95	89	17
Is the defendant guilty?	53	86	100	100	17

the subjects who voted "not guilty" said they had done so because there had been no harm, no crime, and no victim. In this case, then, objective factors were preeminent for roughly half the subjects, whereas subjective factors dominated for the other half. What differentiated case 1 from cases 2, 3, and 4? In all four cases, the individual made a mistake, yet the mistake in case 1 led to exoneration approximately half the time, whereas in cases 2, 3, and 4 it almost never led to exoneration. We can get at the answer by asking, "What if the mistake had not occurred?" What if, in case 1, the defendant had realized before firing that his target was a tree stump and not a man? What if the fortuitous death, in case 2, had not occurred? What if the husband, in case 3, had double-checked his pistol, and the wife, in case 4, had double-checked her sugar cubes? The answer in cases 2, 3, and 4 is the same: a murder would almost certainly have occurred. But not so in case 1, where the myopic marksman would have had to search for a new victim. Cases 2, 3, and 4 involved immediate danger to the victim: had it not been for the defendant's mistake, a homicide would surely have taken place. Case 1 lacked this "objective" element of "potential for immediate harm."

The importance of the lessened danger in case 1 becomes even clearer when we see to what extent objective factors dominated in case 5: 83 percent of the subjects found the defendant not guilty, whereas 17 percent found her guilty. The latter group of subjects cited the subjective factor of "intent." Among the former group, most noted the objective fact that sticking pins in an effigy could not produce harm; hence, there was no real danger to the intended victim. A few of the subjects who voted "not guilty" cited a subjective factor: they made a distinction between "intending to kill" and "wishing the victim dead," and found the latter "intent" to be nonculpable.

These empirical results concerning impossible acts bolster our conceptual, theoretical, and jurisprudential doubts that punishment can be justified as a response to a criminal act. These results strongly suggest that people weigh inner intent heavily and that *subjective liability* is a necessary condition for guilt and punishment. Historically, the factor of evil or criminal intent has been known as *mens rea;* to the subjectivist it is the most important element for establishing guilt and the State's right to punish. *Mens rea* is what makes the action and the actor morally blameworthy and legally subject to punishment; the act merely functions to demonstrate the "firmness of the actor's resolve and to provide one among many sources of evidence of the particular intent."[9] Yet few who espouse subjective liability would go so far as to say that *mens rea* is the only thing that matters. To go that far would entail punishing people merely for their thoughts and intentions. This may be an accepted function of certain religions, but it is not the function of modern law. The reasons for rejecting intention alone as the criterion for punishment involve more than the daunting evidentiary burden of proving intent in the absence of an overt act, particularly if the defendant did not confess. Rather, it strikes us as unfair and unjust to punish intent without an act. Thus, we come to the conclusion that punishment must be justified on the basis of both objective and subjective elements—both a criminal act *(actus reus)* and a criminal intent *(mens rea)*.

Using these two elements, we can begin to see where and why the State's right to punish is constrained. In cases of mistake, the defense denies the *mens rea* element, claiming no blameworthy intent: "I didn't *know* I was sleeping with my mother!" Oedipus would say. In a case where someone is accidentally killed by a ricocheting bullet, there is a lack not only of *mens rea* but also of *actus reus*: the person who fired the gun committed no *criminal act,* as we legally and psychologically understand that term. And when a defendant claims he is innocent, saying, "You've got the wrong man," he is in effect saying, "I didn't commit the act, so of course I didn't have the intent."

Even when an individual does know that he or she is taking a life, the law still may be prevented from punishing. Here the paradigmatic claim is self-defense, which is different from claiming to have made a mistake. The defendant is not saying, "I didn't know the gun was loaded," or "I didn't know I was shooting at a person." Rather, he is appealing to the law's recognition that there are certain quite specific and extraordinary circumstances in which individuals may have to either take a life or lose their own. Under ordinary circumstances such actions and intentions are punishable, as murder or manslaughter. But under extraordinary circumstances, the claim is that such actions are justified; if they are, there is no guilt, and the law may not punish.

A successful insanity claim likewise bars the State from punishing, but does so in a different way. Insanity is a claim of *nonresponsibility*. A defendant who claims self-defense contends that he or she is a responsible person under the law, but one caught in a maddening situation. When a defendant claims insanity, it is not the circumstances but the individual who appears mad—whose capacity to make responsible choices, like that of a child or a severely retarded person, falls below some legal threshold. If such people are not responsible agents, their acts are not morally blameworthy and the law will excuse them. Thus, in cases of insanity and self-defense, although the defendants apparently knew they were taking a life, the law's power to punish is curtailed.

Having surveyed the field and set aside those conditions that justify certain actions and excuse certain defendants, let's look at those individuals who have no excuse or justification for their actions but who raise a claim of a different sort. They have been found guilty by a jury of their peers, and thus do not challenge their guilt; nor do they challenge the State's right to punish per se. Rather, they challenge *particular* punishments as "cruel and unusual."

The Eighth Amendment

When we think of cruel and unusual punishments, we generally think of barbarisms long removed from the legal landscape, at least in Western societies. When the authorities in Singapore caned an eighteen-year-old American, Michael Fay, for alleged acts of vandalism, the *Washington Post* titled its editorial "Singapore's Shame."[10] But the *Washington Post*'s sentiment did not match that of the American community, at least according to a *Newsweek* poll, which found that "more than half of American surveyed . . . indicated that caning was appropriate punishment for spray-painting cars."[11] Whereas caning produces sentiment on both sides of the "cruel and unusual" debate, burning at the stake, boiling in oil, drawing and quartering, and cutting off hands—more tortures than punishments, to our mind—are far more likely to produce uniform sentiment asserting that these are indeed cruel and unusual punishments.

But what about a prison sentence of, say, fifty-four years? The quick answer is apt to be that such a penalty is reasonable, since there are even more extreme sentences in the United States: one can be sentenced to life in prison, or even to death. The more reflective answer is likely to be a question: "Fifty-four years *for what?*" To ask the question is to recognize that the rubric "cruel and unusual" involves not just judgment of a punishment but judgment of the *relationship* between a punishment and a crime. In *O'Neil v. Vermont* (1892), known as the "fifty-four-year punishment" case, the defendant was convicted of 307 counts of "selling liquor without authority."[12] In the opinion of the majority justices in *O'Neil,* the Eighth Amendment was inapplicable because the punishment was in no way barbaric. But Justice Stephen Field found that the Eighth Amendment was "directed . . . against all punishments which by their excessive length or severity are greatly disproportioned to the offenses charged."[13] In Field's view, disproportionality, not barbarism, is what determines whether a punishment is cruel and unusual. Though Field's position was expressed in a dissenting opinion, it soon became the accepted view.

In *Weems v. United States* (1910),[14] a Philippine case involving an official who made false entries in an official document, the defendant was found guilty and sentenced to pay fines and to wear chains *("cadena temporal")* for twelve years. When the case was appealed, the U.S. Supreme Court embraced Justice Field's view that "in interpreting the Eighth Amendment it will be regarded as a precept of justice that punishment for crime should be graduated and proportioned to the offense."[15] Although *Weems* established the principle of proportionality, the case is even more noteworthy because it forged an empirical link between the definition of "cruel and unusual punishment" and an evolving community sentiment. The Court stated that "the Eighth Amendment is progressive and does not prohibit merely the cruel and unusual punishments known in 1689 and 1787, but may acquire wider meaning as public opinion becomes enlightened by humane justice."[16]

This position was radically different from the one put forth in the privacy debate in *Griswold*. In *Weems* the Court was in effect saying that even though we might have perfect understanding of the Eighth Amendment's words and of the meanings contained in the penumbras, those words and meanings do not define "cruel and unusual" once and for all. They cannot. For what is "cruel and unusual" changes, "as public opinion becomes enlightened by humane justice."[17]

Just as the nineteenth century's "corporal punishment" became the twentieth century's "child abuse," the concept of "cruel and unusual" continues to evolve over time. Whereas notions of privacy seemed fixed and whereas modern justices could claim to understand these notions much the way a Framer like Madison did, the concept of cruel and unusual punishment lies in the empirical world, changing as society changes. When it comes to Eighth Amendment matters, the Framers' reference, time, and context dwindle in interpretive relevance, while current context assumes hegemony.

Weems presents us with an assessment problem: How do we determine if a punishment is disproportionate to the crime? We could apply our individual judgments to the fact pattern and decide that the specter of a man dragging about in chains for more than ten years for two expenditure falsifications of 408 and 204 pesos is highly incongruous. But although we might think we're being objective here, our "objectivity" consists of little more than giving our subjective sensibilities free reign and rationalizing this license with the dictum, "We all believe that." The Court in *Weems* recognized the problem, and the majority did not declare the punishment disproportionate on its face. Rather, the Court conducted a proportionality analysis, making *Weems* a landmark in yet another way.

In trying to assess proportionality empirically and objectively, the Court performed comparisons within and between jurisdictions. For example, it looked at punishments for embezzlement under various penal laws in the United States, and found that individuals committing offenses similar to Weems's would generally be punished by a fine "double the amount so withheld and imprisoned not more than two years."[18] Thus, when the Court compared Weems's punishment to punishments for similar crimes in different jurisdictions, his punishment seemed disproportionate.

Likewise, when the Court compared Weems's crime and its punishment with other crimes and punishments in the *same* jurisdiction, it found that there "are degrees of homicide that are not punished so severely."[19] Implicit here is the notion that we have some sort of scale on which we can ordinally array crimes by their blameworthiness and severity, and that we agree about our relative judgments on crime. Thus, if all forms of homicide are worse (more blameworthy) than this form of embezzlement but the latter is punished more severely than some types of homicide, a disproportionality exists.

Deliberately or not, the Court was committing itself to an objective, empirical jurisprudence in regard to Eighth Amendment claims. In dissent, Justice Edward White expressed some "perplexity,"[20] which was farsighted of him, for he seemed to recognize that determining proportionality places justices not only in a supervisory role over state legislatures but in the role of social scientists. Justice White's hesitancy here reminds us of Justice Black's dissent in *Griswold,* where he claimed that the Court was not set up to take Gallup polls. Whether the Court was ready or not, though, the empirical door had been opened, and a future in which justices would act as social scientists was not far away.

Following *Weems,* the Court did not expand its Eighth Amendment provisions; if anything, it was quite circumspect, rejecting claims of cruel and unusual punishment in *Graham v. West Virginia* (1912),[21] *Badders v. United States* (1916),[22] and *Francis v. Resweber* (1947).[23] But the empirical evolution picked up steam with *Trop v. Dulles* (1958),[24] a case involving a soldier who had deserted during World War II and whose punishment was the loss of his U.S. citizenship. In contrast to its decision in *Weems,* the Court recognized in *Trop* that since "wartime desertion is punishable by death, there can be no argument that the penalty of denationalization is excessive in relation to the gravity of the crime."[25] Since

Trop dealt with a U.S. soldier, federal law, and a military court, interjurisdictional comparisons would have been inapt. Still, the question was "whether this penalty subjects the individual to a fate forbidden by the principle of civilized treatment guaranteed by the Eighth Amendment."[26]

The Court decided it did. Without the sort of empirical evidence it had marshaled in *Weems,* the majority simply declared that this sort of punishment and loss of "the right to have rights"[27] is "a fate universally decried by civilized people."[28] But in *Trop v. Dulles,* the Court's decision was at odds with its process. In an oft-repeated quote from the case, the Court claimed that the Eighth Amendment "must draw its meaning from the evolving standards of decency that mark the progress of a maturing society."[29] Thus, the meaning of "cruel and unusual" was directly hinged to society's current standards. The implications for legal process and assessment were clear: the Court must gauge current community sentiment and make proportionality judgments against the backdrop of that sentiment. Yet although the Court's intrajurisdictional assessment found no disproportionality, the Court's judgment did. On what basis did the justices reach their conclusion? They clearly did not rely on empirical confirmation, for the demonstrable evidence did not support the decision. To use Justice Scalia's phrase, it was a "philosopher-king decision,"[30] in which justices made a decision according to their conscience. In the words of Learned Hand, it was a Platonic Guardian decision.

Trop left two related issues unresolved. What place should objective decisionmaking and philosopher-king decisionmaking have? The danger with philosopher-kings and Platonic Guardians is that they substitute their own subjective judgments for those of the community. At the other extreme, should justices follow a purely objective jurisprudence, measuring community sentiment empirically but adding not a whit of their own opinion to the mix? Such a jurisprudence leaves justices functioning as social scientists or bean counters, and makes the empirical evidence not just informing but determinative. Justices may not wish to go that far. These issues are debatable. What is indefensible, however, is the dupery of claiming to be engaged in objective jurisprudence while applying one's personal conscience instead.

In *Coker v. Georgia* (1977),[31] the Court moved even further away from the subjective judgments of individual justices. In finding that the death penalty for rape violated the Eighth Amendment's prohibition against cruel and unusual punishment, the Court noted that "Eighth Amendment judgments should not be, or appear to be, merely the subjective views of individual Justices; judgment should be informed by objective factors to the maximum possible extent."[32] This view took the Court a step closer to social science jurisprudence. Had it not added "to the maximum possible extent," which allows some leeway for subjective factors, it would in fact have attained such jurisprudence.

Did the Court in *Coker* practice what it preached? It did perform an interjurisdictional analysis, and the results were readily interpretable: Georgia was the only jurisdiction that made the crime of rape a death penalty offense, a fact that appeared to make the punishment at least "unusual." But in *Coker,* as in other cases, it was the intrajurisdictional comparisons that presented problems, for we still have no agreed-upon severity scale for crimes.[33] Is rape more severe than, equal to, or less severe than murder? Answers may vary; the likeliest is "less severe." Yet would it continue to be so if rape were compared to a variation of first-degree murder? Suppose the comparison is with a case of accessory felony-murder: the defendant was a getaway driver who was sitting in the car while a store clerk died of a heart attack at the sight of the triggerman's empty gun. Given this comparison, we may not be sure if rape is less severe than this form of murder. What we do know is that in the years since *Coker,* the Court has come to rely more on interjurisdictional comparisons than on intrajurisdictional ones.

A Life Sentence in the Balance

In judging whether or not a punishment is proportionate to the crime, we must do some sort of comparative weighing. Though it is difficult to make intrajurisdictional assessments without a valid severity scale for crimes, and although interjurisdictional assessments may be difficult to read, especially when differences among state laws are minimal, the variables we have thus far been discussing have been simple: "punishment" and its relation to "crime." Now the situation gets more complex. Consider Jerry Buckley Helm, who committed a seemingly minor crime: he wrote a check for a hundred dollars on a nonexistent account.[34]

An interesting thought experiment would be to imagine the average sentence ordinary people would impose for this offense, if they were provided with no sentencing guidelines whatsoever. Would they specify some mild penalty such as probation, a suspended sentence, a small fine? Or would they give jail time—six months, a year or two, or a lengthier imprisonment? How severe would they be?

They would not impose life imprisonment without possibility of parole. I can state this confidently, since I've run the experiment. Yet that was the sentence Helm received in 1979 under South Dakota's recidivist statute. Helm, as it turns out, was punished not because he had committed this one crime but because he had six prior felony convictions—three convictions for third-degree burglary, one for obtaining money under false pretenses, one for grand larceny, and one for third-offense driving while intoxicated.[35] Thus, when recidivist statutes and cases are taken into account, the relation between punishment and crime can become anything but straightforward.

In recidivist cases, according to one view, the crime itself widens and worsens. Unlike the first-time offender, the recidivist has been punished before yet does not heed the law's lesson; he seems to be thumbing his nose at the law, adding insult to injury. Although the act appears the same for the first-timer and recidivist, the *mens rea* seems more serious for the recidivist. Parents understand this. The child who breaks the same rule over and over again provokes greater anger and harsher punishment than does the first-timer.

According to an alternative view, in recidivist cases the crime does not become more severe; rather, the State may punish the *criminal* and not just the crime. A host of new variables come into play: the number and severity of prior convictions; background factors such as the defendant's age, work history, community ties, family stability; whether there is a history of violence, drug abuse, alcohol, and so on. Acting on the basis of this view and using current sentencing guidelines, judges function like actuarials, consulting tables to add or subtract points for the myriad variables and then calculating the final sentence. Whether this calculus produces commonsense justice, we have yet to determine. Whether, in the assessment of the Supreme Court, it produced proportional justice or cruel and unusual punishment for Jerry Buckley Helm, we shall see. But first we need to reiterate an important point about context.

In a courtroom trial, where the issue is the defendant's guilt or innocence, the law generally adheres to a "tight" context. That is, the jury may not hear, and the attorneys may not introduce, evidence that the judge rules irrelevant. The defendant's prior crimes, under ordinary circumstances, are not admissible, since the context consists only of the facts surrounding the particular crime under consideration. Jurors are asked to pass judgment on whether a specific defendant committed a specific crime, and their judgment should be untainted by knowledge of his or her past actions. Context can likewise restricted with regard to the plaintiff: in cases where an alleged rapist claims consent on the part of the victim, the victim's past sexual history is typically shielded. Her past sexual partners and practices become irrelevant, for the context is narrowed to the particular incident in question, to the specific moment of the act, and to the question of whether she said no to the defendant who is on trial.

When guilt is the issue, the image of blind justice prevails, as context is controlled and narrowly defined.

When punishment becomes the issue, the context expands. Justice now rips off her blindfold and scrutinizes the defendant and the actuarial tables. Whether she should do so is debatable. If one views punishment as retribution for the specific crime in question, then the expanded context is of dubious legitimacy. But if one takes a wider view of retribution, or takes the view that punishment is legitimately motivated by desires for retribution, deterrence, and rehabilitation, then the wider context becomes permissible, as well as necessary for precise calculations. Yet when one expands the context, one risks including factors that should not be given any weight. As we will see, this risk has the most serious potential consequences in cases involving the death penalty, because in such cases the stakes are highest, the death decision rests with the jury (in most states), and there is no established procedure for choosing what may be weighed in the aggravating or mitigating mix and for determining how the jury should perform its calculations.

How did the Supreme Court weigh all the factors in *Solem v. Helm?* In a five-to-four decision, the Court ruled that a life sentence without possibility of parole was disproportionate in Helm's case and did violate the Eighth Amendment's prohibition against cruel and unusual punishment. Justice Lewis Powell, writing for the majority, first stated that the Eighth Amendment did apply to "excessive fines imposed" and not only to barbaric punishments or death sentences. He noted that the Eighth Amendment had its roots in the Magna Carta of 1215 (which devoted three clauses to "amercements"—fines that may not be excessive), in the English Bill of Rights, and in common-law rulings against excessive and exorbitant fines.[36] But having set aside history and *stare decisis,* Powell stressed the empirical evolution of the Eighth Amendment: "courts should be guided by objective factors."[37] More specifically, he enumerates three criteria: "(i) the gravity of the offense and the harshness of the penalty; (ii) the sentences imposed on other criminals in the same jurisdiction; and (iii) the sentences imposed for commission of the same crime in other jurisdictions."[38]

Concerning point (i), Powell maintained that "courts are competent to judge the gravity of an offense, at least on a relative scale."[39] As we have seen, one can look at the harm caused or threatened, or at the culpability of the offender. And Powell named other acceptable principles: for example, we generally believe that stealing a million dollars is a more serious crime than stealing a hundred dollars—an attitude incorporated in statutes distinguishing petty larceny from grand theft.[40] Judged on the basis of these principles, Helm's crime was "one of the most passive felonies a person could commit," since it "involved neither violence nor threat of violence to any person."[41] But here, with respect to criterion (i), the Court seemed to be looking at the crime and not the criminal, or the crime abstracted from the defendant's prior history and the recidivist statute that generated the punishment. Powell recognized this when he said that "Helm, of course, was not charged simply with uttering a 'no account' check, but also with being a habitual offender."[42]

The "priors" had to be taken into account, and these complicated the analysis, said Powell.[43] He did note that all the priors were "relatively minor. All were nonviolent and none was a crime against a person."[44] Next came the intrajurisdictional comparisons, according to criterion (ii). In South Dakota, people who committed first-degree murder, second-offense treason, arson, and kidnapping received mandatory life sentences; those who committed manslaughter, attempted murder, first-degree rape, and aggravated assault might get life imprisonment, but the judge had discretion; a third group, convicted of "very serious offenses," were not subject to life imprisonment. Taking this context into account, Powell found that all of the crimes which South Dakota punished with a life sentence were more deserving of that punishment than writing a no-account check. A supporter of recidivist statutes, however, might well point out that Powell was not adequately weighing the priors and the fact that Helm was a repeat offender.

The results of the interjurisdictional comparison—criterion (iii)—were much clearer. "Helm could have received a life sentence without parole for his offense in only one other state, Nevada . . . Therefore, it is clear that Helm could not have received such a severe sentence in 48 of the 50 States."[45] Summing across all three criteria, the majority concluded that Helm's sentence "is significantly disproportionate to his crime, and is therefore prohibited by the Eighth Amendment."[46]

The minority phrased its dissent this way: "Today's conclusion by five Justices that they are able to say that one offense has less 'gravity' than another is nothing other than a bald substitution of individual subjective moral values for those of the legislature."[47] In other words, so much for objectivity. But to appreciate the minority's point and the Court's conflict, we must turn to a case that had been decided three years earlier—*Rummel v. Estelle*—for it was *Rummel* that was central to the minority's opinion.[48]

William James Rummel was convicted of obtaining $120.75 by false pretenses under Texas' recidivist statute. It was his third offense; his first two offenses involved fraudulent use of a credit card to obtain $80.00

worth of goods and services, and passing a forged check in the amount of $28.36. He received a mandatory life sentence. Although *Rummel* and *Helm* appear similar, some small differences are worth noting: whereas Helm had six priors, Rummel had only two; whereas Helm's punishment was life imprisonment without parole, Rummel had the prospect of parole; and by a margin of one vote, Rummel's sentence was found proportionate and not in violation of the stricture forbidding cruel and unusual punishment.

The *Rummel* majority did a scanty objective analysis, noting that Rummel's crime was a felony in at least thirty-five states and that many states authorized lengthy terms of imprisonment for Rummel's other two offenses. This seems to have been the extent of its interjurisdictional comparison.[49] Rummel had presented interjurisdictional data indicating "that he might have received more lenient treatment in almost any State other than Texas, West Virginia, or Washington," but the majority found the data unconvincing: "The distinctions . . . are subtle rather than gross."[50] The Court acknowledged that recidivist statutes created an assessment nightmare: "It is one thing for a court to compare those States that impose capital punishment for a specific offense with those States that do not . . . [It] is quite another thing for a court to attempt to evaluate the position of any particular recidivist scheme within Rummel's complex matrix."[51]

The majority seemed to be not only beating a hasty retreat from the "complex matrix" of recidivism but undercutting the possibility of a clear objective reading, even from apparently clear interjurisdictional data.

> Even were we to assume that the statute employed against Rummel was the most stringent found in the 50 States, that severity hardly would render Rummel's punishment "grossly disproportionate" to his offenses or to the punishment he would have received in the other States . . . Until quite recently, Arizona punished as a felony the theft of any "neat or horned animal," regardless of its value . . . [and] California considers the theft of "avocados, olives, citrus or deciduous fruits, nuts and artichokes" particularly reprehensible.[52]

The *Rummel* majority was trying to have it both ways. On the one hand, the justices were clearly seeking a way out of the assessment labyrinth, which seemed to be inhabited not by the Minotaur but by bovines and assorted fruits and nuts. On the other hand, they were simultaneously seeking to maintain the illusory thread that consistently tied their decision to community sentiment, which they had not gauged. Claiming that sentiment was on their side, they cited (and deferred to) the Texas legislature, for legislative enactments are one reputed gauge of community sentiment. But this sort of reasoning was tautological. If the statute was automatically assumed to reflect community sentiment, then the statute itself constituted the entire Eighth Amendment analysis. There was no reason to undertake inter- and intrajurisdictional comparisons, if the statute alone conferred constitutionality.

The minority in *Rummel* resumed their objective analysis, particularly the interjurisdictional type. They noted that "only 12 States have ever enacted habitual offender statutes imposing a mandatory life sentence for the commission of two or three nonviolent felonies and only 3, Texas, Washington, and West Virginia, have retained such a statute."[53] To put this another way, "three-quarters of American jurisdictions have never adopted a habitual offender statute that would commit the petitioner to mandatory life imprisonment."[54] Those that had required more than three offenses, or at least one violent crime, or limited the mandatory penalty to less than life, or granted discretion to the judge. Through these comparisons, Texas' statute appeared extreme and "unconstitutionally disproportionate."[55]

The minority's intrajurisdictional comparison was also unfavorable, since Helm had been given the penultimate criminal penalty for committing three offenses in which he had defrauded others of about $230, whereas people who had committed murder, aggravated kidnapping, or aggravated rape had received lighter sentences. But calculating the vague recidivist factor was still a problem. To what extent could the justices legitimately inflate the punishment, given that the defendant had committed a third offense and was a habitual offender? The Court had neither an answer nor any way to get an answer.

Community Sentiment is Clear

To find out where community sentiment stands on such recidivist cases, my associates and I conducted the following experiment.[56] We created two cases. The first was a disguised form of *Solem v. Helm* that we called "Stevens v. Idaho," in which the facts from *Helm* (the defendant's last crime, plus his six prior offenses) were reproduced without alteration. Since there might have been something unique about *Helm* which may have produced atypical punishments, we created a second recidivist case, called "Walters v. Texas," involving a woman defendant who had been caught shoplifting a gold bracelet worth $100. We gave her six priors as well, all shoplifting offenses; the total retail worth of the goods she had taken in all seven crimes was $810. Subjects were told that a jury had found the defendant guilty of the last crime, and were asked to impose a sentence.

Subjects received one of the two cases, under one of six conditions. The first condition was a control in two ways: first, the subjects heard only about the last crime and had no knowledge of any priors, so the punishment they gave reflected just one crime; second, the subjects were given no legal guidelines as to the typical or maximum sentence for this sort of crime, and thus the punishment they gave reflected just their judgment of proportionality. Thus, the question here was: What sort of sentences would subjects impose for either the no-account check or the shoplifting, with no knowledge of priors and no legal guidelines? Under the second condition, subjects received the full crime picture (the last crime plus the six priors), but they were again given no legal guidelines. Here the question was: How much more severe would the sentences be in the second group than in the first group? Would the severity of the sentences increase in some additive fashion? That is, would subjects with a knowledge of the defendant's six priors impose sentences seven times longer than would subjects who knew of only one offense? Or would the sentences increase more dramatically—perhaps geometrically or exponentially? Under the third condition, where again all seven offenses were presented, the subjects received legal guidelines. They were told, in the *Helm* case variation, that the maximum punishment for writing a no-account check was five years in jail and a $5,000 fine. In our shoplifting case, the legal standard was one month in jail and a $300 fine. The question here was: How would the subjects use these legal guidelines? Would they use only the sentences recommended by law, or multiply these by the number of offenses, or perhaps use some other calculation?

Under the fourth condition, we tested to see how sentences would change when the prosecution emphasized the defendant's recidivist tendencies. This time, subjects were given the full crime picture plus legal guidelines, but the prosecution labeled the defendant a recidivist or habitual offender and argued that the State had the right to punish a repeat offender far more harshly than a first-timer. The prosecution asked that the State impose life imprisonment without the possibility of parole. What would happen to the average sentence under these circumstances?

According to the recidivist argument, individuals who keep committing crimes show that they are unrepentant, that they are more criminal and more dangerous to society than other offenders, and that they therefore deserve more severe punishment. But there is another way of looking at repeated crime that leads to the opposite conclusion. The fact that someone keeps writing bad checks or continues to shoplift may indicate a psychiatric disorder rather than an incorrigible criminal nature. As the number of priors grows, so too might one's tendency to see the individual as "disordered." Under condition five, in contrast to having the prosecution underscore the accused's recidivism, we had the defense make a strong plea for the defendant as a psychiatrically troubled man who deserved a lighter sentence and professional treatment.

Finally, we set up a sixth condition, pitting the recidivist argument against the psychiatric-disorder argument. The prosecution asked for life imprisonment without parole (as under condition four), and the defense asked for leniency and psychiatric treatment (as under condition five). How would the average sentence change in this situation?

Table 8.2 presents the mean sentences imposed by the subjects in the two cases, under each of the six conditions. The differences in the facts of the cases had a significant effect on the results: the shoplifter received significantly lower sentences than the writer of a no-account check. But let's look more closely at one of the cases—say, the *Helm* variation—to

Table 8.2. Mean sentences (in months) for the Helm variation and the shoplifting case, by condition.

| | Cases | | |
Conditions	*Helm* variation	Shoplifting case	Totals across cases
1. One crime, no sentencing guidelines	10.4	3.6	7.0
2. Seven crimes, no sentencing guidelines	86.0	61.0	73.5
3. Seven crimes, with sentencing guidelines	143.0	2.7	72.8
4. Seven crimes, with sentencing guidelines and recidivist emphasis	355.3	123.6	239.5
5. Seven crimes, with sentencing guidelines and psychiatric-disorder argument	64.8	18.3	41.5
6. Seven crimes, with sentencing guidelines, recidivist emphasis, and psychiatrics disorder argument	185.8	12.0	98.9
Totals across conditions	140.9	36.9	

see what happens as the conditions change. Under the first condition (one offense and no sentencing guidelines), the average sentence was 10.4 months, which was quite a bit lower than the legal standard of five years and a $5,000 fine. Under condition two (seven offenses and no sentencing guidelines), the mean prison sentence jumped significantly—to 86 months, or just over seven years. Clearly, subjects were not just punishing the last crime but were factoring in the six priors; yet, just as clearly, the defendant did not receive anything approaching life imprisonment without parole. It seems almost as if subjects had some idea about what one such crime was worth in terms of punishment and then multiplied that number by the total number of crimes.

Now let's see what happened when the subjects were given sentencing guidelines. The legal standard in the *Helm* variation was five years in jail and a $5,000 fine; in the shoplifting case it was much lower—one month and a $300 fine. In the *Helm* case, introducing the guidelines raised the sentence from 86 months to 143 months, or from seven years to almost twelve years. Subjects were not taking the legal standard and multiplying it by the number of crimes (seven), for that would have yielded a sentence of thirty-five years; nor were they giving the defendant anything close to life imprisonment without parole. For the shoplifting case, interestingly enough, the guidelines worked to lower the sentence.

The key condition involved the recidivist emphasis. Here the sentences were the highest, and significantly so. In the *Helm* variation, the mean sentence was 355.3 months, or almost thirty years. Many subjects in this condition followed the prosecutor's recommendation, although a sizable number were reluctant to impose extreme punishment.

Under the fifth condition, in which the defense made a made a plea for the defendant as psychiatrically disordered, the mean sentence was significantly shorter: 64.8 months, which was about one-fifth what it had been under condition four. Under condition six, in which subjects were presented with both the recidivist emphasis and the psychiatric-disorder argument, the mean was 185.8 months—somewhere between the results for conditions four and five, but closer to the latter.

To summarize: subjects did take prior offenses into account when making sentencing judgments, and their punishments increased whether or not they were given sentencing guidelines and whether or not they were reminded that the accused was a repeat offender. But on the other side, their punishments did not escalate through the roof. Many recommended light sentences, citing the principle of proportionality and the fact that no violent crime had been committed. Most acknowledged that a repeat offender deserved more severe punishment than a first-timer, but did not want the punishment to be extreme. While they cited the need for deterrence, they also were willing to consider the defendant mentally disordered, particularly under the seven-crime conditions, even when the defense didn't push this approach in its argument.

Community sentiment, when not steered by the recidivist emphasis (in conditions two and three), did not come close to favoring life imprisonment without parole. Had Helm been sentenced by this community of subjects, with or without legal guidelines, his sentence would have been somewhere between seven and twelve years. Only when there was a strong recidivist emphasis uncontradicted by a claim of psychiatric disorder did the sentence jump dramatically, but it still did not approach life imprisonment without parole. Across all conditions, only a small percent of subjects (5.2) gave the defendant life imprisonment without parole.

Current Tides and Enduring Themes

The theme of proportionality, which I have called an enduring theme, threads through the subjects' sentencing decisions and their reasons for those decisions. Under the high-resolution microscope of the experimental method—where very specific case facts and subtle variations are arrayed under controlled conditions—the golden thread of proportionality appears bright, strong, and unbreakable, even when the weight of a recidivist argument alone tests its strength. This thread may lead us from the labyrinth yet. But the larger labyrinth of sentiment contains dangers that may dash the hope and rend the thread. The threat now comes not from the mythical past but from the year 1994, when political elections, public opinion polls, and politicians spoke to the topic of punishment and preached a sentiment for the community that was very different from the golden one.

As we saw in Chapter 1, politicians in 1992 were reading opinion polls religiously. Although this was a new religion then, it was orthodoxy by 1994. These opinion polls, despite their simplistic and abstract questions, gave consistent results, and the politicians responded. The new current— a strong countercurrent by all appearances—can be dubbed "harsher-stiffer-deadlier."

The polls indicated that the public wanted more punitive sentences for crimes ("harsher"); mandatory sentences that eliminated discretion, such as those found in legislation prescribing "three strikes and you're out" ("stiffer"); the death penalty for more offenses and offenders ("deadlier"). And the politicians have been giving the public just what it apparently wants.

The 1994 election results seemed to reinforce the theme of greater punitiveness, and appeared to contradict the experimental results that strongly favored the so-called enduring theme of proportionality. Pundits declared that the election results represented the public's across-the-board ire with the status quo and its strong sentiment for movement out of gridlock. But the change had selectivity and direction: the election drove only Democrats from office, sweeping Republicans, with their Contract with America, into control of the Senate and House. And the part of their contract that dealt with punishment promoted the "harsher-stiffer-deadlier" approach.

One of those swept out of office in November was Governor Mario Cuomo of New York, who in December gave a speech before the National Press Club in which he sounded warnings to both the public and the politicians. For the public, he evoked an old adage in new language: "Beware of what you wish for in opinion polls, for the politicians will surely give it to you." As to the politicians, who had once been shepherds leading the flock, Cuomo said they were now following the sheep, jumping to every bleat. The Contract with America, said Cuomo, is "not a plan—it's an echo of selected polls . . . It makes absolutely no demand on our political leadership, other than that they set sail in whatever direction the political winds appear to be blowing at the moment."[57]

Regarding the community's sentiment on punishment, experimental results yield one picture, whereas public opinion results and election results yield quite another. This phenomenon illustrates the point made in Chapter 1 about the difficulties in gauging sentiment—the problems inherent in using abstract questions or specific cases, in picking up shallow and transient sentiments, and in missing the deeper, more enduring sentiments. When sentiment appears divided or too difficult to glean, someone is apt to call for the Platonic Guardians.

Chapter 2 dealt with nullification and the questions of where and why jurors might nullify. Yet we also examined three cases involving judges and the issue of nullification: one judge apparently nullified the law; a second wanted to nullify the sentence but restrained his own sentiment and followed the law; and a third judge partially nullified by creating a new defense, "partial self-defense," that had not previously existed. The current "harsher-stiffer-deadlier" trend appears to be on a collision course with the Eighth Amendment. It is already bringing these new punishment cases before judges. And more judges are nullifying.

"A legal battle is taking shape in California's highest court over a judge's defiance of the state's 'three strikes' criminal sentencing law because he said it would constitute cruel and unusual punishment."[58] In the case, defendant Jeffrey Dean Missamore pleaded guilty to a felony charge of possessing eight grams of marijuana while he had been serving a 120-day misdemeanor sentence for stealing twelve dollars' worth of food from a grocery store; he had a prior felony, burglary, for stealing his roommate's video cassette recorder. The sum of these crimes put him under the state's tough "three strikes" law, and Missamore should have received a sentence of eight to sixteen years. Sonoma County Superior Court judge Lawrence Antolini called the sentence "insane." A municipal judge in Santa Barbara added his opinion, calling the law a "piece of junk." More important is the fact that nullification is on the rise among judges in cases involving mandatory sentencing.

As these and like cases wend their way to the High Court for an Eighth Amendment showdown, our themes and questions follow in their wake. Are such severe punishments in accord with community sentiment, or do they conflict with a deeper sentiment grounded in the principle of proportionality? Have such punishments gone beyond the bounds of acceptability, in a society enlightened by humane justice? If punishment is hinged to evolving standards of decency, what happens if a progressive maturing society enters a period of regress? The justices must decide. And the question becomes: How will they decide?

The Eighth Amendment's prohibition against cruel and unusual punishment establishes a limit on the State's power to punish. The U.S. Supreme Court's Eighth Amendment jurisprudence has tended to favor objective analysis as the means of sounding society's opinion on the matter. An objective determination of sentiment may be difficult, especially if one is trying to determine whether a punishment is disproportionate in recidivist cases. Although the recidivist matrix is labyrinthine, the subjects in the recidivist experiment, like Theseus and Ariadne, seemed to take the bull by the horns, follow the golden thread, and tie their calculations to an enduring theme: proportionality. And based on those calculations, the punishments that courts have meted out to defendants such as Rummel and Helm do seem at odds with community sentiment, at least as it has been gauged here.

Justices may balk at a completely objective jurisprudence for a number of reasons. For one thing, they may not be comfortable with social science methods. For another, some questions cannot be answered by empirical means. Still other questions can be answered empirically only in part. Yet the Court has repeatedly endorsed objective jurisprudence in its Eighth Amendment cases, to the maximum extent possible. Even if the empirical evidence offered here is not fully determinative but only informing, it brings a humane perspective to the recidivist problem—a perspective that may influence the community's assessments of what is and is not cruel and unusual punishment.

According to our experiment, the community would agree with the Supreme Court's decision in *Helm*—namely, that Helm's punishment was disproportionate to his crime and therefore cruel and unusual. But these results also refute the Supreme Court's decision in *Rummel,* where the Court affirmed Rummel's sentence. Overall, ordinary people seem to prefer judgments that preserve rather than unravel or sever the ties that bind crime and punishment. To put this another way, the Gordian Knot holds for this community. Some subjects do not count prior crimes, for these offenses have already been punished. When subjects do take prior offenses into account, their punishments increase gradually rather than jump dramatically to life sentences.

By keeping their calculations simple, subjects seem to indicate they are making a *moral* judgment, not a judgment in sociology, psychology, economics, politics, or penology. When the law turns to actuarial tables that reflect these other issues, it departs from commonsense justice. When subjects repeatedly emphasize the importance of subjective factors—the intent of the defendant, the *mens rea*—their focus affirms that crime is a moral issue and that the punishments they impose are a form of retribution. When the law lets this retributive motive mix and mingle with other, more suspect motives and unusual metaphors—such as bovines, avocados, nuts, and artichokes—punishments may increase dramatically and disproportionately. When measured against commonsense justice, such methods seem nonsensical, and the punishments they yield, like a no-account check, are worthless.

With the aid of some examples of "impossible" crimes, we've seen that community sentiment generally assigns greater importance to subjective factors than to the manifest act. When the defendant *intended* to kill a human being in a feasible way, he or she is almost always pronounced guilty, even if the killing could not possibly have occurred. And in criminal attempt cases in which the act was feasible and harm quite likely, the defendant is typically found guilty even when no harm resulted. Thus, considerations of *mens rea* motivate determinations of guilt and the severity of punishment. With this in mind, let's consider the following situation.

Tinker deliberately attempts to kill Evers by firing his pistol at Evers. But for some reason that is not beyond the realm of possibility (Tinker is a bad shot, or Evers flinched at the last instant), the bullet misses Evers but hits and kills a bystander, Chance. Tinker had no intention of killing Chance; in fact, Tinker may have been unaware of Chance's existence at the time of the shooting. But Tinker *did* intend to kill Evers. There are three main questions here: Is the shooting a crime? If so, what sort of crime is it? And *why* is it that sort of crime? (A fourth question—So who's on first?—will not be discussed.)

The first two questions are easy. Yes, the shooting is a crime, and the crime is murder. But why is it murder when the defendant, Tinker, did not intend to kill Chance? To solve this problem, the law essentially substitutes one *mens rea* for another. It is clear that Tinker attempted to commit murder, although the victim was supposed to be Evers. The law substitutes the intent to kill Evers for the absent intent to kill Chance, and thus concludes that the act was murder. By such a transfer of intent, Tinker is not let off the legal hook, since neither his poor aim nor Evers' fortuitous flinch will exonerate him. Both law and commonsense justice would back this straightforward solution. But when we turn to felony-murder, the complexities and conundrums will complicate the analysis, leading community sentiment and the law to part company.

Let's consider another scenario. A woman named Spring—no shrinking violet, this one—enters a liquor store brandishing a loaded (or unloaded) gun, with the intent to commit a robbery.[1] Something goes wrong. The storekeeper, at the sight of the gun, has a heart attack and dies.[2] Spring has certainly committed a crime, but what sort of crime has she committed? The answer is felony-murder. And the answer continues to be felony-murder in the following variations: Spring's loaded gun accidentally goes off, killing the storekeeper; the storekeeper grabs at Spring's gun, and in the ensuing wrestling match the gun goes off, killing the storekeeper; the storekeeper grabs his own gun and accidentally shoots himself while trying to fire at the fleeing Spring; a police officer accidentally shoots the storekeeper while aiming at Spring. The immediate question is: Why are these crimes classified as murder?

The law states that if in the course of a felony (say, armed robbery or kidnapping) a death occurs, even an unintended death, then the crime is felony-murder. But where is the *mens rea?* We know that, in the above example, Spring intended to rob the liquor store but she did not intend to murder anyone. In view of the fact pattern, Spring's conviction for armed robbery is assured, yet how can we convict her for felony-murder when she had no intent to murder?

Three unsatisfactory answers have been put forth.[3] The least satisfactory is to claim that *mens rea* is unnecessary because felony-murder is simply a strict-liability crime, like selling liquor to intoxicated persons without knowing they're intoxicated. Strict liability focuses exclusively on prohibited acts, regardless of intent. But strict-liability offenses are "generally viewed with great odium,"[4] since they sever "the required connection between culpability and criminal liability."[5] The law and the jury are supposed to judge the culpability of the act and the intention; yet in observing this formal felony-murder rule, it seems we bypass intention and go straight to jail, an expedient that seems to fly in the face of fairness and justice.

The other two justifications for felony-murder do deal with intent.[6] In the first the intent is transferred, meaning that the mental state required for the underlying felony (say, robbery) substitutes for the mental state required for the homicide. But note the crucial difference between this transfer and the case in which Tinker meant to kill Evers but killed

Chance: in the latter situation, the intent to kill Evers is substituted for the absent intent to kill Chance, whereas in the former an intent to rob is substituted for an intent to kill. Yet these two crimes (robbery and murder), in their acts and their mental elements, are quite different, legally, conceptually, and pragmatically. They are also logically distinct, such that we can infer nothing about Spring's wanting to kill from the fact of her wanting to rob. Transferred intent, which has been criticized as having "no proper place in criminal law,"[7] appears to relieve the prosecution of having to prove the *mens rea* element of the crime, since that element is now a given: by illogically linking robbery and murder and creating a *mens rea* (if there was intent to rob, then there was intent to murder), we remove a sizable weight from the prosecutor's burden and the jury's consideration, placing that conclusion beyond dispute.

According to the third view (the second that deals with intent), we presume the malice for the homicide from the mental state required for the commission of the underlying felony. Known as constructive malice, this is a "one size fits all" notion in which a generalized malice is stretched to cover all particulars. But the stretch doesn't work: the malice to commit robbery—or even a generalized malice, whatever that is—may be quite far removed from the intent to commit murder.

The felony-murder rule, supported by insupportable justifications, manufactures murder. Once an accusation of felony-murder has been raised, it is one of the easiest to prove. If you give jurors a conclusive presumption—that if the defendant intended to rob, and if a death occurred, then the defendant is guilty of felony-murder—then the prosecution is relieved of the burden of proving every element of first-degree murder, including *mens rea*. In light of our discussion in the previous chapter, we reach the first of our major questions here: Does the felony-murder rule lead to punishment that is disproportionate to the offense and thus cruel and unusual under the Eighth Amendment?

Let's compound the basic felony-murder scenario by giving accomplices to our triggerman Spring, the one chiefly responsible for planning the liquor store robbery. Imagine that there are three accessories, all of whom are in on the robbery attempt: Summer is the sidekick who enters the liquor store with Spring but does not fire a gun; Autumn is the lookout, stationed outside the liquor store to warn her fellow conspirators if danger approaches; and Winter is the getaway driver, sitting and warming behind the wheel with the motor running.

We know that when the storekeeper dies of a heart attack at the sight of Spring's gun, Spring's crime escalates from armed robbery to felony-murder. But what of the accessories? According to the principle of accessorial liability, the triggerman's culpability is transferred *undiminished* to all the accessories. Thus, Summer, Autumn, and Winter are about to take the fall: they face felony-murder charges as well.

Am I my brother's keeper? The biblical answer, in the case of Cain and Abel, is yes. The legal answer, in the case of sisters-in-crime Summer, Autumn, and Winter, is yes, and then some. Consider this variation: at the sight of Spring's gun, the storekeeper whips out his own gun, fires, and kills Spring. Although the scenario changes dramatically, the outcome is the same, since Summer, Autumn, and Winter may face felony-murder charges for the death of Spring![8] Other variations: if Autumn got trigger happy and shot a police officer outside the store, or if a police officer shot Autumn, the outcome would be the same for the surviving felons. And if Winter got cold feet and decided to speed away from the scene but struck and killed a pedestrian, the fate of one would still be the fate of all. In the eyes of the law, these sisters-in-crime become fungible clones.

Combining the accessorial-liability rule and the felony-murder rule produces "equalist" justice: all of the perpetrators are equally guilty. Yet this equalist outcome seems to contradict the notion of proportional justice, which would have us weigh each defendant's actions and intentions individually. And this brings us to our second major question: Under equalist justice, is the punishment disproportionate to the crime and thus cruel and unusual under the Eighth Amendment?

The Law's Conflict with Itself

The felony-murder rule defines a most serious crime, murder, to which a severe punishment attaches. It does this by turning a felony into murder without demonstrable proof of the requisite intent. When the felony-murder rule combines with the accessorial-liability rule, it ascribes the same crime and equal punishment to all participants, regardless of their individual actions, intentions, and culpability. In applying these legal rules, the law appears at odds with itself. It seems that sacred legal principles are being sacrificed on the felony-murder altar: the principle that we weigh *mens rea;* that we eschew strict-liability offenses; that we take each person's intent into account; that we grant supreme importance to individual justice, rather than "one size fits all" justice; that the burden of proving *mens rea* belongs with the prosecution. How did it happen, then, that the law reached this curious and conflicted outcome?

The legal roots of felony-murder are obscure and in dispute, but some say a judicial blunder by Lord Edward Coke may have been the genesis of the felony-murder rule.[9] The thirteenth-century English jurist Henry de Bracton had made a distinction between cases of *lawful* and *unlawful work* leading to the death of another: "blame is not imputable"[10] to the defendant in the former case, he wrote, but is in the latter. In translating and interpreting the passage, Lord Coke had taken "unlawful killing" to mean murder ("murdrum"), which Bracton did not intend.[11] Escalating an unlawful killing into murder seems to have spawned the "essential non-logic of the rule."[12]

Writing almost three hundred years later, Judge James Fitzjames Stephen found Lord Coke's statements on felony-murder to be "entirely unwarranted by the authorities which he quotes."[13] In his eyes, the doctrine was "astonishing"[14] and "monstrous,"[15] and appeared to gain credence "only from repetition."[16] Courts and judges on this side of the Atlantic have been equally critical. One California court stated that the rule "anachronistically resurrects from a bygone age a 'barbaric concept.'"[17] Another stated that it "erodes the relation between criminal liability and moral culpability."[18] Legal commentary has also been decidedly negative:[19] "Writers have raised conceptual and constitutional challenges to the doctrines' substantive assumptions and procedural presumption, and have called for limiting, revising, and abolishing the doctrine . . . Yet, after all is said, the doctrine is not done."[20]

If legal commentary and dicta are so one-sided in their disparagement, why hasn't felony-murder long since faded from the legal landscape? One answer is that there is a natural constituency within the law that favors the retention of felony-murder: prosecutors. The felony-murder rule is a powerful arrow in a prosecutor's quiver. Since *mens rea* can be easily manufactured, and since it may automatically entail a conclusive, unrebuttable presumption of guilt, a charge of felony-murder often virtually guarantees conviction—or at least makes it as much of a sure thing as a prosecutor is likely to get. Moreover, when accused of felony-murder, a defendant is more likely to plead guilty to a lesser but substantial charge and more likely to cooperate by testifying against accomplices. Thus, whether the prosecutor uses felony-murder as threat, ploy, or charge, convictions are likely to increase. And prosecutors understand that convictions are the ticket to stay in office or reach higher office, particularly when frightened citizens want the "bad guys" put away.

The pragmatics of convictions and reelection, however, are at odds with weightier principles of justice. On principled grounds, the law seems unable to reconcile itself with felony-murder. When this "curious doctrine" came before the Supreme Court in *Enmund v. Florida*[21] and *Tison v. Arizona*,[22] Justice Brennan, in an oxymoronic phrase, called felony-murder "a living fossil."[23] It not only still lives but continues to produce deep divisions within the law and the Court.

The Law and Psychology at Odds

How do average citizens apportion responsibility and blame in felony-murder cases? Although justices may be at odds and the law may be in conflict, attribution theory yields a nearly uniform set of insights and predictions regarding ordinary people's reactions to such situations. According to Fritz Heider,[24] when people attempt to discern the "personal dispositions" of another—his or her temperament, character, or personality, or whether he or she is responsible or blameworthy—these dispositions "are more readily inferred from intentional actions."[25] We infer intentionality when an actor (1) appears goal directed, (2) appears to be the originator of the action, rather than a passive recipient, and (3) appears to strive to achieve intended effects. Heider's theory would predict that, in the eyes of average citizens, the felony-murder triggerman would not be as blameworthy as the premeditated murderer, since the triggerman neither intended nor sought the victim's death. And the accomplices would be viewed as even less blameworthy, since they neither originated the deadly action nor exerted themselves to bring it about.[26]

The correspondent inference theory, which assumes that people have preconceptions about causality, would yield predictions identical to those of Heider's theory, only stronger.[27] Edward Jones and Keith Davis maintain that dispositional attributions are made *only* on the basis of intentional behaviors; thus, the unintended death in the prototypical felony-murder situation would not lead to strong condemnation. Moreover, an act is perceived as intentional when the perceiver believes the actor knew the behavior would produce the deadly consequences, and believes the actor had control over the consequences. But although the defendant is perceived as *knowing* and *controlling* the deadly outcome in the typical premeditated-murder scenario, he is not seen this way in the felony-murder scenario. This is even clearer in the case of the felony-murder accessories, who often claim they did not know that killings would occur, and who, if they were not at the scene, could not have exerted any control over the outcome.

In felony-murder cases, the law asks jurors to render a judgment of murder and to find all of the participants equally guilty. Psychological theory tells us that this is not how people are likely to perceive and judge such situations. When the law and commonsense justice are significantly at odds, jury nullifications sometimes follow. Jurors may refuse to bring in guilty verdicts on the felony-murder charge, and may nullify completely with a "not guilty" verdict or partially nullify by convicting the defendant on a lesser charge.

Two Cases, Two Rulings, and Too Many Doubts

Is the death penalty a disproportionate punishment for accessory to felony-murder? Let's look at the Supreme Court's opinions in *Enmund v. Florida* and *Tison v. Arizona*.

In the first case, Earl Enmund was the getaway driver, sitting in a car when Sampson and Jeanette Armstrong tried to rob a farmhouse in Florida. In the attempt, the Armstrongs shot and killed Thomas and Eunice Kersey. Enmund was charged with felony-murder. Under Florida law the accessorial-liability rule also applied, making accessories like Enmund just as guilty as the triggerman. Enmund was found guilty of felony-murder and sentenced to death.[28]

In the second case, Ricky and Raymond Tison helped their father, Gary Tison, and his cellmate, Randy Greenawald, escape from Arizona State Prison without a shot being fired. Two days later, while driving, they had a flat tire. Since they had no spare, Gary Tison instructed his sons to flag down a passing motorist in order to steal a car. The Lyons family stopped and was taken into the desert at gunpoint. John Lyons asked the Tisons to leave his family there with some water, and Gary Tison sent his sons to get some water. As the sons were returning, they heard shots. All four members of the Lyons family were killed. Ricky and Raymond were found guilty of felony-murder, armed robbery, kidnapping, and auto theft. They were sentenced to death as accessories to felony-murder.

In *Enmund* and *Tison* an Eighth Amendment challenge was raised. Was the death penalty disproportionate, and hence cruel and unusual punishment for accessory to felony-murder? In line with the Court's desire to use objective measurements to the maximum extent possible in Eighth Amendment cases,[29] the Court analyzed related interjurisdictional legislative enactments and jury decisions in order to gauge community sentiment.

In summing up its analysis, the *Enmund* majority concluded that recent judgments by legislatures, juries, and prosecutors revealed a strong tendency to reject capital punishment.[30]

Only a small minority of states—eight—allowed the death penalty to be imposed solely because the defendant somehow participated in the robbery in the course of which a murder was committed, but did not take or attempt or intend to take life, or intend that lethal force be employed. The Court found overwhelming evidence that American juries had repudiated imposition of the death penalty for crimes such as Enmund's, the statistics demonstrating that juries—and perhaps prosecutors—considered death a disproportionate penalty for those who fall within Enmund's category.[31]

It seems, then, that the empirical evidence provided an open and shut case: legislative enactments and jury decisions both indicated a substantial and solid repudiation of the death penalty for individuals in situations such as Enmund's. Moreover, the Court connected the empirical data to inadequate proof of *mens rea,* with phrases such as "did not take or attempt or intend to take a life, or intend that lethal force be employed."[32] This goes beyond the issue of whether the death penalty is cruel and unusual in these circumstances, and brings our earlier questions to the fore: Was the Court considering whether the death penalty might be unconstitutional when the defendant had no intention of killing? What was in the justices' minds is speculative. What the five members of the majority did was clear, and was grounded in data. Or so they claimed.

But the four-member *Enmund* minority reached the opposite conclusion using the same objective data. For example, when the majority found eight jurisdictions that allowed felony-murder *simpliciter,* the minority took issue. "The Court's curious method of counting the States that authorize imposition of the death penalty for felony murder cannot hide the fact that 23 States permit a sentencer to impose the death penalty even though the felony murderer has neither killed nor intended to kill his victim . . . In short, the Court's peculiar statutory analysis cannot withstand closer scrutiny."[33]

If we use fifty-two as the number of jurisdictions (that is, the fifty states plus the District of Columbia plus the U.S. Code), then the *Enmund* majority found that in only 15 percent of the jurisdictions (8/52) could the death penalty be imposed. The *Enmund* minority found that in 44 percent of the jurisdictions (23/52) the death penalty could be imposed. How is it that the majority and minority can look at the same legislative enactments data, yet come up with such disparate numbers and conclusions? The main reason is that they ask and answer different questions. "The majority, sticking close to the *Enmund* facts, asks, in effect, 'How many states would allow for the death penalty when the defendant does not kill or intend to kill, and where the other circumstances are *similar* to Enmund?'"[34] In the minority analysis, the question broadens because "the minority (a) allows the circumstances of the killing to vary in any way (e.g., a second unrelated death, police officer dies), (b) permits a judgment of defendant's participation to reach the substantial or major level, and (c) assumes culpability to be reckless indifference."[35] With these assumptions, permissions, and allowances, the incidence of the death penalty increases and different answers result.

Although part of the problem is interpretive—reasonable people can disagree over how to characterize Enmund's actions and culpability—the disparities that resulted reveal more than legitimate disagreements: they reveal bad social science. A more defensible social science analysis puts the proportion of jurisdictions allowing for the death sentence in Enmund-like situations at 15–37 percent, which is far less than a majority.[36]

What the Court did with jury decisions data was even more suspect. According to the *Enmund* majority, the evidence was *overwhelming* that American juries repudiated the imposition of the death penalty for crimes such as Enmund's. The Court cited the same statistics in both *Enmund* and *Tison:*

> Of 739 death row inmates, only 41 did not participate in the fatal assault. All but 16 of these were physically present at the scene of the murder and of these only 3, including Enmund, were sentenced to death in the absence of a finding that they had collaborated in a scheme designed to kill. The Court found the fact that only 3 of 739 death row inmates had been sentenced to death absent an intent to kill, physical presence or direct participation in the fatal assault persuasive evidence that American juries considered the death sentence disproportional to felony-murder *simpliciter.*[37]

This claim is not only suspect but fatally flawed. To see why the evidence is not only *not* overwhelming but quite inconclusive regarding jurors' sentiments, we must first realize that all the numbers cited are numerators (for example, 3 and 739; and 739 − 3 = 736). Now let's hypothesize the following denominators to bring home the point. For the *Enmund*-like cases, let's assume that five such cases were brought to trial and that three resulted in the death penalty; thus, the proportion of death sentences would be 3/5, or 60 percent. For the 736 cases that did not resemble *Enmund,* let's assume that 1,472 such cases came to trial and that 736 resulted in the death penalty—that is, 50 percent. In this hypothetical example there is a slight difference in the results for the two groups, 60 percent versus 50 percent, but the discrepancy is the opposite of that claimed by the *Enmund* majority, and certainly no indication of overwhelming societal rejection of the death penalty in such cases. The purpose here is to bring home a simple social science fact—a fact that was lost on the Court: only by knowing the denominators can we run statistical tests and draw legitimate conclusions about cases that resemble *Enmund* versus cases that don't. Perhaps the denominators couldn't be obtained? Then the Court, although claiming to have been doing social science, ought to have said nothing, for the data on jury decisions was inapplicable to the issue at bar.

Tison was different but displayed the same flaws. In a five-to-four decision that took the opposite view from *Enmund*, the *Tison* majority held that the death penalty for Tison-like defendants was constitutional, and cited empirical evidence which "powerfully suggests that our society does *not* reject the death penalty as grossly excessive under these circumstances."[38] Why did the Court's opinions in the two cases differ? To the *Tison* majority, the Tison brothers, unlike Enmund, fell into an intermediate class of accessories to felony-murder. The majority put forth two distinctions, one based on participation and the other based on culpability: the Tison brothers were "more major" participants in the crime than the getaway driver Enmund; and the Tison brothers had, or may have had, a more culpable mental state than Enmund, one that could be characterized as showing "reckless indifference to human life."[39]

The *Tison* minority challenged the majority's distinctions, believing that the Tison brothers' level of participation was not legally discriminable from Enmund's and claiming that the "creation of a new category of culpability is not enough to distinguish this case from *Enmund*."[40] In addition to the disagreement over the outcome, there was again disagreement over the objective data.

The *Tison* majority held that for such midrange felony-murder cases, "the majority of American jurisdictions clearly authorize capital punishment and . . . the majority of American courts have not been nearly so reluctant to impose death as they are in the case of felony-murder *simpliciter*."[41] To the minority, the legislative enactments gave just the opposite reading. "The Court would thus have us believe that 'the majority of American jurisdictions clearly authorize capital punishment' in cases such as this . . . This is not the case . . . Thus, contrary to the Court's implication that its view is consonant with that of 'the majority of American jurisdictions,' . . . the Court's view is itself distinctly the minority position."[42]

The social science analyses of both the majority and the minority remain riddled with error. In analyzing enactments data, neither side can agree on how to categorize states, or on the correct question to ask. From a more objective analysis,[43] the range of states that might support the death penalty for Tison-like defendants turns out to be 13–44 percent, not all that different from the Enmund range of 15–37 percent. These ranges are still shy of a majority (51 percent), and certainly shy of the *Tison* majority's claim of an *overwhelming* difference.

As for data on jury decisions, the same inadequate numerators in *Enmund* were trotted out in *Tison*. The *Tison* majority acknowledged the point about denominators, but responded with doubts about "whether it is possible to gather such information."[44] Still, acknowledging that the data were inadequate to sustain any conclusion did not lead the majority to relinquish its unwarranted and illegitimate claims. In both cases, then, conducting a social science analysis proved easier than conducting it well. And when the sound and fury of *Enmund* and *Tison* subsided, community sentiment was still unknown.

Community Sentiment, When Sounder Readings Surface

My associates and I ran a series of experiments aimed at gauging community sentiment on the felony-murder rule, the accessorial-liability rule, and the death penalty for accessory to felony-murder. Would the community support felony-murder convictions, equal punishment for the principal and the accessories, and the death penalty for various types of accessories?

In the first experiment, a getaway driver, Gordon, a lookout, John, a sidekick, Bob, and a triggerman, Dick, tried to rob a liquor store.[45] Mock jurors received one of four case scenarios, each of which described a different series of events leading to the storekeeper's death (that is, we manipulated the *case* variable). In the first scenario ("Heart"), the storekeeper died of a heart attack at the sight of the gun. In the second ("Struggle"),[46] the elderly clerk grabbed at the gun in Dick's hand, and in the ensuing struggle the gun went off and the clerk was killed; the manner of death in this case may have suggested more culpability for Dick. In the third scenario ("Heinous"), Dick pulled away after the elderly clerk grabbed at the gun, and then proceeded to smash the gun into the clerk's face again and again. As the clerk lay on the floor covered in blood, Dick fired six shots in rapid succession into him, and the clerk died from the wounds. By manipulating the facts of the case, we were asking: Does the heinousness of the killing affect the severity of the sentence? And does it do so for just the triggerman, or for all accessories as well? The fourth scenario ("Premeditated") was a control. Just when Bob and Dick got the money from the storekeeper and Bob said, "Let's go," Dick, springing a trick on his sidekick Bob, said, "No, I've been waiting to nail this old guy for two years, and I'm not leaving any witnesses around." With that, Dick opened fire as Bob stood by, and the clerk, hit with six bullets, subsequently died. In this scenario Dick was charged with premeditated first-degree murder. How would that effect Dick's sentence, as well as the sentences imposed on Gordon, John, and Bob, who were charged with felony-murder?

There were two measures of verdict: mock jurors had to decide whether each defendant was guilty or not guilty on the armed-robbery charge, and whether each was guilty, not guilty, or guilty of a lesser offense on the charge of felony-murder (or first-degree murder, in the case of Dick in the "Premeditated" scenario). We were looking for signs of nullification, either complete nullifications (such as a "not guilty" verdict) or partial nullifications (such as a "lesser offense" verdict). But since nullifications can occur for different reasons—sometimes because jurors judge the crime unjust and sometimes because they judge the penalty too severe—we created two conditions to help determine why nullifications were occurring, if they were. Half of the subjects received a scenario in which the State was seeking the death penalty for all the defendants ("capital" condition), and the other half received a scenario in which the State was not seeking the death penalty ("noncapital" condition). If the nullifications were roughly equal under the two conditions, then we would know that it was not the death penalty that was causing the nullification effect but some factor related to the crime or to equalism. If, however, nullifications greatly increased under the *capital* condition, then the possibility of the defendants' receiving the death penalty would be the obvious cause.

There were more than two hundred mock jurors, a relatively large number. They included not only students but adults, so that the sample would be more representative of the general population. And to make the subjects even more like actual jurors in a capital case, we had all of them answer *voir dire* questions. We classified jurors according to their attitudes toward the death penalty: (1) those who would always vote for the death penalty (called ADPs—"automatic death penalty" types), (2) those who would never vote for the death penalty (called "Witherspoon excludables"), (3) those who would be unwilling to follow the law (nullifiers), and (4) those who would be substantially impaired in making their decision ("Witt excludables"). Subjects who fit into none of these categories were termed "death qualified," or DQs. These amounted to 73.1 percent of our sample—a fraction that corresponds to the national figure. In this experiment and the ones that follow, there were no significant verdict or sentencing differences between students and adults.

Concerning the verdicts, there was agreement on the underlying felony charge of armed robbery. For example, "guilty" verdicts for Bob and Dick were 98 percent and 99 percent, respectively. If subjects were following the felony-murder rule, then the percents of "guilty" verdicts on the felony-murder charge should have been about the same as the figures for armed robbery, since the defendants were guilty of the underlying felony and it was uncontroverted that a death occurred in the course of the felony. But the numbers were not at all similar. On the felony-murder charge, Gordon was found guilty 2 percent of the time, John 15 percent, Bob 48 percent, and Dick 77 percent.[47] These figures were significantly smaller than those for the verdicts on robbery, and the declines occurred under both the capital and noncapital conditions. The "not guilty" verdicts revealed the nullifications: Gordon was acquitted 89 percent of the time, John 40 percent, Bob 15 percent, and Dick a mere 2 percent. Not only was there a nullification effect, but that effect revealed proportional rather than equalist justice: jurors were judging Gordon the least culpable, John more culpable, Bob even more culpable, and Dick the most culpable.

As the killing grew more brutal and eventually came to involve premeditation (that is, as the scenarios went from "Heart" to "Struggle" to "Heinous" to "Premeditated"), the "guilty" verdicts for the triggerman, Dick, on the felony-murder and first-degree murder charges increased, from 63 percent to 79 percent to 88 percent to 92 percent. But the incidence of "guilty" verdicts stayed roughly the same for the three accessories. Thus, although subjects judged the triggerman harshly, they did not transfer their judgments to the accessories. In other words, judgments of the principal and the accessories remained distinct, whereas in the law they are linked (through accessorial liability). Moreover, the incidence of "guilty" verdicts for Dick across the felony-murder cases was 77 percent, whereas it reached 92 percent when Dick had committed first-degree murder. Thus, we began to see two unmistakable patterns: first, subjects clearly differentiated the triggerman from the accessories and made individual and separate determinations of guilt; second, subjects distinguished the triggerman who committed premeditated murder from the one who committed felony-murder.

The number of death sentences and two "death rate" percents (D/N and D/FM)[48] were calculated for each defendant by case. Concerning D/N, we first saw a sizable difference between the figure for the triggerman guilty of premeditated murder (64.3 percent) and the one for the triggerman guilty of felony-murder (16.5 percent): the former received the death sentence approximately four times more often than the latter. Second, focusing only on the felony-murder triggerman, we did see an increase in the death sentence rate as the scenarios progressed from "Heart" (4.3 percent) to "Struggle" (12 percent) to "Heinous" (29 percent), indicating an increasingly harsh judgment of Dick's culpability; but this increasingly harsh judgment did not transfer to Gordon, John, and Bob, whose death rates were fairly constant across the cases and considerably lower than Dick's. Third, when we compared the death rates for Gordon (zero), John (1.9 percent), and Bob (5.6 percent) to the rate for the felony-murder triggerman (16.5 percent), we clearly saw that subjects were judging the defendants individually and proportionately, and not administering equalist punishment.

The effects we observed were large and powerful, and demonstrable in different ways. For example, we presented the same scenarios to subjects under what we called the "ninth-justice" paradigm. We told subjects that defendants Gordon, John, Bob, and Dick had been sentenced to death and were appealing their death sentence as cruel and unusual punishment. We further told them that eight of the justices were evenly divided on whether to uphold or to reverse and remand the death sentence, and that the subjects should put themselves in the position of the ninth justice. They were given two lists of reasons, one in favor of reversing and remanding the death sentence and one in favor of upholding it; these lists consisted of quotes taken from Supreme Court cases. Subjects then had to decide whether to uphold or to reverse and remand, and were asked to give their reasons. The "reverse and remand" figures for the four defendants were 97 percent (Gordon), 83 percent (John), 69 percent (Bob), and 53 percent (Dick) across all cases. Only in the "Heinous" case, and only for Dick, were there more subjects voting to uphold (68 percent) than to reverse and remand. Using this paradigm to reveal nullifications, we saw that subjects overwhelmingly chose to reverse and remand the accessories' death sentences.

The getaway driver, Gordon, bears the closest resemblance to Enmund; and Gordon was never given the death sentence. Moreover, the lookout, John, who was not immediately present at the scene of the death, seems most like the Tison brothers (although some might argue that the sidekick, Bob, fits the Tisons' situation better). If the lookout, John, is taken as the Tison parallel, then the triggerman received the death penalty approximately nine times more often; if the sidekick, Bob, is used as the Tison parallel, then the triggerman received the death pen-

alty approximately three times more often. Either way, community sentiment saw a big difference between the principal and the accessories, and
refused to follow accessorial liability to its equalist conclusion.

There is one problem with generalizing these results to *Tison:* the
Tison majority could claim that the hypothetical accessories, Gordon,
John, and Bob, were less culpable and not the more involved participants
that the majority claimed the Tison brothers were. Though I would disagree with this, particularly in regard to Bob, who was at the scene of
death whereas the Tisons were not, my associates and I ran a second experiment in which we increased the culpability and participation level of
both John and Bob. In the new scenario, both carried loaded guns; the
sidekick, Bob, pointed his weapon at the storekeeper and fired recklessly
over the head of the storekeeper when the latter hesitated in opening the
cash register. We tested six different cases, even two cases where a police
officer died, which did not obtain in *Tison.*

The results were much the same as in the previous experiment. Though
all subjects found all defendants guilty of the underlying felony, sizable
and proportional nullifications occurred on the felony-murder charge: the
"not guilty" figures were 56 percent (Gordon), 42 percent (John), 20 percent (Bob), and 5 percent (Dick). The death sentence rates also showed
the proportional effect: zero (Gordon), 1 percent (John), 8 percent (Bob),
and 18 percent (Dick). And the death sentence rate for the triggerman
who committed premeditated murder was 94 percent, which was about
five times what it was for the triggerman guilty of felony-murder.

In subsequent experiments, we used the *Tison* case directly.[49] In addition, we created a third Tison brother who was even more reckless, culpable, and involved and who was at the scene of death. We asked subjects
to try the defendants separately, or in trials with multiple defendants. But
no matter how we varied the cases, defendants, and trial conditions, we
obtained the same basic results. The death sentence rates for the three
accessories were always low, varying between zero and 10 percent, and
five to seven times lower than they were for the *Tison* principal.

We also repeated our ninth-justice paradigm, in which subjects had to
uphold or reverse and remand the death sentence for each defendant.
Two things were different: subjects received the actual *Tison* case and
were given no list of reasons—they had to write out their own reasons for
deciding as they did. Decisions to uphold the sentences occurred about as
often as they had in previous experiments: 10 percent (A), 15 percent (B),
26 percent (C), and 83 percent (D). The reasons subjects gave for their
decisions were illuminating. Those who voted to uphold the sentences
said that the defendant (1) could have prevented the death but did not, (2)

intended to kill, and (3) was a major participant in the killing and had a prior criminal record. These reasons apply to the *Tison* triggerman more than to the accessories, and they stress *intent* and *control,* which attribution theorists consider central factors in people's culpability judgments. Subjects who voted to reverse and remand cited the fact that the defendant (1) was a minor participant and could not control the situation, (2) did not have a criminal record, and (3) did not intend to kill. These reasons fit the accessories more closely than the triggerman, and highlight the absence of intent and control.

Finally, we designed an experiment to test whether the proportionality principle or equalist justice rules at early developmental ages. Kindergarten pupils, second and third graders, and fifth graders were given two scenarios resembling cases of felony-murder and asked to make culpability and punishment judgments.[50] To avoid frightening the youngsters with scenes of deadly violence but to maintain a parallel to felony-murder, we gave the children descriptions of situations in which a "crime" was plotted and "something worse" then happened. In one of our two cases, the ringleader plotted to steal a math test from the copy room while the teacher was at lunch; he persuaded several accomplices to go along, but unknown to the accomplices the ringleader also stole money from the teacher's purse. In our second case, the ringleader persuaded his accomplices to trespass, and a fight occurred in which a boy was injured by the ringleader. In both cases, the children agreed to do something they knew was wrong and then something worse happened. Even at the kindergarten level, subjects clearly discriminated the principal from the accessories, and by the second and third grades the proportionality principle of punishment was quite evident for the accessories as well.

Proportionality Reigns Supreme

The legal category of felony-murder, based on error and contrivance, manufactures a charge of murder for principals and accessories alike. It may be a response to murder most foul or monstrous; it may be an anachronistic remnant, a barbaric concept, and a legal fiction. But this fossil lives, divides the Court, and continues to produce death sentences. It prescribes a most curious way of assessing and assigning guilt, one that appears to detach criminal liability from individual culpability and that seems quite foreign to the way in which ordinary people make such judgments.

In *Enmund* and *Tison* the Supreme Court had to make a judgment regarding the death penalty for felony-murder accessories. As in other

Eighth Amendment cases, the Court's judgment of cruel and unusual punishment was inextricably bound with community sentiment: the latter had to be gauged before the former could be determined. On the face of it, the Court now appears committed to social science analysis as a means of gleaning community sentiment from objective measurements. Social scientists might applaud the intent, but they decry the "science." The Court restricts itself to two suspect gauges, legislative enactments and jury decisions, while ignoring other sources of information.[51] Based on such sanctioned gauges, majority and minority readings are far apart, off the mark, or indefensible on their face.

Yet the Supreme Court in *Tison* affirmed the equalist position, upheld the death penalty for Tison-like defendants, and claimed that community sentiment supported this conclusion when reckless indifference and more major participation by an accessory were demonstrated. In the experiments described here, the Court's empirical claim was undermined across a wide variety of cases and conditions. Community sentiment strongly opposed the death penalty for felony-murder accessories and rejected accessorial liability that would have created an equalist outcome. It appeared to differentiate, in terms of guilt and punishment, defendants guilty of felony-murder from those guilty of premeditated murder. And community sentiment overwhelmingly favored proportional justice, which was based on each person's actions and intentions.

In cases in which the law conjoined two formal rules, the felony-murder rule and the accessorial-liability rule, the legal outcome (equal guilt and punishment) and the process (no individual assessment of *mens rea*) struck subjects as unjust and unfair. When this is the community's perception, nullifications are likely, and our experimental results did in fact show many nullifications. But as Fletcher reminds us, nullifications represent the jury's power not just "to defeat the law, but to perfect the law, to realize the law's inherent values."[52] Commonsense justice seems to be saying, loudly, clearly, and consistently, that the law is wrong and ought to be changed. In more specific terms, the law has distanced itself from justice by creating formal rules (if felony and death, then murder; if one, then all) for judging guilt and assigning punishment that sever the principled threads of proportionality. To this, commonsense justice continually registers its disapproval.

The verdicts and sentences obtained in our experiments suggest that change is likely to be directed not toward anarchy but toward proportionality and coherence in the law. For example, Gordon, John, and Bob were found guilty of the underlying felony, whether it was armed robbery or, in the *Tison* experiment, armed robbery, kidnapping, and auto theft.

These are not minor crimes. None of the defendants emerged from the courtroom free; but they were not punished for murder. Subjects did view the triggerman as primarily responsible for the death and were willing to punish him more harshly than his accomplices, but not as harshly as the man guilty of premeditated murder. There was a difference in *intent* in the two cases, and intent ought to matter. It clearly matters to the community.

When intent is ignored or manufactured, "murther most foul" results.[53] When we sever the crucial link between the act of killing and the defendant's intent—a link commonsense justice finds fair and just—the tragedy for the law turns from *Hamlet* to *Macbeth*, for fair now becomes foul "and foul is fair."[54] With felony-murder, we seem to regress to a more distant time—the days of the Saxons, perhaps—when strict liability still rules; to a more anachronistic and barbaric time (as modern courts have recognized) when crucial links between act and *mens rea* are severed; to a time when curious fossils live.

In Chapter 8 we saw that commonsense justice grabbed tight hold of the golden thread of proportionality to negotiate the cruel and unusual labyrinth of recidivism cases. Here, in felony-murder cases, we've seen that commonsense justice uses the principle of proportionality, joining it with the principle of individualized culpability and punishment assessments, to navigate these cases of "murther most foul" to a fair end. In embracing individualized and proportionate punishment principles, it keeps intent *(mens rea)* in mind and at the heart of things, and discards equalism and one-size-fits-all punishments as "bad fit" and bad law. But the law has not caught up or caught on.

When commonsense justice and the law are "out of joint,"[55] justice and the law loosen their relationship. Justice begins to hang "like a giant's robe upon a dwarfish thief";[56] and when it slips away it reveals a diminished law, oddly more formal in appearance but curiously more naked. And community sentiment, playing the part of Birnam Wood, does not sit still. Common sense—seeing fair from foul, connecting the intent to the act, and making the punishment commensurate with the crime—marches toward the law to a proportionate beat, with a more fitting robe in hand.

Death Is Different

10

In 1972 the Supreme Court's decision in *Furman v. Georgia* opened, closed, and reopened the era of the death penalty in twentieth-century America.[1] Just one year earlier, in *McGautha v. California*, the Court had apparently resolved the procedural issue regarding the penalty, ruling that the jury's absolute and untrammeled discretion in imposing the death sentence did not violate any provision of the Constitution.[2] But in *Furman*, Justice Douglas wrote that the Court was "now imprisoned in the *McGautha* holding."[3] If this was so, then *Furman* not only opened what was closed but represented a full-scale breakout: the *Furman* Court struck down every death penalty statute in the nation as violating the cruel and unusual punishment clause of the Eighth and Fourteenth Amendments. Death was not only different in kind and degree from other penalties, but now it had ceased, as *Furman* imposed a moratorium on the states' ability to give or carry out the death sentence.

Furman is the lengthiest opinion ever written in the history of the Supreme Court. More precisely, it is not *an* opinion at all but nine separate opinions, with each justice proffering his views on the death penalty and related matters. Those matters covered history, philosophy, morality, legal cases, constitutional law, community sentiment, theories of punishment, and a host of empirical data relating to death sentences. Rather than dealing straightforwardly with issues and specific points, *Furman* has the feel of an anthology desperately in need of an editor. Although a five-vote majority emerged on the procedural question, only two justices, Brennan and Marshall, were willing to declare the death penalty per se unconstitutional. This meant that the *substantive* issue was closed.

Justice Marshall tried vainly to discount the Gallup poll findings indicating community support for the death penalty (see Chapter 1), but other justices were not persuaded. Without sentiment in favor of the defendants—sentiment of the sort that obtained in Eighth Amendment recidivist cases and accessory felony-murder cases—the substantive case against the death penalty lost a vital empirical leg. And it lost another when *Furman* shifted the prime reason for the death penalty from deterrence to retribution. For if the State kills in order to deter others from killing, and if social science can show that the death penalty does not deter killings, then the death penalty's mission fails. But when the Court stated that the death penalty was the criminal's just reward, it left deterrence out of the determinative equation.

What *Furman* did open was the *fairness* issue. In ending the substantive debate, it began the procedural debate—over how to write a constitutionally sound death penalty statute and how to administer death penalty justice in ways that were not freakish, arbitrary, or capricious. Whereas statute writing is in the hands of legislators, death penalty decisions are most often in the hands of juries—the conscience of the community. Yet *McGautha* and *Furman* present contrasting views of that community. In *McGautha* the Court shows faith in juries and confidence in their discretion; in *Furman* it expresses doubt and ambivalence.

Trusting Jury Discretion?

Both *McGautha*[4] and *Furman*[5] retell a segment of America's history of jury nullification. They describe how citizens were in "rebellion against the common-law rule imposing a mandatory death sentence on all convicted murderers," and how this sentiment (which is portrayed as the noble, correct sentiment) was brought to bear on lawmakers, via lobbying attempts to restrict the death penalty to certain offenses such as premeditated murder. But if commonsense justice could not change the law swiftly enough through the legislature, then the community had another way to spare a defendant—namely, through jury nullification. And nullifications had indeed occurred, as juries "took the law into their own hands."[6]

McGautha recounts this history of nullification, which could have been portrayed negatively as a tale of anarchy, with pride and admiration: jury discretion rescued defendants and the law from gallows injustice. *McGautha* then traces the subsequent events which expanded and affirmed that discretion. "Tennessee was the first State (1837–38) to give juries sentencing discretion in capital cases . . . but other States followed suit, as did the Federal Government in 1897."[7] In 1899, the Supreme

Court dealt with that federal statute in *Winston v. United States*.[8] The Court reversed a murder conviction because the trial judge had instructed the jury that it should not recommend mercy unless it found certain mitigating circumstances. But this "direction" from the judge was seen as interfering with the statute's aim of entrusting the whole question of capital punishment "to the judgment and the consciences of the jury." As to the tension between "judicial direction" and "jury discretion," the *Winston* Court came down unequivocally on the side of the latter:

> How far considerations of age, sex, ignorance, illness or intoxication, of human passion or weakness, of sympathy or clemency, or the irrevocableness of an executed sentence of death, or an apprehension that explanatory facts may exist which have not been brought to light, or any other consideration whatever, should be allowed weight in deciding the question whether the accused should or should not be capitally punished, is committed by the act of Congress to the sound discretion of the jury, and of the jury alone.[9]

The Court's faith in the "sound discretion of the jury" echoes the sentiments of John Lilburne the Leveller, William Penn the Quaker, and Alexander Hamilton the Founding Father, all of whom advocated the jury's right to determine law as well as fact. But here the jury is not determining law; it is, rather, exercising complete discretion to determine life or death, free of judicial guidance or direction. *McGautha* affirms that juries "do little more—and must do nothing less—than express the conscience of the community on the ultimate question of life or death."[10] It upholds jury discretion as a means "to maintain a link between contemporary community values and the penal system—a link without which the determination of punishment could hardly reflect 'the evolving standards of decency that mark the progress of a maturing society.'"[11]

McGautha wasn't all rosy optimism. The Court recognized that discretion could result in whimsy and caprice as well as the quality of mercy. But the disadvantages of jury discretion weren't nearly so much of a problem as the difficulty of fixing legislative and judicial standards. Cautioning future Courts against trying to define standards or making meaningless "boiler-plate,"[12] *McGautha* placed its faith in the untrammeled discretion of the jury.

It was otherwise with *Furman*. Just one year after *McGautha*, the Court was singing a new tune—a counterpoint in which praise for the "soundness" of juries' discretion blended with calls for the need to curtail "untrammeled" discretion. Chief Justice Burger gave voice to the shift: "It seems remarkable to me that with our basic trust in lay jurors as the keystone in our system of criminal justice, it should now be suggested that we take the most sensitive and important of all decisions away from them."[13]

Yet a number of majority justices, particularly Douglas and Marshall, could not ignore the numbers and the empirical facts, which powerfully suggested that discrimination was a factor in the implementation of the death penalty. Douglas believed that death penalties were disproportionately imposed on members of minorities and unpopular groups, and on the poor, young, sick, ignorant, powerless, and hated.[14] Marshall likewise saw the poor, the illiterate, the underprivileged, and minority group members as "society's sacrificial lamb."[15]

"Untrammeled discretion" represents one end of a continuum. At this end, where the jury is given no judicial guidelines, the context is wide open and prejudices may determine the jury's course. This wide open context was praised in *McGautha* as the source of mercy, milk, and honey. In *Furman,* the description includes words like "wanton," "freakish," "capricious," and "arbitrary."

In *The Maltese Falcon* Sam Spade says, "We need a fall guy." In *Furman* the Court seems to have chosen jury discretion. Some defendants get the death penalty whereas others do not, and the pattern seems "wanton and freakish" to Justice Stewart.[16] To Justice White, "there is no meaningful basis for distinguishing the few cases in which it is imposed from the many cases in which it is not."[17] But, briefly, let's muster an oblique defense of this fall guy by rounding up another suspect for consideration.

It is interesting to note, in *Furman*'s din of criticism aimed at jury discretion, that few fingers are pointed at *prosecutorial* discretion. Juries take the blame, while prosecutors—who decide which cases and defendants become capital cases—remain out of the line of fire. In trying to answer Justice White's implied question "What distinguishes the few cases that get the death penalty from the many that do not?" a social scientist or legal detective should seriously entertain the prosecutorial-discretion hypothesis. More than entertain: the investigator should look at the data to see if prosecutors bring capital charges disproportionately more often in cases where the defendant is poor, illiterate, ignorant, sick, powerless, hated, or a member of a minority group, when other crime factors appear equal. But prosecutorial discretion has never been subjected to as much searching analysis as jury discretion.

Balancing Discretion and Direction

Following *Furman,* many states hastened to write constitutionally acceptable legislation, and four years later, in 1976, a spate of cases enabled the Court to consider new solutions to the designated problem of jury discretion.[18] The simplest solution was proposed in *Woodson v. North Carolina:* if discretion was the problem, then it should be eliminated completely.[19] North Carolina had enacted a law mandating the death penalty for certain crimes: if someone was convicted of one of these crimes, then the death penalty directly and invariably followed. Simple and clean. This scheme removed from the context a host of defendant variables such as age, prior convictions, mental disorder, race, and socioeconomic status— variables permissible and impermissible. Jurors had no chance to exercise discretion , since the context was restricted to one element: the crime.

If the Court wanted a simple and clean answer to Justice White's question of how the death penalty can be equitably administered, North Carolina provided it. And if the Court wanted to eliminate the arbitrary, capricious quality of death sentences, well, the scheme offered in *Woodson* was hard to beat, since the penalty would be imposed automatically. The Court certainly had the opportunity to eliminate jury discretion entirely at this point, if it had wanted to. But its ambivalence about such discretion clearly emerged: it declared North Carolina's scheme unconstitutional.

The pre-*Furman* situation and the *Woodson* scheme represented the extreme solutions to the problems of context and discretion. At the pre-*Furman* end of the continuum, context was widest and discretion was unfettered. At the *Woodson* end, context was tightly narrowed to the crime per se, as variables relating to the criminal and his history and to jury discretion itself were eliminated. Taken together, *Furman* and *Woodson* defined the range of procedures according to which death penalty decisions could be made. Jurors would operate somewhere in the region between complete discretion and no discretion, with guidance from the legislature. This guided discretion was just what the *McGautha* Court had warned against, foreseeing that such legislative directives would quickly turn troublesome. But despite the warnings, the general method was set, although the particular procedural guidelines would eventually take a number of forms. The most prevalent form was sanctioned by the Court in *Gregg v. Georgia* in 1976.[20]

The Georgia scheme endorsed in *Gregg* reduced the number of crime categories for which death could be the penalty, and established that every death sentence was to be reviewed by the Georgia Supreme Court. But these strictures were peripheral to the real import of the case. Georgia's scheme may be labeled a "balancing test" in the area of guided discretion: it asked jurors to weigh the "aggravating" factors offered by the prosecution against the "mitigating" factors offered by the defense. Ten aggravating factors were established by statute.[21] These related to (1) the criminal's history, including whether the person had prior convictions for serious criminal assault; (2) whether the crime was committed while the person was engaged in a felony; (3) whether the criminal knowingly created a great risk of death to others; (4) whether the motive was money; (5) whether the defendant killed a judicial officer; (6) whether the defendant committed a murder or caused another person to do so; (7) whether the crime was outrageously or wantonly vile, horrible, or inhuman, involving torture, depravity of mind, or aggravated battery; (8) whether the defendant killed a peace officer; (9) whether the defendant was trying to escape; and (10) whether the defendant was trying to avoid capture. Jurors had to find at least one aggravating factor in the defendant's circumstances and had to specify it; this was necessary but not sufficient for a vote in favor of the death penalty. The jury also had to find that aggravating factors outweighed the mitigating ones.

One could criticize this scheme from either end of the procedural continuum. Gregg attacked it from the side of unlimited discretion: he claimed that the "direction" given to the jurors was only cosmetic, since the statute was "so broad and vague as to leave juries free to act arbitrarily and capriciously."[22] To illustrate, he cited items (7), (1), and (3), which included the troubling phrases "outrageously or wantonly vile, horrible, or inhuman [involving] . . . depravity of mind," "substantial history of serious assaultive criminal convictions," and "[creating a] great risk of death to more than one person." All of these phrases, claimed Gregg, were too vague and subjective and therefore could be too easily construed by jurors as having been met. Gregg's objection was that despite guidance, the legislature did not go far enough to specify, and thereby eliminate, the sort of discretion that so troubled the *Furman* Court.

Another attack could have been mounted in *Gregg*. The crime in the case was unclear, since Troy Leon Gregg and a traveling companion told different stories. We know that robbery and two murders were committed, but the order of events differed in the two accounts. The trial judge submitted the charges to the jury with the statement that the crime might or might not be considered felony-murder. For my point, let's assume that the crime committed in *Gregg* was felony-murder. We can also assume felony-murder in *Furman,* since the defendant in that case, William Henry Furman, tried to break into a home at night and fatally shot a householder through a closed door.[23]

Now, in *Furman* and *Gregg,* under Georgia's new statute, the felony-murder defendant automatically started off with one strike against him, because felony-murder was in fact *defined* as a murder committed during another felony (item 2 on the list of aggravating factors). This amounted to double counting, because the crime per se not only was the charge but became an aggravating factor by definition, rather than some additional aggravating factor. But it could get worse. If we assume that the underlying felonies were robbery in *Gregg* and burglary in *Furman*, then defendants were *automatically* given a second aggravating factor: "offender committed the offense . . . for the purpose of receiving money or any other thing of monetary value" (item 4). But this was merely part of the definition of robbery and burglary, rather than a superimposed aggravating factor. In contrast to Gregg's challenge, mine proceeds from the opposite direction: some of the guidelines appear to involve duplicity and double counting, taking crime definitions and turning them into aggravating factors which impermissibly load the aggravating side of the balance scale while limiting the jury's discretion.[24] Thus, this attack finds that not enough jury discretion remains to offset death's aggravating and unfair advantage.

In *Gregg*, the Court recognized that "death is different"[25] and affirmed the constitutionality of a number of procedurally different methods for implementing the death penalty. Defending its actions against *McGautha*'s warnings, the Court claimed that guidance is not something novel but natural, a hallmark of the American legal system. This Court rejected *McGautha*'s pessimistic prediction and held that fair, objective standards could be crafted to reduce the likelihood of arbitrary and capricious sentencing.

The Supreme Court endorsed the statutes in *Gregg* and in two other related cases, *Proffitt v. Florida* and *Jurek v. Texas* (both 1976). Florida's scheme in *Proffitt* was similar to Georgia's balancing test, with one significant difference: whereas in Georgia juries themselves made the final death or life decision, in Florida juries merely made a recommendation to the judge. By making the jury's decision penultimate rather than ultimate, Florida curtailed jury discretion far more than Georgia did, since the judge could second-guess and overturn the jury's recommendation.

The schemes endorsed in *Gregg*, *Proffitt*, and *Jurek* (the last of which we'll examine more closely below) must have met the justices' expectations. But whether these schemes would work in reality as well as in the justices' minds remained an open empirical question. Since the Court could not foresee the future, it espoused only a prediction, betting that these statutes would produce procedural justice.

Unmitigated Discretion

In *Lockett v. Ohio* (1978), Sandra Lockett was charged with aggravated murder.[26] In terms we are more familiar with, she was an accessory to felony-murder—the getaway driver, to be specific. She was given the death sentence, since the judge found one statutory aggravating factor but no *statutory* mitigating factor. And this was the point of contention. Ohio law specified only three mitigating factors, relating to (1) whether the victim had induced or facilitated the offense; (2) whether the offender had been subject to duress, coercion, or strong provocation; and (3) whether the offender's crime had been the product of psychosis or mental deficiency. Lockett claimed that this scheme prevented her from introducing other mitigating aspects (such as her age, character, prior record, lack of specific intent to cause death, and relatively minor part in the crime) and therefore prevented the sentencer from considering all relevant mitigating factors that an individualized type of sentencing required under the Eighth and Fourteenth Amendments. A plurality in *Lockett* agreed.

In arguing for "individualized sentencing," Lockett was extending *Woodson,* for one of the reasons the justices had rejected *Woodson*'s mandatory-sentencing scheme was that it treated all defendants alike, allowing no room for discretion in individual cases. But the *Lockett* Court appeared to be reversing the direction of *Furman* and *Gregg,* for it was saying, on the mitigating end, that there could be no guidelines for channeling and directing jury discretion. While Chief Justice Burger, writing for the plurality, admitted that "there is no perfect procedure,"[27] Justice White was far less charitable in his characterization: "The Court has now completed its about-face since *Furman* . . . held that as a result of permitting the sentencer to exercise unfettered discretion . . . the penalty was then being imposed discriminatorily, wantonly and freakishly . . . Today it is held, again through a plurality, that the sentencer may constitutionally impose the death penalty only as an exercise of his unguided discretion."[28] Justice Rehnquist also inveighed against what he saw as a return, at least on the mitigating end, to unfettered discretion:

> If a defendant as a matter of constitutional law is to be permitted to offer as evidence . . . any fact, however bizarre, which he wishes, . . . the new constitutional doctrine will not eliminate arbitrariness or freakishness in the imposition of sentences, but will codify and institutionalize it. By encouraging defendants in capital cases, and presumably sentencing judges and juries, to take into consideration anything under the sun as a "mitigating circumstance," it will not guide sentencing discretion but will totally unleash it.[29]

As one commentary put it, "The *Lockett* decision thus does more than merely expand the number of factors that must be considered by a capital sentencing authority; it alters the process . . . in its requirement that the sentencer give all mitigating factors offered by the defendant independent mitigating weight."[30] Contrary to Justice White's view that *Lockett* was an about-face, another commentator saw it as consistent with the line of death penalty cases because it "recognizes that a consistency produced by ignoring individual differences is a false consistency."[31] Whether this is an about-face, a full circle, or merely a consistent extension, the accent on individual differences and individualized sentencing does alter the procedural implementation of the death penalty. As Stephen Gillers put it, "This emphasis on the differences between people, their 'uniqueness,' . . . necessarily denies legislatures power substantively to determine or to influence who will be executed. Legislatures may still, of course, decide who cannot be executed, but they no longer have power to tell the sentencer how to decide who will be executed. That power . . . belongs entirely to the sentencer."[32]

Following *Lockett*, the jury could hear any mitigating factors the defendant wished to present. Moreover, the jurors had to weigh these factors independently and decide *how* to weigh them, since the State was not allowed to provide a formula. Likewise, in deciding the balance between aggravating and mitigating factors, the jury alone was responsible for the decision, without a guiding rule. Do jurors simply add and subtract factors, like an accountant doing the books? Do they construct life-and-death stories and find the best fit? Or do they use calculus or perhaps flip a coin? We do not know. But we do know that *Lockett* widened the mitigating context and shifted the "guided discretion" tension from the "guided" to the "discretion" end of the continuum. It may also represent a process of "coming full circle," constitutionalizing "Justice Harlan's practical recognition in *McGautha* [that] it is impossible to set down standards in advance for deciding who among those convicted of these crimes shall die."[33]

With a knowledge of *Lockett*'s holding and import, we can now situate many of the more recent death penalty decisions as legacies of *Gregg*, *Woodson*, or *Lockett*. For example, *Sumner v. Shuman* was a 1987 Nevada case involving a defendant who, while serving a life sentence without the possibility of parole, killed a fellow prisoner.[34] Nevada statute mandated the death penalty, but the Supreme Court, adhering to *Woodson*, ruled that such mandatory punishment violated the Eighth and Fourteenth Amendments. In *Maynard v. Cartwright*[35] and *Clemons v. Mississippi*,[36] the issue derived straight from *Gregg*. Like Gregg, these petitioners believed that aggravating statutes containing words like "especially heinous, atrocious or cruel" were unconstitutionally vague, for they allowed far too much subjectivity and provided far too little guidance for discretion. And *Mills v. Maryland*[37] and *McKoy v. North Caro-*

lina[38] can be classified as *Lockett* legacies, for they established that it is impermissible to require unanimous agreement among the jurors in order for particular mitigating circumstances to count, since such a requirement limits the jurors' discretion to weigh any and all factors. Thus, in the post-*Furman* age these early cases set the course of procedural justice, sometimes by what they said and sometimes by what they left unsaid. But the effort to find a balance between too little discretion and too much discretion continued.

Jurek: The Worst of Both Worlds

The Texas statute at issue in *Jurek* advocated guidance rather than unrestricted discretion. The statute asked jurors to answer three questions: (1) In committing the conduct that caused the death of the deceased, was the defendant acting deliberately and with the reasonable expectation that the death of the deceased or another would result? (2) Was it likely the defendant would commit criminal acts of violence that would constitute a continuing threat to society? (3) In killing the deceased, was the defendant responding unreasonably to provocation, if any, by the deceased?[39]

Under Texas law, all twelve jurors had to answer yes to all three questions; thus, the prosecution needed thirty-six affirmative votes to secure the death penalty. Though it appears that a single negative vote could enable the defendant to escape death, this impression is deceptive. To begin with, it could be argued that questions (1) and (3) are moot, for if the defendant was provoked or did not kill deliberately, the State would be charging him with manslaughter or some lesser crime that would not involve the death penalty. In other words, questions (1) and (3) have been asked and answered in the charge and in the verdict of guilt. Now we are down to the rub, question (2), and the practical fact that only twelve affirmative votes are needed.

Two different lines of attack have been mounted on this scheme in general and on question (2) in particular, lines emanating from the opposite extremes of "too guided" and "too discretionary." Let's take the former first. With *Lockett* as backdrop, how is the Texas jury to hear and *weigh* all relevant mitigating factors when the decision boils down to a single question, one that involves a prediction of future violence? To claim that the defendant is free to present any and all mitigating factors is misleading; for if jurors are not free to *give weight* to what they hear and actually *decide on the basis of what they hear,* then what they hear cannot determine the life-or-death outcome, which will be decided solely by the answer to question (2). This line of attack is illustrated in cases where defendants claimed that their history,[40] mental retardation,[41] and juvenile status[42] were improperly excluded from being weighed as mitigating factors under question (2) of Texas' statute, although *Lockett* had established that they must be taken into account.

The second line of attack focuses on what question (2) lets in—namely, psychological and psychiatric predictions of future violence, made by "experts." The lightning rod for this criticism has been "the ubiquitous Doctor Grigson," as Justice Blackmun called him.[43] Known in wider circles as "Dr. Death,"[44] Grigson has testified for the prosecution in more than 120 capital cases; and whether he is judged by his success rate or his presentation, even his critics grant that he makes a very compelling expert witness. He tends to make unequivocal statements such as "Defendant X will present a continuing threat to society by continuing acts of violence," or "X has a lack of conscience," or "X is as severe a sociopath as you can be," or "X is a ten plus" (on a one-to-ten scale, where "tens" are "individuals with complete disregard for human life").[45]

In terms of both style and results, Grigson is a compelling witness. Yet the critics of Dr. Death—who include the American Psychiatric Association and most scientists who study predictors of violence—believe that evidence based on such predictors is very far from compelling. That evidence was presented in *Barefoot v. Estelle* (1983),[46] where the Supreme Court concluded that predictions of violence are no more accurate than the toss of a coin; in fact, they're less so, being wrong two out of every three times.[47]

This line of attack points out that question (2), the answer to which almost certainly determines life or death, allows jurors to hear dubious and unreliable testimony, presented by a most forceful and credible "expert" to whom they may likely defer. One expressed goal of the *Furman-Gregg* line was to eliminate impermissible testimony from the process. Yet the *Barefoot* Court let stand such testimony on the grounds that it did not want to "disinvent the wheel," even when scientific evidence showed that the wheel was broken. The Court took its disinclination to an absurd extent when it stated that "neither petitioner nor the [American Psychiatric] Association suggests that psychiatrists are *always* wrong with respect to future dangerousness, only *most* of the time."[48] The Court bolstered its position by citing procedural remedies within the adversarial process itself: since the defense could cross-examine the likes of Grigson and put its own experts on the stand to offer rebuttals, the Court was willing to allow such testimony and let the jurors sort wheat from chaff.

Although many justices have been skeptical of the *Jurek* statute,[49] others have relied on reassurances from the State of Texas that question (2), despite its very narrow content, is actually interpreted very broadly. This "faith" in judicial discretion seems counter to the thrust of *Furman*, which touts statutory guidance as the means to channel discretion. When we look at how *Jurek* has worked, the results are not reassuring. It has been condemned because it limits permissible mitigating factors when it should not, and also because it permits what some regard as impermissible and error-prone predictions by so-called experts.

In limiting the contextual field when it should not be limited, and in widening it when it should not be widened, the law both wrongly limits and wrongly extends jury discretion. If juries cannot weigh what they ought to weigh, yet are expected to predict the future and apportion guilt in the present, then they are unfairly disadvantaged in their task of making life-or-death decisions.

Bias and Discrimination

Furman's aim of limiting discretion is surely defensible, particularly in light of the troubling data on the death penalty. When death is meted out in ways that seem racially discriminatory and given especially to those who appear to be society's scapegoats, then discrimination and bias are legitimate suspects. Although it is willing to take a human life, the Court has pursued two conflicting goals: it has wanted a fair process, free from bias, discrimination, and impermissible factors; and it has wanted to preserve jury discretion in some form to ensure individualized sentencing, so that the conscience and judgment of the community can be brought to bear on decisions. At its best, such a process allows juries the discretion to nullify death for merciful reasons, but hopefully not to give death sentences for vengeful, biased, or discriminatory reasons. Once the discretionary right has been granted, however, a legally sanctioned crapshoot is underway.

The *Furman* Court's hope (or illusion) was that guidance could improve the situation; the *McGautha* Court, not sharing that illusion, claimed it would not. The *McGautha* Court was pessimistic about the ability of the law and the state legislatures to craft such guidelines, yet it was optimistic about jury discretion. In *Furman* and its progeny, the reverse is true: the Court feared that bias would influence jurors' decisions. A potential source of such bias was at issue in the pre-*Furman* ruling of *Witherspoon v. Illinois* (1968).[50] This source of bias is more troubling than the vague wording of statutory aggravating factors (such as whether the defendant committed a "heinous" crime), since a legislative corrective can sharpen this wording. Correctives can also be crafted for bias arising from questionable testimony (for example, predictions of the defendant's future dangerousness). But there is a certain source of bias that is more pervasive than others, because it may be endemic to jurors themselves.

Consider the tenet that jurors are the "conscience of the community." This dictum is not exactly true, since the "community" is not perfectly represented on jury rolls. Not everyone gets a driver's license or registers to vote, two of the principle ways of entering the jury pool. Furthermore, in the process of jury selection, exemptions and exclusions create additional differences between the jury sample and the original community population. But when it comes to *capital cases,* death-qualified jurors (DQs) differ from the community to a far greater extent than do jurors in ordinary cases, and the differences are neither random nor benign. According to research conducted by J. B. Kadane, approximately 79 percent of all Americans would be death-qualified jurors; therefore 21 percent are excluded from serving on juries, for various reasons.[51] Death-qualified jurors tend to be "demographically distinctive": they "are more likely to be male, to be white, to be well-off financially, to be Republican, and to be Protestant or Catholic."[52]

These facts were not the central issue in *Witherspoon v. Illinois.* Rather, petitioner Witherspoon, who shot and killed a policeman in order to escape arrest and who was found guilty and sentenced to death, contended that when potential jurors were eliminated because of "conscientious scruples" (and nearly half the venire was eliminated for expressing qualms about the death penalty) the death-qualified jurors who remained were biased toward conviction.[53] Witherspoon backed up his claim by citing "three preliminary reports of three unpublished studies showing a relationship between attitudes toward capital punishment and propensity to convict."[54] Although the *Witherspoon* Court acknowledged that the question was an empirical one, it rejected the data as "too tentative and fragmentary."[55] But as more and more data were collected, they found their way into a series of cases,[56] which culminated in *Lockhart v. McCree* (1986).[57]

In an *amicus curiae* brief for the American Psychological Association in *Lockhart,* some fifteen studies were presented; they all used different methods but reached the same conclusions.[58] In general, when compared with other experimental subjects, death-qualified subjects are predisposed "to view evidence in a manner more negative to the defense."[59] More specifically,[60] they tend to trust prosecutors and distrust defense attorneys; they regard prosecution witnesses as more believable, credible, and helpful than defense witnesses; they tend to consider inadmissible evidence even if the judge instructs them not to; they tend to infer guilt if the defendant does not testify; they are suspicious of, if not hostile to, psychological claims of mental disorder or distress; and they are oriented more to "crime control" than to "due process"[61] or mercy considerations. The bottom-line conclusion was that death-qualified subjects tend to be conviction prone.[62]

If these results gleaned from studies, simulations, and experiments reflect the behavior of death-qualified jurors in the real world, then a pernicious bias exists—the bias that remains after the more obvious and objectionable biases have been removed during *voir dire*. This bias not only affects verdicts, but probably also operates to the disadvantage of the defendant in the ultimate life-or-death decision. Yet the *Lockhart* Court rejected the uncontroverted findings. Phoebe Ellsworth called the decision "lamentable": "Justice Rehnquist, writing for the majority, first attacked the research in ways that suggested that the majority Justices had either not understood it or not read it, or that they just didn't care. He then declared that it didn't matter how compelling the data might be, because it is constitutionally permissible to try capital cases before juries that are biased toward guilty verdicts. In short, 'we don't believe the data, but if we did it wouldn't matter.'"[63]

Thus far, we have considered two empirical questions on which social science research has failed to persuade the Supreme Court: "Are death-qualified jurors biased?" and "Can experts accurately predict a defendant's future dangerousness?" Let us turn now to another issue—racial discrimination—which has entailed a similar failure.

In *Furman*, Justices Douglas and Marshall highlighted the fact that racial bias is an impermissible factor in death penalty decisions. In more than a dozen empirical studies since *Furman*, the evidence has powerfully suggested that racial discrimination still pervades the process by which capital punishment is meted out.[64] Two particular findings recur: decisions are affected by the race of the victim, and are also strongly affected when there are certain combinations of race of defendant and race of victim. To put this in plainer terms, death sentences are significantly more likely when the victim is white rather than black (known as a "race-of-victim effect"). And death sentences are significantly more likely when a black kills a white than when a white kills a white(known as an "interaction effect"). Not only are these effects apparent in final jury decisions—they permeate the entire criminal-justice process, from the arrest, to the drawing up of charges, to the prosecutor's decision to seek the death sentence, to the imposition of the death sentence by the jury.

In *McCleskey v. Kemp* (1987), Warren McCleskey was a felony-murderer who shot and killed a police officer while robbing a store.[65]

What puts the case in this chapter, rather than in the felony-murder chapter, is that Warren McCleskey was a black man and the police officer was white. McCleskey presented the evidence from more than a thousand Georgia homicide prosecutions, drawing on research conducted by David Baldus and his colleagues.[66] The race-of-victim effect and the defendant-victim interaction effect were clearly evident in the decisions of both the jury and the prosecution. Baldus and his associates controlled for more than 250 variables, but none could account for the racial effects. To commonsense judgment, the "racial effects were due to race,"[67] but the Supreme Court chose to call these effects "unexplained" and said, "We decline to assume that what is unexplained is invidious." The Court declined to overturn McCleskey's death sentence.

The Court held that McCleskey failed to offer "evidence specific to his own case that would support an inference that racial considerations played a part in his sentence."[68] But the Court was demanding evidence that could not be provided—unless a prosecutor or juror had been dumb enough to exit the courtroom, walk up to a battery of TV and press microphones, and proclaim, "We got the black man!" The Court was in effect barring the racial challenge from ever succeeding. An irony is that had McCleskey presented the same sort of data in a job discrimination case, he would most likely have won. But in the U.S. Supreme Court "empirical evidence that would be sufficient to protect McCleskey's job was not considered sufficient to save his life."[69]

Why did the *McCleskey* Court do what it did? Craig Haney found an answer in a statement by Justice Powell.[70] "Taken to its logical conclusion," Powell said, McCleskey's challenge "throws into serious question the principles that underlie our entire criminal justice system . . . Thus, if we accepted McCleskey's claim that social bias has impermissibly tainted the capital sentencing decision, we could soon be faced with similar claims as to other types of penalty."[71] This would require changing course too drastically, for "there is no limiting principle"[72] here to restrict the change to a modicum. Justice Brennan, in his dissent, noted that "on its face, such a statement seems to suggest a fear of too much justice."[73]

The Payne and Aggravation of It All

The Court may have had not a "fear of too much justice" but a fear of too many repercussions—too many "closed cases" returning for another round. A victory in *Barefoot* on the basis of social science data would have had substantial impact on all capital cases involving predictions of dangerousness; a victory in *McCleskey* would have raised questions in all cases where the victim was white and the defendant black; and a victory in *Lockhart* would have had the most profound consequence of all, throwing into question all death decisions involving death-qualified juries. After *Furman* established general death-sentencing procedures and its progeny refined them, the Court showed little inclination to undertake major revisions, even when empirical evidence strongly suggested that the procedures were flawed.

The Court has been willing to overturn death sentences when the repercussions were limited. For instance, in *Parker v. Dugger*, a Florida judge overrode the jury's recommendation of life imprisonment and imposed the death sentence.[74] The judge apparently ignored the nonstatutory mitigating factors that the jury had found, and the Supreme Court held that the judge's decision was arbitrary and capricious. This sort of situation is unlikely to arise very often. Rarer still is the situation represented in *Lankford v. Idaho*,[75] where the State of Idaho declined to seek the death penalty, but the judge, in a surprise move, gave Lankford the death sentence. The Supreme Court held that this "death out of the blue" violated due process. And in *Yates v. Evatt*, a case involving accomplice murder, the judge's instruction to the jury about "malice" involved a presumption which the Court, in a rare nine-to-zero decision, ruled had unconstitutionally shifted the burden off the prosecution.[76] In these cases the death sentence was overturned, but their scope was limited and few repercussions were likely.

In an effort to refine death-sentencing procedures, the Court has drawn most clearly on *Lockett* and *Gregg*. The *Lockett* line of cases keeps the mitigating context wide open, allowing the defendant to present his or her best case for life and giving jurors almost unfettered discretion in weighing mitigating circumstances. The *Gregg* line focuses on aggravating circumstances, narrowing the aggravating context to a specific set of concrete factors—a strategy that the Court hopes will eliminate arbitrary, capricious, discriminatory, and generally impermissible factors from impinging on jurors' decisions. Thus, jurors have limited scope when considering aggravating circumstances and a great deal of freedom when dealing with mitigating ones. The playing field is not level for the two contexts. But up to this point levelness has not been the goal; rather, the goal has been *fairness*.

In a five-to-four decision in *Booth v. Maryland* that was consistent with the *Gregg* line of cases, the Court held that victim impact statements presented during the capital-sentencing phase introduced "irrelevant" aggravating information that might turn a reasoned decision into an emotional one.[77] Such statements—which gave a detailed picture of the harm that the murderer had caused the victim's family—would create a constitutionally unacceptable risk that the jury would impose the death penalty in an arbitrary and capricious manner. But the dissent strongly questioned the "irrelevancy" of victim impact statements. Justice White did not think it unusual that a punishment decision should take into account not just the *intent* and the *crime,* but the *harm* as well.

Justice Scalia, in dissent, likewise questioned whether the Court should link punishment only to the defendant's personal responsibility and moral guilt. "It seems to me, however—and, I think, to most of mankind—that the amount of harm one causes does bear on the extent of his 'personal responsibility.' We may take away the license of a driver who goes 60 miles an hour on a residential street; but we will put him in jail for manslaughter if, though his moral guilt is no greater, he is unlucky enough to kill someone during the escapade."[78] Moreover, two people may aim guns at victims and pull the trigger, but if one person's gun misfires, then fortuity rather than a moral distinction spares that person from becoming a murderer and eligible for the death penalty. And in the case of the Tison brothers, who were accused of accessory to felony-murder, the actions of the father (triggerman) made the sons (accessories) death eligible.

Finally, Scalia pointed to "community sentiment," the "outpouring of popular concern for what has come to be known as 'victim rights'—a phrase that describes what its proponents feel is the failure of courts of justice to take into account in their sentencing decisions not only the factors mitigating the defendant's moral guilt, but also the amount of harm he has caused to innocent members of society."[79] This paved the way for his argument in favor of leveling the playing field: if all mitigating evidence can be heard, why should "the debate on the appropriateness of the capital penalty" occur "with one side muted"?[80]

Two years later, in *South Carolina v. Gathers,*[81] the Court apparently brushed aside the level-field argument, for it extended *Booth*'s holding to prevent prosecutors from introducing victim impacts into the State's closing argument. But just two years later (four years after *Booth*), in *Payne v. Tennessee,* a new Court, with new personnel, reversed *Booth, Gathers,* and *stare decisis* and held that victim impact statements were permissible.[82] To Justice Scalia, a rational balance had returned to the Eighth Amendment, with "parity between mitigating and aggravating factors."[83]

To the minority in *Payne,* this was power politics, "not reason," for the only thing that had changed in four years was "the personnel on this Court."[84] Justice Marshall said that the majority's decision "charts an unmistakable course,"[85] whereas Justice Stevens, in dissent, showed why it was the wrong course, founded on an "argument [that] is a classic non sequitur"—the argument that the State, for reasons of fairness, must be allowed to present evidence about the *victim*.[86] The victim was not on trial, and evidence about the victim could not be equated with evidence about the defendant. Moreover, the sentencing procedure was not unbalanced, because the State was entitled to rebut the defendant's mitigating evidence and present its own aggravating factors, provided they were well defined so as to limit jury discretion. Justice Stevens then attacked the underlying premise of "evenness": "The premise that a criminal prosecution requires an even-handed balance between the State and the defendant is also incorrect. The Constitution grants certain rights to the criminal defendant and imposes special limitations on the State designed to protect the individual from overreaching by the disproportionately powerful State. Thus, the State must prove a defendant's guilt beyond a reasonable doubt . . . Rules of evidence are also weighted in the defendant's favor."

After clarifying the difference between "fairness," the prime goal, and "evenness," which had never been a goal, Stevens attacked the notion that *harm* must properly be weighed. He distinguished direct harm from indirect and unforeseeable harm; the harm suffered by many victims was of the latter type. To punish the defendant for harm that he or she had not foreseen or intended or directly produced was impermissible, he claimed.

But "evenness" carried the day in *Payne,* and death-sentencing procedures were radically altered as a result. A context in which aggravating factors had been well defined and jury discretion limited now opened wide to let in feelings, sentiments, and melodrama. And so long as such testimony was presented in the form of a victim impact statement, it could not be disallowed. Though U.S. law has never precisely answered the question of what factors the jury is permitted to consider in setting punishment (see Chapter 8 on recidivist cases), *Payne* significantly expanded the context in which "harm" could be made an issue, and thereby allowed those who had been indirectly harmed to shed tears and show pain before the jurors. As the field has been leveled in this manner, the "guided" part of "guided discretion" has shrunk while the "discretion" part has grown. This is what the *Furman* Court feared and the *McGautha* Court praised.

A Morality Play within a Morality Play

Death sentencing is messy. It makes determination of guilt look almost surgically antiseptic in comparison. Juries decide guilt according to rules that were established and agreed upon long ago. The procedural context is limited, and the issues center narrowly on *act* and *intent*. Once guilt has been determined and the capital-sentencing phase begins, a new and different drama opens for the jury.

If prototypes and story construction were central in the determination of guilt (see Chapter 4), it's a good bet they'll be central in the decision on punishment. As Martin Kaplan has said, there are decisions that are "argument rich," based on facts and information, and there are decisions that are "argument poor," relying on moral judgments and values.[87] Decisions to impose the death penalty are argument poor.

When penalty deliberations begin, jurors already have a story that they endorsed in the guilt phase.[88] They now have to decide if the defendant deserves life or death. But recent research has shown that the process is not very evenhanded, since juries returning the death sentence tend to operate on a "presumption of death,"[89] meaning that they presume the death penalty ought to follow unless the defense convinces them otherwise. Thus, the burden here is on the defense, whereas in the guilt phase it was on the prosecution, since "innocent until proven guilty" is the guiding presumption. Other research has shown that death-qualified jurors give more credence to aggravating factors and less to mitigating factors than do other jurors, and that jurors in general have poorer comprehension of mitigating factors than aggravating ones.[90] So the "credence" and "comprehension" factors, because they affect the "life side" more, may further unbalance evenhandedness and make the "death side" the weighty favorite from the outset. Furthermore, jurors who have to decide whether to impose the death penalty and who may already presume that it will be imposed are likely to have in mind a prototype of the "criminal who deserves to die."

In the morality play that is beginning, one that will be highly emotional, jurors may engage in a task of matching, trying to decide if the defendant fits the prototype they have conceived. Then come the arguments and emotional pulls. Not all the arguments are good ones; sometimes they're not even fair. For example, in *Brooks v. Kemp* (1985), a Georgia case that was decided in accordance with the touted mandatory review, the appellate court found that the prosecutor made twelve specific statements deemed erroneous and in violation of the defendant's constitutional rights.[91] These included statements indicating the prosecutor's own belief in the death penalty, reminding the jurors of the cost of imprisoning Brooks, suggesting that Brooks, not the jury, would be pulling the switch at the execution, and so on. Yet the Court of Appeals deemed these "harmless errors." When researchers tested this notion by presenting subjects with the original case (incorporating the twelve errors) and another version that lacked the twelve errors, they found that 67.5 percent voted for the death sentence under the former condition but only 40.4 percent voted for it in the latter condition. The errors weren't so harmless after all.[92]

Jurors, who are free of neither predilections nor prototypes and who are caught in the Sturm und Drang of life-and-death arguments, are now permitted to hear the victims' side of the story. If the previously untold story of harms is now told, it may elicit anger, rage, and the urge to punish to the maximum. If the story elicits compassion, and it usually does, jurors feel sympathy for the victims and want to do something for them. The *bot* is out of the question: you can't bring back the dead. But the *wer* is possible, enabling jurors to compensate the victim through the only discretionary choice they have—the choice to impose the death sentence. But according to the dictionary, "discretion" involves the ability to make *responsible* decisions, and these are quite distinct from emotional decisions based on momentary sentiments.

Whether jurors can make responsible decisions about death is an open question—one that has remained open for a very long time. History and literature provide some perspective. Among Charles Dickens' finest works is his historical novel *A Tale of Two Cities*, which takes place during the French Revolution.[93] With Dr. Guillotine's invention looming overhead, juries of Citizens make life-and-death decisions not on the basis of thoughtfully considered reasons but according to momentary passions, long-held prejudices, and peevish whims. At the beginning of the novel the narrator says, "It was the worst of times, . . . it was the age of foolishness,"[94] and these lines accurately describe the legal chaos of the period. In our own day the *Furman* Court, though more prolix and less elegant, nonetheless reached a Dickensian conclusion: the evidence indicated that jury decisions were discriminatory, arbitrary, and capricious. This led to the shutting down of the death penalty process until the due-process course could be fixed. Under the moratorium, the death boats would be constitutionally tied to the dock.

Furman's five-justice majority did more than just shout "Stop!"; it also gave a stage whisper "Go" for a particular direction—toward guided discretion. Once *Furman* rejected Brennan and Marshall's argument that the death penalty per se was cruel and unusual punishment, the substantive issue was dead and the death possibility was alive—if states could set the correct constitutional course in their statutes. Whispered or not, the message was loud and clear: a death boat could sail if conditions were right. *Furman*'s rejection of *McGautha*'s procedural course of untrammeled discretion gave another hint as to the proper direction. And once *Wood-*

son put an end to the mandatory death option, then the procedural course was set. If *McGautha*'s untrammeled discretion was Scylla and if *Woodson*'s mandatory death was Charybdis, then the Court was setting a course midway between them.

Why were the justices selecting this course for the jurors? Was the decision grounded in empirical findings, was it a strictly Platonic Guardian decision, or was it some combination of both? Justice Brennan, for one, saw that many of these procedural decisions seemed to result from political considerations, sentiments, and untrammeled discretion, while significant and compelling social science data were ignored. In Justice Brennan's words, the Court steered away from "too much justice." Thus, although a majority on the Court doubted whether jurors' discretion was up to the task, at least one justice was having the same doubts about the Court's discretion.

In the matter of the death penalty, there is a morality play within a morality play. In the morality play that is the capital-sentencing drama, jurors ultimately decide who will die. In the morality play of the Supreme Court, with an apparently never-ending string of death penalty cases, justices ultimately decide which rules regulate death, and how much guidance and discretion should prevail. But with *Payne*—the case that introduced victim impact statements, which can inflame passions and turn a supposedly reasoned decision into an emotional one—even the fundamental purpose of these procedures is called into question. Are we pursuing fairness or level playing fields?

There is also the old question involving the proper relationship of *punishment* to the *act, intent,* and *harm,* and the meaning of "harm." Following *Payne,* jurors may be hearing about wider harms, indirect and unintended harms, and more pain; on the other hand, jurors may have been considering these factors even before *Payne* made them permissible. Yet even with "harm" more powerfully weighted in the equation, and even if jurors have a predilection toward the death penalty and presume that it will be used, they nevertheless have rarely imposed it. In the wake of *Payne,* however, they may do so more often. If that occurs, appeals will increase, and the Supreme Court may have to decide whether those death sentences resulted from responsible discretion or the worst kind of discretion. In this play within a play, the actions of jurors drive the actions of the justices, and vice versa.

That the Supreme Court may be caught on a death course that never ends was apparently recognized by Justice Scalia. Writing a "scathing dissent" in a 1992 death penalty case, *Morgan v. Illinois,* he bemoaned the course and sounded like a death-weary justice caught on board a ship that would never reach port: "Today, obscured within the fog of confusion that is our annually improvised Eighth Amendment, 'death-is-different' jurisprudence, the court strikes a further blow against the people in its campaign against the death penalty."[95] Twenty years after *Furman* set the course, justices are still at sea among never-ending death cases. Scalia is not the only one with a lament.

Justice Harry Blackmun, who, despite his own moral reservations about the death penalty, always voted to allow legislatures to impose death if those sentences were imposed fairly, wrote in a 1992 case, *Sawyer v. Whitley*, of his anguish and "'ever-growing skepticism' about the fairness of the death penalty."[96] Regarding his assumption of fairness, he said: "Today, more than 20 years later, I wonder what is left of that premise underlying my acceptance of the death penalty."[97] And Chief Justice Rehnquist voiced his frustration with a death course that affords endless appeals, which "would interfere with the 'finality' necessary to administer the death penalty."[98]

In the early-morning hours of January 5, 1995, Jesse DeWayne Jacobs was executed in Texas by lethal injection. As a *Washington Post* editorial said, "It is a convoluted story, but even if its twists and turns, factual inconsistencies and constitutional aspects are comprehended, it still doesn't make sense."[99] Jacobs had confessed to killing Etta Urdiales, the estranged wife of the boyfriend of his sister, Bobbie Hogan. Before his trial began, Jacobs recanted his confession; he said that his sister had done the killing, that he had been outside the house where the deed was done, and that he never knew his sister had had a gun. He claimed that he had only assisted in burying the body. Nevertheless, a jury convicted him and sentenced him to die.

Then came the complexity. The very same state attorney who prosecuted Jacobs had a change of mind, coming to believe that Bobbie Hogan, the sister, had actually committed the murder. He charged Mrs. Hogan with the killing; she was convicted of involuntary manslaughter and sentenced to ten years. "But the state took no steps to vacate Mr. Jacob's conviction or to explain why he should die when he didn't kill the victim or intentionally act in concert with his sister to do so, either of which is required before a capital sentence can be imposed."[100] Jacobs' final appeal was turned down by the U.S. Supreme Court by a six-to-three vote.

Justice Stevens, in dissent, called the Court's decision "fundamentally unfair": "It would be fundamentally unfair to execute a person on the basis of a factual determination that the state has formally disavowed."[101] As the *Washington Post* reported, "An editorial in the Vatican newspaper, *L'Osservatore Romano*, condemned Jacobs' execution as 'monstrous and absurd,' and compared the Supreme Court's ruling to that of Pontius Pilate, the Roman leader who allowed Christ to be crucified. The court 'preferred the way of Pilate,' the editorial said, 'by just washing its hands of the matter.'"[102] In his commentary, under the heading "The Supreme Court Has Diminished Itself," Nat Hentoff relates a colloquy in which he and a philosopher tackle the question: What has been mankind's greatest achievement?[103] Both give the same answer: due process. But due process, and Jacobs, would die that day, sacrificed to swift "finality." The ultimate comment belongs to Jesse DeWayne Jacobs: "I have news for all of you—there is not going to be an execution. This is premeditated murder by the state of Texas."[104]

The Court has long traveled on this death course, but whether it has gotten very far is an open question. In 1995, twenty-three years after *Furman,* the Court's upholding of Jacobs' execution seems arbitrary and capricious, lacking in the very same "due process" that *Furman* sought to guarantee. As the Court came about, and came back around in *Payne,* where victim impact statements were let in after being barred in two prior rulings, Justice Marshall claimed that it was charting "an unmistakable course," substituting power politics for reason. And when the Baldus data on racial discrimination in the State of Georgia failed to persuade in *McCleskey*—perhaps because, as Justice Powell feared, it would throw "into serious question the principles that underlie our entire criminal justice system"—we wonder about the principles that are guiding this ship. Justice Brennan's comment, that "on its face, such a statement seems to suggest a fear of too much justice," tells us that this justice does not find justice at the helm. And when the *Barefoot* Court allows experts to testify to the defendant's future dangerousness despite empirical evidence that strongly suggests more misses than hits, and when it justifies this with Justice White's freakish phrase (the data are not "always wrong . . . only most of the time"), we suspect that the ship has hit the rocks.

The phrase "death is different," which set this chapter in motion, has now acquired new meanings, and some of those meanings neither flatter the law nor do justice. According to the Supreme Court, jurors are to navigate by "guided discretion"—a direction that would produce due process and fair and conscionable sentences. And in the morality play that is a capital-sentencing hearing, a play that prosecutors are putting on more and more frequently, jurors, using their discretion, give prosecutors their desired death ending only a small percentage of the time. Although wrongful death sentences are handed out, and these mistakes must be acknowledged, the responsibility is seldom the jurors' alone; incompetent defense counsel, overzealous prosecutors, "harmless errors," and judicial rulings all play a part. Jurors may fashion the "death-deserving story." But who supplied the elements for that story, and who failed to offer a strong "life-deserving story"?

And there is another morality play over death that takes place in the Supreme Court, where death penalty decisions are handed down each term. From *Furman* to the present, the death course, which began simply enough as the middle course, has twisted and turned in curious and sometimes contradictory ways. The simple starting principles have been joined and obscured by the principle of level playing fields, the desire for finality, and fears of too much upheaval or too much justice. The Court, which rules on fair play, is divided, at sea, lacking clear wind, and in a foul mood. Had this navigational metaphor been set on dry land, the Court's path would have led into a dark forest; had the metaphor been set underground, we would be back in the labyrinth, without the golden thread. Whether underground, on ground, or at sea, the Court appears stuck. The final words are those of Justice Scalia's dark summation: in its Eighth Amendment jurisprudence, the Court remains obscured within a "fog of confusion."

The Juvenile
Death Penalty

11

The *Wall Street Journal* called them "the young and violent," a new generation of kids who are committing violent crimes at unheard-of ages.[1] Statistics compiled by the Federal Bureau of Investigation confirm the observation, finding "a huge increase in violent crime by juveniles."[2] This poignant and alarming fact, however, comes "as no surprise to any frequent watcher of the evening news, where the faces of the criminals seem to keep getting younger."[3] The "crime facts" are stark, but what to do about such violent juveniles, some of whom are kids who kill, is anything but clear.

In the eyes of many—politicians who feel the heat, citizens who feel the fear, and even those who have toiled in "juvenile justice"—the reform-based juvenile-justice system seems not to be working. According to critics, it severs the nexus between act and consequence; the juvenile thus learns that crime pays, since punishment does not follow. The "system" becomes an apprenticeship program, where juveniles make errors with impunity, learn the trade, and proceed to adulthood more hardened, violent, and valueless than they were before. The critics want to do something different.

Massachusetts remains one of a minority of states that does not have the death penalty. It is a state that has been viewed as "liberal" by some, a "hotbed of liberalism" by others, but certainly not a "hotbed of punitiveness." Yet tough and punitive rhetoric has come from Governor William Weld, who has called for "a man-sized punishment for a man-sized crime."[4] As it turns out, Weld and Massachusetts were latecomers to the movement toward harsher penalties. "According to the National Center for Juvenile Justice, since 1979 more than two-thirds of the states have amended their juvenile codes to make it easier to transfer children to adult court."[5] Whether this movement is driven principally by putative facts or primitive fears, it is nonetheless changing the image of the juvenile offender from "victim" to "villain." As a consequence, with easier transfers to adult court and "man-sized" punishments in the offing, some of these "villains," the killing kids, now face a greater risk of receiving the death penalty.[6]

In the history of the United States, death penalties for juveniles have been rare, and juvenile executions rarer still, comprising less than 2 percent of all executions. In the twentieth century, juvenile executions have almost disappeared.[7] But sentiment may be changing. If the new trend toward "man-sized" punishments—including the most "man-sized" of all, the death penalty—truly reflects community sentiment, then killing the kids who kill may soon become more frequent. But whether the sentiment that politicians are responding to is truly community sentiment remains an open, and empirical, question.

When it comes to punishment, and the death penalty in particular, what society wishes to do is limited by what it constitutionally may do. The Eighth Amendment's clause on cruel and unusual punishment establishes a boundary, barring some punishments as disproportionate to the crime[8] or the criminal.[9] This prohibition has been successfully invoked to bar the death penalty for the crime of rape,[10] for certain accessories to felony-murder,[11] for death row inmates who become insane,[12] and for certain juveniles.[13] Thus, society's desire to inflict adult-sized punishments on juveniles—if there truly is such a desire—may be constitutionally thwarted by the Eighth Amendment.

In Search of Sentiment

Since *Weems v. United States* (1910), the Eighth Amendment has been hinged to the community's evolving standards of decency: as the latter evolve, the very meaning of "cruel and unusual" changes.[14] Thus, the constitutional line separating proportionate from disproportionate punishment is not firmly set by the Eighth Amendment, *stare decisis,* or dicta. The import of this is far-reaching. For one thing, it means that there is no sacred, canonical, once-and-for-all textual interpretation of "cruel and unusual." With an evolving Eighth Amendment, the plain-fact view of law[15] must plainly fall on its face. For the Eighth Amendment is a living, evolving thing that acquires new meanings and shadings as social standards change. Time, then, rather than text, grounds and contextualizes "cruel and unusual." But time per se, like a penumbra, is too ethereal, relative, and impersonal to provide the context for the concrete demands of death adjudication. It is community sentiment, distilled from time and ordained by *Weems,* that gives context and concreteness to "cruel and unusual."

Although community sentiment and the Eighth Amendment evolve over time, there is one static fact that does have significant bearing on the juvenile death penalty question—a fact that sets juveniles apart from adults. Historically, common law at the time of the Bill of Rights drew an "age line" stipulating that children under seven could not be executed.[16] This created an important distinction between adults and juveniles. In capital cases involving adult defendants, age might be a mitigating factor but could not constitutionally preclude imposition of the death penalty. In juvenile cases, however, age was not only likely to be more central and mitigating but could constitutionally bar the death penalty on cruel and unusual grounds.

Even in the current climate, where "man-sized" punishments for juveniles are being proffered, we can make a reasonable guess that most citizens would reject the death penalty for a child of seven, eight, or ten.[17] We strongly suspect that the line at age seven has moved upward, but the current question is, "Where is it now?" Some recent polling results indicate that public opinion is overwhelmingly opposed to executing those younger than eighteen.[18] But polls, as we saw in Chapter 1, may pose the question badly, and fail to pick up fine-grained distinctions. A recent poll asked, "Would you favor or oppose the state's passing a law to allow the death penalty for juveniles over fourteen years of age convicted of murder?"[19] The proportions of people responding "oppose" in their two samples were 69 percent and 65.3 percent. But we do not know if those subjects opposed the death penalty for fourteen-year-olds or for all juveniles. Would subjects have been opposed if the hypothetical age had been fifteen, sixteen, or seventeen? In today's "man-sized punishments" climate, is the line perhaps moving downward, such that society is more willing to consider the death penalty for juveniles of lower ages? Hunches and intuition tell us that the line grows clearer and firmer as the age of the juvenile drops, but hunches and intuition do not fix the line precisely.

Where, in fact, *is* the line? That was the substantive question in *Stanford v. Kentucky* (1989), where two defendants aged sixteen and seventeen challenged their death sentences as cruel and unusual punishment.[20] The substantive question was a factual, empirical question, the sort that social scientists routinely tackle. For scientists to answer the question adequately, and to have their answer accepted by the scientific community, they would have to agree on which methods are acceptable and which are invalid, inapt, and unreliable. Thus, agreeing about procedural methods is the first hurdle. One must decide which data count and which do not, and which methods of analysis are acceptable and which are not. In *Stanford,* the procedural hurdle became the major battle. Justice Scalia, writing the plurality decision, defined the Eighth Amendment playing field in such a way that hunches, intuitions, and suspicions would be relegated to the sidelines and would carry no weight; rather, the objective indicia would reveal where community sentiment stood, and that sentiment would be dispositive.

Scalia's position was itself evolutional. In some matters of privacy (see Chapters 6 and 7), community sentiment counted for little in the Court's decisions, whereas in other privacy matters, those relating to search and seizure, the community's reasonable expectations were considered relevant. In the Court's Eighth Amendment jurisprudence, whether related to recidivist cases (Chapter 8), accessory felony-murder cases (Chapter 9), or the death penalty in general (Chapter 10), decisions were to be based on objective indicia to the maximum extent possible, thereby giving community sentiment an even more dominant say. But in *Stanford* Scalia apparently went all the way: the Court was to make a completely objective decision, using only empirical analysis to answer an empirical question.

Social Scientists and Philosopher-Kings on the Sidelines

Whereas *Weems*[21] and *Trop*[22] forged the nexus between "cruel and unusual punishment" and "community sentiment," and *Coker*[23] explicitly held that "Eighth Amendment judgments should . . . be informed by objective factors to the maximum possible extent,"[24] Justice Scalia pushed "objective jurisprudence" to a new extreme in *Stanford,* where it was not just preeminent but preempted the field.[25] In deciding whether the death penalty for the sixteen-year-old Wilkins and the seventeen-year-old Stanford was cruel and unusual, Scalia first cleared away all irrelevancies. The first irrelevancy turned out to be "socioscientific evidence concerning the psychological and emotional development of 16- and 17-year-olds":[26] "The battle must be fought, then, on the field of the Eighth Amendment; and in that struggle socioscientific, ethicoscientific, or even purely scientific evidence is not an available weapon. The punishment is either 'cruel *and* unusual' . . . or it is not. The audience for these [social science] arguments . . . is not this Court but the citizenry of the United States. It is they, not we, who must be persuaded."[27]

This is an unusual argument. The Court's analysis was supposed to be objective and empirical, and justices were supposed to function like social scientists, yet Scalia rejected scientific evidence that may have directly informed the question at issue. This pushed "objective jurisprudence" not only to a new high but to a new low, for it gave a meaning to "objective" that was anything but. This so-called objective jurisprudence, then, had to be amended: only *some* of the evidence would be dispositive. Scalia cited no basis for his rejection, no scientific studies questioning the validity or reliability of such studies and findings; only his own claim that it was "an uncertain foundation upon which to rest constitutional law." Paradoxically, then, in what was to be a social science analysis, social scientists had been relegated to the sidelines. They were about to have heady company.

Justice Scalia went on to reject decisions based solely or in part on conceptual or moral grounds. That sort of analysis—a so-called proportionality analysis—would, as Scalia saw it, end up replacing "judges of the law with a committee of philosopher-kings."[28] Extending this view, Scalia chided the *Stanford* dissenters for doing just such a proportionality analysis, for "reaching a decision supported neither by constitutional text nor by the demonstrable current standards of our citizens,"[29] and for failing "to appreciate that 'those institutions which the Constitution is supposed to limit' include the Court itself."[30] In taking only a bit from social science, and not a whit from proportionality analysis, Scalia left philosopher-kings and social scientists in foul territory, since his Eighth Amendment field was occupied exclusively by his sanctioned objective data.

His brethren were not quite in accord. In *Enmund v. Florida,* Justice White recognized that empirical evidence ought to "weigh heavily in the balance, [but] it is for us ultimately to judge whether the Eighth Amendment permits imposition of the death penalty."[31] In her *Enmund* dissent, Justice Sandra Day O'Connor also refused to yield the decision solely to a social science analysis, claiming that the "concept of proportionality involves more than merely a measurement of contemporary standards of decency,"[32] and in her majority opinion in *Tison*[33] she stated that the Court must do "its own proportionality analysis." In the opinions of White, O'Connor, and others on the Court, justices ought to be more than "bean counters" and should bring their moral and judicial judgments to the playing field, even at the risk of being branded a philosopher-king or philosopher-queen.

This battle continued in *Thompson v. Oklahoma* (1988), a death penalty case involving a fifteen-year-old.[34] Scalia, in dissent, championed his two positions: the Court should use only selected objective data and should avoid proportionality analysis. The majority rejected his position.

In *Stanford,* writing for a four-vote plurality, he again maintained both positions. Justice Brennan not only rejected Scalia's proportionality position in his dissent,[35] but was also unwilling to restrict the evidence solely to Scalia's selected data. Justice O'Connor pointedly rejected Scalia's position on proportionality, again claiming that the Court had "a constitutional obligation to conduct a proportionality analysis."[36] If one adds her opinion to those of the four dissenters, Justice Scalia's plurality position on proportionality becomes a minority position.

Why this concern for what counts and what doesn't, for what is permissible and what isn't? Why not simply cut to the chase—to the substantive question of where community sentiment stands? Scientists understand that the way you frame a question is likely to determine the answer. The methods you bring to the playing field, leaving certain other methods on the sidelines, may yield answers that are disparate, off the mark, or patently false. If a researcher investigating the sky were allowed to view the heavens only in daylight, the "data" would reveal no stars. And if the task were to read the stars (or the states' laws or legislative enactments), and one group of justices looked east and counted while the other group looked west and counted, well, by dawn's early light, such star-crossed justices might end up in a brawl.

The Scrimmage over Stanford

Scalia's analysis of the data on legislative enactments began with the fact that "of the 37 States whose laws permit capital punishment, 15 decline to impose it upon 16-year-old offenders and 12 decline to impose it on 17-year-old offenders."[37] These states and numbers were not disputed by the minority. Scalia followed this fact with his conclusion: "This does not establish the degree of national consensus this Court has previously thought sufficient to label a particular punishment cruel and unusual."[38]

If we look at Justice Scalia's data and analysis (see Table 11.1), we see that only 40.5 percent of the states would bar the death penalty for a sixteen-year-old (such as Wilkins), whereas only 32.4 percent would bar the death penalty for a seventeen-year-old (such as Stanford). These percentages are not even a majority, let alone a "consensus."

Justice Brennan promptly challenged the plurality's conclusion, calling it "a distorted view of the evidence of contemporary standards that these legislative determinations provide."[39] Brennan labeled it a "distorted view" because Scalia left out fifteen states "in which capital punishment is not authorized at all."[40] If these fifteen states were taken into account, and the minority believed they should be, then "the governments in fully

Table 11.1. Justice Scalia's plurality analysis in *Stanford* of states having the
death penalty and states having no death penalty for offenders aged
sixteen and seventeen.

| | States categorized as | | | | |
| | Having no death penalty | | Having the death penalty | | |
Offender	Number	Percent	Number	Percent	Total states
Wilkins (age 16)	15	40.5	22	59.5	37
Stanford (age 17)	12	32.4	25	67.6	37

27 of the States have concluded that no one under 18 should face the
death penalty,"[41] and "a total of 30 States . . . would not tolerate the execution of petitioner Wilkins"—that is, a juvenile under seventeen.[42]

Justice Scalia strongly objected to the dissent's inclusion of non–death
penalty states, claiming that "it is quite irrelevant to the specific inquiry in
this case."[43] He went on to claim that the dissent had confounded the
question: "The dissent's position is rather like discerning a national consensus that wagering on cockfights is inhumane by counting within that
consensus those states that bar all wagering."[44]

But Scalia's analogy was inapt, for the legislation in the non–death
penalty states surely spoke to the death penalty question for juveniles and
adults. In rejecting the analogy, which would have eliminated states from
the analysis, the dissent kept the "data set" intact. The sidelined social
scientist would have applauded this, but not Justice Brennan's next move,
for Brennan now took his turn at eliminating states. Brennan focused on
the nineteen states where the death penalty was allowed but where "no
minimum age for capital sentences is set in the death penalty statute."[45]
He argued that those states had not addressed the issue of the juvenile
death penalty explicitly, as the other states had. After making this distinction between statutes that were explicit and those that were implicit, he
claimed that "the decisions of legislatures that are only implicit, and that
lack the 'earmarks of careful consideration that we have required for
other kinds of decisions leading to the death penalty,' . . . must count for
little."[46] Actually, they counted for nothing, since Brennan subtracted the
nineteen implicit death penalty states, which left a denominator of 33 (see
Table 11.2). If we place Brennan's baseline numerators, 30 (for age sixteen) and 27 (for age seventeen), over this denominator, we get extremely
high percentages, 90.9 and 81.8, which reflect the proportions of states

Table 11.2. Justice Brennan's minority analysis in *Stanford* of states having the death penalty and states having no death penalty for offenders aged sixteen and seventeen, when "implicit" states are removed.[a]

| | States categorized as | | | | |
| | Having no death penalty[b] | | Having the death penalty | | |
Offender	Number	Percent	Number	Percent	Total states
Wilkins (age 16)	30	90.9	3	9.1	33
Standord (age 17)	27	81.8	6	18.2	33

a. "Implicit" states are those that do not explicitly daw a line at a specific age below which the death penalty may not be imposed.

b. Vermont is counted as a non–death penalty state.

that, after explicitly considering the matter, had barred the execution of sixteen- and seventeen-year-olds, respectively. Justice Scalia's response was terse: "The dissent again works its statistical magic by refusing to count among the States that authorize capital punishment of 16- and 17-year-old offenders those 19 States that set no minimum age in their death penalty statute, and specifically permit 16- and 17-year-olds to be sentenced as adults . . . We think that describing this position is adequate response."[47]

In comparing plurality and minority analyses, we see different numerators, denominators, and control groups, and, most of all, different questions being framed. It is small wonder that different answers resulted. The plurality obtained answers of 40.5 percent (for age sixteen) and 32.4 percent (for age seventeen), clearly less than a majority. The minority obtained 90.9 percent (for age sixteen) and 81.8 percent (for age seventeen), clearly a substantial majority.

Legislative Enactments Reanalyzed

In order to answer the substantive question, we must answer the three methodological questions that so divided the Court in *Stanford*. What is the appropriate denominator? What is the appropriate control group? And what is the essential question? The appropriate denominator is 52, the total number of states and jurisdictions (including the District of Columbia and the federal jurisdiction, in which Congress passes its laws) where elected legislators—the representatives of the people—legislate. There are two arguments for this denominator (52), both of which derive from Scalia's own positions. First, in his analysis in *Thompson v. Oklahoma* (1988), Scalia rejected data on other countries' policies concerning the juvenile death penalty, stating that those numbers were "totally inappropriate as a means of establishing the fundamental beliefs of this Nation."[48] Scalia clearly drew the relevant boundary line around "this Nation," implying that the number of states to be considered was fifty-two, not thirty-seven, as he had claimed in his *Stanford* analysis. The second argument stemmed from Scalia's critique of the dissent's removal of the so-called implicit states. If excluding states is impermissible, he wrote, then his own defense for excluding the non–death penalty states must collapse as well. Therefore, all fifty-two jurisdictional statutes will be used in this reanalysis of the *Thompson* and *Stanford* data.

An assumption must be made about how to "read" legislation. The simplest and safest assumption is to assume that what the legislation says is what the legislators meant. To do otherwise, to go beyond the statutory language and guess at what the legislators may have meant, entails several risks. One risk is loss of reliability: as we have seen, this problem occurred when the plurality eliminated one set of states and the dissent eliminated another set, and neither could agree on what was relevant. A second risk is subjectivizing what was supposed to be objective: if both plurality and dissent turn the objective legislative-enactments index into a Rorschach-like subjective index, then interpretations will vary depending on who is holding the cards; the decision comes down to judicial sentiment, for whichever side can muster five votes for its interpretation wins the hand. But this is not objectivity. If this index fails the test of objectivity but remains the prime if not sole index used, then the Court's quest for objectivity will fail.

Let's categorize the fifty-two states in terms of what they permit and do not permit in regard to the death penalty for juveniles and adults (see Table 11.3). If juveniles are the group in question, then adults are the control group. The distinction between adults and juveniles, which was made at the time the Bill of Rights was adopted, drew the common-law line at age seven. In the cases of the fifteen-year-old Thompson, the sixteen-year-old Wilkins, and the seventeen-year-old Stanford, the question is whether the line has moved to sixteen, seventeen, and eighteen, respectively. In broad terms, the question is: Does the treatment of juveniles and adults under death penalty laws show a significant difference? That is, are juveniles liable to the death penalty in significantly fewer states than adults?

Table 11.3 categorizes the states as either having or not having the death penalty for adults, and as either having or not having the death

Table 11.3. Comparisons between juveniles and adults on the death penalty issue for cases involving defendants aged fifteen, sixteen, and seventeen.

| | States categorized as | | | | |
| | Having the death penalty | | Having no death penalty | | |
Offender	Number	Percent	Number	Percent	Total states
Adults (older than 18)	37	71.2	15	28.8	52
Stanford (age 17)[a]	25	48.1	27	51.9	52
Adults (older than 18)	37	71.2	15	28.8	52
Wilkins (age 16)[b]	22	42.3	30	57.7	52
Adults (older than 18)	37	71.2	15	28.8	52
Thompson (age 15)[c]	19	36.5	33	63.5	52

a. $X^2[1, N = 52] = 5.74, p < .05$.
b. $X^2[1, N = 52] = 8.81, p < .01$.
c. $X^2[1, N = 52] = 12.5, p < .001$.

penalty for seventeen-year-old offenders (such as Stanford). A chi-square (X^2) test was run to test for differences, and the results showed a significant difference ($X^2[1, N = 52] = 5.74, p < .05$) in regard to how the death penalty statutes treat adults and seventeen-year-olds. For example, whereas 51.9 percent of the states would bar the death penalty for the seventeen-year-old, only 28.8 percent of them would bar the death penalty for someone eighteen or older.

For adults and for sixteen-year-old offenders (such as Wilkins) the chi-square test was again significant ($X^2[1, N = 52] = 8.81, p < .01$). Here we see that the difference is even larger: 57.7 percent of the states would bar the death penalty for a sixteen-year-old, whereas only 28.8 percent would bar it for an adult. Last, as shown in Table 11.3, the chi-square test was again significant ($X^2[1, N = 52] = 12.53, p < .001$) for adults and for fifteen-year-old offenders (such as Thompson). The difference again grew: 63.5 percent would bar the death penalty for fifteen-year-olds, but only 28.8 percent would bar it for adults.

Our ultimate question is: Do majorities and significant differences constitute a national consensus? But let's look first at another objective index—namely, jury decisions.

Jury Decisions Data

Little can be made of the jury decisions data. Whether we look at the number of juveniles given the death sentence or the number of actual executions, these numbers are so small that they "carry little significance,"[49] says Scalia. In this instance, his conclusion is right, but for the wrong reason. The social scientist would say that these numbers tell us nothing about the question at bar, for these numbers are merely numerators, when what we need for statistical and comparative purposes are the denominators—the number of such cases brought to trial or the number of cases that resulted in conviction. Only by having the appropriate denominators can we run legitimate statistical tests and draw legitimate conclusions about whether substantial disparities exist between adults and juveniles under death penalty laws.

The statistics used by the dissent in *Stanford* were all plagued by the denominator problem—having either no denominator or the wrong denominator. The *Stanford* dissent concluded too much from too little: that the death penalty is *rarely* given to juveniles. But concluding too much from too little still turned out to be too little. In his *Thompson* dissent, Scalia first exposed the fallacy of the *rarity* argument via an analogy to women defendants.[50] He noted that executions of women are rare and that over time the phenomenon has become even rarer. "Surely," he said, "the conclusion is not that it is unconstitutional to impose capital punishment upon a woman."[51]

Scalia's rebuttal was on the mark in one sense but missed the mark in another. First, *rarity* is not the entire issue at bar. It needs to be established to substantiate *one part* of the claim—that the death penalty for juveniles is rarely given and thus might be "unusual." But in addition to *rarity* one must show *disparity*—that a significant difference exists in the way juries (and legislatures) treat juveniles as opposed to adults in terms of the death penalty. Justice Scalia makes too much of the rarity argument and too little of the disparity argument.

But even rarity and disparity do not completely circumscribe the issue, for if they did, Scalia's analogy to women might be more apt than it is. If it were just a matter of showing rarity and disparity, a woman given the death penalty could probably show both and then claim that a national consensus exists. But what makes Scalia's analogy a straw-woman argument is the fact that the claims of juveniles and women differ in a crucial way. The juvenile's "cruel and unusual" claim is based on the fact that an *established line*, set at age seven, was recognized at the time the Bill of Rights was adopted. No such historical, common-law, or constitutional

claim can be put forth for women. That line for juveniles is a jurisprudential fact of law and life, yet the question for the law, and for the lives of
Thompson, Wilkins, and Stanford, is: Where is that line situated now?

We sense intuitively that the line has moved, but Justice Scalia insists
that guesses and intuitions are impermissible, since the question must be
answered empirically, using only objective data. The second index, jury
decisions data, gives no answer. The first index, legislative enactments,
gave wildly divergent and faulty readings, depending on which justice did
the counting; when the enactments were reanalyzed, however, significant
differences emerged between juveniles and adults. But significant differences are not the same as a national consensus. The question now becomes: What is the significance of significance? Put another way: What is
the criterion or threshold for declaring a national consensus?

The Philosopher-King Takes the Field

In his reputed empirical analysis, Justice Scalia put forth an argument that
not only could not be refuted by empirical data but that made such data
completely irrelevant. The seeds of his argument were first sown in his
Thompson dissent, where he reframed the issue to require the defendant
to show "that no one so much as a day under 16 can *ever* be mature and
morally responsible enough to deserve that penalty."[52] By extension, Wilkins and Stanford would have to prove that no one so much as a day
under seventeen and eighteen, respectively, was ever mature and morally
responsible enough to deserve the death penalty. This burden required a
categorical showing—that no one under age *x* is ever deserving, or that
no jury would ever give the death penalty to someone under age *x*. Science could not certify the former, and the fact that Thompson, Wilkins,
and Stanford stood before the Court refuted the latter.

This categorical argument played fast and loose with the foul lines that
defined the Eighth Amendment field. What were to be considered fair
play were permissible empirical data determined by the objective indexes,
said Justice Scalia; all else fell in foul territory. But the categorical argument moved the foul lines and made the empirical data irrelevant, so that
"fair is foul, and foul is fair."[53]

Requiring the defense to show that no seventeen- or sixteen- or fifteen-
year-old is *ever* fully responsible was to ask the impossible, and Scalia
knew it, acknowledging that "it is not demonstrable."[54] Although the social scientist might show that the evidence supports a hypothesis at the 95
percent, the 99 percent, or even the 99.9 percent level of confidence, the
100 percent level is beyond the earthly reach of any scientist.[55]

Somewhere betwixt midgame and endgame, *the playing field changed* and the philosopher-king seized the field. In changing the requisite, Scalia transmuted an empirical question into a conceptual one, but by doing so his own social science analysis became moot. For in this setup, the null hypothesis could never be rejected, and this contravenes the philosophy of science,[56] which requires hypotheses to be stated in such a way that they are capable of being tested and refuted. This is what saves science from "dogmatism."[57]

At the level of jurisprudence, Scalia's categorical requisite led to tautology and contradiction. If juvenile offenders given the death sentence had to show that no one under a certain juvenile age was sufficiently responsible, their task was impossible. For the Supreme Court to declare the death penalty unconstitutional, it would need a case at bar. But the very case at bar would show that one jury had given the death penalty. Under this stricture, *the fact of the case would defeat the case.* This would lead to the conclusion that the juvenile death penalty could never be judged unconstitutional.

"Statistical magic"[58] was the term Scalia used to describe the *Stanford* dissent's sleight of hand, by which certain states were made to disappear from the analysis. In *Stanford,* with the aid of a far more potent magic, Scalia made the issue, the case, and the empirical playing field vanish as well. From the vantage point of science, though, what Scalia did in science's name "he cannot buckle . . . within the belt of rule."[59]

The Empirical Playing Field Reappears

In *Stanford* the rule of law was applied and the cases of Wilkins and Stanford were settled. Yet the empirical question at the heart of these cases remains decidedly unsettled. Looking at the legislative-enactments data, we are still unsure whether significant differences constitute a national consensus, and we have no clues from jury decisions data about where community sentiment stands. When we scrutinized the Court's so-called objective jurisprudence, we found that "statistical magic" reigned where social science was to rule. For the moment, let's ignore Scalia's arbitrary limit on social science evidence and look at some experimental results that directly address the questions of the juvenile defendant's age, the juvenile death penalty, and community sentiment.

The contradictory readings of community sentiment by both plurality and minority in *Stanford,* coupled with indefensible conclusions, underscore the need for a more systematic, objective, and experimental approach. P. B. Gerstenfeld and A. J. Tomkins[60] have taken such an approach. They presented their subjects with hypothetical death penalty cases in which they manipulated three variables. The crucial variable was *age:* the defendant was twelve, fourteen, fifteen, sixteen, seventeen, nineteen, or twenty-two. The second variable they manipulated was the *heinousness* of the crime: the defendant's actions were judged as being either very heinous or not very heinous. And the third variable involved *prior offenses:* the defendant either had a criminal record or had none. The researchers found that age did have a significant mitigating effect on death sentences, but the effect was not straightforward, since age interacted with heinousness as well as with previous offenses. For example, if the crime was seen as extremely heinous, heinousness seemed to mute the age effect, particularly if the defendant was sixteen or older. If the youth had a history of previous offenses, this likewise reduced the mitigating effect of age. Age, then, was not a monolithic variable having a well-defined and static effect; rather, age existed in a complex context of variables, where interactions and case-specific factors determined whether or not there was an age effect and how large it would be. Thus, although age may be a major determinant in general, its effect may be moderated, muted, or perhaps obliterated when examined in a specific and more realistic matrix of variables.

In an experiment that I conducted with three associates, mock jurors received three cases in random order.[61] These cases were thinly disguised versions of *Thompson, Wilkins,* and *Stanford* in which the defendants' names were altered but the fact patterns remained the same. We were thus investigating the *case* variable, because we suspected that these cases differed not only in the age of the defendant but, among other things, in the perceived *heinousness* of the crime. If that was so, different cases would produce different death sentence rates, independent of the age of the defendant. Whereas the Supreme Court seemed to be treating defendants Thompson, Wilkins, and Stanford as if age were the only difference, it may have been that age was confounded by the heinousness of the crime.

The second crucial variable was age: three juvenile ages (fifteen, sixteen, and seventeen) were used, corresponding to the ages of Thompson, Wilkins, and Stanford, respectively, plus two adult ages, eighteen and twenty-five. Each of the three cases given to subjects involved a defendant of a different age. The dependent measures were the verdict on a first-degree murder charge and the number of death sentences given. Our questions were these: Was there a case effect? Was there an age effect, and where did it begin to show? And was there an interaction effect between age and case, such that as the case increased in heinousness, the age effect was wiped out?

There were significant case effects for verdict and for death sentences. The percentages of death-qualified subjects who found the defendants guilty of first-degree murder in the three cases were 55.2 for *Stanford*, 88.1 for *Thompson*, and 97.0 for *Wilkins*. The percentages of death-qualified subjects rendering death sentences for the three cases were 22.4 for *Stanford*, 43.3 for *Thompson*, and 56.7 for *Wilkins*. Overall, then, the case variable affected death sentences directly and indirectly. There was an indirect effect in that far fewer defendants (55.2 percent) in the *Stanford* case were found guilty of first-degree murder, meaning that there was a reduction (by 44.8) in the percent of those who would be exposed to the risk of capital punishment. And there was a direct case effect, since even those who had been found guilty in *Stanford* had a death sentence rate approximately 50 percent lower than the rate in *Thompson*, and approximately 60 percent lower than the one in *Wilkins*. Thus, it would have been a mistake to compare cases as if one were simply comparing ages, for age interacted with the *perceived heinousness of the case*.

There was an age effect, but the picture here was more complicated than for case. The age effect was significant for verdict: the fifteen- and sixteen-year-olds were treated alike, and differently from the defendants aged seventeen, eighteen, and twenty-five, who had higher conviction percentages (see Table 11.4). For the death sentence measure, age was again significant, but only barely so. When we assessed the age effect for each case separately, we found a significant age effect only for the *Stanford* case; for the *Thompson* case it was marginal, and for *Wilkins* it was clearly not significant at all. Thus, as heinousness increased it became the dominant factor, and the effect of age became less and less significant.

In order to answer the question of where community sentiment stands, one must first define "community." If by "community" one means jurors, the "conscience of the community," as the Supreme Court does when it looks at jury decisions data, then "community" is the subset of this sample that consists of individuals who are death-qualified and who can serve on capital juries. All of the analyses the Court presented were based on that subsample. But one could advance the argument that "community" means everyone, both death-qualified people and excludables. This meaning is consistent with the one used in legislative enactments (the first of the objective indexes), in opinion poll readings, and in the Court's pronouncements in landmark cases such as *Weems, Trop,* and *Furman.*[62]

Over the total sample in our study, the case effect and the age effect

Table 11.4. Percentages of "guilty" verdicts (F%)[a] and death sentences (D/F%)[b] in cases resembling *Stanford, Wilkins,* and *Thompson* by age of defendant.

Case	Age 15		16		17		18		25		Total	
	F	D/F	F	D/F	F	D/F	F	D/F	F	D/F	F	D/F
Stanford	44	11	40	10	57	36	72	22	67	50	55	22
Thompson	96	32	83	33	92	58	81	44	82	55	88	43
Wilkins	93	53	100	56	100	71	91	46	100	56	97	57
Across cases	85	35	71	32	83	55	80	36	85	54		

a. The F% is the number of death-qualified subjects rendering a "guilty" verdict on the murder charge, over the total number of subjects rendering verdicts.

b. The D/F% is the number of death-qualified subjects giving the death sentence, over the number of first-degree murder verdicts.

were larger for both verdict and death sentences than they were in the death-qualified sample. To illustrate with the age effect, only 8 percent of the total sample was willing to give the fifteen- and sixteen-year-old defendants in the *Stanford* case the death penalty, whereas 11 percent of the death-qualified sample gave the death penalty to these defendants in this case. And only 25 percent of the total sample gave the death sentence to the fifteen- and sixteen-year-old defendants in the *Thompson* case, whereas 32 percent of the death-qualified subjects did. However, the interaction effect between age and case recurred in the most heinous scenario *(Wilkins)*. Here, the age effect disappeared for the total sample, as 49 percent gave the two youngest defendants the death sentence—a number that matched the overall percentage across all ages for that case.

Based on the results of the first experiment, the case that subjects had judged most heinous and that had produced the highest death sentence rate *(Wilkins)* was selected for further refinement. We created three versions in which the *type of defendant* varied: the defendant was (1) the principal murderer (that is, the one who did the stabbing, as in the original case), or (2) the accessory to the murder (the one who held the victim down while the principal stabbed her to death), or (3) an accessory to felony-murder (the getaway driver who remained outside the store but who knew that an armed robbery was taking place). These variations allowed us to see whether type of defendant would affect the death sentence rate. The importance of the felony-murder charge in our study is underscored by the fact that felony-murder crimes produce a sizable portion of death sentences for adults[63] and that 92 percent of juveniles currently sentenced to death are convicted under the felony-murder law.[64]

The age variable was extended. The defendant in our second study was thirteen, fourteen, fifteen, sixteen, seventeen, eighteen, or twenty-five. There were three dependent variables: the verdict on the underlying felony (armed robbery), the verdict on the main charge (first-degree murder or felony-murder), and the number of death sentences given (the main variable). Our questions were: Would type of defendant have an effect? And would the sentences subjects imposed on the accessory to murder be more like the ones they gave the principal murderer or more like the ones they gave the accessory to felony-murder? Would there be an age effect? Would it be between juveniles and adults, or would there be several effects as the juvenile age decreased still further? And would there be an interaction effect between type of defendant and age? Finally, subjects had to give reasons for their life-or-death decisions, and those reasons were categorized and analyzed to determine which reasons best predicted life versus death decisions.

For the death-qualified subsample and for the total sample, there were significant main effects for type of defendant for all dependent measures. Whether we looked at the verdict for the underlying felony (robbery), the verdict for first-degree murder or felony-murder, or the death sentence rate, the accessory to felony-murder was judged less blameworthy and less deserving of the death penalty than either the principal or the on-scene accessory. To illustrate, the guilty percentages for the first-degree murder charge were 67.7 percent for the accessory to felony-murder, 78.8 percent for the on-scene accessory, and 85.9 percent for the principal; for the death sentence percentages, the rates were, respectively, 11.4 percent, 40.4 percent, and 49.8 percent—differences that were quite significant.

For the age variable, there was a significant effect for both the murder verdict and the death sentence measure. Looking at the death sentence percentages (see Table 11.5), we see that there appear to be three distinct groupings. At the lower juvenile end (ages thirteen to fifteen), the death rates were 23.8 percent (thirteen), 30 percent (fourteen), and 25 percent (fifteen), with the death rate ranging between 23 and 30 percent. For older juveniles and those who were just barely adults (sixteen to eighteen), the death rates were 37 percent (sixteen), 29.6 percent (seventeen), and 40 percent (eighteen), with the rate ranging between 30 and 40 percent. And for twenty-five-year-olds, the death rate was close to 60 percent. The analyses showed significant differences among these three groups on the murder verdict and death sentence measure, with planned comparisons revealing a significant difference between the younger group

Table 11.5. Percentages of "guilty" verdicts (F%)[a] and death sentences (D/F%)[b] rendered by death-qualified subjects on charge of murder, by age and type of defendant.

Type of defendant	Age of defendant							
	13–15		16–18		25		Total	
	F	D/F	F	D/F	F	D/F	F	D/F
Principal	75.0	38.1	90.0	48.1	100.0	69.2	85.9	49.2
Accessory	73.1	31.6	78.1	44.0	100.0	50.0	78.8	40.4
Felony-murder accessory	58.6	5.9	81.5	9.1	55.6	40.0	67.7	11.4

a. The F% is the number of death-qualified subjects rendering a "guilty" verdict on the murder charge (either first-degree murder or felony-murder), over the number of subjects rendering a verdict.

b. The D/F% is the number of death-qualified subjects giving the death sentence (D), over the number who rendered a "guilty" verdict for the murder charge (F).

and the middle and older groups combined, and a significant difference between the younger and middle groups combined versus the older. Thus, there were two "discriminable" breaks in the death sentence rate by age.

Reasons for Life-or-Death Decisions

In order to categorize subjects' reasons for their life-or-death decisions, we developed a reliable and inclusive scheme that consisted of fourteen specific constructs for death and fourteen for life. Construct 1 involved the balance between aggravating and mitigating factors: the death reason (D1) gave greater weight to aggravating factors, whereas the life reason (L1) gave greater weight to mitigating factors. Construct 2 involved the subjects' perception of the defendant, in light of his past, as either a hardened criminal (D2) or not a hardened criminal (L2). Construct 3 involved a rehabilitative prediction: subjects saw the defendant either as beyond rehabilitation (D3) or not (L3). Construct 4 involved a prediction of future dangerousness (high versus low probability). Construct 5 involved the youth factor—whether subjects thought that youth was or was not a valid argument. Construct 6 involved the hardship factor—whether or not subjects a hard life a mitigating circumstance. Construct 7 involved a mental-disorder factor: whether or not a history of mental disorder, if believable, was a mitigating factor.

Construct 8 was the principal-versus-accessory factor: Did the defendant do the killing or not? Construct 9 involved intent: Was the killing committed deliberately, with premeditation, and in cold blood? Construct 10 involved control—whether the defendant was perceived as controlling the action or not. Construct 11 involved the parole factor: some subjects gave the death sentence if parole was possible, whereas others gave life if parole was not possible. Construct 12 cited deterrence: subjects either gave death because they believed it would deter, or gave life because they believed it would not deter. Construct 13 was the heinousness factor: How heinous or gruesome did the murder seem? And construct 14 involved the felony-murder factor: Did the murder while another crime was being committed?

Table 11.6 presents the most frequently cited death and life reasons. For subjects who decided to impose the death penalty, premeditation (D9), heinousness of the crime (D13), aggravating factors outweighing mitigating factors (D1), no rehabilitation possible (D3), and hardened criminal (D2) were the predominant reasons. For those reaching the life decision, the youth factor (L5) was cited most frequently, followed by the accessory factor (L8), the possibility of rehabilitation(L3), hardship as a mitigating factor (L6), and mental disorder as a mitigating factor (L7).

To identify higher-order factors, we performed a cluster analysis. The death reasons (see Table 11.6) divided into four clusters, accounting for 57.4 percent of the total proportion of the variance. The first cluster, with only one construct, was labeled "intent," and spoke to the traditional *mens rea* concern. Cluster 2, which we called "heinous/aggravated crime," focused on the gruesome crime, committing during another crime (robbery), in which aggravating factors outweighed mitigating ones and youth was not a valid factor. Cluster 3, which we called "hardened criminal," applied this label to the defendant, admitting no mental disorder and no rehabilitative possibilities. Cluster 4, with one construct, was called "control" and viewed the defendant as controlling the action. These clusters—especially 1 and 4, and to some extent 3—fit the picture of the principal most closely, and fit the accessory to felony-murder least of all.

For the life reasons, three clusters emerged and accounted for 52.4 percent of the total proportion of the variance. Cluster 1, called "youthful accessory," cited youth, the defendant's accessory status, and the fact that, on balance, mitigating factors outweighed aggravating ones. Cluster 2, called "rehab," cited a history of mental disorder and a belief that rehabilitation was possible. And cluster 3, called "hardship / no intent," found a background mitigating factor combined with the lack of "deathworthy" *mens rea*. Across these clusters, although youth was a central

Table 11.6. Cluster analyses of subjects' frequently cited reasons for deciding to impose the death penalty or to grant life.[a]

Reason	Percent citing
Death decision	
Cluster 1: Intent	
(D9) Intent	16.7
Cluster 2: Heinous /aggravated crime	
(D13) Heinousness of crime	16.1
(D1) Aggravating factors	12.6
(D5) Youth an invalid factor	7.5
(D14) Another crime committed with the murder	8.1
Cluster 3: Hardened criminal	
(D3) Beyond rehabilitation	10.9
(D2) Hardened Criminal	10.3
(D7) No mental disorder	8.1
Cluster 4: Control	
(D10) Defendant had control	3.5
Life decision	
Cluster 1: Youthful accessory	
(L5) Youth	26.7
(L8) Accessory	18.3
(L1) Mitigating factors	8.9
Cluster 2: Rehab	
(L3) Rehabilitation possible	15.7
(L7) Mental disorder	12.0
Cluster 3: Hardship / no intent	
(L6) Hardship	13.1
(L9) No intent	2.6

a. The analyses account for .5742 (death decision and .5237 (life decision) of the total proportion of the variance.

factor, there were past and future concerns (hardship and rehabilitation), along with a crime concern which found no intent for that accessory-type defendant.

In this second experiment, we purposely used the most heinous case, which in the first experiment muted if not obliterated the age effect. But even at this high level of heinousness, two main effects were discernible. First, type of defendant had an effect: the principal was judged more blameworthy and death-worthy than the accessory to felony-murder. This finding, under different conditions, replicated work on accessory to felony-murder which showed that community sentiment judged principals and accessories to felony-murder proportionally rather than equally, and thereby punished the former far more severely than the latter. The new finding added a caveat: when the accessory was not an accessory to felony-murder but was on the death scene, intended to kill, and assisted the principal in committing the murder, subjects saw no significant difference between the defendant who held the victim down and the one who did the stabbing.

The second main effect was for age, which emerged again despite the heinousness of the crime. In extending the age range, we noted two discriminable breaks: compared to the death sentence rate of the twenty-five-year-old adult, the rate for those who were sixteen, seventeen, and eighteen was significantly lower; and the rate for young juveniles of thirteen, fourteen, and fifteen was even lower. From the first experiment, where we found both a heinousness main effect and an interaction effect between age and heinousness, we speculated that with cases less heinous, and with the age range extended downward, we would get an even more pronounced age effect. Such speculation might be off the mark, however. For example, since we did not investigate cases of low heinousness, we do not know if the relation between age and heinousness is linear or curvilinear. Perhaps subjects would not give the death penalty at all for cases of very low heinousness, regardless of the defendant's age, and thus age might have its most pronounced effect in the midrange of heinousness.

The analysis of subjects' reasons for their life-or-death decisions removes any doubt that age of the defendant was the primary factor in life decisions, accounting for the largest segment of variance. The accessory factor weighed heavily as well in subjects' construal of the crime, since in such cases the defendant did not intend to kill, wasn't on the scene of death, and couldn't control the outcome. These subjects who decided against imposing the death penalty also pictured the defendant as having suffered hardship and mental disorder, yet not so severely that he couldn't be rehabilitated.

The subjects who imposed the death penalty saw the crime and the defendant not through polar-opposite constructs but through orthogonal ones. They accented intent and the heinousness and aggravated nature of the crime, and the fact that the defendant had control over the situation. In comparison to the focus of the "life" subjects, then, theirs was restricted far more to the moment of the act, the nature of the act, and the *mens rea*. Even when they looked to the past or the future, their picture was quite different from that of the "life" subjects: they saw a hardened criminal whom they did not think could be rehabilitated. When they cited "youth," it was to discount it as a factor.

In the Supreme Court's Eighth Amendment jurisprudence, community sentiment is given a central if not dispositive place in judgments of whether punishments are disproportionate or not. The problem has been determining which gauges to read, and how to read community sentiment accurately. Although newspaper articles, call-in radio shows, and unsolicited phone opinions may get the politician's eye and ear, the self-selected samples in these indexes do not represent the community. And even opinion polls that tap a representative sample may ask such broad, open-ended questions that the results tell us little about the crucial specifics. When the Supreme Court turned to legislative enactments, the plurality and minority analyses in both *Thompson* and *Stanford* were so far apart and so riddled with impermissible assumptions that no accurate reading emerged. And when the Court turned to jury decisions data, the data were inadequate to the task.

In controlled experiments where the fact patterns were clearly defined and manipulated, where heinousness, prior offenses, type of defendant, and age of the defendant were systematically varied, and where college students and adults, death-qualified subjects and all subjects made life-or-death decisions, and gave reasons for their decisions, a picture did emerge. In an extremely heinous case, where we expected the age effect to be most muted and where approximately 60 percent of subjects gave the death penalty to a twenty-five-year-old, approximately 25 percent gave it if the defendant was thirteen, fourteen, or fifteen, and approximately 35 percent gave it if the defendant was sixteen, seventeen, or eighteen. Thus, for the latter two groups, 75 percent and 65 percent of the death-qualified community refused to give the death penalty.

In *Stanford*, the majority concluded that there was no national consensus against the death penalty for sixteen- or seventeen-year-olds. Our results, for the most heinous case, showed 65 percent of subjects refusing to give the death penalty. This 65 percent figure, which would be called a landslide in an election, is conservative, and likely to understate the case against the juvenile death penalty for at least three reasons. First, the figure comes from an artificial experiment, a paper-and-pencil task that made it emotionally easy to decide in favor of the death penalty. If subjects had been actual jurors confronting a live juvenile, with all the emotions that attend such a case, the opposition figure of 65 percent might have been even higher. Second, the 65 percent figure comes from the death-qualified subjects; when we look at the total sample, the figure climbs higher. Third, from the earlier results, we would expect that 65 percent figure to climb as the case became less heinous. These results, then, although far from conclusive and perhaps understated, do appear to contradict the *Stanford* Court on the issue of where community sentiment draws the line in applying the death sentence to juveniles.

Line Drawing and Death

Social scientists can determine significance, but determining the significance of significance lies with the Supreme Court. In the matter of killing kids, it is not gauge readings per se but the justices who say whether these results reveal a societal consensus against the death penalty. It is the Court, finally, that draws the ultimate line. But there is one way in which the entire endeavor of line drawing runs into contradiction. Perhaps Justice Scalia understood this, even as he continued on his own contradictory course.

Scalia recognized that a fifteen-year-old murderer might be as morally culpable as an eighteen-year-old, perhaps even more so. Yet as J. L. Hoffmann noted, one of the "perils of line-drawing" is that "ordinal" proportionality is ignored, since offenders whose "just deserts" are equal are treated unequally.[65] Thus, if we drew the line at sixteen, the morally culpable fifteen-year-old, though as blameworthy as the eighteen-year-old, would not get the death penalty whereas the latter would. Moreover, when we draw lines at particular ages, we are no longer dealing with the actions, intentions, and history of a particular defendant. We are dealing with the "average fifteen-year-old," who exists only as an aggregate—a "statistical juvenile" who is only as real as the "average man."

In important yet troubling ways, legal labels such as "average person" or "average fifteen-year-old," and legal notions of finding an "age line" for the juvenile death penalty or creating some general "rule," are discordant with the way in which commonsense justice thinks about defendants and goes about deciding. This was discernible in the research findings on the juvenile death penalty; it was also evident in cases of accessory to felony murder (Chapter 9) and recidivist cases (Chapter 8). In recidivist cases, a labyrinth in which the Supreme Court became divided and lost, commonsense justice threaded its way through using the principle of proportionality. In applying the principle, ordinary citizens hinged the severity of the punishment not to a label ("recidivist") but to the moral blameworthiness of the actor.

In cases of felony-murder and accessory to felony-murder, commonsense justice made two distinctions that the law did not make. One distinguished the felony-murderer from the person who commits first-degree, premeditated murder: commonsense justice did not punish them equally, for it did not consider the actor who killed unintentionally to be as culpable as the actor who killed deliberately. The second distinction differentiated the felony-murder principal (triggerman) from the accessories: commonsense justice rejected the rule of equalism, where a one-size-fits-all punishment was meted out for the principal and the accessories. Again, the principle of proportionality was dominant, but now that principle was combined with the principle of individualized assessment of each defendant's culpability.

In the research presented on juveniles and the death penalty, statistical tests were run and a main effect for *age* was found. But isolating on the main effect distorts the true picture, for it eliminates complexities; and it is in the complexities, rather than in the oversimplifications, that a more interesting story emerges. The numerous "interaction effects" showed, for example, that the main effect for age decreases and evaporates as the heinousness of the case increases. Thus, three fifteen-year-olds who kill will not be judged and punished alike, if the first happens to be the *Stanford* defendant, the second the *Thompson* defendant, and the third the *Wilkins* defendant. Two sixteen-year-olds will likely receive differing percentages of death sentences if one has no prior record but the other has a history of prior offenses. And two seventeen-year-olds, one the principal doing the stabbing and the other the felony-murder accessory in the getaway car outside, are likely to be treated differently. Thus, *age* is one significant factor, but it is embedded in a shifting context of factors.

Perhaps the most enlightening findings come from the subjects' reasons for their decisions. Here we most clearly see complexity rather than simplicity in the factors they weigh. Whether they reach the "death" or the "life" decision, the "intent" factor (Was there an intent to kill?) looms large. Although this traditional *mens rea* concern comes to the foreground, it does not dwarf other concerns, since subjects also weigh the heinousness of the crime, aggravating factors, and whether the defendant was controlling the action; these factors are balanced against the age of the defendant, whether the defendant was an accessory or the principal, and other mitigating factors. Moreover, subjects also look at the defendant's past history, present mental state, and probable future. Did the defendant suffer hardships in the past? Was the defendant suffering from some mental disorder at the moment of the act? Is this a hardened criminal who is beyond future rehabilitation? Thus, commonsense justice considers complexity—which seems antithetical to simplistic line drawing.

Yet the Supreme Court, in *Thompson* and *Stanford,* tried to find such an age line. In *Stanford,* Justice Brennan's minority opinion claimed that the age line was eighteen, whereas Justice Scalia's plurality opinion asserted that the line had not advanced from *Thompson,* which held it to be sixteen. But even though Scalia defends his reading of the data and the line that he believed reflected community sentiment, his opinion revealed doubts and misgivings about line drawing at all.

We have seen the Court draw lines before. In *Coker,* the Court established a line beyond which the crime of rape was not death-worthy. In *Enmund* it declared that certain accessories to felony-murder, those who do not kill or intend to kill, cannot receive the death penalty. And in *Ford,* it drew yet another line, stipulating that death row inmates who go insane cannot be executed. But there are other lines, such as those based on intelligence quotient or age, that are different from and more troubling than the ones above. For example, in *Penry v. Lynaugh* the Court held that the death penalty was not prohibited for a mentally retarded defendant who had an IQ of between 50 and 63.[66] A number of justices indicated that they would have voted differently had Penry's IQ been lower. But how much lower? Is the line to be set at 45, or 40, or 30? If you draw the line at 45, are you willing to justify the death penalty for someone with an IQ of 46 but not for someone with an IQ of 44? We begin to realize that IQ, like chronological age, correlates imperfectly with moral culpability. This sort of ruler makes for a poor rule.

Perhaps our Founding Fathers, with a line already drawn at age seven, established the line-drawing course that the current Court is stuck on and is merely following as it seeks the new line. But that sort of *stare decisis* determinism denies choice. In *Furman,* the Court certainly had the choice and opportunity to abolish the death line completely, but did not. In *Thompson* and *Stanford,* it had the opportunity to end the juvenile death penalty line, but did not. In all likelihood, kids who commit murder will increasingly face man-sized punishment, and some judges and juries will no doubt impose it.

Our society is likely to continue killing kids until community sentiment establishes clearer and brighter lines on the Eighth Amendment playing field. This may mean a main effect for *age* that does not decrease or disappear when other factors are thrown into the mix—an age line that is unmistakably bright under all conditions. Such an effect does not obtain yet. But whether our society continues to impose the death penalty on kids who kill does not depend only on the community's sentiment; for the community may have clear and convincing sentiment, but the Supreme Court must see it and acknowledge it. Thus, sentiment must be accurately gauged and interpreted by Supreme Court justices, acting as good social scientists. And this has not yet happened. Making the "objective indicia" dispositive has not been matched with sound science, because the Supreme Court's "social science" cannot withstand social science scrutiny.

At the other extreme, our society may stop killing kids not because community sentiment evolves but because Supreme Court justices decide that they would rather be philosopher-kings than social scientists. For example, if five justices reject Justice Scalia's position and decide the matter based solely on their own moral proclivities, then death may be declared "cruel and unusual" based upon a majority of proportionality analyses. But the results could go the other way: a majority may declare death for juveniles proportionate and constitutional. Either way, a complete turn toward proportionality would not only be abrupt; it would rupture the long-standing connection between the Eighth Amendment and community sentiment. As a result, subjective Platonic Guardian decisions might come to rest on the moral consciences of five unelected individuals—a ground less firm than it would have been, had the decision rested on the conscience of the community.

The community's sentiment on age and the death penalty is not perfectly clear; but neither is it indistinct, or as disparate as the Court would have it. It is complex rather than simple. If there is a "rule," it may be "There is no simple rule." The life-or-death decision, the jury's final act, comes after the "story" is fashioned, a story in which many factors are weighed. In one story, age may dominate; in another story, age may be muted; in still another, it may be irrelevant.

Jurors make individualized judgments based on the case-specific facts. They do not draw generalized lines. We can ignore the particulars and statistically average their judgments across cases to find a general line, but this "average sixteen-year-old" composite doesn't exist in the flesh-and-blood, life-or-death drama of a real case, with a real defendant and a unique set of facts. Applying the average to particular cases may be courting considerable error. Yet the Court seeks a rule—a generalized rule that works across particular cases—and the justices would like to ground the rule on community sentiment.

The problem, then, is that the Court is seeking what citizens don't do: it is trying to discern community sentiment's "age line," but citizens do not typically draw a general age line, at least not with age as the only variable. Still, if the Court remains committed to line drawing and seeks the "average" sentiment, a reanalysis of the data along with experimental findings suggests that the Court in *Stanford* has not gotten it right. Legislative enactments show that significant differences exist in the way states treat fifteen-, sixteen-, and seventeen-year-olds, as contrasted with adults, in regard to the death penalty, and mock-juror experiments with death-qualified subjects likewise show significant differences.

In *Stanford*, Justice Scalia relegated social scientists to the sidelines, along with their "socioscientific," "ethicoscientific," and even "social science" evidence. He preferred that such evidence be presented to the court of public opinion, not the Supreme Court. Thus, social scientists could only watch the scrimmage that was *Stanford*—and what a spectacle it was. Supreme Court numerology and statistical magic fought it out on the Eighth Amendment playing field; the old hidden-ball trick was employed by both sides, as first one group of states was made to disappear, then another; cockfight analogies and straw-woman arguments were punted about. After half-time, alchemical magic was employed: the empirical issue was transmuted into a categorical one and the defendants vanished from their own case. And as the clock wound down, with grand sleight-of-hand the empirical playing field itself was made to vanish. In the end, as petitioners Heath Wilkins and Kevin Stanford were led off to death row, and as the social scientists rubbed their eyes in disbelief, perhaps all wondered whether this was justice, science, or just a bad dream.

On Self-Defense Justice

12

We first encountered the topic of self-defense in Chapter 3, where we looked at the case of the "subway vigilante," Bernhard Goetz. As in Akira Kurosawa's classic film *Rashomon,* interpretations of the incident varied depending on whose perspective each interpreter took; jurors moved from the illusory certainty of objective reality into the subjective minds of the actors, and ultimately into the sort of subjective stories that everyone constructs. In Chapter 8, concerning the question of when the State may punish, we saw that simple answers, such as "when the defendant has caused *harm*" or "when the defendant has committed a *criminal act,*" were contravened by accident, mistake, attempted crimes, and impossible acts. There again, simple answers involving observable events in objective reality gave way to more complex answers, involving *mens rea* and the unobservable intentions and perceptions of the defendant. In this chapter, the topics of self-defense and of the justification for punishment are conjoined. When we are finished, we will once again see a subjective plunge into intentions and stories, for the story of self-defense will be neither complete nor intelligible without it.

The chapters on punishment showed that the Eighth Amendment is constantly changing: the meaning of "cruel and unusual" evolves as community sentiment evolves, since the latter drives the former. We will see that the notion of self-defense is likewise mutable, but community sentiment is not the primary driver here; cases and case law commentary are the prime movers of change. In its common-law beginnings, self-defense law evolved from two distinct situations, one entailing justification and one entailing excuse. Over time, these two contexts would blur into one defense. Historically, attitudes would fluctuate concerning which perspective—objective or subjective—should dominate, and jurists would propose contradictory and inadequate schemes for handling "mistaken self-defense." As the "objective reasonable man" test assumed greater importance, jurists developed a stringent set of preconditions that sharply limited the number of successful self-defense claims. Yet despite the fact that the self-defense claim has had a long evolution and is still based on reasonable preconditions and the reasonable-man perspective, a question remains: Does self-defense law make sense, and is it reasonable, in terms of commonsense justice? To focus the question, we will use two exemplars that common-law judges foresaw, "felony prevention" and "chance medley," and one that they surely did not foresee: the case in which a battered woman kills her spouse.

Three Exemplars

The scene is eighteenth-century England. A man riding alone in his carriage is waylaid by a robber on horseback. The robber stops the carriage, pulls his knife, and announces his intention to rob. The man gets down from his carriage and the robber gets down from his horse. Instead of turning over his possessions, however, the man pulls his knife. Robber and victim face off in silence several yards apart, neither one making a move. Suddenly, the victim lunges and the fight begins; when it ends, the would-be robber is dead. At the trial, the man pleads self-defense. In this "felony prevention" case, the man is claiming not only that his act was justifiable but that he did what the law, public duty, and morality demanded of him: he prevented a felony.[1] He should not be punished for his act; in fact, he ought to be commended. The jury finds him not guilty.

From our perch as invisible observers, let's note a few things about this act and the defendant's "self-defense" claim. First, at the time the two men "fell to," it was unclear whether the robber intended to kill or merely intended to rob, as he had announced, or whether he was contemplating how to save face and exit. Second, it was the victim, not the villain, who initiated the fight that would take a life. Third, consider the alternatives not taken. What if the man had just stood there, maintaining the face-off, or announced that he would fight to the death if attacked? Might the robber have simply left, and looked for easier pickings elsewhere? What if the man had backed away, or taken to his heels? Perhaps the robber might have settled for the carriage and not pursued the escaping man at all. In sum, the defendant had options that he did not take, including warning, doing nothing, and retreating. From this perspective, his deadly actions do not appear to have been necessary.

In taking a life, this defendant claims to have achieved a higher good—namely, the prevention of a felony. The act may have been justified, but it does not appear to resemble self-defense as we ordinarily think of it. One of the preconditions for self-defense, and one of the ways we define a self-defense situation, is that there must be a *serious threat* to body or life; yet here, we are not sure that the man was threatened, let alone threatened seriously. A second precondition involves *imminence*, yet again we do not know if the threat (if there was one) was imminent, since the robber made no aggressive move. And third, since the man's back was not literally to the wall, he had the option of retreat, which he chose not to take. *Impossibility of retreat* is another precondition. If we ask whether the preconditions were met—whether the man was in a "take a life or lose your own" situation—the answer appears to be no. So, in this felony prevention situation, it seems that many of the usual self-defense requirements do not apply.

Situation two takes place in nineteenth-century America, in a town in the wild West. Two strangers are playing cards in a saloon when they begin to have words. Words are followed by push and shove; then fists and objects start flying. One man apparently goes for his gun, and the second man quickly reaches for his gun and fires. The first man is shot dead, never having gotten his gun out of the holster. The second claims self-defense.

In evaluating this claim, we see that there are a number of differences between this situation—called a "chance medley"—and the felony prevention situation. In felony prevention there is a villain who attempts a robbery and an innocent victim who does nothing to provoke. In a chance medley, both parties engage in the quarrel, and thus the defendant bears some responsibility for provoking, continuing, or escalating the situation. Under common law, chance medley was treated in one of two ways. If the defendant had killed "on the spot," the act was considered "homicide chance-medley, or manslaughter."[2] But if the defendant had retreated and had his back to the wall before killing, then it was seen as "homicide *se defendendo,* in which case there was no conviction but only forfeiture of goods."[3]

If impossibility of retreat is a precondition for the claim of *se defendendo* ("defending oneself"), then our defendant's claim must fail, unless he can meet one of the exceptions to the retreat precondition. If by some chance he owns the saloon, he might claim the *castle* exception: common law recognized that if there was one place a man should feel safe and secure and should not have to retreat, it was his castle. If our defendant does not own the saloon, he might claim the *true-man* exception (which is now out of favor but which was well regarded in nineteenth-century jurisprudence). Why should a good and true man have to turn and run, rather than do the "manly" thing of standing and meeting the aggression? But without some psychological character analysis, we cannot tell whether our defendant is a good and true man, or even any better than the guy he plugged. One legendary true man was Wild Bill Hickock, who, before becoming a U.S. Marshall, was twice tried for murder and twice acquitted by reason of self-defense. In one of those cases, a man had come to Hickock's home to collect some money owed, and "Hickock, hiding behind a window curtain, shot him down from inside the house as the man stood, without having drawn his gun, on the front porch."[4] The jury nonetheless acquitted on grounds of self-defense. Perhaps this is a variation on the true-man exception, or a front-porch extension of the castle exception. Then again, maybe it's an instance of jury nullification, indicating that "law in fact" may depart from "law on the books" for self-defense claims.

In the felony prevention case it is easier to apply the castle and true-man exceptions, since we can view the man's carriage as an extension of his castle (an eighteenth-century mobile home) and see the felony as burglary; in addition, we can more easily view the innocent as a true man. In the *se defendendo* case, which is more likely to take place in a barroom or on the street, the castle exception is improbable and the defendant's innocence ended when his participation in the quarrel began. Thus, historically, *se defendendo* was regarded differently from cases of felony prevention, and the fact that defendants were punished with forfeiture of their goods indicated that the law judged them more culpable than defendants who claimed felony prevention. With the differences highlighted, *se defendendo* looks more like a claim to *excuse* the person rather than to *justify* the act. There is no noble motive of attempting to thwart a felony; rather, the defendant commits a wrongful killing and argues that, for reasons peculiar to him and the situation, he should not be blamed or punished.

There is another precondition, which we can introduce by varying the chance medley situation slightly. What if the man who was killed was not reaching for his gun at all? What if he was reaching for a knife, or just intending to throw a punch, when the defendant fired and killed him? The precondition requires that the defendant be faced with *equal force* or a *proportional response*. If the facts of the case are altered, a number of things change: the fist is not likely to be seen as a *serious threat*; perhaps the knife is not a serious threat as well; and if the threat decreases, then *imminence* is lacking. When the gun-to-gun situation changes to a fist- or knife-to-gun situation, an imbalance appears: the defendant is no longer using a force equal or proportional to the threat. These preconditions are not independent of one another. Change one, and others are likely to change as well. In addition, we see another reason for the requirement that there be no possibility of retreat, and another argument against the true-man exception: if someone retreats, rather than impetuously firing on the spot, he has more time to appraise the situation accurately. In sum, the law of self-defense is a demanding law, under which the defendant must satisfy a lengthy list of preconditions in order to make a successful claim of self-defense.

The common-law distinction between felony prevention and *se defendendo,* and between justification and excuse, disappeared in the nineteenth and twentieth centuries as courts and legal writers conflated the two into one self-defense doctrine. As different as these two roots are, it is important to note the similarities. Both of our exemplars involve strangers; both involve men; both involve armed men. In these cases, the incident has no "history" to speak of, since the narrative begins only a few moments prior to the act. Thus, the whole story of self-defense can be described briefly, and just a few actions tell us all we need to know about whether the self-defense preconditions were met. Now we meet the third situation.

The girl is in love and marries young, even though her parents disapprove of her choice. Several months later, while drinking, he slaps her around. She cries and threatens to leave. He apologizes profusely, professes his love, swears that it will never happen again; she believes him. He does it again a month later, causing a bit more physical damage. Words of contrition, gifts, and promises of love follow, and she believes him again. Her parents, unwilling to come to the rescue, wash their hands of her—"You made your bed, now lie in it." She gets pregnant in the hope that a child will help him mature. He grows more tyrannical instead. He controls all the finances, comes to dictate every phase of her life, and isolates her socially. Verbal abuse, humiliation, threats, and physical and sexual abuse become more and more frequent and severe. She begins making trips to the emergency ward for broken bones, supposedly caused by falls.

She calls the police, but his beating stops when they arrive. The police leave after giving him only a warning. He beats her more savagely for the call. She moves out of the house, but he tracks her down. He tells her that if she does not come home with him, he will kill the child; she goes with him, and is beaten. As time goes by, she becomes more depressed, feeling hopeless and suicidal. After one brutal beating and humiliation, he says that he's going to kill her later, but first he's going to watch television while he drinks himself into a stupor. One hour later, while he is watching television, or perhaps sleeping in front of the television, she takes one of his guns, walks up behind him, and shoots him in the head. He dies, and she pleads self-defense.

At first glance, the case of the battered woman who kills seems the weakest of all. In many ways it is quite different from felony prevention and chance medley. For one thing, this is not a situation involving strangers; it has a long and significant history, which, from a psychological or dramatic point of view, is absolutely essential to an understanding of the deadly denouement. If we were to foreshorten the tale, beginning at the moment of the act or even just one hour earlier, with the beating and threat, the story would become skewed, distorted—almost a parody of what really happened. Second, this "relationship case" takes place in the home, not out in public, yet the castle provided no special sanctuary or privileged retreat for the defendant, since the husband owned half the castle. Third, this case does not involve two men of roughly equal size, with equal arms at the ready; throughout the long history that preceded the killing, as well as in the brief moment of the killing, the size, strength, and arms of the two parties were never equal. Still, if the law's focus is a narrow one, foreshortening context to an hour's worth of action, and if the law's perspective is an objective one, judging the action through the eyes of the reasonable man, then the preconditions of serious threat, equal force, imminence, and no possibility of retreat have not been met. In these circumstances, the woman's claim of self-defense claim will fail.

Enter Mistake, and the Subjective Perspective

Up through Blackstone's time, the common-law position seemed to be that "mistake," reasonable or unreasonable, excuses a harmful action. It excuses, according to the jurist Sir Matthew Hale, because "an act done in ignorance of the true facts is 'morally involuntary.'"[5] In the two centuries following Blackstone, courts and commentaries began to differentiate reasonable from unreasonable mistakes, claiming that the former constituted a defense but not the latter.[6]

Where does mistake in general fit with the specifics of self-defense? Let's assume that the robber in our felony prevention case had a change of heart during his silent face-off with the victim—that he had given up the goal of robbery and, fearing for his own life, was looking for a safe way out. If so, then the innocent man was mistaken about the highwayman's intent and the danger he posed, and was acting on that mistake. In our case of chance medley, let's assume that the first man was reaching not for his gun but for a handkerchief, intending to pacify his assailant. In these circumstances, the second man who draws and fires is acting under the mistaken view that the situation is life threatening. And if, in our third example, the husband's threat was idle, just bullying bluster that would have been forgotten in the haze of his hangover, then our defendant was acting on a mistaken perception.

There are no mistakes in external reality. Mistakes exist only in the mind. It is the perceiver who construes and interprets events mistakenly, and therefore mistake is located in the realm of the subjective. So if mistakes (reasonable mistakes) excuse the actor or justify the act, the law must be willing to enter the defendant's subjective perceptions in order to judge whether the mistake is reasonable or not. Thus, the objective, reasonable man cannot continue to view events from his detached and distant perch, because from that distance and angle he might fail to detect the intentions and motives of the key actors. No, mistake requires the objective, reasonable man to climb down and stand in the shoes and subjectivity of the defendants, in order to see what they see.

"Seeing what they see" does not mean he has to give up his objective, reasonable judgment. Yet in the following cases, the observer is asked not just to see what they see but *to be what they be*. In an 1830 case, *Grainger v. State*,[7] the victim, a man named Broach, was described as a "reckless bully"[8] who "designed to commit trespass and battery to the body of Grainger, without intending to kill him."[9] Grainger, who killed Broach, was described as "a timid, cowardly man."[10] Grainger's fear might relate to our felony prevention or chance medley defendants, but the case is most applicable to the battered woman who kills. The court held that Grainger had acted in self-defense, even if the danger he perceived was the product of an unreasonable belief. "The court made clear that it was the defendant's mental state, and not that of a reasonable man . . . , that was to be assessed."[11]

According to this ruling, our reasonable man, who has stepped into the defendant's subjective viewpoint, must now make a Proteus-like transformation from reasonable man to timid coward in order to understand the fears and actions of the defendant. Moreover, in light of the *Grainger* court's view that the mistake could be unreasonable or reasonable, another Proteus-like transformation is required: the reasonable man must now ask himself not if *he* would have construed the events as life threatening, but if it is *possible that Grainger construed* the events that way, even if that construal was unreasonable. This final transformation all but erases the last vestige of "objectivity" from our objective, reasonable man and leads to an almost completely subjective approach to self-defense, mistake, and justification.

While influential cases and commentary were still insisting that the mistake in self-defense must be reasonable,[12] a trend toward subjectivizing the reasonable man was becoming evident. For example, in *Hill v. State* (1908),[13] the court noted that although an attack with fists is ordinarily not regarded as a serious threat, there "may be many cases in which the disparity between combatants is so overwhelming that the one of superior power may inflict great bodily harm."[14] And in a 1934 case, also involving two men, the court commented that the deceased was 6 feet 1 inch tall, weighed 200 pounds, and was "powerful and aggressive," whereas the defendant was 5 feet 6 inches tall and weighed 155 pounds.[15] These cases involving size disparity relate more to the battered woman who kills: the two parties are typically very different in height, weight, and strength. So now the reasonable man is asked to make another Protean change—namely, to assume the shape and size of the defendant. And when the defendant is a woman, the reasonable man must become a reasonable woman. This in fact is what the court said in the 1977 case of *State v. Wanrow,*[16] which "involved a small woman who was on crutches because her foot had been broken and who shot a much larger male whom she believed to be threatening to sexually molest her children."[17]

Our reasonable man is required to change gender, shape, size, and perspective as the case dictates. Other cases have endowed the reasonable person with disabilities and handicaps: a defendant suffering from a severe hernia,[18] another who was in poor physical condition,[19] another who was missing three fingers and had a bandaged hand,[20] yet another who was a sixty-five-year-old man.[21] In the *Goetz* case, the defendant's history, particularly his previous muggings, and his knowledge of crime on the New York City subways were deemed relevant and appropriate to the jury's deliberations. And in *Wanrow,* social acculturation became a factor. The court "took the view that women are acculturated not to use non-deadly force when they are threatened; rather, they are socially trained either to submit totally to a male, or to resort to deadly force."[22] Thus, the defendant's past experience, developmental history and acculturation, traumas and scars all may play a part in how he or she perceives events. The reasonable person must take an almost thoroughly subjective perspective in order to judge the defendant's subjective culpability.

This subjective line on self-defense and mistake, along with the view that reasonable and unreasonable mistakes both lead to justification, was and still is the minority position. The majority of jurisdictions embrace the standard of the objective, reasonable person, and the majority of cases distinguish reasonable mistakes, which excuse or justify, from unreasonable ones, which do not. But making a distinction between two types of mistake leads to an unreasonable outcome, a result illustrated by the case of the battered woman who kills.

Let's consider what charge the prosecution will bring. Since the victim was asleep, heat of passion or provocation are irrelevant, so manslaughter is out. The charge is likely to be murder, in the second or first degree. If the reasonable person or reasonable juror thinks that the defendant made a reasonable mistake (in believing that she was in imminent danger of being killed), then her act will be seen as justified. But if the jurors view her mistake as unreasonable, then there is no justification and they will find her guilty of murder. Note, first, that there is no middle option: when justification and excuse merge into justification, then either the defendant is justified or she is not; in this scheme, there are no partial excuses. Second, consider that the jurors may judge her mistake unreasonable and find her guilty of murder. Does this outcome make sense? Is she really just as culpable as the more typical murderer? Wasn't she acting *in extremis,* caught in a "maelstrom of circumstance,"[23] rather than acting coolly and coldly, with deliberation and perhaps premeditation? She may not even have wanted to kill at all; perhaps she merely wished to end the threat to her life. If these notions regarding her intent are near the mark, then there is a difference in culpability between this defendant and the cold-blooded murderer. Yet according to the dominant legal view, she will be judged and punished like the murderer if her perceptions are deemed "unreasonable."

Is Self-Defense Law Biased against Women Who Kill?

C. K. Gillespie puts forth a number of strong conclusions: "the law of self-defense is a law for men";[24] "the law of self-defense discriminates against women";[25] and "where self-defense is involved, . . . it is difficult to avoid the conclusion, looking at convictions, that jurors frequently are unwilling to believe that it is *ever* reasonable for a woman to kill her mate."[26] The first two conclusions assert a bias *in the law,* whereas the third asserts a bias *in the jurors.* The next chapter presents an empirical evaluation of those claims. First, however, we must see why such claims have been put forth.

Researchers who have examined verdicts in cases where a battered woman killed her mate and claimed self-defense,[27] as well as legal advocates who defend such defendants and comment on their trial experiences,[28] have shown that acquittals on the basis of self-defense are rare. This rarity is not necessarily the result of bias in the law or bias in the jurors. Yet statistics that reveal disparities in charging and sentencing have been marshaled to support the "bias hypothesis."

> Women charged in the death of a mate have the least extensive criminal records of any female offenders. However, they often face harsher penalties than men who kill their mates. FBI statistics indicate that fewer men are charged with first- or second-degree murder for killing a woman they have known than are women who kill a man they have known. And women convicted of these murders are frequently sentenced to longer prison terms than are men. The following case illustrates the discrepancies in attitudes that may lead to this uneven sentencing:
>
> In 1978 an Indiana prosecutor, James Kizer, refused to prosecute for murder a man who beat and kicked his ex-wife to death in the presence of a witness and raped her as she lay dying. Filing a manslaughter charge instead, Kizer commented. "He didn't mean to kill her. He just meant to give her a good thumping."[29]

Women do kill far less often then men, which is one reason there are so few women on death row. But when women kill, their pattern is different. Unlike men, women rarely kill strangers; most kill people they know—a family member or a mate. This sort of familial killing is more often regarded as heat-of-passion rather than cold-blooded premeditated murder, and it seldom becomes a capital case.[30] So type of killing, in addition to infrequency, contributes to the fact that few women receive the death sentence. But if we look *within* this type of crime, we see that gender disparities in charging and sentencing are hard to reconcile with blind justice and strengthen the prima facie case claiming the existence of bias in prosecutorial discretion, jurors' decisions, and the law.

The case asserting bias in the law is most evident when we examine the preconditions for self-defense in light of the reasonable-person standard. Although there has been a subjectivizing trend, the objective standard of reasonableness still remains dominant. Let's begin with the precondition that the defendant must show she was threatened with serious harm. From an objective point of view, a man advancing on a woman with his fists, or even hitting her with his fists or kicking her with his feet, may not be regarded as presenting serious harm under the law. To those who have worked with battered women, or who have studied the problem, this legal construal of the harm as "not serious" is crazy—seriously out of touch with reality.

In Lenore Walker's studies of battered women, the overwhelming majority of injuries to these women were inflicted by men's hands, fists, and feet.[31] And such assaults cause more than just injuries: M. E. Wolfgang's study of homicide reveals that one fourth of female homicide victims died from beatings delivered by hands, fists, and feet.[32] Thus, what the law may regard as nonlethal and not serious seems to produce a high percentage of deadly outcomes. But the legal outcome is absurd, say the critics, for if a woman picks up a knife or a gun and uses it on the man advancing with his fists, she can—according to the reasonable-person standard—be seen as overreacting, using unequal force to counter the so-called nonlethal threat. Yet if the *Wanrow* court is to be believed, she is not socially acculturated to resolve the dispute with a fistfight. Even if one rejects that court's foray into developmental-psychology theory, one must still think through the pragmatic aspects of the situation. Since the contest will probably involve a lightweight against a heavyweight, the woman's fists are likely to be ineffective against the raging bull, and may in fact only enrage him so that he inflicts more "nonlethal" blows. If he sees red, she's going to see black-and-blue, if she lives to see anything.

The precondition requiring that the defendant show she could not retreat is particularly problematic from a strictly objective point of view, a view embedded in the most frequently asked question in such cases: Why didn't the abused woman leave the premises?[33] After all, says the objective, reasonable person, if the abusive man was sleeping, she could simply have walked out the door and driven away. But the facts are that most battered women, including that very small subgroup who kill, have tried to leave. Some returned because they were physically dragged back, and some because of threat and coercion. In addition to trying to leave, many have called the police, or even gone to court to get the man out of the castle; the results have been ineffective more often than not. Even when ordered by a court to stay away, some batterers violate the court order with impunity, showing the woman that she has no control and that he cannot be controlled. Whereas outsiders see the exit door unblocked, the insider, with her history of trying and failing, comes to see no escape. Angela Browne has reported that 98 percent of battered women who kill and 90 percent of battered women who do not kill believe that they could not escape.[34]

There is still another component to the escape possibility. Many batterers let these women know that if they try to escape they will be killed. A study conducted by G. W. Bernard and colleagues has shown that attempting to leave is a high-risk factor—that is, it significantly increases the probability that the woman will be killed.[35] In other words,

many of the batterers make good on their threat. Battered women sometimes become good psychologists—that is, they become adept at reading
the subtle cues which are likely predictors of imminent violence; and if
they read the "I'll kill you if you try to leave" threat as genuine, then
subjectively they can believe that the unblocked door offers no escape.

If the case of the battered woman who kills is viewed as more akin to
felony prevention than to the chance medley situation *(se defendendo)*—
where she acts to prevent the felony of assault, battery, manslaughter, or
murder—then the retreat requirement no longer holds. And it certainly
does not hold when the felony was committed in the defendant's own
castle. It appears, then, that the case of the battered woman who kills is
viewed not as akin to felony prevention but more as a derivative of
chance medley, even though this "derivation" stretches the notion of *mutual* combat between rough and ready equals to the surreal and unreal.
Yet according to this view she must retreat even though the castle is hers,
because it is also his. Still, one could argue that the case of the battered
woman who kills corresponds more closely to felony prevention than to
chance medley.

In "confrontational" cases, where a man advanced on a woman with
his hands, fists, and feet at the ready or advanced with a knife or gun in
his hand, the objective, reasonable person is almost certain that mayhem,
and perhaps murder, was likely to follow. The objective, reasonable person needs to make a decision on three issues before judging the
defendant's self-defense claim. First, was the threat a serious one? This
may have been clear if the man was holding a gun, but less clear if he had
no weapon other than his hands. Second (depending on the weapon he
was holding and the weapon she picked up to defend herself), were the
forces equal or unequal?. And third, could she have retreated or not before using deadly force?

In "nonconfrontational" cases, where a woman killed a man while he
was passively watching television or sleeping, she runs into the imminence requirement, which is likely to undermine her defense. If "imminence" is construed narrowly as "impending," "ready to take place," or
"immediately," then the objective, reasonable person would claim that
there was no immediate threat and hence no immediate cause or
justification for deadly force.

A narrowly construed imminence requirement can lead to some absurd
conclusions. In confrontational cases, does the woman have to wait until
her assailant's hands are around her throat, or until he lands his first
punch or kick, before being justified in defending herself? Does a rape
victim have to wait until the attack is underway and the rapist is on top

of her? If imminence is defined that narrowly, then the woman is allowed to defend herself legally only at the point when that defense is most likely to be ineffective. *State v. Schroeder* (1978) involved a male prisoner who killed his cellmate as he slept, after the cellmate—a larger and stronger man—had threatened to rape him the next morning.[36] The Nebraska court found that Schroeder had not acted in self-defense, since the attack was not imminent. But Schroeder knew that his cellmate would and could make good on his threat and that telling a prison guard was not a realistic alternative, since such "snitching" would only have invited deadly reprisals from other inmates. From Schroeder's subjective point of view, with no alternative and no way out of the cell, the attack was as good as imminent.

Different Voices, a New Disorder, and an Old Problem

Feminist jurisprudes are generally in agreement that self-defense law, on the books and in application, works to the disadvantage of female defendants who have killed a man. When it comes to recommendations, though, there are different voices, proposing quite different and sometimes incompatible solutions.[37] Perhaps the least challenging perspective advocates *equal treatment* under the law: whatever the law and its standard, it should be applied in nondiscriminatory ways. This call for fairness and equal justice is difficult to disagree with. "While not insensitive to differences in the power and opportunities of women in many of the situations of contemporary life, equal treatment feminists worry that rules intended to accommodate those differences, to adjust for disadvantage, or to promote affirmative action will perpetuate negative stereotypes, reinforce adverse cultural messages, and therefore operate to the ultimate disadvantage of women."[38]

A more radical perspective stresses *different norms,* claiming that men and women view morality in distinctly different ways. This position builds on Carol Gilligan's influential study *In a Different Voice: Psychological Theory and Women's Development,* which identifies a male pattern grounded in abstract rights of equally capable and equally powerful autonomous individuals, and a female pattern grounded in connection and caring, acknowledging a complex context, and emphasizing ongoing relationships and responsibilities.[39] Gilligan was suggestive; she and other researchers have recognized that males and females are not bimodally split and that, in fact, both males and females use *both* patterns or "voices." But some advocates of this position extend and polarize

Gilligan's views. If one sees laws and standards as male laws and standards, then one will call for different norms. This position, for example, would support *Wanrow*'s substitution of a reasonable-woman standard for the reasonable-man standard. But this position, which views the law as revealing a male orientation toward abstract rights, sees "gender bias in its very structure," and eliminating such bias would require "a radical change in the methodology of moral and legal analysis."[40]

The third perspective, which stresses *different situations,* recognizes that there are "crucial differences in the life situations of women and men."[41] Beyond the fact that women can bear children and men cannot, there are less sharp though no less important differences in acculturation, role stereotyping, socioeconomic status, opportunities for advancement to the highest professional levels, and the use of force and aggression in interpersonal relationships. A perspective emphasizing different situations would applaud the *Wanrow* court's recognition of an acculturation difference and would favor not just a reasonable-woman standard but a battered-woman standard, which is not all that different from *Grainger*'s standard of the "cowardly, timid man." One might wonder whatever happened to the concept of reasonableness, and argue that we ought to formulate a standard of the "reasonable battered woman." This might be an oxymoron, or it may be a distinction without a difference; for could we reliably distinguish the reasonable battered woman from the unreasonable battered woman? And if we adopt this distinction, have we gone so far into the subjective that anything goes and anything justifies?

In the past decade, one direction taken by legal advocates has been to try to get testimony supporting the "battered-woman syndrome" (BWS) admitted into evidence—an effort that has met with great success. A "battered woman," as defined by Lenore Walker, is "one who is repeatedly subjected to any forceful physical or psychological behavior by a man in order to coerce her to do something he wants her to do without concern for her rights."[42] But beyond battering, the woman is also likely to suffer social isolation, almost complete subjection to the batterer, threats, humiliations, and sexual abuse. A battering cycle—of minor abuse, followed by a major battering incident, followed by loving contrition, followed by all these stages repeated again and again—can reinforce the relationship in a perverse way. In such a climate, the woman may enter a state of "learned helplessness" in which she comes to believe that nothing she can do will matter.[43] Depression and lower levels of response ensue.

Let's see what such testimony is likely to do for the defendant, and what it is not likely to do. If the prosecutor asks and the jurors wonder why the woman didn't leave her batterer, then expert testimony on battered-woman syndrome can help the jurors understand her subjective psychological state. Through testimony about learned helplessness, and about the way in which the defendant came to believe that she was helpless and that the situation was hopeless, the jurors can understand her "apparent apathy and passivity." In testimony concerning depression, jurors will hear how depression inhibits activity; moreover, they will hear that depressives come to view themselves negatively, believing that nothing will change for the better and that the future will be worse. Such testimony may be indeed helpful in answering the most frequently asked question: Why didn't she leave?

But this is *not* the most important question at trial. The important question is: Why did she pick up the weapon and kill? Here, testimony on battered-woman syndrome (1) provides no answer, (2) provides a contradictory answer that undercuts her self-defense claim, (3) suggests an answer that leads to improbable results, or (4) suggests an answer that neither defendant nor counselor intends. Battered-woman syndrome paints a portrait of a woman who is extremely passive—dependent, beaten into submission, offering no resistance, seeing even an unobstructed exit door as blocked. Yet how can we explain the fact that this extremely passive woman suddenly turns active and violent, and uses deadly force to kill her batterer? The syndrome does not seem to furnish the answer. It explains why she didn't leave; but the more the testimony stresses her passivity and helplessness, the greater the contradiction between her putative psychological state and her active, violent killing.

As for improbable effects, consider four situations in which a woman kills.[44] The first is the confrontational killing that occurs during a serious battering. One study found that such cases represented only a third of the killings; the other three situations were nonconfrontational and accounted for two-thirds of the cases.[45] In the second situation, the battered woman leaves, files for divorce, gets an court order of protection, but is repeatedly stalked, pursued, and beaten by her husband; eventually, in desperation, she kills. This pattern fits about 40 percent of the cases. The third situation involves the battered woman who kills her mate while he sleeps—a scenario that corresponds to about 21 percent of the cases. And the fourth is the battered woman who hires a killer to shoot her mate (about 6 percent of the cases).

Setting aside the confrontational killing (since this is the easiest context in which to support a self-defense claim), note what happens in some of the other cases with learned-helplessness testimony. In the second case, where the woman takes active steps to leave her batterer and end their relationship, her behavior, which we may applaud, contradicts assertions that she was in a state of learned helplessness. In this case, testimony on battered-woman syndrome may be ruled inadmissible because it doesn't fit, or attacked on cross-examination because it neither fits nor explains. The "contract killing" case, where the defendant looks most culpable and the self-defense claim appears weakest, may turn out to be "the strongest case of all"[46] with BWS testimony. "The utter passivity, the inability to act even when the abuser is sleeping, the apparent dependence on the intervention of a male support figure, all reinforce a diagnosis of battered wife syndrome."[47]

Such testimony may have an unintended effect. Let's say an expert tells the jurors that the defendant has a syndrome which fits within the category of post-traumatic stress disorders, as characterized by the American Psychiatric Association in its *Diagnostic and Statistical Manual of Mental Disorders* (DSM-III-R).[48] A juror might say, "Oh, so you're telling me she's crazy—she's got a mental disorder." This interpretation moves the defendant closer to the insanity plea than to self-defense. Whereas the defense counsel is trying to claim that the act was self-defense and justifiable, BWS testimony gets the jurors to focus not on "what she did" but on "who she is."[49] Thus, in the light of psychological-disorder testimony, her beliefs that the attack was imminent and that the unblocked exit door was nonexistent now look like unreasonable and mistaken beliefs at best, or outright delusions at worst. If she were pleading insanity, or diminished capacity, or guilty but mentally ill (GBMI), jurors might reach for a mitigating or excusing verdict after hearing such testimony; but since she is claiming self-defense, testimony on the battered-woman syndrome may be misdirected.

On Flunking, Failing, and Passing

The battered woman who kills in a nonconfrontational situation is likely to flunk the "objective, reasonable person" test; even in confrontational situations, it may be difficult to pass all the self-defense preconditions. The battered woman's advocates, however, are likely to claim that it is the law that fails her. In seeming to demand reasonableness *in extremis*, the law may be asking human nature to be what it is not. Justice Holmes, long associated with the "objective, reasonable man" standard, was referring to this unrealistic expectation when he stated that "detached reflection cannot be expected in the presence of an uplifted knife."[50]

We wonder, then: Is "reasonable" reasonable? Does the law of self-defense make sense to commonsense justice? Or does the objective perspective fail as good justice? On preconditions and perspective, the law remains divided. As to whether unreasonable mistakes can excuse as well as reasonable ones, different cases and commentary produce different answers. And the law is far from working out a coherent middle ground for "imperfect self-defense."[51]

To one who stands outside the law, all the nuances of self-defense can seem like much ado about nothing. Shakespeare, who had little love for lawyers and less "for this kind of legal hairsplitting,"[52] satirized *se defendendo* in Hamlet, where two clowns discuss Ophelia's suicide by drowning, and one comes up with a way in which, *se offendendo,* she can get a Christian burial nonetheless: "If the man goes to the water and drowns himself, it is, will he, nill he, he goes; mark you that? But if the water comes to him and drown him, he drowns not himself: argal he that is not guilty of his own death shortens not his own life."[53] The humor of this passage is likely to be lost on a woman who is being threatened not by the water but by the man coming at her, for if she stops the man with deadly force and pleads self-defense she will likely find herself in difficult legal waters.

The Self-Defense Drama

13

Some people have asserted that there is a general bias against women who kill their mates. If these people are right, then we should find evidence of that "general bias" in the verdicts subjects render: we would predict few "not guilty by reason of self-defense" (NGRSD) verdicts in cases where women kill their mates. Yet even if NGRSD verdicts turn out to be few, this fact may not necessarily indicate bias; few such verdicts may be reasonable, given the case and the perspective. If subjects view self-defense preconditions from the perspective of the objective, reasonable person, particularly in a case where a woman killed a sleeping husband, NGRSD verdicts should be rare—but not because of bias. To document bias, then, we need to rule out other hypotheses that could account for such findings. When we ask more specific questions in experimentally controlled ways, a richer, more revealing story emerges.

One specific question is whether subjects will take an objective or subjective perspective when considering whether the defendant faced a serious threat, used equal force, and had the option of retreat. Similarly, will they define "imminence" narrowly and objectively, or will they allow subjective context and history to affect their judgments? And will they render the NGRSD verdict far more often in confrontational cases than in nonconfrontational cases, because the latter fail the objective test? Or will we find (contrary to the hypothesis of bias and the demands of reasonableness) that subjects generally support nonconfrontational cases, despite the fact that such cases fail to meet the objective test?

Beyond the alleged general bias against a woman who kills a man and pleads self-defense, C. K. Gillespie asserts yet another bias: jurors expect the woman to "plead that she was temporarily insane."[1] In an early cause célèbre, the "Burning Bed" case, which became a book and then a Holly-wood movie, Francine Hughes was accused of setting her sleeping hus-band on fire and killing him; the jury found her not guilty by reason of temporary insanity.[2] To some, the defense strategy of pleading insanity rather than self-defense was indicative of that bias. If this "insanity" bias exists, we would predict that subjects would choose a "not guilty by rea-son of insanity" (NGRI) verdict over a "not guilty by reason of self-defense" (NGRSD) verdict, if they could choose between them.

When the issue changes from bias to remedy, the question becomes: Does expert testimony correct the alleged general bias against women who kill their mates, or does it reinforce the insanity bias?[3] Testimony for the battered-woman syndrome (BWS) may reinforce the self-defense por-trayal by explaining to jurors why the defendant did not leave the house and how she could see the situation as life threatening, imminently dan-gerous, and affording no escape; but jurors who hear such testimony may more readily move to an insanity portrayal. Does such testimony help correct the alleged general bias? If so, whom does it help, and why? In evaluating the helpfulness of expert testimony, we might expect BWS tes-timony to be of little help in straightforward, confrontational self-defense cases; in fact, such testimony might muddy the waters and make the case worse by turning the jury's attention from what the defendant did to who she is. Expert testimony is most needed in the "hard cases"—for instance, the nonconfrontational cases in which the woman kills her batterer while he's sleeping. So the more important question is: Does BWS testimony help in the cases where help is most needed?

No Bias—But No Strict Objectivity Either

In an experiment looking at factors that predict verdicts when a battered woman kills her husband, Diane Follingstad and her colleagues created a detailed "battered-woman" case.[4] Subjects received a scenario describing the couple's courtship and marriage, how and when the husband began abusing his wife, and how his physical abuse escalated in frequency and severity from shoving to punching and kicking. Incidents leading to stitches and broken bones were documented with hospital records. The scenario detailed the cycle of violence alternating with promises of re-form, along with the husband's jealousy and the social isolation he im-posed on his wife. The wife made three calls to the police but never signed a warrant against him; she claimed at the trial that he had threatened her with violence if she were to do so. On three occasions she moved out of the house and went to a shelter, but returned out of fear.

The night of the death, the husband had been fired from his job, was enraged, and threw food in her face. At this point in the narrative, subjects were given three variations that manipulated how the husband died. The researchers called this variable FORCE. Level one was a straightforward self-defense scenario involving a confrontational killing: the husband advanced on the wife with a weapon, and she used a weapon to kill him. At level two, the husband verbally threatened his wife and advanced without a weapon; she picked up a weapon and killed him. At level three, the husband had beaten and verbally threatened his wife, but had gone to bed saying he would "finally give her what she deserved" when he awoke; and in this nonconfrontational scenario, she killed him while he was sleeping.[5]

In addition to the manner of death, the researchers manipulated two other variables, one dealing with expert testimony and the other with juror instructions. In half the cases, there was an expert witness who gave testimony concerning the battered-woman syndrome; no expert testified in the other half. For the instructions variable, half the subjects received instructions for verdicts of self-defense (NGRSD), murder, and manslaughter; the other group received instructions for verdicts of insanity (NGRI), murder, and manslaughter. Thus, the researchers created a $3 \times 2 \times 2$ design, with three levels of FORCE, two different testimony conditions, and two different instruction conditions.

Subjects first rendered a verdict where the choices were murder, manslaughter, and either NGRSD or NGRI. Then subjects were given an expanded choice, where all the subjects had murder, manslaughter, NGRSD, and NGRI as options. In the first verdict choice, 60 percent of the verdicts were either NGRSD or NGRI, with significantly more "not guilty" verdicts resulting with the NGRSD instructions than with the NGRI instructions. These findings suggest two answers: first, the high percentage of "not guilty" verdicts across cases (60 percent) suggests that there is no bias against a woman who kills her spouse; second, the fact that there were more "not guilty" verdicts under the NGRSD than under the NGRI condition suggests that there is no bias toward seeing the battered woman as insane.

The expanded verdict results reinforce these readings: the "not guilty" verdicts jump from 60 percent to 80 percent, with most of the change coming from subjects under the NGRI condition who first rendered a manslaughter verdict but who changed to NGRSD. This suggests that when subjects have a wider set of verdict options which includes the NGRSD option, NGRSD is even more clearly the option of choice; these results contradict the hypothesis that there is a general bias against the

NGRSD verdict. Second, when the NGRSD option was pitted against NGRI, subjects clearly preferred the former—a result that again contradicts the "insanity bias" hypothesis.

There is a methodological problem here, however. By not balancing order (that is, always giving subjects the three-verdict choice first and then the four-verdict choice), the researchers may have inadvertently created a "demand characteristic": subjects may have inferred that the experimenters wanted them to use the new, fourth option, and they merely complied. This may have inflated the overall "not guilty" rate, but this would not explain why the verdict shifts went mainly one way—toward NGRSD—and not toward NGRI. A more plausible answer is that subjects under the NGRI condition could not find the verdict they wanted, but when they found it under the expanded condition they switched.

With regard to the FORCE variable the researchers, as expected, found the highest percentage of NGRSD verdicts in the confrontational case (where the man advanced with a weapon). Although the percentages were significantly lower in the other two cases (confrontational—no weapon, and nonconfrontational—sleeping), half the subjects still rendered "not guilty" verdicts, and, surprisingly, there was no significant difference between these two conditions. These findings suggest that subjects were not viewing these cases through the lenses of the objective, reasonable person. If they had been looking at the serious-threat and equal-force issues strictly objectively, then the no-weapon condition should have produced few NGRSD verdicts, and the nonconfrontational case should have produced even less. Moreover, if they had been interpreting the issues of imminence and retreat in a strictly objective fashion, then NGRSD verdicts in the nonconfrontational case should have fallen dramatically, but that is not what happened.

No single experiment can answer all questions. For example, in the level-one FORCE case, we cannot tell if the weapons used by the husband and wife were of the same type; thus, it is unclear whether they used equal or unequal force. Although the level-three case (man sleeping) can be seen as showing less force than levels two and one, this nonconfrontational case was not strictly a "less-force" case: the factors of imminence and retreat also varied here. We know that NGRSD verdicts dropped for level three in comparison to level one. But did the drop result from less serious threat, the fact that the imminence precondition was not met, or the fact that the option to retreat was available but not taken?

The expert-testimony variable produced mixed results. When the researchers analyzed the subjects' verdicts, they found no significant differences between the BWS-testimony and no-testimony conditions. But when they asked subjects what factors affected their verdicts, 59 percent of the subjects said they relied on the psychologist's testimony and 90 percent said they believed the testimony. Why were subjects' verdicts (no difference in the percentages for BWS testimony and no-BWS testimony) so greatly at odds with their beliefs about what affected their verdicts (they believed that testimony made a difference)? Perhaps subjects did not really know why they did what they did, or said they were affected by testimony because they believed this was what they should say. On the other hand, perhaps they were affected but the effects were subtle and diffuse, affecting perceptions that a gross measure such as verdict could not detect. This research was unable to answer these questions.

There are caveats with all experiments, and this one was no exception. Perhaps the surprisingly high proportion of NGRSD verdicts under the expanded-option condition (80 percent) resulted from the fact that the mock jurors tended to be "liberal" and sympathetic (they were college students at a southern university). It would strengthen our confidence in the experiment if these results could be replicated with other groups of subjects. Another possibility involves the fact that only one case was used and only the ending varied; perhaps the case was an atypical one in which the history of beatings was so horrendous that the jurors felt more than ordinary sympathy for the defendant. Testing with other cases would again strengthen these findings.

Psychological and Subjective Instructions

In an experiment conducted by J. P. Greenwald and colleagues, subjects were given one of two detailed cases involving a battered woman and her husband.[6] The cases described his heavy drinking; the severe physical, sexual, and psychological abuse he inflicted on her; her social isolation; his cycle of abuse followed by contrition; her attempts to leave; and her belief that there was no escape. Although the details of the two cases varied slightly, the scenarios were essentially the same. They were non-confrontational: he beat her and threatened to beat her later, but was asleep when she killed him.

The experimenters were primarily interested in the effect of instructions to the jurors concerning the NGRSD verdict. It has been hypothesized that one reason for the low percentage of NGRSD verdicts in actual cases may be the narrow wording and focus of self-defense instructions: the language focuses exclusively on physical danger. Charles Ewing proposed a "psychological self-defense" test[7] which would justify deadly force when it "appeared reasonably necessary to prevent the infliction of extremely serious psychological injury."[8] Ewing defined "serious psychological injury" as "gross and enduring impairment of one's psychological functioning which significantly limits the meaning and value of one's physical existence."[9] Such a test broadens the meaning of "self-defense." One critic, in fact, has claimed that it makes the concept too broad, too vague, and unworkable.[10] But Greenwald tested various instructions, including Ewing's psychological self-defense theory.

Subjects were placed in one of four instruction groups. The first received instructions on Physical Self-Defense only; the second received instructions on Psychological Self-Defense only; the third received both Physical and Psychological Self-Defense instructions; and the fourth, a Control condition, received no self-defense instructions. After reading the case, subjects rendered a verdict: first-degree murder, second-degree murder, voluntary manslaughter, or not guilty. The Control condition produced only 10.4 percent "not guilty" verdicts. The Physical Self-Defense only produced 20 percent "not guilty" verdicts. But the Psychological Self-Defense only and the Physical-plus-Psychological produced 43.8 percent and 46 percent "not guilty" verdicts, respectively. It was the Psychological Self-Defense instruction that made the difference: when subjects received a liberalizing test, they used it, and the "not guilty" verdicts more than doubled.

If we exclude the Control condition and sum across the three self-defense instructions conditions, 36.7 percent of the verdicts were "not guilty." This is a sizable percentage, given that the cases were non-confrontational—the hardest type of case in which to make a self-defense claim. Like the Follingstad results, these figures seem to show that there is no bias against a woman who kills her husband. Across all four groups only 4.1 percent of the subjects rendered a first-degree murder verdict, yet these nonconfrontational cases offered the easiest opportunities to claim premeditated first-degree murder. If subjects had been biased against the woman in these cases, there would probably have been a much higher percentage of first-degree murder verdicts.

Ewing's psychological self-defense test, which produced the big difference in this research, has not been accepted by any jurisdiction, and it is not likely to be accepted in its current, wholly subjective form. If all the defendant had to do was say, "I believed it was necessary to use deadly force to prevent extremely serious psychological injury to me, injury that would significantly limit the meaning and value of my existence"—well, how is that to be refuted? Though the test may be unrealistic, it does indicate that subjects will think and decide along wider psychological lines *if instructed*. But it may indicate that they are already thinking along those psychological lines yet finding no legal avenues available. This is similar to the outcome in Follingstad's experiment: in the expanded-verdict option, when subjects apparently found the verdict that fit their construal of case, approximately 20 percent switched from voluntary manslaughter to NGRSD.

Another caveat remains the subjects, who once again were college students, this time at a midwestern university. Moreover, since the two cases they were given differed only slightly, amounting to one, non-confrontational test, we still can't tell whether this case might not have aroused much greater sympathy in comparison to typical cases that go to trial. On the other side, the cases here and in the Follingstad experiment were modeled on actual or prototypical cases, a fact that suggests they were typical rather than atypical.

Subjectivity and Context

My students and I conducted an experiment that incorporated three cases, one of which involved a battered woman who killed.[11] We designed a prototypical case, a composite drawn from actual cases, that developed and described typical background facts, as in the Follingstad and Greenwald experiments. The case had five different endings, three confrontational and two nonconfrontational. In the first confrontational scenario (GUN), the husband approached with a gun; the wife was backed into a bedroom corner, reached for a gun, fired, and killed. Here the threat was unarguably serious, there was equal force, the retreat requirement was satisfied, and the threat was clearly imminent. In the second confrontational killing (KNIFE), the husband approached with a knife; the woman retreated as above, but killed with a gun. Here the question was whether the knife would be regarded as a serious threat (one California court found that it was not)[12] and whether the lack of equal force would matter. In the third confrontational case, the husband advanced with his fists (FISTS); the wife retreated, but killed with a gun. Again the question was whether fists would be regarded as a serious threat and whether the unequal force would matter. In the two nonconfrontational cases, as in Greenwald's cases and Follingstad's level three of FORCE, there was a beating and a threat to beat and kill later; but here the husband was either awake, drinking, and watching television (AWAKE) or was sleeping in front of the television (SLEEP) when the wife killed him. Not only was serious threat in doubt here, but imminence and retreat as well.

Along with the five different endings, the cases had one of three levels of expert testimony. One group had no expert testimony of any kind (NOEXP). A second group had expert testimony, with the expert giving diagnostic testimony regarding battered-woman syndrome (EXPDIAG). The third group had the expert going beyond diagnostic testimony to describe the defendant's psychological and subjective state—the extent to which she felt under attack and unable to escape (EXPSYCH). It was through this sort of testimony, we argued, rather than through a new test like Ewing's, that the subjective perspective would probably be injected into the trial. Thus, we had fifteen combinations (five weapon/threat scenarios, multiplied by three levels of expert testimony).

In this research, there were two groups of subjects, a student group from an eastern university and an adult group; the mean age was forty-two. One question we were asking was: If the subjects had a wide range of verdict options—from the most culpable verdicts like murder to verdicts that mitigated to verdicts that exculpated and justified—how would their verdicts distribute? At the extreme of highest culpability, subjects could render verdicts of first-degree murder (FDM) and second-degree murder (SDM). If they wanted to show partial mitigation of culpability, they could render a verdict of voluntary manslaughter (VM), which mitigated due to provocation, or guilty but mentally ill (GBMI), a verdict that may perhaps mitigate due to mental illness. At the exculpatory end was insanity (NGRI), and at the justificatory end was self-defense (NGRSD). The results for the subjects' verdicts are shown in Table 13.1. First, the NGRSD verdict percentages were high for each of the five weapon/threat conditions, averaging 63 percent across conditions and ranging from 80 percent in GUN (confrontational) to 42 percent in AWAKE (non-confrontational). Second, the three confrontational conditions (GUN, KNIFE, and FISTS), in which the NGRSD percentage was about 75 percent, were significantly different from the two nonconfrontational conditions (AWAKE and SLEEP), in which the NGRSD percentage was about 44 percent. Thus, when serious threat, retreat, and imminence preconditions did not appear to have been met, the NGRSD verdicts dropped by about 40 percent. But this drop was not as great as might have been anticipated from the perspective of an objective, reasonable person; for despite the drop, NGRSD *remained the verdict of choice* under these two nonconfrontational conditions.

To better understand the drop in NGRSD verdicts for the non-confrontational cases, let's look at these results from the extreme of greatest guilt. What we see, overall, is that very few subjects rendered verdicts of first-degree or second-degree murder. This finding was expected in confrontational cases but surprising in nonconfrontational ones, where

Table 13.1. Subjects' choice of verdict, by condition, in the case of the battered woman.

Condition	Number of subjects	First-degree murder	Second-degree murder	Voluntary manslaughter	Guilty but mentally ill	Not guilty by reason of insanity	Not guilty by reason of self-defense
Seriousness and imminence[a]							
GUN	54	5	2	4	2	7	80
KNIFE	50	2	0	12	8	0	78
FISTS	56	4	4	4	11	7	71
AWAKE	50	8	6	12	28	4	42
SLEEP	55	5	6	13	18	13	45
Average	265	5	3	9	13	6	63
Presence of expert,[b] and type of expert testimony[c]							
NOEXP	81	7	5	10	17	4	57
EXPERT	185	4	3	8	11	8	66
EXPDIAG	99	4	1	5	15	3	72
EXPSYCH	86	3	5	12	7	13	60

a. Conditions GUN, KNIFE, and FISTS were not significantly different from one another, but they were significantly different at p<.05 (using log-linear X^2 tests, with planned comparisons) from AWAKE and SLEEP. There was no significant difference between AWAKE and SLEEP.

b. There was no significant difference between NOEXP and EXPERT.

c. There was no significant difference between EXPDIAG and EXPSYCH.

the husband was watching TV or asleep in front of the TV; under these circumstances, intent to kill, the *mens rea* element of murder, should have been easiest to prove. Although the NGRSD verdicts did drop in these nonconfrontational cases, the mock jurors did not reach for the most culpable verdicts (murder); rather, there was an increase in the mitigating verdicts, VM and GBMI. Mock jurors, then, discriminated between the deliberate, intentional murderers (who would have received a high percentage of verdicts for first-degree or second-degree murder) and these defendants (who did not), even though objective appearances might have suggested no difference.

In cases where the subjects mitigated the defendant's guilt with a verdict of voluntary manslaughter, we might ask: Where did the subjects find provocation when the husband was asleep or watching TV? The same issue presented itself in Chapter 4, when our Hamlet tried to claim self-defense or provocation when the King was passively sitting on the thrown, apparently presenting neither threat nor provocation. The claims of mitigation or justification did not fit, from the objectivist perspective. Perhaps this voluntary-manslaughter verdict was an instance of partial nullification: subjects sympathetically and generously bent the law to lighten the punishment. This possibility could not be ruled out. Or subjects may have taken a subjective view of provocation which stretched time and context beyond the moment of the act. For example, they may have found provocation in past incidents, which were numerous, or in the threat to kill that the husband uttered before he fell asleep. If those threatening words did not fade and die in the seconds after they were uttered, but remained in the atmosphere with a half-life of their own, then the threat may have been present for the subjects as well as the defendant.

To return to the three confrontational cases, the slight differences in NGRSD percentages among GUN (80 percent), KNIFE (78 percent), and FISTS (71 percent) turn out to be nonsignificant. Subjects, then, were judging a knife and fists as serious threats, and they did not seem to be concerned about equal force here. If fists were as serious as a gun, and subjects' verdicts indicated that they were, then subjects were taking a more subjective view and not just objectively weighing the deadliness of each weapon.

The verdict patterns of the adults were not significantly different from those of the college students. This finding lends further support to the view that jurors, in imposing the NGRSD verdict, display no general bias against the woman who kills her mate, and it contradicts the view that these and earlier findings resulted from the fact that the college students were more sympathetic. In addition, there was no significant difference in the verdict patterns between males and females; if the bias was not general after all but limited to males, we found no evidence of that here. Moreover, we classified subjects as death-qualified or not, to see if that dimension, and its associated crime-control orientation, would lead to significantly harsher verdicts on the part of the death-qualified subjects. Put another way, if neither the subject's age nor the subject's gender produced different verdicts, would the subject's attitudes do so? Would those who had a due-process attitude favor NGRSD while death-qualified subjects, with more of a crime-control attitude, would favor guilt? They did not. The subjects who were death-qualified rendered essentially the same verdicts on these cases as those who were not, strengthening our claim that we did not have an unusually sympathetic sample.

There was no evidence for an insanity bias. Quite to the contrary: when subjects had both self-defense and insanity verdicts available to them, they chose the former over the latter by a ten-to-one ratio. These results disprove Gillespie's claim that jurors expect the woman to plead temporary insanity,[13] and Schneider and Jordan's belief that jurors are more willing to excuse because of impaired mental state than justify on grounds of self-defense.[14] In an experiment conducted with Canadian college students, Marilyn Kasian and colleagues did find greater support for a plea of automatism than for either self-defense or psychological self-defense.[15] But their case factors certainly pulled in the automatism direction, since their defendant had suffered a head injury from a blow, could not remember events that had occurred on the night of the homicide, and had slipped into a dissociative state—all of which suggested a temporary-insanity situation. Reaching an automatism verdict seems realistic based on facts rather than bias. The results from other experiments do not show a bias toward insanity.

Finally, the presence or absence of expert testimony had no significant effects on the verdicts here, replicating Follingstad's results. In addition, there was no significant difference between diagnostic testimony and subjective, psychological testimony. To make sure that a significant effect was not being masked by the confrontational cases, we retested to see if expert testimony had an effect where it was most needed, in AWAKE and SLEEP. The results again indicated that expert testimony and type of testimony produced no significant effects.

A Subway Shooting, with Limited Context

It is time to broaden our case focus, for the questions regarding perspective and preconditions go beyond the narrow confines of cases involving battered women who kill their mates. My associates and I tested a second case, based on *Goetz*. A nurse finished her night shift and was riding home on the subway when she was confronted by four youths, one of whom said, "Give us some money." Six months earlier, this woman had been mugged, beaten, and stabbed by two youths. The incident had occurred on the subway when she was going home from work; it had sent her to the hospital and kept her out of work for two months. Although the physical trauma had since healed, the psychological trauma had not. She was plagued by chronic fear, flashbacks, nightmares, sleep disturbance, depression, and anxiety—symptoms that an expert witness called post-traumatic stress disorder (PTSD). One other fact: she now carried a pistol in her handbag.

In this case, three variables were manipulated: threat/weapon, escape/retreat possibility, and expert testimony. For threat/weapon, there were three levels: the youth who said, "Give us some money," had a gun in his hand (GUN), a knife in his hand (KNIFE), or nothing in his hands

(HAND). The woman reached into her handbag, pulled out a gun, and fired four shots, killing the youth who had spoken; we thus had unequal force in both the KNIFE and FISTS scenarios, as well as doubt about the seriousness of the threat in the latter two scenarios.

As to the second variable, our no-escape (NOESCAPE) condition had the subway doors closed; the four youths surrounded the woman as she was sitting. Our possible-escape condition (ESCAPE) had the subway doors open as the train was at a station; the four youths were off to the side, not blocking the exit door. Here the question was: Would it matter if she didn't try to escape/retreat when an opportunity was available?

The third variable was the same as in the case of the battered woman who killed: one group received no expert testimony; a second received diagnostic testimony about post-traumatic stress disorder, and a third received diagnostic testimony plus psychological inferences about how that trauma could have affected her subjective construal of threat, imminence, and escape possibilities.

The results, presented in Table 13.2, revealed some interesting differences between this case and the one involving the battered woman who killed. When GUN, KNIFE, and HAND were averaged, the percentage of NGRSD verdicts was only 27 percent, compared with the 63 percent average for the battered-woman case. Although this was a substantial and significant drop, the NGRSD verdict still remained the verdict of choice, although the distance between NGRSD and the second-choice and third-choice verdicts (voluntary manslaughter and guilty but mentally ill, respectively) narrowed considerably.

What accounted for the drop-off? One answer, we believed, was context. In the battered-woman case there was a good deal of context, revealing the history of a relationship in which many beatings and injuries had occurred. It was a history not only of the defendant but *of the victim, and of their relationship.* In the subway case, subjects had only a brief history of the defendant (her prior mugging, her post-traumatic stress), but the youths remained anonymous, their motivation was unknown, and their relationship with the defendant began and ended in a few seconds. It was unclear what were they up to. Were they just harassing the woman, or were they trying to intimidate her into giving them money, or was the threat more serious? In the subway case there was some doubt; but there was no doubt for the subjects in the battered-woman case, for the history and context made it quite plain who was the victim and who was the villain.

A second difference between the subway and battered-woman cases appeared under the weapon/threat conditions. Whereas there were no

Table 13.2. Subjects' choice of verdict, by condition, in the case of the subway shooting.

			Verdict percentages				
Condition	Number of subjects	First-degree murder	Second-degree murder	Voluntary manslaughter	Guilty but mentally ill	Not guilty by reason of insanity	Not guilty by reason of self-defense
Seriousness[a]							
GUN	90	3	12	24	18	0	42
KNIFE	83	18	14	19	16	4	29
HAND	93	6	22	27	29	4	12
Average	266	9	16	24	21	3	27
Escape/retreat possibility[b]							
NOESCAPE	143	10	13	27	20	4	27
ESCAPE	123	8	20	20	23	2	28
Presence of expert,[c] and type of expert testimony[d]							
NOEXP	94	11	21	26	12	1	30
EXPERT	172	8	13	23	26	3	26
EXPDIAG	74	4	12	22	35	3	24
EXPSYCH	98	11	14	23	19	4	28

a. Conditions GUN and KNIFE were significantly different from HAND at $p<.05$ (using log-linear X^2 tests, with planned comparisons, but GUN and KNIFE were not significantly different.

b. NOESCAPE and ESCAPE were not significantly different.

c. NOEXP and EXPERT were significantly different at p<.05.

d. EXPDIAG and EXPSYCH were not significantly different.

significant differences among GUN, KNIFE, and FISTS in the battered-woman case, there was a sizable and significant difference between GUN (42 percent NGRSD verdicts) and KNIFE (29 percent) versus HAND (12 percent). Why was there a difference here?

Again, this finding appeared to relate to context. When there was no historical context to identify the dramatis personae as victims or villains, and insufficient current context to determine what the youths were really up to, then subjects used the objective perspective to judge serious threat, with GUN and KNIFE considered more serious than HAND. But in the battered-woman case, the subjects knew, because of the contextual history, that when the husband advanced with just his hands he was going to inflict severe damage. So "hands" were not seen in isolation in the battered-woman case; the subjects did not, for example, associate them with the beatific hands in Michelangelo's *Creation of Adam* on the Sistine

Chapel ceiling. No, they were the *husband's* hands; and in the light of the husband's history, they were seen by defendant and jurors alike as presenting an imminent and serious danger. This was a subjective view, colored by historical conditioning. The defendant and the jurors came to believe, with virtual "certainty," that those hands were threatening severe harm.

Context can tell jurors not only about the batterer but about the woman. Follingstad and her colleagues conducted another experiment involving a case in which a battered woman killed her spouse.[16] They manipulated background information such that the woman was seen by family and neighbors as (1) a good wife and mother, or (2) a dysfunctional wife and mother, or (3) a bad wife and mother. With the guilt rate set at 1.00 for the good wife and mother, the guilt rate rose to 2.49 in the dysfunctional case and to 6.24 in the case of the bad mother and wife. Although such contextual information may not have been legally relevant to the question of what had happened at the moment of the act, subjects did incorporate this information and it did affect their verdicts.

Kasian and her colleagues, in their experiment, manipulated the history of abuse, giving subjects either a severe-abuse or moderate-abuse condition. They found that juries "were twice as likely to find the defendant guilty in the moderate abuse condition as compared to the severe abuse condition when either the self-defense or the psychological self-defense pleas were used."[17] An interesting point is that if the jurors had been following the law and focusing on the *moment of the act* to evaluate the self-defense claim, then background abuse should have been irrelevant. Yet it turned out to be quite relevant and significant. It did, however, turn out to be irrelevant in their automatism plea. This, I suggest, is because automatism turns most directly on an assessment of the defendant's mind *at the moment of the act*, and history of abuse would be irrelevant to evaluating her mental state at the moment of murder. In cases where the defendant was pleading self-defense, it is again clear that subjects widened the context.

Returning to the subway case, we do not find any difference between the ESCAPE and NOESCAPE conditions. One possibility is that the escape/retreat requirement matters little to mock jurors. There is some support for this interpretation in the battered-woman case, for in AWAKE and SLEEP she could, objectively, have walked out the door, yet jurors were still rendering NGRSD verdicts about 44 percent of the time. On the other hand, perhaps the escape manipulation in the subway case was weak; that is, even if the youths were standing off to the side and the subway doors were open, the woman may not have seen any realistic escape possibility. After all (subjects might ask), if she made a dash for it, how far would she get if the youths pursued her? If subjects decided that she would still be trapped in the subway, then both ESCAPE and NOESCAPE would amount to the same thing.

For this case, there was no significant difference between men and women in their verdicts. Again, no gender bias was found. As for the alleged bias against women who kill their husbands, that was again contradicted by the finding that NGRSD verdicts were significantly higher when the woman killed her husband than when she killed a male stranger on the subway. There was a significant difference between adults and students in the subway case that goes against the claim that students are more liberal than adults: the adults rendered significantly more NGRSD verdicts here. It is likely that, given their age and the fact that they were probably more familiar with subway dangers, they had a greater subjective appreciation than the students of the terror the defendant claimed to have experienced.

In the subway case, we found that having an expert testify did make a difference, but type of expert did not make a difference. The expert-testimony difference did not produce an increase in NGRSD verdicts; rather, such testimony shifted some first-degree and second-degree murder verdicts to guilty but mentally ill (GBMI). Although the shift may have mitigated guilt and muted punishment, this effect seems to substantiate the concern that expert testimony persuades jurors to see the defendant as disordered rather than as justified for her actions.

Thus, in the battered-woman case, expert testimony had no direct effect on verdicts, but in the subway case it did. There was also an *indirect* effect. After reading each case, subjects made ratings about the defendant and the case on a number of dimensions. Some of these dimensions were highly predictive of verdict. For example, subjects were asked to rate, on a scale of 1 to 11, how much mitigation her self-defense claim warranted, where 1 was none at all and 11 was complete mitigation. On this dimension of "mitigation by reason of self-defense" (MITSD), subjects who rendered verdicts of first-degree murder rated her 3.71, on the average, whereas NGRSD subjects rated her 9.46. Another dimension, called PREMED, asked the subjects whether the defendant had acted with complete premeditation (rating of 1) or no malice at all (11); as expected, subjects who found her guilty of first-degree murder rated her at 2.73, whereas subjects rendering a verdict of NGRSD rated her at 8.17. These two dimensions, MITSD and PREMED, related quite closely to her self-defense claim.

The next three dimensions related to her mental state. They involved a rating of whether she had had the capacity to make responsible choices or whether she had been incapacitated (CAP); the second was whether her thinking had been distorted or clear (THINK); and the third asked whether she was culpable or not for bringing about her mental deterioration and the actions that followed (CULP). Expert testimony does not move subjects' perceptions on MITSD and PREMED toward acquittal by reason of self-defense; what it does do is move the subjects' perceptions of the defendant on CAP, THINK, and CULP toward "mentally disordered." If an insanity verdict (NGRI) did not quite fit, then GBMI seemed to, since the subject could register a verdict that acknowledged both guilt and disorder. But this was not what defense advocates had in mind when they fought to get expert testimony admitted into such trials.

R. A. Schuller and her colleagues, in a recent experiment involving a case in which a battered woman killed, found a verdict effect for the type of expert they called "specific"—that is, one who interviewed the defendant and related the battered-woman syndrome to that specific person.[18] But they did not find a verdict effect for the "general" expert—one who did nothing more than present syndrome evidence. This was arguably a confrontational case, however, so we still have no solid evidence for a *verdict effect* in nonconfrontational cases. Schuller also found that expert testimony had an indirect effect—shifting the subjects' evaluations of threat, fear, imminence, escape, and the need to act—toward the subjective end, closer to the defendant's claim. Kasian also found no main effect of expert testimony, but did find indirect effects on perceptions. All of these research findings, taken together, suggest that expert testimony has a marginal direct effect on verdicts and a modest, indirect effect on perceptions, but it is clearly not a testimonial trump card for the defense. The research also suggests that the *form* of the testimony may matter more than testimony per se: there may be ways of presenting such testimony that can substantially increase its potency.

In the experiment that I conducted with my students, there were five dimensions that were predictive of verdict in all cases. But there was one dimension that was predictive in only the battered-woman case: the dimension called OTHER, where subjects made a rating as to whether others were at fault or whether others were not responsible for what had happened. Clearly, in the battered-woman case, the "other" who is judged quite responsible is the husband, the victim.

Different Ways of Constructing Stories

In the experiments described above, subjects seemed to be weighing the defendant's culpability and responsibility against the husband's; specifically, they were weighing both party's actions, motives, mental states, and conflicting interests. In some ways, then, subjects were viewing this matter as more like a tort case than like a criminal case.[19] In criminal law's dramatis personae, the man is the "victim" and the woman is the "alleged felon." But in light of the history of these two individuals, which provides context for the subject's "story," she is likely to wear the mantle of "victim" while he wears the mantle of "villain." In criminal law, of course, his character matters little, or not at all; we do not charge a defendant with first-degree murder if she killed a saint, and only second-degree murder or voluntary manslaughter if she killed a sinner. Yet to the subjects, his character and past actions clearly matter, and are weighed against hers. These two players in the drama are more like "protagonist" and "antagonist," or "plaintiff" and "tortfeasor," in a situation where the jurors attempt to figure out who's who.

When reading, hearing, or watching stories, we are generally uncomfortable with ambiguity, for we like to know who is the hero, who is the villain, and who did what; this is one reason Akira Kurosawa's film *Rashomon* is discomforting. In the first part of our battered-woman story (that is, up to the moment of the act), which we'll call Story 1, the roles are fairly clear: she is the protagonist and he the evildoer, and although we may not admire her unreservedly (perhaps thinking her weak for not leaving him), she nonetheless gets our sympathy and he our antipathy.

Now begins a courtroom drama in which the prosecution tells Story 2. This story opens with a double message: jurors are reminded that the defendant is presumed innocent, but then are immediately told that the State is bringing first-degree murder charges against her and hopes to punish her to the maximum extent possible under law. Somebody thinks her guilty—very guilty. The prosecution then seeks to paint her as the villain and the husband as the victim. In Story 2, not only are the victim-villain roles reversed but the victim's character is largely irrelevant: he functions as a prop, merely attesting to the fact that an unnatural death has occurred. Furthermore, history is largely irrelevant, since the key legal questions telescope time to the moment of the act. This narrow slice of time, detached from time past, becomes the focus; all else is deemed legally irrelevant. Overall, then, the prosecution's story, which coincides with the law's story of self-defense, fragments and foreshortens both time and history; it leaves one character's character out of the drama entirely; and it partitions the defendant's story into one act and a few narrowly defined categories of intent *(mens rea)*.

Although this legal mode of story construction may be appreciated by lawyers, modern novelists, and avant-garde filmmakers, it is not the way ordinary people construct stories. Jurors trying to understand the motivation of the defendant intuitively understand that time past and time future are both contained in time present. Some defense attorneys show that they understand this as well, when they employ the strategy of trying the victim. That is, they attempt to put the deceased on trial; they raise the issue of his character at every opportunity, and hope the jurors get so angry that they'll want to dig him up and shoot him. This strategy, more akin to the tort situation, seeks to create a story that is much fuller, much richer in detail, history, and character than the preceding stories. This narrative, which we'll call Story 3, bears a closer resemblance to Story 1 than to Story 2.

The jurors' story, as we glean it from the experimental findings, tends to be more like Stories 1 and 3 than like Story 2, particularly when there is a good deal of context. When there is little context, jurors focus on the finite moment of the act, from which they try to gather all the crucial information. On the basis of that moment, they judge whether the threat was serious and imminent, and whether deadly force was necessary, from an objective view of weapon and circumstance. Still, if the subjects are older and have had experience traveling on the subway, their objective judgments will be colored by their subjective experiences. Where there is history and context to the story, as in the case of the battered woman who kills, a much more subjective perspective dominates—whether the jurors are judging the seriousness of the threat, its imminence, or the possibility of retreat. Although the subjective view remains dominant, the objective view is not absent completely; for in the nonconfrontational cases, jurors do not take an entirely subjective view of imminence, since we do see a significant drop in the NGRSD verdicts from what obtained in the confrontational cases. But they do not view imminence from an entirely objective perspective either, for they still render NGRSD verdicts here more often than any other verdict. It is fair to say, then, that they construe "imminence" more broadly than the legal construction, mixing objective and subjective perspectives.

Quite apart from legal particulars and preconditions, this is a story, a drama of two people, that turns deadly. One dies, but two were involved, and each played a part. Each person's moral culpability is weighed, and balanced against the other's. Though the woman fired the shot at the moment of the act, the reasons for that culminating act lie far back in time, linking past events with perceptions, beliefs, and feelings. Long ago, Freud told us that events were multiply determined, sometimes having causes that stretch far into the past and deep into the psyche. Jurors seem to know this, particularly when they know the historical context, and they reject simple determinism, and simplistic legal verdicts based solely on actions in a moment of time.

One of the theoretical problems with the self-defense justification is its either-or quality: either you get the defense, or your claim fails. The problem is that a defendant charged with first-degree murder whose self-defense claim fails may be treated just like a first-degree murderer, even when the intent *(mens rea)* is not the same. Aside from the doctrine of "imperfect self-defense," which has had "limited acceptance,"[20] there is no middle ground. Similarly, if the defendant's self-defense claim rests on an honest mistake, she gets the defense if the mistake is judged "reasonable" but loses it entirely if it is judged "unreasonable."[21]

What if some jurors are in a quandary? What if they have constructed a story that fits the facts and the defendant's *mens rea,* as they understand it, but now they are searching for a middle-ground verdict category that fits their judgment of her moral culpability—and they cannot find one. There seems to be evidence that a number of subjects create a middle ground, by using the verdicts of voluntary manslaughter and guilty but mentally insane. In the experiments described above, these two verdicts were the second- and third-choice verdicts overall, but they consistently became more frequent in the hard cases, such as when the battered woman killed her sleeping husband or when the youths in the subway displayed no weapon. Do the subjects really mean "guilty but mentally ill"? It's highly doubtful. Even among jurisprudes who debate the nuances of this peculiar verdict,[22] and among legislators who enact GBMI legislation, there remains great confusion about what it means and how it is practiced.[23] It is more reasonable to assume that subjects have very little idea what "guilty but mentally ill" means. We already noted that verdicts of voluntary manslaughter were hard to reconcile, since the sleeping victim had not provoked the defendant. If some jurors in the hard cases are unable to go all the way to a verdict of NGRSD and unwilling to go all the way to a verdict of first-degree murder, they may use the GBMI and VM verdicts as the mitigating, middle-ground position. In other words, these jurors are partially nullifying, finding a verdict among the options that fits their sense of the moral culpability of a particular defendant.

At the end of *Rashomon,* the firewood dealer, who has been telling the story of the stories, asks his listener, "Just think, which one of these stories do you believe?" The listener, shaking his head in confusion, replies, "None makes any sense." The firewood dealer, having the last word, says, "Don't worry about it! It isn't as if men were reasonable." Our conclusion here is not quite so despairing.

Most experimental subjects construct reasonable stories, though their constructions reveal that they take the subjective view, particularly when historical facts are plentiful. This is no more than what all good novelists, dramatists, and psychotherapists do: they account for the present in light of what they believe about the past and the future. In their subjectivity, they do not lose sight of reality completely, for objectivity matters, and matters a great deal when history is missing and ambiguity is great. Although subjects compose stories differently from the way the law would have it, one could defend the argument that the subjects' way is more reasonable and commonsensical than the legal way. It is the law, after all, that dissociates history, represses a major character's character, and compartmentalizes the whole into pieces and preconditions.

Stories are the penultimate step. The final step is to fit the story into a verdict category. But this final step may be a stumbling block for jurors, if the law's verdict categories in self-defense cases are too few or if they fail to fit well with the subject's story. And when the defendant's *mens rea* is judged to be less than murder but more than justification, subjects appear momentarily stuck. Something similar might have occurred in the *Goetz* case, where the jury never got to the self-defense issue, finding *mens rea* lacking for attempted murder instead.[24]

Subjects may resolve their quandary by refashioning verdicts to suit their purposes, at the expense of verdicts meaning what the law says they mean. This can be dubbed ignorance, willfulness, or nullification, but such a dismissal misses the instructive message that commonsense justice is sending the law. The perceived quandary and the creative-refashioning solution are neither foreign nor unfamiliar to the law. In Chapter 2 we saw a judge engaging in creative refashioning, constructing the previously nonexistent category of "partial self-defense" in a case involving a borderline retarded teenager who killed his sleeping father.[25]

It may be that subjects are not looking at self-defense as a *justification* at all. The research evidence seems to show that subjects do not take a detached, objective, reasonable-person view of each and every self-defense precondition. Rather, they seem to look at the situation as a whole—as a violent, sick drama with mixed motives and a disturbing history, whose troubled characters were caught in the maelstrom of the moment. Taking a predominantly subjective view, subjects perhaps understand that the defendant did not *intend* to kill in the maelstrom of the moment but merely wanted to escape the threat to her life.[26] If subjects are looking at motive and intent to understand the story (and the story model, as we saw in Chapter 4, suggests that this is exactly what people do), then this mode of interpretation is not some radical departure from the law. On the contrary, it is an old and respectable strategy, grounded in the concept of apportioning guilt to the level of *mens rea*, which in this case is less than murder.

Thus, on the basis of context, characters, and the events at the moment of the act, commonsense justice fashions a story and an answer grounded in *mens rea*, yielding a reasonable dramatic judgment of the defendant. In finding the reasonable law unreasonable and unyielding, commonsense justice bends the law to make justice. Yet bending the law does not take us further away from justice in this instance; for in rediscovering the *mens rea* basis for deciding guilt, we actually get closer to one of the law's more enduring precepts.

The Maddening Changes in Insanity Law

14

In 1723 "Mad Ned Arnold" shot and wounded Lord Onslow, claiming that Onslow had bewitched him with devils and imps. In 1800 James Hadfield—a man who literally had a hole in his head, the result of a war wound he'd received while defending King and country—conceived the notion that the King had to be removed from England's throne in order to pave the way for Christ's Second Coming; with delusion in mind and pistol in hand, Hadfield fired at the mad monarch, George III, but his aim, like his belief, proved untrue.[1] In 1840 Edward Oxford fired a pistol at young Queen Victoria, who in her long reign was fired upon five more times, and once was struck on the head with a brass-knobbed cane by an insane officer in her army.[2] In 1843, after being seized for shooting a man, Daniel M'Naghten was asked if he knew the gentleman he had shot. He replied, "It is Sir Robert Peel, is it not?"[3] It was not. And in 1981 John Hinckley, Jr., shot and wounded President Ronald Reagan and three others, reportedly to win the love of actress Jodie Foster.[4]

These were all "insanity" cases, and except for "Mad Ned Arnold," arguably the maddest of the lot, they were found "not guilty by reason of insanity." In their time, these cases created a great stir: public officials, the press, and the populace all reacted, usually with outrage. Issues of safety were on the minds of many, particularly monarchs and ministers, who seemed to be favorite targets of the mad. But since those who reigned and ruled were also favorite targets of assassins—who clearly "knew what they were about"—suspicions arose that assassins might simulate madness to get off the hook and that doctors might aid and abet in this ruse. Practical questions were raised as to whether doctors could distinguish sanity from insanity, or insanity from feigned madness, and whether jurors would be dazzled and duped by medical testimony.[5]

In legal and legislative circles, acquittals for reasons of insanity were repeatedly seen as "wrongful" verdicts, and from this mistaken conclusion a tenuous logic followed: "if the verdict was wrong, then the standard [must have been] wrong."[6] This increased pressure to change the law. In charting insanity's new directions, legal and psychological experts competed over who would lead and control, as well as which theories, legal or psychological, best explained human nature and should best govern future insanity law.[7] This debate, which involved far more than just law and science scrapping, was overlaid with symbols, myths, politics, and fear—just the sort of "hydraulic pressure" that distorts judgment, as Justice Holmes warned.[8] Nonetheless, pressures mounted for change. These "great cases" were about to make "bad law."[9]

Exculpating Insanity, but Missing Its Essence

In Anglo-American jurisprudence, insanity has been a fixture for nearly a thousand years. In tenth-century England, the laws of King Aethelred provided that "if it happens that a man commits a misdeed involuntarily, or unintentionally, the case is different from that of one who offends of his own free will, voluntarily and intentionally . . . Likewise he who is an involuntary agent of his misdeeds should always be entitled to clemency and better terms owing to the fact that he acted as an involuntary agent."[10] This appears to be the familiar *mens rea* claim, the long-standing view that we should not punish where we cannot impose blame. If we excuse for accident and mistake (runs the argument), so too should we excuse for insanity, since the person does not offend with free will, or voluntarily, or intentionally.

Investigating this claim, we find that insanity rests on two analogies that lead in different directions. One analogy links the insane with children: both, it might be said, lack a threshold level of competence—a capacity to understand what is what. Without this legally minimal capacity, their actions become involuntary, unintended, and excusable. If the insane are like children, then insanity is a *condition,* a *non compos mentis* (no power or possession of mind). This argument invokes a deeper incapacity than mere lack of *mens rea:* it is not that the insane person does not know that he is shooting at a person rather than a tree, or is unaware that he is squeezing a gun rather than a guava; rather, this *mens* argument asks whether the individual is a "response-able" actor[11] and whether he has the deeper capacity to make responsible choices. If it is decided that the individual lacks the capacity, then the argument can be made for setting criminal adjudication aside[12] and going directly to disposition, where the issues are treatment and deterrence, not blame and punishment.

The second analogy, made explicit in a thirteenth-century treatise by H. D. Bracton,[13] distinguishes insane people from children and likens insanity to the defense of "not guilty by reason of duress": "For a crime is not committed unless the will to harm be present . . . And then there is what can be said about the child and the madman, for the one is protected by his innocence of design, the other by the misfortune of his deed. In misdeeds we look to the will and not the outcome."[14] "Misfortune" emphasizes that mental or physical distress has caused the act. The term encompasses the individual who rages *(furiosus)* like some wild beast when under a severe psychological stressor, but who at other times may be sane, sound, and responsible. Unlike the child who lacks capacity across the board and throughout the age of innocence, this insane person had the capacity but now has fallen below threshold responsibility. Under this *duress* analogy, the legal inquiry tends to narrow to the moment of the act, to the particular *mens rea,* and to the question of whether the symptoms of insanity were great enough to defeat the specific intent requirement.

Under either analogy, insanity exculpates, although it does so differently from the claim of self-defense. Those who plead self-defense assert that they are responsible actors caught in maddening circumstances. They knew what they were doing and knew the likely outcome of their actions, but in order to evade punishment they offer a reason that supersedes the injunction against killing. Insanity defendants, on the other hand, claim that they are not responsible actors—that their actions are the result of disordered or defective minds.

Within conventional jurisprudential theory, self-defense is regarded as a "justification," whereas insanity is an "excuse." But these distinct categories begin to break down and blur if we add mistake to the self-defense mix, and make the mistake more and more unreasonable. Take a man on the subway who is approached by a youth who has a gun in his hand and who demands five dollars. If the man pulls a gun, fires, and kills the youth, he may well get off on grounds of self-defense, even if the police discover that the youth's gun was a toy. Reasonable mistake may justify. But what if the youth is sitting across from the man, doing a crossword puzzle, periodically tapping his pencil. Now the man again pulls his gun, fires, and kills the youth, claiming, as in the first version, that he believed his life was about to end, since the pencil tapping was a signal of imminent death. As the actor's subjective belief becomes more unreasonable to the reasonable person, we tend to see his action as the result of delusion and insanity, rather than self-defense. But subjectively, from his own point of view, he acted in self-defense and is claiming justification.

Delusion illustrates how the law's essential principle of insanity, which changed repeatedly throughout history as a result of great cases and wrongful-verdict claims, continued to miss the mark. Consider "Mad Ned Arnold," who was clearly delusional: his brother, other family members, and people from the local community all attested to his insanity at his trial.[15] But the insanity standard that governed his case was the "wild beast" standard—a test that exempted a man from punishment only if he was "totally deprived of his understanding and memory, and doth not know what he is doing, no more than an infant, than a brute or a wild beast."[16] This standard, which had been endorsed by the such distinguished jurists as Bracton, Coke, and Hale across nearly five centuries, required complete impairment in awareness and perception at the moment of the act, a total lack of comprehension. All the prosecution had to do, and did, was show that Arnold bought the powder and the shot, which indicated planfulness and *mens rea*. Under the "total deprivation" standard, any signs that could be construed as indicating intentional acts were enough to defeat the insanity claim, even if they resulted from crazy beliefs.

From the standpoint of alienists (the forerunners of psychiatrists), this was a wrongful verdict, for not only was the wild-beast standard overly restrictive but it missed the essence of insanity. Still, "insanity" was a legal concept, not a medical one, and the law remained leery of turning over the standard to the medical profession. On the other hand, "insanity" was clearly related to madness, whose types and shadings were foreign to most judges. When judges confronted a defendant who had "mental problems" and faced up to their own amateur standing, few of them could entirely ignore the advice of professionals. Over the next two centuries, as psychiatry's scientific status became established and its dominion over the characterization of madness ever more firm, psychiatry would often take the lead in efforts to change the law. But in the slaying of the wild beast, the telling blows were delivered by a delusional man, his brilliant lawyer, and an overlooked jury.[17]

Consider a case that was tried in 1800—that of James Hadfield, who also had a delusion and, like Arnold, bought pistol and shot.[18] As further indication of intent, Hadfield learned that the King was headed for Drury

Lane Theatre and took up a position inside the theater with a clear line on the royal box. When apprehended after he had fired and missed, he appeared quite rational, more so than Arnold. So why was Arnold convicted whereas Hadfield was found not guilty by reason of insanity?

Hadfield's attorney was Thomas Erskine, regarded as the greatest lawyer of the age. Erskine derided the wild beast and the notion of total insanity as illusions. He made great play with the "total-deprivation" standard: if this meant, for example, that a man must not know his own name, or a husband not know that he is married, or a father not remember that he has children or not remember the way to his house, "then no such madness ever existed in the world."[19]

Erskine then went on to define what he claimed was the true essence of insanity. The madman is deluded, reasoning from false premises, "because a delusive image, the unseparable companion of real insanity, is thrust upon the subjugated understanding, incapable of resistance because unconscious of attack."[20] Erskine's reframing shifted the symptom focus from perception to reason. Beyond this cognitive shift, Erskine's focus on delusions redefined insanity as being far less sweeping than "total deprivation," since a delusion could represent a narrow realm of "crazy thinking."

Erskine had to tiptoe, since his "theory" was neither the law of the land nor the standard that governed the case. The wild beast ruled, and a blatant call to the jury to disregard the rule would have run afoul. But Erskine did grandstand when he invited the jurors to inspect Hadfield's exposed brain, which they could see by looking through the hole made by his war wound. And in his closing summary, when he rubbed Hadfield's head, he was no doubt reinforcing his message that Hadfield's capacity had been shot. Although history credits Erskine with wounding the beast and bringing in the acquittal, it overlooks the jury; for no matter how masterly Erskine was, if his views had not fit with the jurors' "intuitive ideas about what is and is not insane,"[21] the case would have been lost.

There is an important footnote to *Hadfield's Case*. The presiding judge, Chief Justice Kenyon, feared for the safety of "every man of every station, from the king upon the throne to the beggar at the gate,"[22] if Hadfield was released. In 1800 Parliament hastily drafted the *Insane Offenders Bill*, requiring that those acquitted on grounds of insanity be taken into strict custody until "His Majesty's pleasure be known." The bill, which was made retroactive to *Hadfield*, "solved" the dispositional issue: "not guilty by reason of insanity" would no longer mean "free." Hadfield, whose actions had triggered the legislation, became the exemplar, spending the rest of his life in Bethlem Hospital.

The Beast Is Slain, but Do the Rules Reign?

Daniel M'Naghten's acquittal had an aftermath similar to *Hadfield*'s: up-roar, wrongful-verdict declarations, and changes in the law.[23] The uproar included a "blame the juror" refrain:

> The *Illustrated London News* decried "the natural tendency of soci-ety to refuse to contemplate them [assassins] in any other light than as acts of madness." An editorialist for *The Times* of London voiced the hope that the "soft headed" would not "twist and torture" minor incidents of peculiar behavior in the accused's background into "symptoms of insanity." Some critics asserted that jurors could not comprehend the judge's instructions, while other critics held that jurors willfully disregarded the instructions. Lord Cooper maintained that jurors simply retire and ask themselves, "Is this man mad or is he not?" no matter what instructions the judge pro-vides.[24]

Let's evaluate these claims in light of the facts of *M'Naghten's Case*. M'Naghten was ably defended by Alexander Cockburn, who called nine medical experts to testify. All said that M'Naghten was insane. The jurors did not have to twist and torture anything, since the "insanity case" was made nine times over. The "blame the jury" hypothesis also ignores the fact that the prosecution was inept: the solicitor general, Sir William Follett, failed to offer any other motive for M'Naghten's act. For exam-ple, Follett never developed the idea that the defendant was a political assassin, even though it was rumored in the press that M'Naghten may have had links to the Chartists or the Anti-Corn Law League, two groups strongly and sometimes violently opposed to the Tory government. Follett failed to ask how it was that this itinerant woodturner had the large sum of 750 pounds in a Glasgow bank, and whether this might not have been an assassin's payoff. Furthermore, when defense experts over-stepped their bounds by testifying to the ultimate opinion, Lord Chief Justice Tindal asked Follett if he was going to object, but Follett did not. Finally, when Tindal asked Follett if he planned to call his own experts to rebut the defense's testimony, Follett threw in the towel, telling the judge that he could not press for a verdict against the prisoner. As if the jurors needed reminding, Justice Tindal pointed out to them that all the evidence was on one side, and practically directed them to reach the insanity ver-dict. In light of what happened, the case against the jurors does not stand up.

Substantively, what fell was the restrictive wild-beast test. The House of Lords took the unusual step of summoning all fifteen justices to explain the law. The new explanation that fourteen of the justices fashioned was the M'Naghten Rules, which shifted the definition of "insanity" from the wild-beast symptoms to a more inclusive cognitive test, simplistically known as the "right-from-wrong" test. The rules were as follows:

1. To establish a defense on the ground of insanity it must be clearly proved that, at the time of committing the act, the party ac cused was laboring under such a defect of reason, from disease of the mind, as not to know the nature and quality of the act he was doing, or if he did know it, that he did not know he was doing what was wrong.

2. Where a person labors under partial delusions only and is not in other respects insane, and commits an offense in consequence thereof, he must be considered in the same situation as to responsibility as if the facts with respect to which the delusion exists were real.[25]

The rules were amplified by commentary. For example, it was noted that knowledge of right and wrong meant knowledge of the "very act charged" rather than "knowledge" in the abstract. According to this particular-versus-abstract distinction, Hadfield knew that killing the King was wrong in the particular and legal sense of the "very act charged," yet he maintained, in his delusion, that his act had been right, in a higher moral sense. But under the new M'Naghten Rules, that higher moral sense or abstract knowledge was no longer the relevant dimension. Thus, if Hadfield had been tried under the wider orbit of M'Naghten, he should have been found guilty.

If we take the completely subjective rule 2 and assume that M'Naghten truly believed that the Tories were out to get him, then he should have been found guilty by his own rules: since M'Naghten walked up *behind* Edward Drummond (secretary to Prime Minister Peel) and shot him in the back as Drummond was walking down a street oblivious to M'Naghten's presence, delusional self-defense would not have been a valid plea, for there was no immediate threat. Thus, even though the rules widened the scope of the insanity defense, they wouldn't have embraced the delusional M'Naghten.

When the justices' new rules were read in the House of Lords, the applause "had barely died down when the doubters and detractors took over."[26] From Queen to commoner, from journalist to jurist, those present voiced doubts, fears, and misgivings about the new rules. One fear was that the broader rules would encourage future acts of murder and mayhem against the monarch. A second fear was that more insanity cases and acquittals would follow. A third fear was that the liberalized rules would encourage fakery, whereby ordinary criminals or mildly disordered offenders would play the role of "crazies" and jurors would be taken in. When these fears are considered together, we see that a myth was coming into being: the myth that insanity is an "easy out." It is one which continues to live despite implausible assumptions and contrary facts. The myth assumes that defendants could easily pull off the charade, and assumes that jurors, either as dupes or co-conspirators, would go along. The myth also ignores the fact that Daniel M'Naghten, like Hadfield before him, spent the rest of his life confined in a mental hospital, so the "easy out" was no out for him.

In the history of the insanity defense, one of the sobering findings is that empirical facts do not seem to deflate myths. To illustrate, take three myths that have enjoyed more than a century of viability, unsustained by substance: (1) insanity defenses are frequently used; (2) they are easily engineered; and (3) they are used in the most heinous murder cases to enable the defendant to escape punishment. Yet when the ten-year period following M'Naghten is compared with the ten-year period preceding the adoption of the M'Naghten Rules, we see no significant increase in the percentage of cases where insanity was alleged, no significant increase in the generally low rate of insanity acquittals, and no significant increase in insanity verdicts in murder trials.[27]

M'Naghten's Case generated other fears that soon assumed mythic status. Since the judge made available to the defense the 750 pounds in M'Naghten's bank account, M'Naghten had one of the best-financed defenses mounted in those days. The myth that insanity is a rich man's defense would persist, repeated as truth in the United States Senate and House hearings following *Hinckley.*[28] Another fear, expressed by the House of Lords, was that the opinions of experts would take on determinative power—that trials would become a battle of experts, and that these "hired guns," with their own agendas, would usurp the jurors' function. These fears were raised following *M'Naghten* and again after *Hinckley;* they have been raised for 150 years, despite evidence to the contrary, elevating empty fears to the status of myth.[29]

Elasticizing the Law

Not all of the criticism was against widening the law. There was a minor chorus that criticized the M'Naghten Rules for not going far enough and for situating insanity on an already outmoded psychology.[30] This chorus was composed largely of medico-psychological experts, along with a few jurists.[31] For example, the influential American doctor Isaac Ray, whose treatise on insanity was quoted by Cockburn at M'Naghten's trial,[32] was highly critical of Coke's and Hale's formulations, which still exerted great influence. Ray viewed these great lawyers as poor psychiatrists who were too unfamiliar with the forms of madness to define its essence adequately. To Ray, the right-versus-wrong test was the wrong test, because most insane defendants knew that their criminal deed, in the abstract, had been wrong. The flaw lay in the way they connected their particular act to the abstract belief. In Ray's formulation, if the disorder embraced the act or if the act emerged as a product of that disorder, he would have voted for acquittal. Although Ray's views became the law in only one state, New Hampshire, they would recur a century later in the Durham Rule.

Other alienists objected to the law's artificial and outdated division of human nature into three separate and distinct realms—those of reason, emotion, and volition. Human nature, they maintained, functioned as a whole, and the law ought to reflect nature rather than create a legal caricature. Moreover, the rules made reason supreme, which created problems for conditions where volition seemed impaired but reason functioned normally. Influential physicians such as Phillipe Pinel and James Prichard were identifying cases of *"manie sans délire"* (lucid mania without delusion) and "moral insanity"—cases in which sudden impulse drove the will.[33] In *Hadfield's Case* Erskine spoke about "motives irresistible," and now medical professionals were documenting it. The irresistible-impulse test ultimately was added to the cognitive test in many American jurisdictions, giving the rules an even wider reign.[34] In England, although the irresistible-impulse addition was debated, it was not incorporated; rather, the courts chose to "elasticize" the M'Naghten Rules, stretching the rules and straining their meaning to embrace such conditions.[35]

Unfortunately, in moving from the wild-beast test to the M'Naghten Rules to the irresistible-impulse addition, the law continued to track *symptoms* of madness rather than identify the *essence* of insanity. In abandoning the beast, it abandoned perception, awareness, and memory symptoms. In adopting the rules, it embraced cognitive symptoms. In adding the irresistible impulse, it sanctioned emotional and volitional symptoms. This trend to embrace, formally or elastically, more symptoms and disorders within the insanity orbit did not satisfy everyone; on the contrary, discontent with the rules continued to grow, despite the additions and stretches. By the mid-twentieth century, on both sides of the Atlantic, the M'Naghten Rules were under sharp attack, chiefly but not exclusively by those in the psychological professions. Justice Felix Frank-furter gave testimony before the Royal Commission on Capital Punish-ment,[36] stating that the "M'Naghten Rules are in large measure shams." He added that he did "not see why the rules of law should be arrested at the state of psychological knowledge of a time when they were for-mulated." The legal concept of insanity was about to be widened fur-ther.

In the United States, this occurred in *Durham v. United States* (1954),[37] where Judge David Bazelon resurrected Isaac Ray's notion of the deed as a product of mental disorder. "The court was convinced not only that his rule was substantively sound but that it would usher in a new era of har-mony between psychiatrists and lawyers."[38] Psychiatrists could now more freely inform the jury about a defendant's mental disease, without confining their remarks to the M'Naghten criteria. Lawyers could ask their experts broader questions about symptoms and their meanings. The jury would hear testimony based on the modern psychological premise of an "integrated personality," rather than on the premise of dissociated parts.

The critics of *Durham* were quick to pounce on the "product rule," rightly noting that it provided no definition of "mental disease." More-over, the so-called integrated personality was still a compartmentalized personality, since prohibited conduct emerged from a separate area of the mind that housed mental disease. The problem was that the same mental disease could produce law-abiding conduct as well, and *Durham* failed to explain why "insane acts" emerged and why they ought to be excused. On the matter of expert testimony, even Bazelon admitted that instead of providing more specific facts, experts merely made their jargon increas-ingly technical and offered more, not fewer, conclusive-sounding state-ments to the jury.[39]

The critics of the *Durham* product rule weighed in with myths as well. Several believed that extremely technical jargon would befuddle jurors, leaving them thoroughly confused. Either the experts would then usurp the jurors' decisionmaking power, or jurors would yield their moral deci-sion to the experts.[40] Commenting on this wider law (a "none rule," to some) and on the prospect of more extensive expert testimony that was likely to confuse jurors, Abraham Goldstein wondered "whether the psy-ches of individual jurors are strong enough to make that decision, or whether the 'law' should put that obligation on them."[41] Such a charac-terization of jurors—which compared them with "cattle being led to slaughter" or "lemmings to the cliff"[42]—though proffered with surety in some quarters, was stated without a shred of fact.

Partial Insanity and Diminished Responsibility

Up to this point, we have spoken of insanity as an all-or-nothing excuse: either you have a total impairment and your criminal deed is excused, or you do not and nothing lessens the guilt. The preeminent jurists of the sixteenth and seventeenth centuries, Coke and Hale, both recognized that madness came in a variety of shadings yet maintained that the impairment had to be "total" to excuse. With regard to "temporary insanity," a condition in which periods of frenzy and lucidity alternated, Coke and Hale again maintained an all-or-nothing position: if the act was committed during *furiosus* it was excused, but if it was committed during a lucid interval the person was as guilty as someone who had no disorder.

In the seventeenth century, the Scottish jurist Sir George Mackenzie (known as "the Bluidy Mackenzie)" formulated a different opinion that would break the all-or-nothing straitjacket of insanity jurisprudence. Mackenzie reasoned that in cyclical diseases, where madness intermittently distorts the judgment, "it cannot but leave some weakness" when lucidity returns.[43] Mackenzie argued "that since the law grants a total impunity to such as are absolutely furious, therefore it should by the rule of proportions lessen and moderate the punishments of such, as though they are not absolutely mad yet are Hypochondrick and Melancholy to such a degree, that it clouds their reason."[44] The Scottish system thus had a third option: a judgment of diminished responsibility, partial insanity, and a culpability lying somewhere between none and full.

In 1800 the Act of Union with England anglicized and submerged this Scottish aberration, and the traditional two-choice, all-or-none notion prevailed. It did so, that is, until 1957, when the British passed the Homicide Act. Although they considered the *Durham* product rule, they rejected it in favor of the more radical concept of diminished responsibility, creating an English version even more generous than the old Scottish one. In the United States, a diminished-capacity defense was evolving through case law in California, which created an option and verdict between insanity and full guilt.[45]

In the United States, *Durham* represented the apogee of the broadening sweep of insanity laws, yet *Durham*'s limited acceptance, its notable definitional deficiencies, and the fears and myths that followed its inception were all harbingers of doom. With *Durham*'s death all but certified, many were looking for a quick fix and a fallback, which they found in the "model penal code" test developed by the American Law Institute (ALI).[46] This test took M'Naghten's definition of sanity—the defendant's ability "to know" right from wrong—and rephrased it as "to appreciate the criminality of his conduct." It also took the "irresistible-impulse" addition and rephrased it as "to conform his conduct to the requirements of the law." These changes were semantic and cosmetic glosses, repackaging the same cognitive and volitional concepts that had already been found wanting. The major reason for the ALI test's quick acceptance may lie in symbol rather than substance, for it appeared that the law was taking back the keys to the courthouse that *Durham* gave away to the experts. In fact, the ALI test did no such thing, as *Hinckley* would soon demonstrate.

Hinckley's act, caught by television cameras and run and rerun on nightly news shows, coupled with the *Hinckley* jury's verdict of "not guilty by reason of insanity,"[47] were enough to inflame passions. The press, the polls, and even the president all expressed opinions on the failings and outrages of the insanity defense. The familiar pattern of chatter recurred: outrage was vented, myths were repeated, and the verdict was branded a "wrongful" verdict. The wrongful verdict signaled that the test had to be flawed, and two years of House and Senate hearings ensued, all directed at creating a new test to set this maddening issue right—once again.

A distinguished group of jurists, jurisprudes, psychiatrists, psychologists, and legislators testified at those hearings.[48] Major organizations such as the American Bar Association, the American Psychiatric Association, and the American Medical Association offered position statements on the insanity matter, and all of the statements differed.[49] At one point, eighteen separate bills were under consideration in the House and eight under consideration in the Senate.[50] These proposals ran the entire gamut, from abolishing the insanity defense, to creating a *mens rea* test that would resurrect the wild beast, to creating an option of "guilty but mentally ill" (GBMI), to doing away with the concept of volition, to fine-tuning the ALI test. In addition to demands for altering the substantive wording of the test, there were proposals to shift the burden of proof, change the standard of proof, limit expert testimony, and tighten dispositional procedures.

Michael Perlin, who has written extensively about how and why persistent myths come to drive insanity law such that incoherence and gridlock result,[51] has culled the following quotes to indicate the fears, superstitions, and myths that were voiced.

Former Attorney General Meese argued that eliminating the insanity defense would "rid . . . the streets of some of the most dangerous people that are out there, that are committing a disproportionate number of crimes." Sen. Strom Thurmond criticized the insanity defense for "exonerat[ing] a defendant who obviously planned and knew exactly what he was doing." Sen. Dan Quayle endorsed constituents' views that asserted the insanity defense "pampered criminals," and that the defense was "decadent," giving defendants the right to kill "with impunity."[52]

"These positions," says Perlin, "parrot medieval views of the mentally disabled criminal defendant: mentally ill individuals are disproportionately dangerous; responsibility-based exculpation is somehow immoral and thwarts the public's right to vengeance; planfulness implies responsibility; the health of our civilization depends on our ability to punish the mentally ill criminal."[53]

Study after study of the mentally ill as a group has shown they are not disproportionately dangerous; on the contrary, the mentally ill are likely to be the victims of crime rather than the perpetrators.[54] As for planfulness, the cases of *Arnold, Hadfield, M'Naghten,* and *Hinckley* illustrate what psychiatry and law have long known—that delusional planfulness does not necessarily mean responsibility. On the legal side, responsibility-based exculpation has been a cornerstone of Anglo-American law, making punishment moral where there is culpability but immoral where there is none. In previous chapters we noted that self-defense, accident, and some forms of mistake exculpate because juries do not find the defendant culpable. An attorney general and U.S. senators may be forgiven for making statements that reflect ignorance of facts, but when lawyers and lawmakers reveal an ignorance of basic legal and civic principles, this is a sign that reason is not running the show.

Regarding the "facts" of the insanity plea, senators Larry Pressler and Orrin Hatch called it "a rich man's defense." Representative John Myers called it a

> "safe harbor for criminals who bamboozle a jury" into thinking they should not be held responsible. Congressman Sensenbrenner portrayed the insanity trial as "protracted testimonial extravaganzas pitting high-priced prosecution experts against equally high-priced defense experts . . ." Former Attorney General William French Smith charged "there must be an end to the doctrine that allows *so many persons* to commit crimes of violence, to use confusing procedures to their own advantage and then have the door opened for them to return to the society they victimized."[55]

Perlin comments, "Each of these mythic statements is a textbook parody of empirical and behavioral reality. The insanity defense is disproportionately used in cases involving indigent defendants; jurors are rarely deceived by simulated pleas; the 'battle of the experts' takes place in a small fraction of insanity cases; the number of defendants who even plead insanity is minute."[56]

These myths turned out to be motives irresistible, for even when testimony debunked the myth,[57] the myth, like some dybbuk, continued to exert a powerful influence over those proposing changes in the law. Contradictory testimony, consisting of basic facts and empirical findings, met a Cassandra-like fate. And the jurors' view of the insanity defense, already maligned following the *Hinckley* decision, was dismissed as revealing ignorance and stupidity. "Laws change for reasons, although not always for the best of reasons."[58] In what followed, we see an example of "making law in the absence of evidence,"[59] a practice that led to bad law. A law, as it turned out, which was "much ado about nothing."[60]

No Choice, False Choice, Old Choice

Congress clearly had a direction in mind, and the title of the Senate subcommittee's report, "Limiting the Insanity Defense,"[61] gave it away. The only question was which limitation Congress would pick. This limiting push was felt at the state level as well: more insanity laws would change in the wake of *Hinckley* than at any other time. The most radical of the limiting proposals favored abolishing the insanity defense entirely—a measure that was adopted by Montana and Idaho. This apparent "no-choice" position is deceptive: it sounds as if the insanity plea has been silenced and is no longer an option. But eliminating the affirmative insanity defense does not stop the defense from asserting that the defendant did not have the requisite *mens rea*. Since the prosecution must prove criminal intent, the defense is entitled to introduce evidence of mental state to disprove intent. Point one is this: the insanity plea is not silenced, for it sounds loudly as a way of defeating *mens rea*.

Norval Morris, who advocates a *mens rea* position, claims that *mens rea* can "carry the freight."[62] Judge Rudolph Gerber also advocates a *mens rea* position.[63] But the historical problem with *mens rea,* which Erskine skillfully mocked—is that the delusional patient apparently has *mens rea* but may be acting out of quite crazy beliefs. Although Gerber and Morris maintain that *mens rea* can carry the freight, both admit that *mens rea* cannot handle the person who believes that God has commanded him to kill. So the second point is this: when the freight is a delusional defendant, *mens rea* drops it—for *mens rea* will wrongfully convict the delusional patient as soon as he buys the proverbial pistol and shot.

A third point is that for special forms of insanity known as automatism cases—where the act was done in a state of sleepwalking, hypnosis, epilepsy, and so on—the notion of insanity can be used to challenge whether an act occurred at all.[64] For example, did the sleepwalking individual "act," as we legally understand this term, or was he or she simply an unconscious body in motion, without foresight or awareness? In special cases, then, insanity can be used to mount a second challenge to the prosecution's case, this time challenging the *actus reus*. So insanity may enter the courtroom drama on two fronts: in the *actus reus* phase in some rare cases, and in the *mens rea* phase in all cases.

Those in favor of abolishing the defense were often the quickest and loudest to voice fears that defendants found not guilty by reason of insanity would find their way back to the community to do harm again. Although "disposition" was on minds of many, the *mens rea* position, in abolishing the special verdict of NGRI, actually left the community less protected. Since the verdict under a *mens rea* scheme would lead to a straightforward "not guilty," the state would have no immediate and automatic statutory power to commit such an individual involuntarily. Although the state could always initiate civil commitment proceedings, the "not guilty" would put the onus and burden clearly on the state. So if the abolitionist mission was really to ensure greater deterrence and dispositional control, the *mens rea* test might paradoxically lead to less.

Quite apart from disposition, those who took the *mens rea* view favored turning the clock back to 1723, when the wild beast roared in *Rex v. Arnold*. But the wild beast proved a paper tiger, inadequate to carry the freight in *Hadfield's Case* and dead on arrival in *M'Naghten*. The arguments for burying the beast were sound, and today they remain sounder than arguments in favor of resurrecting the beast.

From the abolitionists' *mens rea* limitation, we move to the verdict of "guilty but mentally ill" (GBMI), which Christopher Slobogin has called "an idea whose time should not have come."[65] But come it has, and frequently. Although Congress rejected this option, eleven states followed Michigan's lead and adopted GBMI, making it the verdict of choice for states enacting reforms. But there are good reasons for suspecting that it is deceptive—both a false choice and a bad choice.

To reveal its true nature, we must contrast GBMI with "diminished responsibility." Diminished responsibility is a genuine third option that denotes less responsibility and culpability than full guilt (as in cases of murder), but more responsibility and culpability than the NGRI defense. Here punishment follows, but it is mitigated, neither full punishment nor complete exculpation. The level of punishment thus "tracks" the level of responsibility and culpability. Not so for the typical GBMI verdict, which is a guilty verdict denoting no diminution in responsibility or culpability. The most dramatic demonstration that nothing lessens the guilt can be seen in a few cases where individuals given GBMI were also given the death sentence, which some courts have upheld.[66] Little did these defendants realize that the letters GBMI were Bellerophontic, calling on the state to kill the bearer of those letters. What then is GBMI?

The American Psychiatric Association has called GBMI a "compromise" verdict:

> "Guilty but mentally ill" offers a "compromise" for the jury. Persons who might otherwise have qualified for an insanity verdict may instead be siphoned into a category of guilty but mentally ill. Thus some defendants who might otherwise be found not guilty through an insanity defense will be found "guilty but mentally ill" instead.
>
> The "guilty but mentally ill" approach may become the "easy way out." Juries may avoid grappling with the difficult moral issue inherent in adjudicating guilt or innocence, jurors instead settling conveniently on "guilty but mentally ill." The deliberations of jurors in deciding cases are, however, vital to set societal standards and to give meaning to societal ideas about responsibility and non-responsibility. An important symbolic function of the criminal law is lost through the "guilty but mentally ill" approach.[67]

To the cynic (and there are many), GBMI is an attempt to fool both the defendant and the jury into believing that the defendant will get treatment for the acknowledged "MI" in GBMI, while assuring the community that the defendant is going to jail for the "G" part. Studies of how GBMI works in practice reveal that the "GBMI verdict seems to provide a means of assuring long terms of confinement for mentally ill offenders who have committed violent offenses . . . [but] that the treatment available to GBMIs is no different from that available to other prisoners with mental health needs."[68] It appears to trade cynically on its name, implying that the "mental illness" will either mitigate or be attended to, though its purpose is to siphon off some who might plead and be found NGRI.

Congress rejected various GBMI proposals, opting instead to lop off the volitional element of the ALI test in its Insanity Defense Reform Act of 1984. On the basis of testimonials but without sound empirical data,[69] it was decided that the reason for wrongful verdicts was the element of volition. Old arguments were rehashed and reiterated as truth (for example, that jurors—and even experts—were incapable of distinguishing irresistible impulses from impulses the defendant simply failed to resist).[70] It followed that if neither expert nor juror could reliably make this "twilight/dusk" distinction, then the distinction should be dropped entirely. Thus, a volitional amputation was performed.

In the wake of *Hinckley,* and after two years of hearings, only the cognitive elements of the ALI test were left, and these were essentially nothing but a semantic update of the M'Naghten Rules. So in 1984 Congress turned the clock back to 1843 and opted for an old alternative, the M'Naghten Rules—a test that had been stretched, elasticized, and amended for more than a century. Yet despite all these tucks, lifts, and cosmetic fixes, and despite the fact that critics called it a sham and much worse, this was the test that Congress resurrected and anointed to set right the maddening matter of insanity.

The Insanity Defense Reform Act (IDRA) is not likely to make matters right. It would not have made *Hinckley* right, since the issue of whether John Hinckley could control his impulses was not central to his insanity claim. Rather, the focus was Hinckley's beliefs, his cognitions, whether in terms of the ALI test or IDRA, and on this issue a dozen experts testified and offered more than a dozen diagnoses. Even on a purely cognitive playing field, the jurors' discrimination task was formidable.[71]

George Fletcher noted that "the definition, administration and ramifications of the insanity defense express the deepest concerns of the Anglo-American legal culture. Vested with significance that goes beyond its practical impact, the issue of insanity requires us to probe our premises for blaming and punishing. In posing the question whether a particular person is responsible for a criminal act, we are forced to resolve our doubts about whether anyone is ever responsible for criminal conduct. And if some are responsible and some are not, how do we distinguish between them?"[72] Not only did Congress fail to probe the premises deeply, but it settled for the shallow and shopworn, adopting a cognitive test that fastened on a symptom rather than the substance of insanity. Rather than breaking new ground, it settled for a retread, reinventing the 140-year-old M'Naghten wheel. Moreover, when seeking guidance in resolving their doubts, senators and representatives seemed far more comfortable with myths than with evidence. And although many cited the public's outrage, or spoke of the "public's dysfunctionally heightened arousal,"[73] this may have been no more than *perceived* public opinion, for *direct evidence* regarding how the public construes insanity was notably absent at the hearings.

Congress not only missed the essence of insanity; it begged the question of partial insanity, which the British had addressed in their diminished-responsibility verdict. Congress wanted to hear from *Hinckley* jurors, but it did not want to heed what they were saying. The head juror at the *Hinckley* trial declared: "If I had had another choice, in fact if we all had had another choice, it would have been different now. It would not have been this way. Everyone knew beyond a shadow of a doubt that he was guilty for what he did. But we had that mental problem to deal with. We just could not shut that out."[74] Striving to limit the insanity defense, Congress was in no mood to open up a third choice that might lead only to more claimants. Thus, the insanity plea would remain what it had always been: an all-or-nothing affair.

How Jurors Construe Insanity

15

Change has been the constant in the insanity defense equation. When a great case produced a "wrongful" verdict, pressure for a new test grew. Legal and psychological arguments were prominent in the equation, though myths, fears, and politics were factors as well. The perspective of the jurors, when this factor was given any place at all in the equation, was usually regarded negatively: their verdicts were denounced, their judgments were maligned, and their thinking was declared soft-headed. Judging from the critical comments, one might think that the defendant's insanity had rubbed off on the jurors. But even as the jurors' perspective was dismissed, another constant appeared: theoretical arguments for a proposed new insanity test seldom made contact with the empirical reality of what jurors do, and why they do what they do. Though defendants were declared "insane" and jurors were dubbed dysfunctional, the *process* of change remained schizophrenically split: discourse between law and commonsense justice fell into silence, or degenerated into a monologue about jurors in which caricature and cliché replaced understanding.

Insanity tests may ignore the jurors' perspective but they eventually confront empirical reality, as when a new test is applied to new cases. Sooner or later, we get an approximate ideas of how it is working and whether it is working as intended. Even before it is applied to the first case, the new test can be viewed as a *prediction*: that is, from the arguments advanced for this test, it is easy to derive predictions about how it should work when compared to some other test. To illustrate, critics claimed that the wild-beast test was inaccurate and misleading because it focused on perceptions and was too demanding in its insistence on total mental incapacity. The advent of the M'Naghten Rules shifted the focus

from perceptions to cognition, and relaxed the standard from total incapacity to "pockets of madness"—delusions. On the basis of these changes
one might predict that, in comparison to the wild-beast test, the
M'Naghten Rules would produce more verdicts of "not guilty by reason
of insanity." This is, in fact, what many predicted and many feared. But
do tests, in practice, work as advertised?

Before turning to that question, let's generate a few more predictions.
The M'Naghten Rules plus the irresistible impulse should produce more
NGRI verdicts than the rules alone. And *Durham*'s "product rule" test,
which critics believed opened the insanity door wider than ever before,
should produce more NGRI verdicts than the M'Naghten Rules plus the
irresistible-impulse addition, the rules alone, or the wild beast. The test
devised by the American Law Institute (ALI), with its cognitive and volitional aspects, should produce fewer NGRI verdicts than the product rule
but more than the M'Naghten Rules alone. And the test instituted by the
new Insanity Defense Reform Act (IDRA), which eliminates the volitional
aspect, should result in fewer NGRI verdicts than the ALI test. But the
empirical question remains: Do tests work in practice as their supporters
intended them to work? Do the predictions hold up?

In a seminal test of tests, Rita James Simon had twenty different mock
juries hear the same case; ten of the juries received "M'Naghten instructions" and ten received "Durham instructions."[1] Even though these two
tests differed in wording and focus, she found no significant differences in
the verdicts. Why? Do jurors (as critics of jurors have argued and Lord
Cooper maintained) ignore the instructions and simply ask themselves,
"Is this man mad, or is he not?" Since Simon tape-recorded the juries'
deliberations, we have an answer to this question. Jurors were not ignoring the instructions, for the instructions were cited and debated during
deliberations. But jurors *construed* the instructions.

To illustrate construing, let's stay with the M'Naghten test and see
how two jurors, one of whom voted "guilty" and one of whom voted
NGRI, construed the key phrase "to know." The juror who voted
"guilty" said: "I think he is a little insane, but I think he knew the nature
of the act, knew he was doing something wrong. The judge's instructions
point out that even though the man may have had perverted notions, if he
knew what he was doing at the time he committed the act, he knew he
was doing wrong, that's all we have to pass on. That's really our decision."[2] First we hear that this juror retained the key phrases and elements
of the M'Naghten instructions, contrary to the critics' assertions. And
second, this juror construed the phrase "to know" quite specifically and
narrowly, in the manner of some legal interpretations. In contrast, the

juror who voted NGRI said that the defendant "knew what he was doing in the sense that he knew how to get into the house, where to find the bedroom, what articles he wanted to take, but he still didn't know the full significance of what he was doing."[3] Again, this juror knew the instructions but construed the phrase "to know" more broadly, invoking a deeper capacity or incapacity to appreciate the overall significance of the particular acts. A third point is that neither of these two jurors construed the phrase in a bizarre or eccentric way.

The juries that received the Durham test likewise engaged in considerable construing, and construed differently according to whether they voted "guilty" or NGRI. But Simon noted that they had little difficulty "construing the instructions to suit their beliefs concerning the centrality of cognition."[4] So even though Durham's language and focus were clearly different from those of the M'Naghten instructions, jurors construed and reached a common denominator—which, according to Simon, was cognition.

Before accepting these results uncritically, we need to consider the limitations of the experiment. Perhaps the sample was unrepresentative in some unknown way, producing results that would ordinarily not occur. For instance, if the one case which was used turned out to be an oddity that strongly lent itself to a cognitive construal, then verdicts might have been similar regardless of which insanity test was used, whereas another case might have shown differences. Moreover, a finding of no difference between the M'Naghten and Durham instructions does not mean that differences would not be found if more insanity tests were tested. These possibilities suggest the need for a follow-up experiment that extends the number of insanity test instructions being examined, and adds more cases for the mock jurors to decide.

In an experiment that my colleagues and I conducted,[5] subjects were assigned to one of six different insanity test instructions: the wild-beast test, M'Naghten, M'Naghten plus the irresistible-impulse addition, Durham, the ALI test, and a proposed new test called the Disability of Mind test.[6] Each subject rendered judgments and verdicts on five different cases, presented in random order. We created an array of hypothetical cases, modeled after real cases, in which the alleged "mental condition" varied from the organic (for example, epilepsy) to the purely psychological (for example, stress disorder). Though the background facts of the cases differed, we held the defendant's gender (female), and the mode and manner of the killing (all picked up a loaded pistol that had fallen to the floor and fired) constant across cases.

Simon found no differences between two tests, and we found no significant differences overall among six tests. This finding is remarkable, given that the tests covered 250 years of insanity jurisprudence and differed markedly in their wording and focus. The finding is also sobering, given the long-running debate over insanity tests and the efforts that have been expended in perfecting a better test. In an attempt to make these results even more up-to-date, I gave a group of subjects the new IDRA test from which the volitional aspect had been eliminated; a second group of subjects was given the full ALI test; and a third group was given a *mens rea* update of the old wild-beast test.[7] Again, no significant verdict differences among the tests were found. Thus, Congress's advertised method of limiting the insanity defense through the IDRA test failed when empirically tested.[8] But it is not just the IDRA test that fails to work as advertised;[9] it seems to make no difference what test you give mock jurors.

If no test works any differently from any other, what would happen if you gave "no test" to subjects? S. F. Handel and I examined this question by setting up an experiment in which we gave subjects "no instruction," telling them simply to use their "own best lights" to decide these cases.[10] Whether we looked at each case or across all the cases, we found no significant differences between subjects who received "no instruction" versus those who received instructions. In several experiments with students and adults, subjects who used their "own best lights" reached verdicts similar to those of subjects who used the wild-beast test, M'Naghten, M'Naghten plus the irresistible-impulse addition, Durham, the ALI test, and the IDRA test. Thus, in terms of the predicted outcomes, tests with markedly different criteria failed to produce discriminably different verdicts, and failed to produce verdicts discriminably different from those produced by a no-test condition. Lord Cooper may have had it partly right: jurors do not ignore instructions but they construe instructions, employing their constructs of "sane" and "insane" to determine their verdict, despite the wording of the legal test given to them.

In the Insanity Defense Reform Act of 1984, Congress not only changed the substantive wording and criterion of insanity but barred experts from giving "ultimate-opinion" testimony. It also changed the burden and standard of proof, requiring the defense to prove insanity by "clear and convincing evidence."[11] Clearly, the prohibition against ultimate opinion, along with the burden and standard shifts, were aimed at making verdicts of NGRI less likely. Quite apart from the theoretical question of whether experts should be allowed to give an ultimate opinion (a continuing debate that dates from *M'Naghten's Case*),[12] we have the empirical question of whether the prohibition will work as advertised.

Christopher Slobogin has argued that the prohibition will not work.[13]

Preventing experts from answering the ultimate question—Is the defendant sane or insane?—still leaves them free to answer the penultimate question: Do you believe the defendant can understand the consequences of his behavior or appreciate the wrongfulness of his acts? Slobogin predicted that jurors who hear penultimate testimony will have no trouble translating that into "Oh, so the expert thinks he's insane." His prediction turned out to be accurate, and then some.

Solomon Fulero and I gave subjects one of four types of expert testimony: ultimate opinion, penultimate opinion, diagnostic opinion, and no expert opinion.[14] There were no significant differences for the three expert-testimony conditions: although having an expert testify did increase the number of NGRI verdicts, it did not matter what level of conclusion the expert reached. Even when the expert gave only diagnostic testimony ("The patient has a delusional paranoid disorder, which is a severe psychiatric condition"), mock jurors seemed to have little trouble construing and translating that into "Oh, he's insane."

James Ogloff empirically tested the changes that the Insanity Defense Reform Act made in the burden and standard of proof.[15] He found no significant difference between placing the burden on the defense and placing it on the prosecution, and no significant difference when the standard was changed. In passing the act, Congress (1) amended the substantive test, (2) barred ultimate-opinion testimony, and (3) altered and shifted the burden and standard of proof. And if we sum up the empirical findings, Congress struck out on all three changes, for none of the three produce the predicted reduction in NGRI verdicts. One important measure of a test is whether it works as intended. The Insanity Defense Reform Act does not. It is not alone, however, since it joins a long list of tests that failed to work as advertised.

Why do these tests fail to produce discriminably different verdicts? The familiar refrain is "Blame the jurors": jurors are indiscriminate, unable to comprehend such legal subtleties; if they remember legal instructions in the jury box, they forget them in the jury room; and even when they remember them, they often ignore or willfully disregard them. The only problem with this familiar refrain is that it is not borne out by empirical research. To cite but one instance, Simon's experiment showed that jurors do not ignore or willfully disregard instructions but that they remember and comprehend them.

In the experiments my colleagues and I conducted, a recurrent finding was that subjects made *case-by-case* discriminations.[16] Most subjects changed their verdicts across cases; they were not indiscriminate and they did not show general sympathy or antipathy to NGRI verdicts. Contrary to the critics' worst indictments, we found that jurors did think. Moreover, the evidence showed that when it comes to the insanity plea, jurors' thinking was deeper and more complex than legal and legislative thinking.

In addition to making verdict discriminations among cases, subjects also discriminated among defendants on items relating to culpability and disposition. They discriminated when asked to evaluate how responsible the defendant was for her act and how much mitigation was warranted for her mental condition. Subjects also discriminated on an item the law does not take into account in insanity cases: the defendant's culpability for bringing about her mental deterioration. For instance, subjects who found the epileptic defendant guilty acknowledged that at the moment of the act she was going into seizure and was unconscious when the gun went off; they did not hold her responsible for the shooting. But they did hold her responsible for ceasing to take her seizure medication two days earlier without consulting her doctor. It was this "negligence" or "recklessness" that they weighed and found blameworthy.

As to disposition—which is an issue the law reserves for the judge and not the jury—it was clear that jurors did think about what should happen to a particular defendant, and they had discriminably different opinions for different defendants. For example, in the paranoid-schizophrenic case and the stress-induced case, where the NGRI percentages were similar (68 percent and 74 percent, respectively), 46 percent of the subjects were willing to set the stress-induced defendant free, whereas only 1 percent were willing to set the paranoid schizophrenic free; 94 percent wanted to see the paranoid schizophrenic confined in a psychiatric hospital. Thus, even when verdicts were similar, subjects sometimes construed cases quite differently, making discriminations about types of culpability and dispositional outcomes.

Some subjects made still another discrimination which was quite germane to their verdict and to the perception that a particular verdict was "wrongful." This involved *contextualizing*. It has been argued that in making an *assessment* subjects must first *contextualize* the problem.[17] In these "insanity" experiments, the problem was contextualized for them: they were told, in many ways, that they were dealing with an *alleged insanity case*. They were given this framing in the prosecution's and defense's opening and closing statements to the jury, in the judge's instructions, and in the verdict options that were presented. Yet in the experiment that I conducted with S. F. Handel, approximately 12 percent of the sample framed the case differently, contextualizing the problem *out-*

side the parameters of NGRI-or-guilty.[18] Some of these subjects saw the epilepsy case as a "tragic accident" and wondered why charges were even brought. Some subjects saw the stress-induced case as one of self-defense, not insanity, and wanted to render an NGRSD verdict. Of the subjects who found the defendant guilty, some wanted to bring in verdicts of involuntary manslaughter or criminal negligence. Though the 12 percent figure was small, it was not insignificant. It highlighted the importance of *contextualizing,* for if jurors' view of a case is different from the law's, they are not likely to find their verdict of choice. This raises the possibility a jury will nullify, or construe a verdict option in ways that do not conform to legal orthodoxy.

The empirical evidence seems to show that jurors make fine-grained distinctions among defendants and cases. The myth that jurors don't think can now put to rest; in fact, they think deeply and broadly, though not always within legal guidelines. We've already seen that many jurors consider and weigh a "culpable negligence" factor, which is germane to their assessment of the defendant's moral blameworthiness yet not part of the legal instructions. There is evidence that some subjects consider disposition, and may reach a verdict "backward": that is, they first decide whether they want to see the defendant in prison or in a psychiatric hospital, and then decide which verdict is likely to achieve that outcome. And there is evidence that they contextualize, sometimes seeing the problem outside the defined parameters and seeking verdicts that are not available.

Whether contextualizing or construing, the subject is constructing the meaning of the case, the meaning of expert testimony, and the meaning of legal instructions. While construing reaches up to the legally lofty realm of instructive words and phrases, it also reaches down to the defendant's *behavior.* One of the questions asked in Simon's experiment was: What separated the jurors who voted "guilty" from those who voted NGRI?[19] More specifically, were the jurors in the former group citing one set of behaviors that indicated "sane," whereas the jurors in the NGRI group were citing a different set of behaviors that indicated "insane"? The answer was no: jurors in both groups cited the same behavior, but construed it in very different ways.

Simon used a disguised version of the *Durham* case, which we discussed earlier.[20] The defendant broke into a house in broad daylight and was caught with a cheap cigarette lighter and cufflinks, together worth less than fifty dollars. When discovered, he was crouching like a duck with a newspaper over his head, in the middle of a room. How were these facts construed? As we saw in Chapter 5, people saw the same set of facts in different ways: the NGRI jurors thought that only a crazy person would do these things, whereas the jurors who voted "guilty" thought they could well be the methods and ruses of a clever thief.

The same behavior, construed differently, led to different prototypes and verdicts. For one group the prototype of the "smart criminal" fit, whereas for the other group the prototype of the "insane individual" fit. Note that in this battle of discrepant prototypes, the "reasonable person" prototype was nowhere to be found—for reasonable people do not break into houses.

Commonsense Insanity

Ordinary people make a variety of discriminations, most of which fall well within accepted legal boundaries. Some discriminations, however, fall outside these boundaries, and some invoke accepted legal principles not found in traditional insanity jurisprudence. Construing seems to be a ubiquitous phenomenon, whether applied to case parameters, testimony, instructions, or the actual behavior of the defendant. What has not yet been shown yet (though the evidence raises a strong suspicion) is that ordinary citizens have intuitive constructs of "sane" and "insane" which are powerful and determinative, more so than the constructs embedded in legal tests. For if jurors are setting the legal test aside, then they must be falling back on their commonsense notions of insanity. And if they reconstrue the test, their commonsense notions of insanity must be giving their reconstructions shape and form.

Some jurisprudes have made a recommendation that is much in line with the research findings: the legal notion of "insanity" ought to rest on the commonsense perspective. These commonsense advocates argue that legal tests have medicalized the definitions of "mental illness" and "insanity" to such a degree that these terms not only stand outside ordinary thinking but remove insanity from its proper moral context. Michael Moore puts it this way:[21] "If the issue is a moral one . . . then the legal definition of the phrase should embody those moral principles that underlie the intuitive judgment that mentally ill human beings are not responsible . . . What is thus needed is an analysis of that popular moral notion of mental illness. What have people meant by mental illness such that, both on and off juries, they have for centuries excused the otherwise wrongful acts of mentally ill persons?"[22] Stephen Morse makes a similar point.[23] He not only rejects "pseudomedicalizations" but criticizes legal and semantic debates that have created a "distinction without a difference."[24] For instance, the word "appreciate" was used in the ALI test in place of the word "understand," which had figured in the M'Naghten test. This distinction may have meaning to legal scholars, but to the jurors who construe instructions it is apt to be meaningless. Morse proposes a "craziness test": "A defendant is not guilty by reason of insanity if at the time of the offense the defendant was extremely crazy and the craziness affected the criminal behavior."[25] This craziness test is similar to Lord Cooper's assertion that jurors ask themselves: Is this man mad or is he not? Lord Cooper's supposition, and Morse's, "is that ordinary citizens are, in essence, invoking such a craziness test," so the law ought to follow the path laid by the community.[26]

Herbert Fingarette and Ann Hasse, who also advocate a commonsense view, believe that traditional legal tests focus wrongly on "symptoms" of insanity and fail to identify its essence.[27] Symptomatic definitions, whether focused on perception, cognition, or volition, all identify the flaw in the *mens rea* but miss the deeper *mens,* which Fingarette and Hasse identify as the individual's "lack of capacity for rational conduct in regard to criminal significance of the conduct."[28] Without such a capacity the person is not "response-able," and this "is central to what we wish to express when we speak of someone as 'out of his mind,' 'out of touch with reality,' 'mentally incompetent,' 'crazy,' or 'mad.'"[29] By invoking the colloquial terms for insanity, terms used by ordinary citizens who sit on juries, Fingarette and Hasse seek a legal definition that comports with the commonsense understanding of insanity.[30]

Judge Bazelon, author of the Durham rule, likewise criticized this focus on symptoms: "The fundamental objection to the right-wrong test . . . is not that criminal irresponsibility is made to rest upon an inadequate, invalid or indeterminable symptom or manifestation, but that it is made to rest upon *any* particular symptom."[31] Bazelon proposed what a minority of ALI draftsmen proposed—namely, a "justly responsible" test. Jurors would be instructed that a defendant is not responsible "if at the time of his unlawful conduct his mental or emotional processes or behavior controls were impaired to such an extent that he cannot justly be held responsible."[32] The "justly responsible" test is significant because it "candidly informs the jury that it is their function to apply the moral standards of the community to what they have learned about the offender."[33] Under this test, jurors would be "free to consider all information advanced by the relevant scientific disciplines."[34]

These commonsense advocates decry the medicalized, legalized, and jargonized notions of "mental illness" and the grounding of the legal concept of "insanity" on symptoms. All of these wrongheaded trends distort the matter of insanity: it *ought* to be a proper moral judgment, resting on the moral principles that underlie ordinary people's understanding of "sane" and "insane." But however commonsensical these commonsense notions sound, they still lack a sound empirical base. What is still needed, as Moore pointed out, is an *analysis* of what people mean by "sane" and "insane," such that they continue to excuse the otherwise wrongful acts of some insanity defendants as morally just.[35]

We need a way to get people to identify and explain their constructs of these terms. In addition, since we're seeking their intuitive concepts, we don't want to give them a legal test which might steer them merely to parrot the test's construct as their own. Thus, in the experiment I conducted with S. F. Handel, subjects received no insanity test but were told to use their own best lights in deciding four insanity cases.[36] For each case they were asked to write out the factors they found most relevant and determinative in reaching the verdict they did, and to explain their reasons. These reasons were categorized by independent raters using a seven-construct schema that proved reliable and captured their reasons.

One end of the construct dimension reflected the "insane" judgment (NGRI), whereas the other end reflected the "sane" judgment (guilty). The seven dimensions were: (1) incapacity/capacity to make responsible choices; (2) impaired/unimpaired awareness and perceptions; (3) distorted/clear thinking; (4) could not control / could control impulses and actions; (5) nonculpable/culpable actions; (6) no evil motive / evil motive; and (7) others at fault / others not at fault. Some of these dimensions consisted of the traditional symptom focus: for example, construct 2 was essentially the wild-beast test, construct 3 reflected the cognitive focus of the M'Naghten Rules and the IDRA test, and construct 4 incorporated the irresistible-impulse addition and the volitional part of the ALI test. Unrelated to specific symptoms is construct 1, which related to the deeper essence of the concept of "insanity." Construct 5 focused on negligence or recklessness before the moment of the act, such as ceasing to take prescribed medication, drinking alcohol while on medication, or dropping out of therapy against medical advice. Construct 6 judged the motivation for the act, and whether the motive was evil or not. Construct 7 assessed contributory blame—that is, whether others were at fault.

The first thing we noted was that subjects invoked a number of relevant and determinative constructs per case, 2.5 on the average. This indicated complex construing rather than simplistic construing; in fact, since most legal tests identify very few constructs (the ALI test used two, and the IDRA test only one), the "simplism" would seem to be in the *legal test,* not in the subjects' minds.

Second, subjects rendering an NGRI verdict and subjects rendering a "guilty" verdict did not construe the same case along identical construct dimensions. Although some dimensions were cited by both groups of subjects, others were relevant to one group but not to the other, and this occurred for every case. Thus, the subjects did not engage in simple, polar-opposite construing, where subjects who voted "guilty" saw "clear thinking" while NGRI subjects saw "distorted thinking." Their construing was orthogonal: some dimensions turned out to be determinatively relevant to one group but not the other.

Third, in making fine discriminations, subjects changed their relevant and determinative constructs from case to case. When we looked at the "symptomatic" constructs—the cognitive construct (distorted/clear thinking), the volitional construct (could not control / could control impulses and actions), and the awareness construct (impaired/unimpaired awareness and perception)—none of these proved to be centrally relevant across cases as a factor for the NGRI or the "guilty" verdict, and in a number of cases they were irrelevant. Two construct dimensions did achieve a number of first rankings as a factor for either NGRI or "guilty" across cases: the capacity/incapacity construct, and the culpable/nonculpable construct. When these two factors were combined, they ranked first in seven out of eight analyses.

But just putting the capacity and culpability factors together does not solve the problem posed by subjects' changing their relevant and determinative constructs from case to case.

> For if jurors keep shifting their relevant and determinative constructs as the case changes, then an empirically derived, common law test of insanity is likely to run into the same problems and meet the same fate as the de jure legal tests: That is, it might work well for one case but not the next, when what is needed is an insanity test that works from case to case. The first question is: Can we find, amidst these shifting constructs, some constructs that seem to hold steady across the spectrum of cases? And the second question is: Given that we can find such steady constructs, will they account for a sizable portion of the variance?[37]

Searching for steady constructs, I ran another experiment in which I again asked mock jurors to write out their determinative reasons.[38] This time, instead of asking independent raters to categorize the reasons, I had the subjects themselves categorize their reasons. This change enabled me to test for one possible source of error: perhaps raters were reading in too much and making it appear as if subjects were more complex in their construing than they really were (the average rating was 2.5). Furthermore, since only the subjects knew exactly what they meant, outside raters may have miscategorized reasons, creating a reliability problem. A test that had subjects categorize their own reasons would be the most reliable gauge; it would tell precisely how many constructs and which constructs they were citing. The results showed that they cited 3.2 constructs per case for their NGRI verdicts and 3.0 constructs for their "guilty" verdicts. Thus, the construct picture was indeed complex; if anything, the independent raters may have underestimated the number of constructs.

These results also showed that traditional insanity tests do not *instruct*. Any insanity test can be viewed as a legal guideline—or, more strongly, a rule—which tells jurors to use that particular construct, and only that construct, in deciding the case. For example, the IDRA test instructs jurors to use a cognitive construct only. The ALI test instructs jurors to use either a cognitive or volitional control construct. And the wild-beast / *mens rea* test directs jurors to focus on awareness and perceptions. When we look at the constructs cited by subjects who received these three tests, plus a group that received no instruction, we find no significant construct differences: that is, subjects essentially cited the same constructs regardless of the legal guideline given or whether they were given one at all. To take but one example, the mock jurors receiving the IDRA test cited the volitional control construct just as often (if not more often!) than the subjects who received the ALI test, even though the IDRA test expressly lopped off the volitional component. The experiment revealed two things: the tests failed to instruct and channel the subjects' constructs along the designated de jure line, and the subjects' intuitive constructs of "sane" and "insane" remained powerfully determinative.

The main question was whether it was possible to find, amid the complex constructs that changed with the case, higher-order constructs that held across cases and accounted for a sizable portion of the variance. Cluster analysis revealed two such constructs, which accounted for a sizable 62 percent of the variance.[39] The first was the capacity/incapacity construct, which related to the deeper meaning of insanity and to the issue of whether the person was capable of making responsible choices. This construct absorbed many of the symptomatic constructs, while tapping something more essential. The second construct was the culpable/nonculpable dimension, relating to actions that occurred *before* the act and to whether negligence or reckless was involved. In a subsequent experiment, these two constructs once again emerged and accounted for a large percentage of the variance, indicating that the finding was both reliable and robust.[40]

This empirical work shows that the arguments of commonsense advocates have a great deal in common with the way in which ordinary people construe "insanity." People evidently believe that "insanity" means more than just *symptoms;* its meaning lies closer to the moral question of whether the actor is responsible or not. But the second construct, involving culpable actions, reflects a divergence between commonsense justice and the way black-letter law views insanity, and it is commonsense justice that takes the more sophisticated approach. P. H. Robinson has noted that criminal law's view of "causing the conditions of one's own defense" is "inadequate, . . . frequently irrational, and is a poor approximation of our collective sense of justice."[41] This doctrinal confusion is evident when it comes to insanity: sometimes the law ignores prior culpability and focuses exclusively on the moment of the act; sometimes it focuses on the earlier conduct and ignores the moment of the act; and sometimes, as in cases of felony-murder (see Chapter 9), it inappropriately substitutes one type of culpability for another, even when the two types are quite distinct. An intoxicating illustration makes the problem quite clear.

Imagine a guest at a party who drinks heavily, gets into his car, and has an accident. Someone is injured or killed. The question is: Can the drunk driver plead insanity and be found NGRI? If we focus our culpability inquiry only on the "moment of the act," the drunk driver's "insanity case" is as good as it comes: his impairments in awareness, cognition, and impulse control are at least as great as those of the most famous "insanity" defendants—Hinckley, M'Naghten, Hadfield, and Arnold. Thus, if we keep the analysis solely on the moment of the act, a verdict of "not guilty by reason of insanity" seems assured.

At this point, however, we are likely to object, and to change the focus from the moment of the act to an earlier time: the time of the party, when there were no impairments and when fateful and fatal decisions were being made. The ordinary citizen is likely to say, "You got yourself drunk," "You put yourself in that condition," "You made foolish choices that were reckless or negligent." The fact that the defendant was completely impaired at the time of the crash *is not the point.* The point, to the ordinary citizen, is that the law's focus in the matter of insanity has been narrowly circumscribed on the moment of the act, whereas commonsense justice encompasses more time and relevant actions in making a culpability judgment. In looking back just a few hours prior to the event, commonsense justice finds some culpability. But what kind of culpability is it, and what should we do with it?

If we take that earlier culpability, merely transfer it to the moment of the accident, and claim that the guest is responsible for the homicide, something is amiss. The guest is clearly not as culpable as someone charged with murder or voluntary manslaughter, since he had no *intent* to harm or kill. In this case there are two separate and distinct actions and intentions—conceptually distinct and separated in time—that require independent culpability judgments.

The problem of two separate actions and intentions is not unique to insanity cases. M. D. Alicke and T. L. David found that in ordinary social situations involving judgments of blame, people do more then merely assign causal responsibility.[42] They will blame and punish an individual more when they attribute capacity-development or capacity-activation responsibility. "Capacity-development responsibility" refers to responsibility for developing an incapacity such as depression, psychosis, or alcoholism. Perhaps this is why cases of chronic alcoholism produce the fewest NGRI verdicts: if subjects consider a defendant responsible for bringing about her disability of mind, then they are saying she has capacity-development responsibility. "Capacity-activation responsibility" refers to responsibility for activating the incapacity. For instance, some subjects in the experiment involving the shooting by the epileptic considered the defendant responsible for her actions, because they saw her decision to stop taking medication as precipitating the seizure that led to the fatal shooting.

A number of experiments dealing with insanity consistently showed that subjects weighed this *culpable-actions* factor, which deals with responsibility and culpability for prior actions and decisions that brought about the person's mental disability. Research findings in social psychology have shown that this capacity-responsibility judgment is common to situations that have little to do with insanity per se, indicating that this culpability judgment is commonplace and widespread. But as G. P. Fletcher noted, criminal law tends to conflate different types of causation.[43] Confusion results not only at the doctrinal level but at the practical level, for jurors who make separate and sophisticated distinctions have no way to register their distinctions in the traditional two-choice (NGRI or "guilty") schema. This was what the head of the *Hinckley* jury was telling Senator Heflin when she said that the jurors were looking for a third choice but couldn't find one.

One Size Misfits All

Not only do people see different types of culpability; they see shadings. If people see "gray" but insanity is defined as a "black-or-white" quality, then jurors have another problem: they must fit "gray" into one of two categories, neither of which matches their judgment. The diminished-responsibility option in England and the "guilty but mentally ill" option in twelve U.S. states create, albeit in quite different ways, a third option. As we have seen, some people fear that jurors will overuse such a category as an easy out, or misuse the category by convicting (with a GBMI verdict) someone who should properly be exculpated (with an NGRI verdict). The American Psychiatric Association has claimed that jurors will use this third verdict as an "easy way out," avoiding "the difficult moral issues inherent in adjudicating guilt or innocence . . . [and] settling conveniently on guilty but mentally ill."[44] Even though experiments have shown repeatedly that jurors make complex moral judgments—more complex than the law's—the charge of simplism and avoidance of moral issues keeps cropping up.

Data from Michigan, the state that first introduced GBMI, provide few insights into what jurors do, since more than 90 percent of Michigan's insanity trials were bench trials, conducted before a judge and not a jury.[45] In an empirical test of GBMI, C. F. Roberts and colleagues found that 66.7 percent of the verdicts across their four cases turned out to be GBMI.[46] They concluded that the frequent use of GBMI (it was used 2.5 times more frequently than either "guilty" or NGRI), coupled with the lack of significant differences across their cases, meant that most "subjects preferred to utilize the GBMI option as a compromise verdict even in the face of very severe mental illness."[47] They reached that conclusion despite the fact that their subjects "who decided GBMI were more confident . . . of their decisions than either subjects who decided NGRI . . . or Guilty."[48]

From these results, it appears as if the critics of jurors and the third option were right. Yet there are reasons to suspect that the experimenters' method may have inflated the use of the third option. Subjects were asked to render a verdict in the traditional two-choice schema, with NGRI and "guilty" being the two choices. But almost immediately thereafter, the researchers gave the third option and asked for another verdict for the same case. Subjects now had a three-choice schema featuring NGRI, "guilty," and GBMI. This second verdict rendering, following on the heels of the first, may have created the impression (known as a demand characteristic) that subjects were expected to use the new, third category. Moreover, since they did not balance "order" by asking half the subjects to do the three-choice schema first and the two-choice schema second, we cannot be sure that an order effect or a demand characteristic did not inflate the results.

K. Duff and I conducted an experiment in which order was counterbalanced: one group of subjects received the three-choice schema first and then the two-choice; a second group was given the schemas in reverse order.[49] Moreover, the two verdict renderings were separated by a week's time. The third option here was called "diminished responsibility" (DR). Subjects were given no legal definition of the term; they were merely told it meant that guilt and punishment were lessened because of the defendant's mental condition. By not giving a legal definition of the concept which might have constrained its use, we maximized the likelihood of overuse, if indeed subjects had a penchant for using it as an easy out.

Across our four cases, we found that the DR verdicts accounted for 41 percent of all verdicts—a far cry from Roberts' figure of 66.7 percent, and one that does not immediately suggest overuse. Furthermore, the DR verdicts were rendered by subjects from both the "guilty" and NGRI groups—a result that contradicted the critics' predictions that subjects would use this verdict to convict defendants who should be exculpated (the NGRIs). A comparison of the two- and three-choice schemas revealed that NGRI verdicts dropped across cases from 59 percent to 35 percent, whereas "guilty" verdicts dropped from 41 percent to 24 percent.

Although DR use across cases was 41 percent, there were significant differences in its use *by case,* evidence that jurors used that verdict *selectively,* not indiscriminately. For example, the DR verdict was the most frequently used verdict for the epilepsy case (51 percent) and the stress-induced case (56 percent), but not for the other two cases; only 28 percent rendered a DR verdict in the chronic-alcoholic case, where the guilty verdict was dominant (69 percent), and in the paranoid schizophrenic case only 28 percent rendered a DR verdict, while NGRI (67 percent) was dominant. Finally, not one subject used the DR verdict for all four cases, again indicating selectivity.

When we looked at the ratings of these defendants, we found that subjects who rendered a DR verdict "saw" the defendant differently from those who rendered either a "guilty" or NGRI verdict. If subjects were using the DR verdict appropriately, one would expect their ratings to have fallen between those of the "guilty" and NGRI groups, and they consistently did. Ratings of responsibility for the act, responsibility for bringing about the mental condition, degree of mitigation warranted, and so forth were significantly different from the ratings of the NGRI and "guilty" groups. Even when two cases, the epilepsy case (51 percent) and the stress-induced case (56 percent), had similar DR percentages, there was evidence that subjects were discriminating. For the epilepsy case, in which the defendant stopped taking her medication without consulting her doctor, DR subjects rated her as being quite responsible for bringing about her mental disorder, whereas they rated the battered woman in the stress-induced case as not responsible for bringing about her disorder. On the rating of responsibility for the act, however, the epileptic was seen as not responsible, but the stress-induced defendant was rated as moderately responsible. Thus, even where similar verdicts resulted, subjects continued to make distinctions about different types of culpability, as well as shaded distinctions of black, white, and gray.

If the DR verdict was a "true" in-between verdict rather than a compromise, as the evidence from the ratings suggested, then we should have seen further evidence of this when examining the determinative constructs subjects invoked. If DR reflected some culpability but a verdict less severe than "guilty," and some mitigation due to the mental condition but a verdict more severe than exculpation (NGRI), then the subjects who rendered the DR verdict should have been invoking a mixture of NGRI and "guilty" constructs. And they did. The subjects who rendered DR verdicts cited a set of constructs that were significantly different from those cited by either the "guilty" or the NGRI subjects: in fact, they mixed NGRI and "guilty" constructs.

These basic results were replicated in another experiment which featured a comparison of the DR option (with no legal test definition) and the GBMI option, in which subjects were given Michigan's legal wording.[50] There were no significant differences in terms of verdicts, ratings, and constructs cited between the DR and GBMI schemas. Usage was moderate overall (40.2 percent for the DR option, and 33.9 percent for the GMBI option), and selective and discriminative by case.

In these experiments, the subjects' *constructs* were more determinative of verdict than particular insanity tests and other variables considered. But it is possible that constructs were not determinative of verdict, but merely an artifact of making a verdict. Perhaps the subject decided on a verdict, and then tried to justify his or her verdict by listing constructs that appear consistent. If so, then constructs became after-the-fact artifacts, self-serving rationalizations created to give the appearance of rationality and consistency. Another experiment by Roberts and colleagues showed convincingly that constructs are not artifacts,[51] and that "the relationship between construals and verdicts exists independent of whether a previous verdict has been articulated publicly."[52] Constructs are real, and they remain determinative. When these researchers looked at the subjects' constructs in regard to the GBMI verdict, they found that subjects used the GBMI verdict "to signify diminished blame and punishment."[53] Thus, although GBMI was supposed to be a "functionally 'guilty'" verdict, subjects did use it as a mitigating midground category, reflecting diminished responsibility.

A Commonsense Test of Insanity

Since subjects appeared to see different types of culpability and different degrees of culpability, I developed a new insanity test that incorporated these culpability distinctions.[54] I then compared this test against a traditional two-choice test (IDRA) and the two three-choice tests (GBMI and DR). The new test asked mock jurors to make a series of sequential judgments, beginning with a *behavioral decision:* Did the defendant's behavior cause the harm that was a criminal offense by law? If subjects answered no, a verdict of "not guilty" followed. If they answered yes, they moved on to the *mens decision:* Was the defendant, at the moment of the act, suffering from a disability of mind, and did that disability of mind play a significant role in the defendant's criminal behavior? If subjects said no, they went on to the *mens rea decision,* considering traditional intent questions that could lead to a verdict of guilty, guilty to a lesser offense, or not guilty. But if subjects said yes to the *mens* question, they had to decide if the disability of mind at the moment of the act was partial or total. Then they proceeded to the *culpability decision:* Was the defendant culpable to some degree for bringing about her disability of mind? If they found culpability, they had to decide if she was partially or totally culpable. Specific verdicts followed from this sequence of decisions. In this schema, subjects would render a verdict of NGRI only if they thought the defendant had a total disability of mind and was not culpable for creating her disability.

In comparison to the three-choice and two-choice schemas, this new sequential schema produced fewer NGRI verdicts. Moreover, it closely tracked subjects' ratings and determinative constructs of the defendant, significantly more so than any other schema. Put in terms of variance, this schema reduced error variance and predicted verdict to a greater extent than any other schema. Since subjects were naturally making different types of culpability judgments and shading discriminations, this schema gave them the vehicle for registering those discriminations. Subjects in the two-choice and the three-choice conditions were making the same responsibility and culpability judgments and invoking the same constructs that subjects were making under the sequential-verdict condition; but they did not have the categories, or all the categories they needed, to register their discriminations. Thus, they had to squeeze and conflate, fitting apples, oranges, and pears into one category. When subjects are forced to do this, the resulting decisions include a few "bad apples" and the appearance of a wrongful verdict.

Finding a way to incorporate the jurors' perspective is the great challenge. Ignoring this perspective does not work, yet it is notably absent from the history of changes in the insanity test. Without it, test after test has failed to cure the ills it was created to correct. New tests that show no significant difference in verdicts from their predecessors turn out to be much ado about nothing. Moreover, when such tests seize and incorporate new substantive standards out of the ether of legal or psychological theory—standards that make little contact with jurors' intuitive constructs of "sane" and "insane"—these new legal constructs consistently fail to instruct.[55]

Maligning the jurors is the wrong answer: the evidence is overwhelming that jurors engage in complex construing and make multiple discriminations. The charge of "simplism" is more aptly laid on the law's doorstep. When jurors' constructs of "sane" and "insane" are elucidated, they are revealed not only as complex but as appropriate and deep. Jurors go beneath the superficial symptoms of insanity, the shallow cornerstones of so many legal tests, to an essence that lies in the defendant's capacity to make responsible choices. They also consider and weigh a dimension akin to negligence or recklessness that has been notably absent or conflated in insanity law: culpability for bringing about one's disability of mind. This is not inapt but quite germane.

George Dix has concluded that "the law, if it is to maintain the community's respect, must grade its condemnation according to the moral turpitude of the offender as the community evaluates it."[56] We know that the community does grade moral turpitude: whenever it sees "gray" in a case it seeks a true diminished-responsibility verdict, not the sham of GBMI.

When an insanity schema is created from commonsense distinctions, the results indicate fewer NGRI verdicts, tighter variance, and a more faithful tracking of culpability judgments. When the law's path is constructed from legalisms unchecked by realism, people do not follow. Rather, commonsense justice follows a path paved with commonsense constructs. If the law followed the path of commonsense justice, understanding rather than dismissing its constructs, that path would lead not to darkness or madness but to familiar legal terrain. On this ground, jurors would make complex yet intelligible culpability distinctions and shadings, providing a moral footing in this maddening matter of insanity. The law could do worse. And it has.

Murderous Passions, Mitigating Sentiments

16

Achilles and Odysseus, heroes of the *Iliad* and the *Odyssey*, both react with murderous passion to certain provocations. When their earthly emotions erupt, Athena meddles, but not with evenhandedness or equal justice: curiously and contradictorily, the goddess of wisdom stays the hand of Achilles yet goads Odysseus to slaughter. From an earthly vantage point, the gods may be crazy or contrary; from an Olympian vantage point, though, humans might be as well. Our legal history reveals that, like the gods, we reach disparate verdicts while remaining confused about the mitigating rationale for manslaughter—why we punish a killing done "in the heat of passion" less severely than we do murder. Still, all is not even between heaven and earth; for whereas Athena proposed and Zeus affirmed exculpation for the slaughter wreaked by Odysseus, modern law seems to have settled on mitigation. Yet the unsettled, earthly question is not *what* we do but *why* we do what we do. Why do we mitigate punishment for manslaughter, rather than punish it fully like murder or excuse it entirely like self-defense or insanity?

A Tangled Web

To understand the law's rationale for mitigation, we must first see how the law relates the concepts of provocation, emotion, time, reason, and action. From this web of psychological strands, the law extracts an *implicit* theory of human nature—a theory that drives its manslaughter jurisprudence. From the same web, the discipline of psychology, backed by research, also extracts theories. And ordinary people, who grant neither law nor psychology hegemony or exclusivity here, have their own implicit theories. In evaluating the law's theory, we need to see if it comports with or departs from psychological and commonsense views. And we must see if the law's implicit theory is consonant or at odds with its own exemplar, the "reasonable person."

The law's implicit theory can be clarified if we look at the story of Achilles. At the beginning of the *Iliad,* the Muse sings of his wrath, the core emotion of the poem.[1] Achilles was seized by red-hot emotion when King Agamemnon took his spoil of war, the concubine Briseis. Achilles would have drawn his sword and killed Agamemnon on the spot had not the goddess Athena "swept down from Mount Olympus and grabbed him by the hair and told him to stay his hand."[2] If the goddess had not intervened and if Achilles' murderous rage had run its fatal course, what would his crime have been? Not murder, for the elements of deliberation, premeditation, and malice aforethought were arguably lacking. More likely, it would have been a crime of passion: manslaughter.

If it was manslaughter, what was the provocation? The answer seems to be Agamemnon's appropriation of Achilles' spoil of war, Briseis. Although this was an affront to Achilles, Agamemnon's action was itself a reaction: Achilles had demanded that Agamemnon give up his spoil of war, Chryseis, to appease Apollo and end the plague on the Achaeans. In losing Chryseis, Agamemnon appears to have played tit for tat, a move that should not have surprised Achilles. What is more important from the point of view of manslaughter is the fact that this provocation does not appear to be an "adequate" reason for killing. Yet Achilles' emotions flared quickly to a red-hot extreme. From a "crime-control" perspective, the law might expect Achilles to have controlled his emotions and not have flown off the handle at mere words or insults, real or imagined. In sum, the law might well have told Achilles that a bruised ego is insufficient provocation for killing. If the law believes that the provocation was insufficient and that the defendant had the ability to control his emotions and actions, then it might remit nothing from the punishment, arguing that this taking of life was as morally wrong as murder and should be punished fully.

But Achilles has a defense. Since the goddess of wisdom needed to intervene, we can assume that his wisdom was nowhere to be found, or insufficient to restrain his murderous emotions at that moment. Isn't his instant wrath and haste to reach for his sword prima facie evidence that he could not control his emotions? Crimes of passion, as ordinary individuals understand them, involve emotions so hot that they distort or obliterate reason, or emotions so strong that reason cannot check them. This is Achilles' claim. Yet if the claim is correct, why not push the claim past mitigation all the way to exculpation, since this view comes close to the irresistible-impulse version of insanity? If we are unwilling to find such a defendant not guilty by reason of insanity, then what is the difference between manslaughter and insanity? Or, to put it another way, where is the blameworthiness in manslaughter?

Compared to the volatile Achilles, the wise and wily Odysseus seems almost phlegmatic. His emotions need goading by Athena. Another difference between these two heroes can be seen in their respective wartime and peacetime contexts: whereas our punitive judgment of Achilles may be mitigated by the fact that he was fighting a war, Odysseus' actions occurred ten years after the war, when there were presumably more civilized means of settling grievances. So what did the suitors do to provoke Odysseus to "clean house" by wreaking murder and mayhem?

The suitors were courting Penelope, Odysseus' wife, but not without ample reason: Odysseus had been gone twenty years and was presumed dead; Penelope was considered a widow. Even her parents were urging her to remarry, and from Homer's description of her, any single man in his right mind would have pursued her. Moreover, the suitors were getting certain encouraging, even provocative signals from Penelope. She was far from the innocent, as she skillfully manipulated the suitors by giving each one in turn the sense that she might pick him.

It is true, though, that the suitors were parasites. They plundered a bit. They were disrespectful nuisances. And they did hurl insults Odysseus' way, even throwing an object at him when he was disguised as a beggar. But such actions seem less like crimes than like misdemeanors and bad manners, and a long way from provocations warranting death. Yet death is what the suitors got; and, as Zeus and Athena determined at the epic's end, Odysseus got *no* punishment—not mitigation of punishment, but no punishment at all. In the eyes of the gods, Odysseus' wrath and vengeance appear justified.

When Achilles' wrath against Agamemnon is compared with Odysseus' wrath against the suitors, some notable differences are evident. Although we have some questions for Achilles about whether Agamemnon's provocation was sufficient to fire up murderous wrath, we have many more questions for Odysseus on the provocation issue. With regard to emotion, Achilles seems to flare red-hot in an instant, and remains angry until the goddess stays his hand. Odysseus' emotions are less extreme and need godly goading to reach murderous heights. A more notable difference is *time*. In the case of Achilles, provocation, emotion (wrath), and action (reaching for his sword) occur in a brief instant, with little time to "think it through" and almost no time for the hot blood to cool. In the case of Odysseus, days go by—not just more time per se, but time for Odysseus to bring his reason to bear on the maelstrom of emotion and provocation, to coolly plan the timing and manner of the mass execution he will perform. From a prosecutor's vantage point, Odysseus' actions are more like first-degree murder than manslaughter.

In Homer's world Odysseus' actions go unpunished in the Olympian High Court, though they might not have escaped punishment had citizens decided the matter. By the time of Aristotle, the court that heard homicide cases took a dim view of any appeal to emotion as a mitigating factor, let alone as an excusing factor. And in our world, the law has not seriously contemplated a complete excuse. To the contrary, the law expects reason to hold anger in check; an individual must not plan and inflict deaths when provocations seem slight, or when time allows hot blood to cool and reason to regain the upper hand. Yet the law lowers its expectations when provocations grow and time shrinks: although "Thou shall not kill" remains the operating ideal, the law recognizes that people function far from the ideal under red-hot emotions—emotions that can get out of control in the face of some provocations. When that happens, murder becomes manslaughter, different in kind and degree from true murder. Though the law understands human nature under heat, and acknowledges this "fact of nature" by mitigating the punishment for manslaughter, it still does not exculpate. This indicates that the law nonetheless expects that reason should and could have controlled the red-hot emotions to some degree. But can reason exert control under such circumstances? Is this expectation, or implicit theory of human nature, realistic?

We associate the "red" emotions of wrath, anger, and rage with crimes of passion, and the "white" emotions of fear and fright with self-defense. This oversimplified red-versus-white distinction allows us to consider the following question: Why is it that red emotions lead to mitigation, whereas white emotions (if certain self-defense preconditions are met) lead to exculpation? If intense emotion, whatever its color and name, can distort perception, apprehension, and judgment and can disable control as well, then why is there a legal difference in culpability and punishment between red and white emotions?

One distinction between the two involves empathy. If a person is frightened, people generally move toward the person, trying to comfort or console. By contrast, when a person is angry or enraged, people generally move back, since the "heat" is frightening. Even when we understand the reason for the rage, we still recoil, especially when the anger leads to violence and death. Perhaps it is our emotional reactions to these emotions—empathy for white, antipathy for red—that produce the legal difference. This answer points to sentiments, and thus raises the possibility that extralegal concerns might be driving the jurors' verdicts.

A second difference between red and white emotions may involve a moral judgment concerning the necessity to act. In the typical self-defense scenario, the defendant is in a situation where she must take a life or lose her own. Action is imperative. There is no similar urgency, typically, when a person is angry and seeking revenge. For example, if a husband hears about his wife's infidelity, or even catches her and her lover *in flagrante delicto*, his revenge might come tomorrow, next week, or next year. Similarly, Achilles could have avenged the slight from Agamemnon in his own good time. Avengers come in a variety of forms—from the impetuous Othello to the coldly calculating Iago to the indecisive Hamlet—and whatever factors drive their revenge, necessity is usually not one of them.

Related to necessity is a third factor. Common in the animal world, and in the human animal, is a flight-or-fight reaction to danger. Moreover, under fear or stress, a "general-adaptation syndrome" kicks in—an emergency reaction by the sympathetic nervous system that involves, among other things, the release of hormones in the brain and certain subsequent actions.[3] If common sense apprehends this, then the white emotion of fear seems more primitive, more basic, more genetically if not phylogenetically "hard-wired" into our nature than the red emotions—as if we had to react the way we did to fear, but we did not have to react that way to anger. Thus, there may be a physiological basis that drives fearful responses, whereas there may be none driving anger. If this is so, then the *necessity* attributed to fear has a physiological as well as a psychological basis, but one cannot say this of anger. The flip side to necessity is choice, and it follows that people are likely to attribute more choice to the angry individual. If the angry individual could have done otherwise, then here is a source of culpability.

This commonsense notion that fear entails greater necessity may be at odds with facts about stress. Hans Selye, the father of modern stress theory, has asserted that the general-adaptation syndrome is *nonspecific*, meaning that any of a great number of stresses or provocations may set off the emergency reaction.[4] Thus, Achilles in the grip of wrath and the individual overcome with fear may be acting under the influence of the same hormones in the brain and may perform the same actions. If each is being similarly impelled by physiological reactions outside conscious control, and if each has the same inability to control and shut down this reaction before violent meltdown, then distinctions concerning culpability and punishment lose their physiological grounding.

At the psychological level, we know that stressors come in myriad forms with a variety of emotions and that these can produce negative psychological and physical effects.[5] For example, when we're under stress, our perceptions may be distorted and our judgment about the meaning of someone's actions or motives may be far off the mark. If "stressors" are viewed as akin to legal provocations, then stressors that lead to anger and stressors that lead to fear may yield the same distortions in perception and judgment. If anger and fear produce like distortions, and if individuals act on those distortions, why should the law mitigate punishment in one case but exculpate in the other?

Though the ancient Greeks, or at least their gods, may have exculpated murder committed under provocation, and perhaps even revenge murder, it is clear that Anglo-American common law never seriously considered exculpation for manslaughter. In trying to situate manslaughter within a mitigating midrange, common law sought to elucidate the boundary conditions and objective rules that mark its playing field.

Common-Law Manslaughter "Rules"

One rule that has been abstracted from case law by legal commentators is that "mere words" are not sufficient provocation.[6] Though "sticks and stones" certainly can harm, names, words, gestures, and the like seem incommensurate with a violent response. In a sixteenth-century case, *Watts v. Byrnes,*[7] "the defendant had been beaten by the victim two days before the slaying . . . [and on] the third day, the victim passed by the defendant's butcher store and 'gave him a wry face,' whereupon the defendant pursued the victim and stabbed him from behind, probably with a butcher knife of some kind."[8] Though the jury ultimately returned a verdict for murder rather than manslaughter—an outcome that can be seen as consistent with the rule that words, looks, wry faces, and other slight provocations are insufficient reasons for violence—the jury's final verdict was not the whole story. The jury first acquitted the defendant of murder, bringing in a manslaughter verdict, but the judge imprisoned the jury and directed them to return a murder verdict, which they eventually did. From the jury's initial perspective, the provocation was mitigating. Given what happened, there appears to have been a split between what the common-law judge and the commonsense jury construed as manslaughter.

In another early case *(Williams)* two strangers met, and one insulted the defendant's Welsh heritage, whereupon the defendant threw a hammer at him; the hammer missed the intended victim but hit and killed a bystander.[9] Here was an insult, plain and simple—mere words leading to deadly violence; but the court held the defendant guilty only of manslaughter. This court seemed to be at odds with the legal rule stipulating that mere words were insufficient. Although some courts were finding defendants in "mere word" cases guilty of murder, *Watts,* and particularly *Williams,* show that the so-called rule was in fact not "common" or uniformly applied.

The "mere words" rule underwent mutation and division. "Insults," which were regarded as insufficient provocation, were split off from "informational" words, which could be regarded as sufficient. An illustration of this is *Royley* (1666), in which a boy ran to his father and informed him that he had just been beaten by the victim.[10] "The father then ran three-quarters of a mile, found the man who beat his son, and killed him. The court, upon a special verdict of the jury, was unanimously of the opinion that 'it was but manslaughter,' because the killing was 'upon the sudden occasion.'"[11] Yet this opinion is problematic on a couple of counts. First, the defendant did not see the provocation: he only heard about the beating from his son. Although the son's words can be considered information, we do not know, and the father did not know for certain, whether the son had embellished the information or even fabricated the story. Thus, we do not know if the father acted on true information.

Next, consider the "upon the sudden occasion" factor. Clearly the attack did not take place upon a sudden, for even if Royley had been a world-class miler, he certainly would have needed some minutes to cover the three-quarters of a mile—minutes in which reason could have regained dominion over affect. Wasn't he thinking at all during his sprint? Couldn't he have done some thinking during that period of time? When he found the man, shouldn't he have paused to consider his options? We would certainly expect a chance medley self-defense claimant to have considered the retreat option, even though such a defendant, unlike Royley, faced a deadly weapon.

Maddy (1672)[12] was a confession-of-adultery case in which the "defendant expressly told others that he would kill the cuckolder."[13] The "*Maddy* court believed that the killing would have been manslaughter except that the time interval and the defendant's declaration demonstrated that the killing was one of vengeance and not done in the heat of passion. Thus, the brief reference indicates that absent evidence of premeditation, the informational words of a confession can be adequate provocation."[14] Adultery cases that involve couples caught *in flagrante delicto* are, for most people, prototypes of "crimes of passion." "No 'rule' of adequate provocation was more firmly entrenched, even by the end of the eighteenth century, than that which proclaimed that a spouse (a husband, of course) who found his wife in bed with a lover, and killed one or both of them, was entitled to a reduction to manslaughter."[15] Yet this well-established "rule" had qualifiers: *only* adultery could be adequate provocation; and a mere suspicion of adultery was insufficient.

Still, even with qualifiers, the rule was already bent in *Maddy's Case*. The defendant, Maddy, did not actually see the act, but he heard informational words about an adulterous act. He may have had a very strong suspicion, given the source, but he had no firsthand, eyewitness evidence. If legal writers were trying to distinguish seeing from hearing, *Royley's Case* contravenes, for that was a "hearing" case in which manslaughter and mitigation were granted. Thus, the line between visual and aural provocations fails to distinguish manslaughter from murder.

The line between insulting words and informational words fails as well, as two hypothetical changes in *Royley* and *Maddy* make clear. What if Royley's son and Maddy's wife both lied, such that the alleged beating and adultery never occurred but Royley and Maddy acted as if they had? Words of information can be misinformation, yet still produce the same *subjective* provocations. Analogous to mistaken self-defense is mistaken provocation, where an honest but reasonable or honest but unreasonable mistake leads to a killing, and to the question of whether the defendant will lose his manslaughter mitigation and receive a murder conviction instead. If, according to the rule, the *substance* of the confession must be true—if the adultery in fact had to occur—then Maddy would lose his case, even though his feelings and beliefs would be identical under both true and mistaken provocation.

There were other "objective rules" that commentators and treatise writers were abstracting, such as the rule of proportionality. As Richard Singer put it, such a rule "declares that regardless of the defendant's actual mental state, and regardless of whether he could have entertained malice aforethought, he will be precluded from arguing that he lacked such malice aforethought—and will therefore be found guilty of murder—unless, in anger, he used a weapon which in some metaphysical sense is 'proportionate' to the provocation."[16] Like the "equal force" rule in self-defense, the proportionality rule makes sense only for *physical* provocation. If the proportionality rule must be met in all cases, then discovered-adultery cases and cases of insulting or informational words would fail the test, for deadly violence would be considered a disproportionate response.

Of all the rules that commentators have abstracted from cases to define the parameters of manslaughter, the rule regarding *time*—killing "upon a sudden," in the heat of passion—seems almost axiomatic, yet it is no less problematic than other rules. The logic of this rule rests on considering the alternative: if the killing was not upon a sudden but occurred after a cooling-off period, judges assumed that the defendant's blood and passions had cooled, his reason had been restored to its full apprehending and inhibiting strength, and full culpability and punishment should follow. By this rule, Odysseus should be fully punished, but not Achilles.

Under common law it was also assumed that the question of how much time must pass for cooling to occur was an *objective* question, one to be decided by the court rather than by the jury.[17] The assumption that "time" inevitably cools passion and restores reason, and that the necessary time interval can be objectively determined by the courts, leaves two sorts of defendants in the murderous cold, unable to claim mitigating manslaughter. We can dub these two types the "brooders" and the "rekindlers."

Consider literature's consummate brooder, Hamlet, who just can't seem to get on with it: he starts and stops, hems and haws, and finally, in Act V, does the deed he was given to do in Act I. Now consider *State v. Gounagias* (1915):[18] "The defendant, a Greek immigrant, had purposely killed the deceased. He sought to introduce evidence that he had been sodomized by the deceased and that for the next three weeks, the defendant's friends, who had learned about the incident from the deceased, taunted him. The Washington Supreme Court held that this evidence had been properly excluded from the trial because, while the defendant might in fact have killed in passion, it was not 'of a sudden.'"[19] The court, having made this curious distinction between "in passion" and "of a sudden," whereby only the latter was granted manslaughter and mitigation, went on to offer an even curiouser and stranger psychological "theory" to justify the verdict: "This theory of the cumulative effect of reminders of former wrongs . . . is contrary to the idea of sudden anger as understood in the doctrine of mitigation. In the nature of the thing, *sudden* anger cannot be cumulative. A provocation which does not cause instant resentment, but which is only resented after being thought upon and brooded over, is not a provocation sufficient in law to reduce intentional killing from murder to manslaughter."[20]

This proposition seems entirely inconsistent with what we know from psychology, and with what common sense tells us about ordinary relationships. People react and abreact, in therapy and out, long after the trauma or stress has faded. Adults who have suffered abuse in childhood, be it physical or sexual, may strongly react in the "heat of passion" in adulthood; others, traumatized by war, rape, and many other human and natural disasters may suffer rekindling, flashbacks, and post-traumatic stress disorder (PTSD), which can feature sudden, passionate, even violent reactions to stimuli that normally do not evoke such responses. Even in "normal" individuals who have no diagnostic label, we often see reactions that seem disproportionately hot. When a parent suddenly rages at a child, a spouse at a spouse, an employer at an employee, or a teacher at a student, these are heat-of-passion responses that clearly relate to the cumulative past, for the intensity of the response cannot be explained by looking only at the last-straw incident. As with certain self-defense cases—the case of the battered woman who kills her spouse, or Goetz who kills on the subway—unless we're aware of the prior traumatic incidents and the cumulative history, the murderous action seems disproportionate and inexplicable.

Brooders and rekindlers have something in common: a new spark, be it internal or external, ignites an old flame. A legal theory that denies what seems fundamental about human nature risks losing common support. The law seems to be embracing a stimulus-response simplism—a view that provocations always produce intense anger on the spot and then "die," becoming insufficient to trigger intense anger that is not premeditated revenge. The Washington court told Gounagias that the sodomy he had suffered was over and done with (claiming that since it was physically over it was psychologically over), that the subsequent taunts (mere words of the insult variety) were insufficient by themselves, and finally that the two events—the sodomy and the taunts—*did not go together or connect in any way;* but these assertions seem preposterous. That sort of legal thinking, where objective rules artificially keep connected events in rigidly separate compartments, would be clinically diagnostic to psychologists. Laymen, who are imprisoned by no such legal reasoning, would likewise probably reject this conclusion. In the experiments involving insanity cases and self-defense cases, we saw that jurors widened the moment of the act purview to include other relevant factors within the context.

When these objective rules are taken together, Singer says, the individual defendant all but vanishes: "A system which precludes evidence of words which actually enraged the defendant to the point of loss of self-control, which precludes evidence of his victim's adultery unless the defendant saw the physical act itself, which focuses on the force used by the defendant in proportion to the battery inflicted by the victim, and which views the question of cooling off as one of law rather than of fact has, for all practical purposes, relegated the defendant to the sidelines. The issue of his culpability has, thus, been transformed into one to be measured by rules, rather than by his actual mental state."[21]

The "final objectification"[22]—the "quintessential 'rule' of objectivity"—is the standard of the "reasonable" or "ordinary" man.[23] The exemplars of the "reasonable person" and the "ordinary person," though often used interchangeably or blended into the "ordinary, reasonable person," must be kept distinct. For as Glanville Williams noted, the "reasonable man" never kills, even under provocation, for his reason and control always find another way of responding to provocation short of murder.[24] And as George Fletcher put it, "in the context of provocation, the reasonable person is hardly home."[25] But in recognizing that many people do kill under provocation, and in deciding that this form of killing warrants mitigation, the law is recognizing a lower standard than that of the exemplary "reasonable man." Here, we settle for the ordinary and average.

Settling for the "ordinary person" and finding the mythical average are two different things. The law can decide that the ordinary man would not resort to killing in the face of taunts, but where does that leave Gounagias? The ordinary person faced with taunts was not sodomized three weeks earlier. If individual variability is left out of the legal equation and if only the actions of the mythical exemplar are considered, then the actual defendant becomes persona non grata at his own trial.[26]

In the latter half of the nineteenth century and the first half of the twentieth, the objective view dominated and the "ordinary person" reigned in manslaughter cases. Yet even where this exemplar was touted, subjective cracks appeared. In *Maher v. People* (1863),[27] where the phrase "ordinary men or the average of men" first appeared,[28] the court referred to the need for provocations to be "adequate or reasonable." If "adequate" meant those legal categories recognized by common law—adultery, battery, chance medley—then "reasonable" seems to recognize another group of provocations which were not recognized as yet by the law. Moreover, as courts began to give juries responsibility for deciding such issues as whether a provocation had been reasonable or whether the defendant had had time to cool down, the jurors' subjectivity came forcefully into play, even as the "ordinary man" was held as the standard.

The apprehension over too much subjectivity and individuality was evident: courts feared "that people with low thresholds would be beneficiaries of a subjective test."[29] In *Jacobs v. Commonwealth* (1888),[30] where psychiatric evidence was excluded, the court wondered why one person should be excused and not another, when the "phlegmatic man may be moved to anger as well as the most nervous." This apprehension led courts to confuse, and fuse into one, the "front-end" and "back-end" issues. We can take individual characteristics into account on the front end—when considering how a person construed and emotionally reacted to a provocation (that is, whether it was a provocation to that person, and how severe); and we can take them into account on the back end—when considering whether the provocation affected the defendant's level of self-control. But a front-end impairment does not necessarily mean a back-end impairment. When no distinctions are made and an exemplar is arbitrarily held aloft, the objective law and the reasonable person—like the defendant in the following case—are rendered impotent.

In *Director of Public Prosecutions v. Bedder* (1954), a seventeen-year-old who had been told by a doctor that he was impotent hired a prostitute in a desperate hope that he might be able to perform.[31] When he could not, the prostitute taunted and ridiculed Bedder, and he killed her "in what was undeniably true rage."[32] But in the instructions to the jury—instructions that the House of Lords affirmed—Bedder's impotence was declared irrelevant, and the jurors were told that they should not take it into account. As Fletcher notes, we "can hardly say that the jury passed judgment on Mr. Bedder if they did not consider the most significant facts that influenced his loss of control."[33] "In effect, this meant that the legal issue to be decided by the jury was whether a reasonably *potent* man would have been incensed to the point of killing by taunts regarding his impotence. The question, of course, was silly."[34]

The *Bedder* decision was promptly attacked, and three years later, via the Homicide Act of 1957, British law took a subjective turn: juries were henceforth directed to consider everything done and said. In the United States, the Model Penal Code introduced "extreme mental or emotional disturbance," which was to be judged "from the viewpoint of a person in the actor's situation under the circumstances as he believes them to be." This turns the question from an objective inquiry into an almost completely subjective one. It does even more, for the narrow moment of the act is widened to include the individual's history as part of the *context*. Context, in turn, is central to an understanding of Bedder's reaction to the taunts and ridicule (the provocation).

Psychological Findings and Theories

The law of manslaughter appears to be based on two implicit theories of human nature. The first, which relates to the front end of the causal chain, involves the effects of provocation on an individual's emotions, reason, and propensity to violence. The second theory, which pertains to the back end of the causal chain, involves the effects of emotions on action and self-control. The front-end theory is evident in the *objective* rules which evolved from case law and commentary and which incorporate the notion that provocations may be ordered in some crude but clear way. Some provocations, like insults, are deemed insufficient to ignite murderous passions or to mitigate. Others, such as informational words that reveal an act of adultery, might send the passions soaring over the killing threshold into the mitigating realm of manslaughter, if the information is true. Still others, such as a punch in the nose, are clearly the right stuff of mitigation, if the defendant's response is proportionate.

The question for the law's implicit theories is this: Does psychological research support or contradict these implicit legal theories? One area of research that has produced consistent findings involves the relationship between stress, emotional strain, and illness. "Stressors," which have been categorized[35] and quantified,[36] can be viewed as an analogue of provocations. The literature tells us that when stressors accumulate and the quantified stress level is high, people often feel emotional strain and are more likely to suffer physical illness (ulcer, heart attack) and psychological problems (anxiety, depression, suicide).

Clinicians and researchers believe that stress has a *cumulative effect,* and the empirical evidence supports this belief. When clinicians make a diagnosis, for example, they routinely consider stresses that have acted on the patient during the previous year or six months; when clinicians perform psychotherapy, the timeline generally extends much further into the past, encompassing even earlier stresses; and in research situations where subjects are given stress rating scales, the stresses they are asked to consider are usually those that have affected them in the previous year. But whereas psychology, supported by research findings, opens the "time window" to the cumulative effect of stresses, the *Gounagias* court closed the time window and rejected the "theory of the cumulative effect of reminders of former wrongs."[37]

Although there is a correlation between stress and illness, the correlations are, oddly, much lower than many researchers and clinicians expected. They fall in the modest-to-low range ($R = .20–.30$), with stress accounting for only a small proportion of the illness variance (4–9 percent). Why these perplexingly low correlations? The main reason, I suggest, is that in doing such scientific, objective, quantifiable research, experimenters have left out the individual person entirely, much the way the defendant is left out when objective rules and exemplars are invoked.

Consider, for example, a major life event: the death of a spouse. On the Social Readjustment Rating Scale, the most frequently used measure of stress, every person whose spouse has died within the past year gets 100 points. But such a rule treats every person like every other person, like the mythical average person, assuming that there is no individual variability among people. But we might well imagine death-of-spouse scenarios that elicit a range of reactions from "devastation" to "relief." We can meaningfully give points to a life event only if we first find out how the particular person subjectively experienced the event. To put this another way, the idiographic approach, rather than one based on generality, yields the more meaningful analysis.

When psychologists attempt to "objectify" that which is subjective or create generalities out of the idiographic, they make the same mistake that objectifiers of the law do. As a consequence they lose individual meaning and variability among individuals, ending up with deceptively low correlations. By establishing the "average person," they end up describing *no person,* for it is clearly false that all people react alike to the same life event. Subjectively, it is not the same life event, save in the most trivial sense of a label. The import is clear for provocations. We can understand whether an event was a provocation, and how much it provoked a certain defendant, only if we conduct some sort of subjective inquiry.

In the legal arena, objectivizing the inquiry by hoisting up the average-person exemplar eliminates the defendant from the assessment and renders moot the moral inquiry into the his or her blameworthiness. Furthermore, it eliminates from consideration the context, which provides the backdrop and ground for a full assessment. For the issue of whether the one taunted was impotent, or had been sodomized, or had been beaten before, or had never laid eyes on the taunter is surely relevant to the question of provocation.

There is yet another lesson to learn from the stress-illness literature. On the Social Readjustment Rating Scale, death of a spouse earns 100 points at the top end of the scale and 11 points attach to a minor violation of the law at the bottom end. But it's possible that for a particular individual, a minor violation of the law may actually be a greater stress than the death of a spouse. Let's use "making obscene telephone calls" as the minor violation of the law. If the person making such calls turns out to be a highly visible, successful, prominent figure, and the event and his picture are splashed across television screens and newspaper headlines throughout the country, and if his shame, embarrassment, and disgrace are acute, and if his friends and colleagues call for his resignation—well, this so-called minor event, worth but 11 points, may in subjective fact be the most traumatic event in that person's life.

Based on the mythical average person, this interval scale holds that one type of provocation is worth 11 points while another is worth 100 points; yet such a scale may not hold at all for a particular individual. At the idiographic and subjective level, one person may give these life events a very different ordering and point value; someone may well react more hotly and passionately to insulting words than to a shove. Therefore, if we try objectively to designate, differentiate, and quantify which events are adequate provocations and which are not, we're bound to fail; for like the objective law, the individual—who, of course, reacts in an individual way to life events, stressors, and provocations—is relegated to the sidelines, replaced by a mythical exemplar. The lesson for psychological research and the law is the same: on the front end, in assessing the level of provocation or stress, we must understand how the particular individual subjectively sees and experiences the event, whether we are treating the person as medical professionals or judging his or her moral blameworthiness as jurors.

The back-end questions ultimately focus on self-control. Can red-hot emotions cause murderous actions that either bypass the controlling reason entirely—like some reflex action, automatism, or unconscious striking out—or, by their heat, disable reason's ability to rein in the resulting actions? On this question, psychologists are divided. On one side of the debate is Robert Zajonc, who has argued for the primacy of affect, claiming that emotion and cognition can be independent.[38] Zajonc believes that there are separate systems in the brain for handling emotion and cognition, and thus that it is possible for affect to "precede cognition in a behavioral chain"[39] or for affect to "be generated without a prior cognitive process."[40] Zajonc's position would be most compatible with heat-of-passion cases, for if affect can precede cognition and initiate the behavioral chain that leads to killing before cognition can enter the chain and restrain the individual, then the individual can hardly be said to be fully culpable for what he or she could not stop.

But Zajonc's position, if pushed to the limit, is compatible more with exculpation than with mitigation. Why not excuse the individual entirely, rather than holding him guilty for manslaughter, if in fact he could not stop the emotional train from running its deadly course? If, as Zajonc wrote in another paper, "preferences need no inferences," then emotions can lead to action *outside* the cognitive process, and presumably outside the individual's ability to exert reason and restrain the process.[41] If these emotional preferences are irresistible, like a train without brakes, where is the blameworthiness, save the possibility of negligence, if the train crashes?

The foremost critic of Zajonc's position is Richard Lazarus, who has argued over the years for the primacy of cognition.[42] As Lazarus writes, "I have taken the strongest position possible, and the most controversial, on the causal role of cognition in emotion, namely, that it is both a necessary and sufficient condition. *Sufficient* means that thoughts are capable of producing emotions; *necessary* means that emotions cannot occur without some kind of thought. Many writers who accept comfortably the idea that cognition is sufficient reject that it is necessary."[43] If, as Lazarus claims, some form of cognition is always present, preceding and causing the emotion, then an exculpatory claim that "I wasn't aware and couldn't control" would fail. Lazarus' view might support the mitigation claim, for he is not saying that the cognitive appraisal that occurs in emotion is necessarily complete or accurate. He is saying only that cognition is there, be it in minimalist form or even in the form of "unconscious appraising."[44]

Zajonc finds that Lazarus is inserting cognition into emotion *by definition,* when it is an empirical question. Moreover, says Zajonc, if one defines the most fleeting, even unconscious registerings as instances of "cognitive appraisal," one moves from science to that which "cannot be observed, verified, or documented."[45]

On the cognitive side, Gerry Parrott and Jay Schulkin have noted that recent neuropsychological findings do not support independent affect and cognitive systems; rather, "centrifugal anatomical wiring suggests that emotion and sensation cannot be independent from cognition."[46] Moreover, from a functional or evolutionary perspective, emotions must serve an adaptive function: if they prepare the organism for action, if they steer action toward satisfaction of a need, then this instrumental function could not occur without cognitive appraisal. Thus, the emotional process must involve operations of "interpretation, memory, anticipation, and problem-solving."[47]

Although psychological research and theory yield no agreed-upon answer as to whether emotions can operate independently of cognition and control, the literature does clear away some of the simplism in this arena—simplistic views of emotion and cognition, for example. As Parrott and Schulkin write, "to consider emotions to be passions (as opposed to reason) is to make two assumptions, both problematic. One is that all emotions are irrational, which flies in the face of experience and, if true, would be highly inconsistent with evolutionary and functional accounts. The other assumption is that the term 'cognition' can be equated with rationality, which is surely not what is meant by this admittedly ambiguous term in contemporary psychology."[48]

James Averill, in his study of anger and the law,[49] takes the view that emotions "are primarily social constructions."[50] If we can judge an emotion such as anger only "by reference to norms and standards"[51] rather than by "individual psychology,"[52] then in judging the meaning and strength of provoked emotions and the actions that result, a jury "may be more 'expert' than most psychologists and psychiatrists,"[53] since they share those social standards. Averill does construct a "partial list" of rules and norms relating to anger, but this is not quite the same as the law's objectifying rigid rules: for the former, general social rules admit to particular exceptions and to the presence of human variability, whereas objective legal rules attempt to hold fast for all, ignoring human variability.

Commonsense Views of Manslaughter's Mitigation

One of Averill's social rules of attribution is that "an angry person should not be held completely responsible for his or her behavior."[54] This is one type of empirical fact, affirming what most people believe. And for some legal questions—such as those involving privacy and people's reasonable expectations, or cruel and unusual punishment and community sentiment—this sort of fact is precisely what the court seeks to gauge and what will likely determine the outcome. But in the matter of murderous passions, manslaughter, and mitigation, the fact that most people share a belief that "anger mitigates" does not establish that belief as true. At this point science cannot say with certainty, either at the level of individual psychology or at the level of physiology, that anger lessens reason and control such that manslaughter rather than murder is always warranted. In the absence of that sort of empirical support, the belief that "anger mitigates" is just a commonsense assumption.

Parrott has looked at the thoughts people have when they are impulsively angry, and from his work we can extract yet another commonsense assumption about why mitigation rather than exculpation should follow.[55] "When people are impulsively angry," Parrott writes, "they just as impulsively think in ways consistent with being angry. When they cease to believe that they have a right to be angry, they stop being angry. So what is remarkable about impulsive anger is not that it can spring into being without *any* beliefs that one has been wronged, but that it can spring into being based on such *flimsy* beliefs that one has been wronged."[56] If jurors believe that there are flimsy beliefs but not full-blown delusional beliefs, this may well be the discriminating reason for mitigating but not exculpating.

These commonsense assumptions, extracted from admittedly inconclusive data, are nonetheless in accord with the law's assumption that manslaughter ought to be mitigated when compared to the crime of murder, and punished when compared to acquittal by reason of insanity. This accord did not always exist, and a reading of history suggests that it was not community sentiment that changed but the law, particularly over whether an objective or subjective perspective should normatively govern the matter of provocation. This difference, once great, is clearly narrowing. The law's subjective about-face in the second half of the twentieth century, after more than two centuries of objectivizing the rules and reifying a mythic exemplar, indicates that the law is taking a path closer to the one laid by commonsense justice. This may be another example of Roscoe Pound's prediction—that when there is a "divergence between the standard of the common law and the standard of the public, it goes without saying that the latter will prevail in the end."[57]

Beyond the issue of an objective versus subjective standard, an issue that is fading, there remains a disparity between commonsense justice and the law concerning the underlying rationale for manslaughter's mitigation. Most people endorse mitigation for manslaughter, as Averill suggests; yet if they were pressed to give a *reason*, their answers would probably be vague: "It feels right," "It's different from murder," "It's not as bad," "The person didn't really mean it." This level of generality and imprecision is not good enough for the law—nor should it be, for the doctrine needs to be sustained by something more substantive than "It feels right." Yet in searching for a rationale, the law has rounded up the usual suspects, none of which precisely fits the bill.

Lord Coke, focusing on *mens rea,* held that manslaughter could not be murder because the essential element of murder—malice aforethought—was lacking. But surely there are manslaughter cases where the defendant, in the heat of passion, did want to kill the adulterous spouse, or cuckolder, or aggressor hurling insults or fists. To say that the defendant never intended killing, never had malice aforethought, clearly seems false.

Another tack is to claim that heat of passion negates malice aforethought. This claim fares no better, however. Surely there are premeditated murderers who kill in the heat of passion, and passions also come into play in self-defense and insanity cases. The issue can't rest merely on a measure of heat, for if passions run high in murder, manslaughter, self-defense, and insanity, then something other than passion produces the discrepant verdicts and punishments. Assuming that "if there is heat, then there is no malice" is clearly false.

Other doctrinal battles—such as whether manslaughter is a partial justification (because the victim somehow "asked for it") or a partial excuse (the law mercifully "indulges human frailty")—do not take us very

far. In the end, we somehow understand that the defendant who committed manslaughter and the defendant who committed murder are not on
the same footing, and this understanding springs more from the subjective
view than from objective rules or doctrinal rationales. Common sense just
seems to understand "that persons in extreme situations normally do not
'intend' very much of anything; they merely wish to end the stressful situation."[58] If the defendant did not intend anything but struck out in blind
distress, we know that this is different from murder.[59] Even if the defendant did intend to strike under provocation, our common sense tells us
that she probably did not contemplate the consequences of her act; this is
different from murder, and also from insanity. Manslaughter, then, is not
merely a crime of passion, as advertised, but a partial failure of reason:
reason may falter either on the front end, in the way provocations are
perceived and construed, or on the back end, where reason's flimsiness
may justify the anger and the act rather than controlling it.

Mitigation, then, appears appropriate. It is not just good policy, but
good principle. That principle, seen again and again in commonsense justice, is proportionality. Mitigation fits with the discriminations people
make between manslaughter and murder, on one end, and with the discriminations they make between manslaughter and nonculpability (be it
from innocence, accident, self-defense, or insanity), on the other. Thus, it
reflects the gradations of culpability that people discern. The law has tried
to reify those abstract gradations with objective rules—rules that have
failed. By abandoning objective rules and giving juries the key questions
(Was the provocation adequate? Was there adequate cooling-off time?),
the law's subjective turn may end up producing a "commonsensical
'rough justice'"[60] that may lack sophistication and exactness but not public support.

In judging the wrath of Achilles and Odysseus, the gods seemed to rely
on whim, trying to whitewash crimes with some exonerating factors that
failed to satisfy. Anglo-American common law never seriously entertained a complete whitewash, where the defendant was exonerated and
found not guilty; rather, the verdict of manslaughter indicated some culpability, and a mitigating midrange evolved. In the course of this evolution, common law reached for some objective rules and an exemplar. But
the rules bent and broke, the exemplar was hardly home, and the defendant was all but absent at trial. As Singer puts it, the effort to find some
"verbal formula to capture [the] distinction" between types of killers has
consistently failed for four centuries. In turning to the subjective element
in manslaughter, the law may perhaps be recognizing that "less really is
more."[61]

In making a subjective veer, the drafters of the Model Penal Code not only shifted toward the direction commonsense justice had been taking all along, but went even further. With its concept of "extreme mental or emotional disturbance" (EED), the code ended up severing all ties to objective reality. The problem with the EED standard is illustrated in two Connecticut cases, *State v. Zdanis*[62] and *State v. Elliot*,[63] both of which dealt with "brooders" who had committed homicide without being provoked by the victims. The appellate court in *Zdanis* made it clear that "virtually any reaction to any stimulus may be considered in an EED jurisdiction,"[64] and the appellate court in *Elliot* went even further: "The defense [which pleads EED] does not require a provoking or triggering event; or that the homicidal act occur immediately after the cause or causes of the defendant's extreme emotional disturbance . . . A homicide influenced by an extreme emotional disturbance is not one which is necessarily committed in the 'hot blood' stage, but rather one that was brought about by a significant mental trauma that caused the defendant to brood for a long period of time and then react violently, seemingly without provocation."[65]

The appellate courts' ruling is good news for the brooder but bad news for the law. This EED construal is based on a naïve and outdated notion of subjectivity, where mental entities float about in the mind. In this sort of mind, as in this sort of subjective law, there exists a disembodied and disconnected EED, severed from its nexus to provocation on the front end, untied from control and action on the back end, yet leaving mayhem, murder, and manslaughter in its wake. And if we are prepared to grant this species of alien such autonomy, it will surely claim mitigation as its due.

The contrast with commonsense justice is great. In self-defense or right-to-die cases, jurors' notions of subjectivity are embedded in interpersonal relationships and interactions, in the current and historical contexts. Subjectivity is thus connected to objective facts, not divorced from them. In sharp contrast is the law's notion of subjectivity, where EED stands in isolation: it is a mental entity which is not interrelated or embedded in any context, save subjectivity itself. Like some alien entity, it erupts without cause, acontextually; what is worse, it erupts without good reason. The EED standard lacks grounding, then, and this sets it apart from commonsense justice.

The drafters of the Model Penal Code, mindful that the objective rules for manslaughter had failed, turned—correctly, it would seem—toward the subjective. This turn promised greater alignment with commonsense justice and held out greater hope for doctrinal consistency. But although the direction was appropriate, the chosen path was not. This new, exclusively subjective path—a solipsistic slide into extreme emotional disturbance that dead-ends in a dark mind—is problematic. Throwing the issue to jurors under these conditions may produce commonsensical rough justice despite the vagaries, or it might promote vague and disparate verdicts.

If there are fewer rules and no one-size-fits-all exemplar, then jurors have greater discretion. If there is an exemplar, jurors must construe that standard to fit the individual particulars of the case and the defendant; thus, it becomes a one-time, one-case, one-defendant exemplar. In the absence of general rules, idiography dominates, and in that realm subjectivity and discretion have wide latitude. In constructing a story of what happened and why, jurors must divine the motivation and intent of the defendant, the way in which the defendant perceived and reacted to provocation, the degree to which his or her emotions flared, and whether reason and control were operating or could be expected to operate in the individual case. On these matters, which involve the essential elements of the manslaughter story, juror discretion is largely unfettered. Whereas in death penalty decisions the Supreme Court since *Furman* has moved to restrict unfettered discretion and give guidance to jurors, in manslaughter decisions it has moved in the opposite direction. And although comparing death penalty and manslaughter jurisprudence may be like comparing apples and oranges, one might still venture the cautious conclusion that less is more.[66]

The Path of Commonsense Justice $\quad$ **17**

Across a number of venues, the paths of law and commonsense justice diverge, sometimes rather sharply. One reason for the divergence is *context*. At times, citizens seem to frame cases in a way that differs from the law's, thereby seeing a different "picture" of what the case is about and of the relevant factors to be included or excluded. An easy generalization, albeit an overgeneralization, is this: the commonsense context is typically *wider* than the law's.

This wider view applies to both current and historical contexts. In cases of self-defense, insanity, felony-murder, and manslaughter, jurors weigh more factors than the law's restricted set of sanctioned elements. This wider view extends backward and forward in time, thereby giving a different historical context to the drama at bar. Whereas the law seems to freeze the frame at the moment of the act and then zoom in on a specific set of determinative variables, the commonsense context, like a motion picture, conveys actions before, during, and even after the moment of the act.

Freezing the frame may produce high resolution when it comes to still pictures, but it may well produce absurdity when it comes to justice, as the failed "manslaughter" cases of *Bedder*[1] and *Gounagias*[2] illustrate. Had Gounagias picked up a weapon immediately and killed his sodomizer, he would have been reacting in the heat of passion and "of a sudden," and the jury surely would have rendered a verdict of manslaughter. But because he waited, brooded, and let time go by, the legal moment of the act passed into the future and the act of sodomy faded into the legally irrelevant past. After three weeks of taunts by the deceased and his friends, Gounagias picked up a weapon and killed. If the killing defined the relevant "moment of the act," then the provocation was no longer the sodomy but the taunts; yet taunts per se, by an objective rule that deemed "mere words" insufficient as a provocation, could not mitigate the crime to manslaughter.[3] In this narrow context—which began with a taunt and ended with a death—the most important "fact," the sodomy, was not even in play.

In the law's frozen moment and high-resolution portrayal, events occur *in time* rather than *in the mind*. In time, events begin, end, and are no more. In the mind, objective events have subjective counterparts; each has a mental and emotional half-life that may linger long after the objective event has taken place. If the *Gounagias* jurors were instructed to take the narrow, in-time view and did not even hear about the "irrelevant" sodomy, can it be said that they really passed judgment on the defendant?

In the commonsense view, the sodomy was clearly in play, in at least one of two ways. First, it may have been in play because a few jurors still viewed it as *the* provocation, despite what the law said and despite the fact that it had occurred weeks earlier; this is a view of time and context akin to the poetic assertion that time past and time future are both contained in time present. This view is not pure fancy, but one that sees time as relative, subjective, and psychological, whereas the law appears to regard it as fixed and immutable.

Second, commonsense justice views the sodomy as part of the relevant context, giving meaning to the provocation of taunts. The deceased and his friends were not taunting the "ordinary person," who had not been sodomized; they were taunting Gounagias, who had been. The taunt was not the same for all, since context colored the stimulus, giving it a shading for Gounagias that it would not have had for the ordinary, nonsodomized person. To treat taunts *acontextually* and *objectively* is to take the subjective and psychological out of the human judgment, and to take the person of Gounagias out of the picture. This typically yields a stimulus-response simplism—an analysis that reduces stimuli to objective and invariate properties, which in turn produce responses that either fit the preordained category of manslaughter or do not. Yet nowhere in such a stimulus-response matrix is there room for a particular person, with a history and context that affects his or her perceptions, judgments, emotions, and reactions.

So in *Gounagias* a relevant action was omitted. The jury judged his reaction to provocative taunts acontextually, unmindful of history, by reference to an ordinary-person exemplar who was a cardboard caricature of the flesh-and-blood Gounagias. This less-than-human way of judging human actions and intentions has been rejected again and again by commonsense justice.

Whereas *Gounagias* omitted a relevant *act* from the context, *Bedder* omitted a relevant *personal fact:* the defendants's impotence. This element of Bedder's personal history may well have been relevant to the way in which Bedder reacted to "mere word" taunts, much as Bernhard Goetz's prior mugging may have played some part in the way he heard the "mere words" addressed to him on the subway, or the way previous beatings affected the way the battered-woman defendant heard her husband's "mere words," when he said he would kill her after his nap. In a legal view that circumscribes context to the moment of the act, batterings, muggings, and acts of sodomy that took place in the past may not matter; but they do matter to commonsense justice.

Why does the law foreshorten context? Not only does an alleged criminal act set the legal process in motion; it also defines its focus. In judging a defendant's responsibility for the act, the law arbitrarily limits the context to a few key elements at the time of the act. This restricted contextual matrix is also a restricted causal or culpability matrix. If the context is widened, jurors may end up weighing everyone's culpability, not just the defendant's. But weighing everyone's culpability is a Judgment Day task, and while God is surely up to it, the criminal law is not. Moreover, such a widening may place causality on an infinite regression into the past. Jurors might reason, "Well, the accused said, but the victim said, but the accused did, but the victim did," and so on; and either the parsing of guilt or the infinite regress might bring law to the brink of paralysis. Limits are needed, and since acts begin and end somewhere, concentrating on the moment of the act may be as good a method as any for setting limits.

There is a diagram called Freitag's Triangle that represents the rise and fall of the action in conventional dramatic narratives. Applying this diagram to the law, we see that the law restricts context to the climax and denouement—to the place on Freitag's Triangle where conflict comes to a deadly resolution.[4] Within this dramatic analogue, the law's context omits the exposition, the beginnings of the conflict, the development of the action, and the increasing complication in the conflict leading to the climax. By contrast, commonsense justice typically widens the context to embrace all the stages of the drama. People want to know what happened before the act. What actions, motives, and emotions pushed the drama to this point? In short, we want to know the *story,* and for this a fuller context is essential. Such a desire is neither overinclusiveness nor voyeurism; rather, it is the view of *storytelling* that writers and dramatists routinely take, a view as old as "In the beginning" or "Once upon a time." Yet the point here is not merely to argue that storytelling is respectable or has a lineage older than the law's. The claim is bolder and broader: it is that the wider context of the story is the *better context* in which to judge human action. Viewing only the last act does not give us enough of the drama for us to render verdicts on the likes of Hamlet or Othello, Antigone or Oedipus.

Widening the context does entail some risks. For one thing, the neatly drawn distinction between criminal law and civil law may blur. Yet as Kalven and Zeisel noted, jurors do not fully embrace this distinction, and often see the culpability context as embracing both victim and defendant.[5] This is particularly so when victim and defendant know each other, as in a case involving a husband and wife in which the criminal act took place within a history of batterings. Here, jurors are likely to be weighing the actions and intentions of both parties. So if they see "black and blue," they may fault the victim and temper their judgment of the defendant, even to the point of exculpation. If they see "red-hot" passion arising from the victim's flagrant provocations, they may mitigate their judgment of the defendant to manslaughter, even if manslaughter does not precisely fit. And if they see "white-hot" emotion, long cooled by time and planfulness, fired by cold-blooded revenge, then they may feel sympathy for the victim and antipathy for the defendant, bringing down the harshest verdict possible.

The law does not ask jurors to parse culpability among participants; to do so might bring extralegal and impermissible factors into play. This may be true in the legal context, but from the commonsense view the case is an *interpersonal* action, a social drama, and to extract one of the parties from the social web and then focus the analysis exclusively on that individual's actions and intentions seems contrived. Much may be lost in such a translation. For example, if we cannot consider the acts, intentions, and culpability of Claudius, can we truly judge Hamlet?

We do not need to consult literature to make the point, for the law provides plenty of exemplars. Let's take an issue that has been of great concern on college campuses in the last decade: date rape. In the prototypical case the young woman alleges rape, whereas the young man claims consent. If, as often happens, there is no physical evidence (torn clothes, scratches and bruises, witnesses who heard her shout "No"), then the jury is left with two stories—hers and his. If this was not a first date but a relationship that had existed for some period of time, then the act in question and the participants have a history, together and apart. Are his history with other women and her history with other men relevant?

Should the jury hear if he had a "reputation," or if some other woman had accused him of a similar offense in the past? Should the jury hear about her "reputation," or if she accused some other man of a similar offense in the past? Are the past facts irrelevant or extralegal?

A clean and simple answer—such as "Yes, they are irrelevant and extralegal"—quickly turns messy and complicated. Under certain conditions, a judge might rule that they are relevant. But we must remember that jurors not only hear testimony but are instructed to weigh and judge the credibility of the testimony; and in a prototypical rape case, this means weighing the credibility of both parties and of their stories. History, then, provides not only a context for evaluating the dramatic and legal act in question, but a context for evaluating the dramatis personae and their subjective narratives.

The law might well argue, as Justice Holmes did, that its business is not God's business: instead of judging all, it judges only the one who allegedly broke the law. When jurors stray from the sole function of judging the individual to apportioning blame, justice will suffer. If the law artificially focuses on a person, an act, and a finite period of time, it does so in order to make a cleaner and more precise culpability judgment. But if the claim is that a wider context produces a messy and less distinct culpability judgment, some lessons from insanity cases contravene this claim.

When a defendant pleads not guilty by reason of insanity, commonsense justice widens the law's narrow context to consider a second type of culpability: the responsibility bringing about the mental disorder. Although such inclusiveness makes the judgment more complex, this type of culpability is consistent with legal assessments in other venues, where the defendant's responsibility for his or her condition is properly weighed, as when drinking leads later to some crime. It is also consistent with attributions of responsibility in social judgments. Thus, it might be said that commonsense justice brings into the context not an extralegal factor, but a legal one that has been overlooked or conflated.

Though one could cite many examples of commonsense justice's wider context, the overgeneralization runs into an apparent exception when judges go about deciding law. This judicial process has been likened to story construction or to writing a new chapter in a continuing story,[6] and has been analogized to the way in which jurors construct a story at trial.[7] The analogy begins to falter, however, when we look at the place of *stare decisis* in judges' and jurors' stories. *Stare decisis* is likely to have a prominent, even dominant place in judges' stories, yet no place in jurors' stories. For the law, then, legal history weighs heavily, creating a context that runs back to the Constitution and to ancient common law. If the question is which system widens context further, the law wins out over commonsense justice by a few centuries.

This *stare decisis* difference, however, is more apparent than real. Jurors do not cite case law in a *formal* way, but this does not mean they do not invoke some age-old notions of justice. If the jury nullification appeals of Antigone, Lilburne, and Penn fell on nondeaf ears, then jurors also must possess such notions of justice. They may not cite them; they may be unable to cite them. But these commonsense roots—about what is fair, right, and just—must be there.

Subjectivity

If *context* defines the field and the factors that are in play, then *perspective* concerns the point of view we take when regarding those factors. The conundrum has been whether to take the outsider's or the insider's perspective, as the dilemma between objectivity and subjectivity continues to bedevil legal theory.[8] The overgeneralization here is this: commonsense justice resolves the conundrum easily, consistently taking a more subjective view, whereas the law remains divided, giving different answers depending upon the issue, the century, and the jurist.

In his analysis of patterns of liability in the law, George Fletcher finds three patterns, which he labels manifest criminality, harmful consequences, and subjective criminality.[9] In manifest criminality, the "particular form of the act . . . is essential to liability."[10] The objective act must show the actor's criminal purpose. In the pattern of harmful consequences, liability for the harmful event "is based on the objective attribution of this harm to a responsible person and the determination of culpability in bringing it about or failing to prevent it."[11] Manifest criminality and harmful consequences begin their focus with the objective—either the act or the harm. In contrast, the subjective-criminality pattern takes "the actor's intent to violate a protected interest as the core of criminal conduct."[12] As Fletcher notes, "The manifest and the subjective . . . interweave in contemporary thinking about criminal law,"[13] but the conflict between these perspectives is "camouflaged by . . . legal maxims that create an image of unity in criminal theory."

In *The Common Law* Justice Holmes sought neither to camouflage nor to reconcile the subjective-versus-objective conflict; rather, he sought to situate the law in the objective sphere.[14] In his jurisprudence, law works "within the sphere of the senses"[15] and remains "wholly indifferent to the internal phenomena of conscience." The subjective realm of intentions and motives—the dark interior that captivates novelists and dramatists, who try to bring, in Roscoe Pound's words, "a restless world of flesh and blood" to life[16]—is of no concern to the law, says Holmes. Subtext is for the literary, not the legal, since "the standards of the law are external standards."[17]

In trying to make this objective jurisprudence work, Holmes deprives terms like "malice" of motive and feeling, leaving a dry logic according to which certain consequences will follow. By invoking the reasonable-man exemplar, Holmes avoids a subjective inquiry into what a specific defendant knew, for it is enough to know that the prototype would have known. According to Holmes, the law makes no "attempt to see men as God sees them."[18] Whether God would approve of Holmes's creation, we cannot say; but we can say that ordinary citizens do not see men as Holmes saw them. His tour de force falls flat: commonsense justice rejects such extreme objectivism.

In constructing a story of what happened and why, jurors seem quite comfortable stepping into the shoes of the defendant and looking at the events subjectively. In fact, the subjective view seems necessary for making an adjudication. If jurors are to construct a story that makes sense, the story must explicate the motive and intentions of the actor. Jurors must plunge into the subjective waters to find those hidden motives, rather than remaining on dry land with easy, prototypical answers.

Perhaps the clearest indication of the subjective preference can be seen in mock jurors' judgments of impossible-act cases. For the manifest-liability advocate, impossible acts—such as shooting at a tree stump while assuming it is a man, firing an unloaded pistol at someone, or mistakenly putting unpoisoned sugar cubes in someone's tea—are not criminal on their face, nor can they produce harm, as the harmful-consequences advocate requires. Though these actions present neither the appearance of criminality nor the possibility of harm, subjects have no qualms about finding guilt when the subjective intent was to kill.

Though jurors may have a preference for the subjective, the law may be able to curb their subjective preference with objective rules and instructions from the bench. An interesting test of subjective preference versus objective rules occurs in cases where the accessorial-liability and felony-murder rules conjoin. Here the law establishes simple rules for judging guilt—rules that involve a transfer of intent from one crime to another and from one defendant to another. Yet in experiment after experiment, subjects have rejected these objective rules, particularly those that transfer one person's guilt onto another. On the contrary, subjects evaluate each defendant's intentions and actions, and consistently nullify equalist justice in favor of proportional justice. When the law dictates that felons are fungible—that accessories and principals are not only their brother's keeper but are identical twins in guilt—jurors see them as separate individuals, with their own identities and levels of culpability. When the law dictates equal punishment, jurors reject equalism for proportional punishment based on assessments of individual culpability. And they perform these assessments by conducting subjective analyses, despite the law's objective directions.

For commonsense justice, "intent" is the cornerstone of culpability, far more than objective acts or rules. Unlike Holmes, who treated intent as a deconstructionist, constructionist, and minimalist, commonsense justice not only gives intent centrality but dresses it with layers of emotion, motive, and meaning that make it very different from the denuded, skeletal remains of Holmes's objective prototype. The thoughts of the defendant become the crucial issue in murder, manslaughter, and self-defense cases; they are the only issue in insanity cases, where the objective act is not in dispute and where the drama turns entirely on the defendant's internal state. When the law erects formal rules, limits the focus to the objective, or props up a prototype to answer questions for the defendant and for the jury, the law runs counter to the jurors' powerful and prevailing subjectivity. When push comes to shove, the jurors are likely to bend and reconstrue the objective rules in subjective ways, or nullify such rules altogether.

"Intent"—when it is neither denuded in a Holmsian way nor formally pulled from a hat in the legal legerdemain called felony-murder—is clearly a subjective factor. The "act," in contrast, is an objective factor. And these two factors, referred to, respectively, as *mens rea* and *actus reus*, are often the only factors under consideration. But there are cases in which these factors are not the only ones on the playing field; in euthanasia and right-to-die cases, for example, a number of other factors come into play. The law may make assisted suicide illegal, or decide that the plug can be pulled only if the condition is terminal, meaning that the patient has less than six months to live. The law can add conditions, such as that the decisionmaking has to be competent and the intent must be clear, as shown by a living will. Furthermore, medicine and science can weigh in, defining the parameters of "terminal" and "irreversible" objectively and tightly. But when ordinary citizens are asked to play juror or judge in such cases, they take a wider and more subjective view.

In cases of so-called assisted suicide, jurors may see the defendant as an extension of the patient and not as an independent actor; the victim then becomes just a person exercising her wish to die. When subjects interpret "terminal" and "irreversible" in terms of quality of life rather than scientifically, they enter a psychological space in which they ask not, "Could I live?" but "Would I want to live?" They are also more willing to *infer* intent than to hinge it exclusively to a legal living will. Overall, most subjects weigh the person's values and feelings more than the objective pronouncements of science and law. In taking into account more than mere matter, subjects want less law and more deference to the privacy rights and the wishes of the individual.

Although jurors' preference for the subjective appears pervasive and weighty, there is a countervailing fear. Giving deference to discretion may lead to ruleless law—an oxymoron that means no law. If each case is an exercise in jury discretion, then there are no rules that transcend the particular case. Even within a case, plunging into a defendant's psychological interior is hardly a sure method, for thoughts, feelings, and motives cannot be seen directly, not even by the likes of Freud. Such a subjective, discretionary enterprise grounds the law not on terra firma but on the unstable and invisible, where all we have are constructions, interpretations, and the stories constructed by jurors and judges. To the objectivist, this is not law but a frightening carte blanche to "do your own thing." In such a realm, Platonic Guardians—and here they may be jurors as well as justices—play their hunches and weave their yarns, as "truth seeking" becomes immaterial and the rule of law becomes irrelevant. Too much discretion, be it in the direction of context or that of subjectivity, arouses a fear of anarchy—a fear that the law has been lost.

Is the prediction of anarchy valid? Will jurors lose their way amid the subjective? The evidence from self-defense cases, and from cases where self-defense shades into mistaken self-defense or delusional self-defense, indicates that they will not. When a case involves two strangers with no history or past context, subjects tend to evaluate the seriousness of the threat objectively rather than subjectively. If they were just taking the subjective vantage point of the defendant, and if that defendant had believed herself seriously threatened, then *belief* would be all that mattered and a verdict of not guilty by reason of self-defense would follow; but it does not. If subjective belief were the only factor, then a mistaken belief should be just as good as a factual belief, an unreasonable mistake as good as a reasonable one, and a delusional mistake as good as a clear-headed one. Yet this is clearly not the case. If jurors yielded entirely to the subjective, then insanity cases in which delusional beliefs triggered the criminal act would have a high acquittal rate; yet we know that acquittals by reason of insanity are rare.

Jurors, then, do not yield entirely to the subjective. They are selective rather than indiscriminate, evaluating a defendant's subjective beliefs by some individualized measure that must be objective, reality-based, and shared; for if each juror applied a totally idiosyncratic standard in judging, then hung juries would be the rule rather than the exception. Since we know that that is not the case, then one juror's standard must comport rather closely with other jurors' standards. This standard may not precisely match that of the objective, reasonable man. But when the reasonable man is off the Holmsian mark, individualized standards may provide jurors with a measure that is psychologically more realistic.

Those who are suspicious of discretion and subjectivity are not likely to be mollified. They will probably claim that when jurors render verdicts, they do so under rules and legal definitions given by the judge. These rules, given by the parental authority, act like the superego reigning in the id, curbing the jurors' penchant for the subjective and discretionary, the wild and the willful. But what would happen if the field were not tightly circumscribed, if the elements were not legally limited, and if the jurors could use their own rules instead of the judge's? This situation, a nightmare for those who fear discretion, is approximated when jurors determine punishment, for the factors, context, and discretion all widen.

Recidivism cases present a particularly good test of whether jurors' discretion and subjectivity will become anarchic. Not only are jurors invited to weigh the defendant's character and prior convictions, but the State and the law argue that they *should* do so, and that they should give the recidivist defendant a punishment that is grossly inflated for the particular crime. Under experimental conditions, subjects overwhelmingly reject excessive, disproportionate punishment, even when urged in that direction by the prosecution. Although punishments increase with the number of prior convictions, they do not inflate at exponential rates. Moreover, traditional concerns regarding the seriousness of the latest crime and the defendant's intent play the major part in setting punishment, and jurors adhere to these concerns even when they are urged to consider recidivism even more. According to these findings, jurors' discretion is bound not by the law but by their good common sense.

The ultimate fear of juror discretion arises when jurors impose the ultimate penalty. In its death penalty jurisprudence, the Supreme Court has revealed its ambivalence, ranging from faith in untrammeled discretion *(McGautha)* to fear of the same sort of discretion *(Furman)*. The conscience of the community must still speak, but it cannot do so freely or unconscionably. In trying to guide the community's mind through an aggravating and mitigating mine field, through a contextual mélange where aggravating factors are more or less defined and where mitigating factors can be anything that comes to mind, this, says the Court, is the right course. Moreover, as jurors weigh and balance specific aggravating factors against indeterminate mitigating factors, they have complete discretion over how they weigh, what they balance, and what sort of math they use. In this "new math," it would be unsurprising if some wrong answers occurred.

When we look at cases in states where jurors do make the final decision, some cautious conclusions emerge. Jurors who are death qualified (who do not have the qualms and scruples that turn them into excludables) do not impose the death penalty readily, or anywhere near the number of times the prosecution asks for it. The death penalty remains the exception, even among citizens who do not take exception to it. From outcome to process, being a juror in a capital case seems to be a highly stressful experience: interviews conducted after the capital-sentencing phase reveal that many members of the jury suffer lasting emotional effects. A giddy lynch mob it is not. Since jurors have the discretionary freedom to give vent to their punitive sentiments if they so desire, their desire must be held in check by their own restraints. And when we look at experimental findings, those restraints turn out to be considerations of intent, the heinousness of the act, the defendant's role in the crime, the defendant's youth, and evidence of abuse in the defendant's childhood—factors well within accepted guidelines, even if these guidelines are not precise.

Internal Guidelines: Shades of Mens Rea

The subjective element upon which guilt or innocence turns, *mens rea*, turns out to have both more and fewer nuances for citizens than for the law. At times, jurors will see more shades to *mens rea* than the law either sees or sanctions, and these distinctions with a difference will create problems when it comes to rendering a verdict. At other times, jurors will focus not on a particular mental state *(mentes reae)* but on a generic concept approximating "evil mind," where the question is whether the defendant "truly acted in a malicious and malevolent way."[19] If the law asks for hairsplitting while jurors cleave to the generic, there will once again be problems in determining the verdict. To understand what jurors understand about *mens rea*, we must examine both ends of the concept, beginning with nuance.

A dramatic example of the shades involved in *mens rea* is the case of accessory to felony-murder. Here, jurors see nuance precisely where the law asks them not to. When subjects are asked to determine *mens rea*, they make that determination *for each defendant* by considering all that was said and done against what might have been said and done. This view rejects formulaic, objective determinations of *mens rea*. Subjects balk at transferring intent from one crime to another, and they outright rebel at transferring intent from one defendant to another. Determining intent is individualized, not generalized, and the law's effort to make felons not only their brother's keepers but their equal-time cellmates proves ineffective.

Though felony-murder may be a living fossil that uses "transfers" to concoct intent, most crimes define a specific intent. But this is where nuance comes into play. What if the juror finds some culpability, but not the specific intent for the offense charged? Jurors are allowed to bring in a lesser, included offense. But what if there is no lesser, included offense? What if jurors are confronted with an all-or-nothing situation?

The insanity defense has been just such an all-or-nothing situation for more than two hundred years. And although the law presents jurors with this black-or-white picture, empirical evidence shows that subjects see shades of gray. One shade is diminished responsibility, a *mens rea* that falls between "completely culpable" and "not culpable at all." Another shade involves an inference: the prosecution may ask jurors to infer the specific intent from an act (for example, from the fact that the defendant bought pistol and shot). But such an inference may not satisfy jurors if they see that intent as having arisen from a delusion, reflecting a deeper incapacity, whereas the law seems to be asking them to judge the surface *mens rea*. The problem for jurors then becomes acute: they must either treat the delusional defendant as if he were guilty of first-degree murder, or else find him not culpable at all. Finally, another shading involves culpability for bringing about one's mental condition—a responsibility which, in insanity cases, subjects recognize but the law does not. When the law's verdict categories conflate two distinct culpability judgments, or conflate gray with either black or white, the verdict may appear wrongful, but this is very different from concluding that the jurors rendered the wrong verdict.

The problem of too few categories cuts across much of criminal law. In self-defense law, for example, where the area of "mistaken or putative self-defense" remains a theoretical backwater, a defendant who makes a mistake can be in very deep water. If we require a defendant pleading self-defense to meet an objective set of prerequisites, then even if a defendant mistakenly believed that a serious threat existed, his or her defense may fail. As a consequence, jurors are asked to regard the defendant as a murderer; since there was no objective threat, hence no provocation, manslaughter is not a likely fit. But neither is the crime of second- or first-degree murder. What can jurors do with such a defendant when the verdict categories do not fit?

In cases of manslaughter we see the same problem. When the verdict of manslaughter is bound tightly to the provocation and to a response that must be "of a sudden," then brooders and rekindlers are not only out in the cold but entrapped by a murder conviction. But a more severe verdict of murder may not fit this defendant's *mens rea*. If jurors can see a difference between the *mens rea* of a murderer and that of the particular defendant, then once again there are too few categories. The jurors are reduced to three unenviable choices: ignore the difference and follow the law, reconstrue the categories to create some de facto fit, or nullify.

These examples illustrate the nuance problem, where citizens see fine distinctions between the defendant's intent and the law's definition of the crime, yet have no way to register these distinctions through the verdict options they are given. In the opposite case, the law asks for a highly specific intent but jurors embrace a generic *mens rea*—a "malice" more evil than "malice aforethought."

In experiments involving active-euthanasia cases where all the elements of first-degree murder were apparently satisfied, only 36 percent of the subjects rendered a verdict of first-degree or second-degree murder. For many of the 64 percent who did not, even though they heard evidence indicating malice aforethought in the legal sense, they did not see malice in the sense of "evil motive." Some saw no malevolence, no revenge motive; some saw no malice at all. Others believed the defendant had acted of affection, a feeling quite the opposite of what we usually attribute to murderers. Whether the defendant's motives were pure and noble or confused and disturbed, they were neither identical to nor as blameworthy as those of a first-degree murderer. In this instance, the legal specifics of intent took a back seat to the blameworthiness of the defendant's motives.

This fusion of "the issues of motive and intent,"[20] which was illustrated in the trial of Bernhard Goetz, moves jurors "closer to a moral conception of intent."[21] But fusion need not mean confusion or nullification; it may represent a broader *mens rea*, replete with moral overtones, which once had an elevated place within the law. So if Goetz's motive was to ward off an attack, then he never had "a malicious motive to kill";[22] and thus no evil motive for killing existed.

The jury in the *Goetz* case was attacked in the press for not following the law's narrow reading of *mens rea,* and for applying a more moral, generic *mens rea.* For a contrasting case—where a jury was attacked for not breaking away from the law's narrow reading of *mens rea* and not embracing the generic—we must return to Los Angeles in 1992, when the jury verdict in the first Rodney King trial sparked a riot and when a videotape again captured apparently blatant crimes. A truck driver, Reginald Denny, was dragged from his cab, beaten unconscious, and hit in the head with a brick. His skull was fractured in some ninety places. But when the jury acquitted Damian Williams and Henry Watson of the most serious charge, attempted murder, the press reacted with a few bricks of its own.

Columnist Richard Cohen wrote: "Even days after the verdict was returned, it remains impossible to get the tape of the assault out of our heads. There is Damian Williams hitting Denny in the head with a brick and then doing a little dance of jubilation. The force of the throw, the damage it did, Williams's evident glee at the maiming of another person—these are all hard to reconcile with his acquittal on the charge of attempted murder."[23] Cohen continues: "We're told the prosecution failed to prove that Williams had intended to kill Denny . . . There was no intent to kill, the jury said. No? Then what in the world *was* attempted?"[24] Cohen, unable to resist some unfounded speculations about why the jurors did what they did, claims that a background of racism, the Rodney King case, an equating of the King case with the Denny case in some way that attempted to balance the verdicts—all "seeped into the jury room."[25] So Cohen's explanation, all without evidence, and contradicted by the statements of the jurors, is that extralegal and impermissible factors drove the verdict.[26]

Columnist Charles Krauthammer also delivered a few blows at this "slap-on-the-wrist verdict."[27] The former psychiatrist returned to his old profession when he said, "Obviously there was fear, fear of touching off another LA riot, fear on the part of the jurors for their own safety. The jurors have stoutly denied this. Some issued these denials on TV—their faces blacked out to conceal their identities."[28] To his eyes, blacked-out faces on TV are sure signs that the denial was not real denial but psychiatric denial. Once we confidently turn jurors' utterances into their opposite through a version of the "unconscious ploy"—where we somehow know what is in their unconscious, and know that it is contrary to what they consciously said—then we can dispense with their statements as misleading self-deceptions aimed at covering their tracks. This interpretive leap, without some validating net, leaves the unrefutable assertion hanging not in the realm of science but in polemics.

The *Washington Post* countered such "polemics" by noting that many commentaries seemed to be premised on the idea that the main defendant was *acquitted*.[29] In fact he was "*convicted* of mayhem, a felony carrying a maximum sentence of eight years in prison," and also convicted "of four misdemeanor assaults, which could bring his sentence up to 10 years."[30] The editorial noted that the jury had been "accused of all manner of sins, including a misplaced political correctness and a willingness to place justice second behind a desire to avoid a verdict that might have started more riots."[31] The *Post* accused the critics of "playing fast and loose with analogies to the Rodney King case," of "linking these two trials as some sort of racial yin and yang," and of invoking "dangerous mythologies."[32]

I would like to offer another hypothesis about what happened—a view that cleaves a bit more closely to the jurors' words. To begin with, let's note that the Denny case was complex; there were not only multiple defendants but multiple charges, many of which seemed to overlap. If we were to stop ordinary citizens on the street and ask them to define and differentiate "mayhem," "assault," and "attempted murder," their answers would probably be quite confused—even if we didn't ask them to distinguish "simple mayhem" from "aggravated mayhem." This is a case of nuance, a case of *mentes reae,* where the law asks jurors to make a series of fine discriminations about subtle shadings of intent.

Concerning the most serious charge, attempted murder, Juror 307 said, "I couldn't see attempted murder because if he attempted to kill him, why did he only hit him once? Why not just keep hitting him?"[33] This juror evaluated what was done against what could have been done. If the prototype of "attempted murderer" involves a more strenuous, zealous, or persistent effort to infer the intent, then the defendant's one-shot effort left reasonable doubt.

Let's also remember that no one asked the jury, "Do you believe the defendants did *wrong?*" No one asked, "Do you believe that the defendants' motives were evil?" Or, "Do you believe that the defendants are blameworthy?" Had the jurors been asked any or all of those generic *mens rea* questions, their answer would probably have been yes, and the fact that both defendants were found guilty of something is some sort of affirmation. The jurors were not asked the general question; they were asked for nuance. Yet critics seem to think that they fudged or finessed the big question, although that big, moral question was never posed.

When jurors reconstrued a narrow *mens rea* into a broader question of malice aforethought, as in the *Goetz* case, criticism followed. And when jurors followed the law's narrow *mens rea,* which they may have done in the Denny case, they were also criticized. The criticism may have been unfair in both cases. We have seen that the subjective element of *mens rea* is one that subjects hold dearly and do not abandon lightly. Moreover, the evidence shows that jurors know both ends of *mens rea,* sometimes seeing greater shadings and sometimes deeper meanings than the law may allow. This star-crossed situation may be changing, not because the path of commonsense justice is aligning itself with the law's but because the resurgence of *mens rea* within the law is turning the law's path back toward commonsense justice.[34]

Internal Guidelines: Proportionality

Mens rea is measured, and the measure for measure turns out to be *proportionality*. Citizens tend to order crimes in a similar way, from most serious to least serious, creating what might be called a blameworthiness scale. If they are asked which crimes should be punished the most and which the least, or to assign punishments to these crimes, their rankings or ratings of punishment are closely related to blameworthiness. To put this more simply, punishment is proportional to the crime. This suggests that people have such a blameworthiness scale in mind, and can invoke it when a task calls for it. Judging guilt and setting a sentence are such tasks.

We see the principle of proportionality being invoked when jurors try to find a mitigating verdict, attempting to match a verdict proportionately to the blameworthiness they perceive. In cases of euthanasia, manslaughter, self-defense, insanity, and diminished responsibility, subjects try to find the right equation for the particular defendant, invoking a contextual scale on which they will situate the defendant below the more culpable and above the less culpable. The punishment decision—which jurors generally do not make and which the judge will instruct them not to consider—is likely to influence the verdict decision despite admonishment from the bench. There is evidence that some jurors reason backward in some cases—that is, they decide what ought to be done with the defendant (determine the sentence) and then decide what verdict will best bring that about. Although this backward decisionmaking is not legally sanctioned, the process seems grounded in proportionalism. Thus, whether jurors go about deciding verdicts in the forward manner or in a looking-glass manner, blameworthiness and punishment do not stray very far from their proportional connection.

When jurors decide the punishment directly, as in death penalty decisions, death-qualified jurors must decide if the defendant fits their deathworthy prototype, and whether a teenage defendant is as deathworthy as an adult. Within this narrow bandwidth of crimes for which convicted defendants are death eligible by statute, jurors must somehow measure punishment proportionally to an imprecise set of factors, some of which include the facts of the crime, the intent, and the harm, as well as the defendant's history, character, and potential for violence. If the jurors' death sentence is deemed disproportionate and challenged on Eighth Amendment grounds, the Supreme Court will do its own proportionality analysis, using objective data only or adding the proportionate scales of its own Platonic Guardians. So proportionalism, which is deeply rooted in commonsense justice, is the applicable standard. And when this standard is applied incorrectly in a particular case, when the punishment is judged disproportionate, it is done so by the standard of proportionality. In this iteration, proportionality regenerates proportionality.

The potency of proportionality can be seen most dramatically in situations where the law tries to forbid it, as in accessory felony-murder, or where the law urges jurors to abandon it, as in recidivism cases. In accessory felony-murder, the law asks jurors to treat the principal and all accessories equally; in capital cases, this might mean death sentences for both. Yet in repeated experiments, subjects have cast aside equalism in favor of proportional treatment of defendants. This is not just an adult phenomenon. In experimental work with children using scenarios resembling felony-murder, we see how strongly and early proportionality reigns. Even kindergartners discriminate between the principal and the accessories in their culpability and punishment judgments, and children who are in second and third grade discriminate proportionately among the accessories as well.

If accessory felony-murder tries to forbid proportionalism in favor of equalism, recidivism cases fly in the face of proportionalism in another way. These cases urge jurors to abandon proportionalism or, more aptly, to embrace and apply its opposite: disproportionate punishments. A defendant is convicted of a crime such as shoplifting or writing a no-account check—a crime that would ordinarily warrant only moderate to light punishment. The jury is then asked to give a disproportionate sentence of life imprisonment, based on the fact that this defendant has committed such offenses a number of times before and is therefore a recidivist. Although life imprisonment for shoplifting or writing a bad check would certainly be disproportionate under the evolving Eighth Amendment, and is disproportionate in the eyes of mock jurors asked to determine a sentence is such cases, the question is whether the punishment calculus changes when prior convictions are thrown into the equation. With such convictions alone, the punishment increases, but proportionately. When the prosecution asserts that the defendant is a recidivist and asks for a disproportionately severe sentence, the jurors' sentences increase but not nearly to the extent that the prosecution would like. And when the recidivist claim is countered by the defense, the punishments drop, reflecting a more proportionate calculus. Left to their own devices and equations, subjects punish proportionately.

That some forget or ignore proportionality is evident in Senator Phil Gramm's defense of a bill entitled the Neighborhood Security Act of 1993.[35] Gramm was concerned about "a relatively small group of predators" who commit a vast percentage of crime. He wanted to target these "hardened criminals" and "chronic offenders," and sought to increase the mandatory minimum punishments that Congress had enacted during the 1980s. But he defined hardened, chronic predators as anyone convicted of a violent crime "while possessing a firearm."[36] This most disputable measure, without factual backing, would snare within its wide net many crimes of family violence, such as those in which a spouse wounds or kills a spouse but in which the self-defense claim could not be met. We know that women who kill their husbands generally have a nonviolent history. But under Gramm's proposal "criminals convicted of a violent crime while possessing a firearm would face no less than 10 years in prison for the firearm violation alone, 20 years if the gun is fired and either life in prison or the death penalty if the gun is used to kill."[37] Disproportionate punishment, based on a dubious definition of "hardened criminal," is the sort of simplism that citizens reject when they are asked for their individualized judgments on the defendant's blameworthiness and the punishment that is due.

In the current climate—or, more aptly, in the perceived current climate—lawmakers will continue to propose legislation for disproportionate sentences. They will claim, in their defense, that community sentiment supports it, a claim resting on that imprecise gauge, the public opinion poll. Some of these proposed and passed pieces of legislation will be contravened by better empirical data, reflecting commonsense justice, but perceptions and myths may continue to weigh more heavily than facts in the drafting of legislation, a phenomenon we have seen in laws concerning the insanity defense. In the case of legislation on mandatory minimum sentences, if facts fail to check the legislatures' rush to enactment, the courts may provide a balance. Judges may refuse to follow the law on Eighth Amendment grounds; or if the punishment does appear to violate the Eighth Amendment's prohibition on disproportionate punishment, the Supreme Court may strike it down. But we have seen that when commonsense justice is allowed to work, jurors can exercise their judgment on crime and punishment, on *mens rea* and proportionate sentences. And where the law's path and the community's path diverge, commonsense justice can devise its own checks and balances, through a variety of nullifications, to exert a corrective.

Though commonsense justice has no exclusive claim to "truth," it nonetheless demands respect—not because it is anarchy waiting to happen but because it invokes the sacred precepts of justice embedded in *mens rea* and proportionality. Rooted in a legal history far older than the U.S. Constitution, the jury, the conscience of the community, speaks: it decides guilt, and sometimes renders a life-or-death judgment. Jurors may not have the right to decide the law in most states, though they certainly have the power in all states. That power has been endorsed and condemned, seen as justice and as anarchy; but in the end, jury discretion remains an established and affirmed fixture within the law.

When jurors' reasons for their verdicts are put under an experimental microscope and examined across a number of legal venues, they seem solid, substantial, and sound. They are rooted in *mens rea* and the principle of proportionality, which have influenced Anglo-American law for centuries. Citizens apprehend a depth to *mens rea,* but also perceive its nuances, and when they see distinctions worth making rather than ignoring, they try to register these distinctions somehow. They also make proportionality distinctions among types of crimes and criminals, and attempt to fit punishment to blameworthiness, while resisting vindictive excesses—excesses that some legislators find hard to resist. *Mens rea* and proportionality constitute a well-worn path. In calling the law to follow the path of the community, we are not urging it to heed majoritarian, transitory, ignorant, or unprincipled sentiment. We are asking it to acknowledge what it may have forgotten or lost sight of: the deeper roots of justice.

Notes

INTRODUCTION

1. O. W. Holmes, *The Common Law*, ed. M. D. Howe (Cambridge, Mass.: Harvard University Press, 1963; orig. pub. 1881), p. 1.
2. Ibid., p. 32.
3. *Stanford v. Kentucky*, 492 U.S. 361, 379 (1989).
4. R. Pound, "The Need of a Sociological Jurisprudence," *Green Bag* 19 (1907): 615.

1. IN SEARCH OF COMMUNITY SENTIMENT

1. H. Dewar, "When Whispers Are Heard as Shouts," *Washington Post*, June 7, 1992, p. A23.
2. Ibid.
3. R. Morin, "Voting against This 'Referendum': Perot Invites a Skewed Response, Public Opinion Researchers Say," *Washington Post*, March 21, 1993, p. A29.
4. E. Goodman, "Not So Fast: 'Instant Opinion Is an Oxymoron,'" *Washington Post*, February 6, 1993, p. A23.
5. ABC News, "Insanity on Trial," *Nightline*, June 22, 1982.
6. V. P. Hans and N. Vidmar, *Judging the Jury* (New York: Plenum, 1986), p. 181.
7. P. C. Ellsworth, R. M. Bukatay, C. L. Cowan, and W. C. Thompson, "The Death-Qualified Jury and the Defense of Insanity," *Law and Human Behavior* 8 (1984): 45–54; R. Fitzgerald and P. C. Ellsworth, "Due Process vs. Crime Control," *Law and Human Behavior* 8 (1984): 31–51; V. P. Hans, "An Analysis of Public Attitudes toward the Insanity Defense," *Criminology* 24 (1986): 393–414; V. P. Hans and D. Slater, "John Hinckley, Jr., and the Insanity Defense: The Public's Verdict,"

Public Opinion Quarterly 47 (1983): 202–212; V. P. Hans and D. Slater, "'Plain Crazy': Lay Definitions of Legal Insanity," *International Journal of Law and Psychiatry* 7 (1984): 105–114; D. Slater and V. P. Hans, "Public Opinions of Forensic Psychiatry Following the Hinckley Verdict," *American Journal of Psychiatry* 141 (1984): 675–679.

8. Hans, "An Analysis of Public Attitudes."

9. N. J. Finkel, *Insanity on Trial* (New York: Plenum, 1988).

10. R. A. Pasewark, "Insanity Plea: A Review of the Research Literature," *Journal of Psychiatry and Law* 9 (1981): 357–401; H. J. Steadman and J. J. Cocozza, "Selective Reporting and the Public's Misconceptions of the Criminally Insane," *Public Opinion Quarterly* 41 (1978): 523–532.

11. Hans and Slater, "'Plain Crazy.'"

12. J. A. Fox, M. L. Radelet, and J. L. Bonsteel, "Death Penalty Opinion in the Post-*Furman* Years," *Review of Law and Social Change* 18 (1990–1991): 499.

13. Ibid., p. 500.

14. *Furman v. Georgia,* 408 U.S. 238, 361, 363 (1972) (per curiam).

15. P. C. Ellsworth and L. Ross, "Public Opinion and Capital Punishment: A Close Examination of the Views of Abolitionists and Retentionists," *Crime and Delinquency* 29 (1983): 116–169; A. Sarat and N. Vidmar, "Public Opinion, the Death Penalty, and the Eighth Amendment: Testing the Marshall Hypothesis," *Wisconsin Law Review* 17 (1976): 171–206; R. M. Bohm, L. J. Clark, and A. F. Aveni, "Knowledge and Death Penalty Opinion: A Test of the Marshall Hypothesis," *Journal of Research in Crime and Delinquency* 28 (1991): 360–387.

16. W. Bowers, "Capital Punishment and Contemporary Values: People's Misgivings and the Court's Misperceptions," *Law and Society Review* 27 (1993): 162.

17. Fox et al., "Death Penalty Opinion," p. 510.

18. E. E. Smith and D. L. Medin, *Categories and Concepts* (Cambridge, Mass.: Harvard University Press, 1981); V. L. Smith, "Prototypes in the Courtroom: Lay Representations of Legal Concepts," *Journal of Personality and Social Psychology* 61 (1991): 857–872; A. Tversky and D. Kahneman, "Availability: A Heuristic for Judging Frequency and Probability," *Cognitive Psychology* 5 (1973): 207–232.

19. V. P. Hans, "Law and the Media: An Overview and Introduction," *Law and Human Behavior* 14 (1990): 400.

20. Ibid.

21. Fox et al., "Death Penalty Opinion," p. 524.

22. E. Rapaport, "The Death Penalty and Gender Discrimination," *Law and Society Review* 25 (1991): 370; also see S. Gross and R. Mauro, *Death and Discrimination* (Boston: Northeastern University Press, 1989). (They report that more than 80 percent of the death penalties given out in Florida and Georgia, and 75 percent in Illinois, were in felony-murder cases.)

The NAACP Legal Defense and Education Fund found that in 1986 more than 75 percent of death-row cases involved felony-murder.

23. N. J. Finkel and K. B. Duff, "Felony-Murder and Community Sentiment: Testing the Supreme Court's Assertions," *Law and Human Behavior* 15 (1991): 405–429.

24. R. Toner, "Politics of Welfare: Focusing on the Problems," *New York Times*, July 5, 1992, pp. 1, 16.

25. R. H. Thomas and J. D. Hutcheson Jr., "Georgia Residents' Attitudes toward the Death Penalty, the Disposition of Juvenile Offenders, and Related Issues," Paper prepared for the Clearinghouse on Georgia Prisons and Jails, 1986.

26. Virginia Commonwealth University, "Commonwealth Poll Regarding Attitudes towards the Death Penalty," *Commonwealth Poll,* May–June 1989.

27. K. C. Haas and J. A. Inciardi, "Lingering Doubts about a Popular Punishment," in K. C. Haas and J. A. Inciardi, eds., *Challenging Capital Punishment: Legal and Social Science Approaches* (Newbury Park, Calif.: Sage Publications, 1988), p. 11.

28. L. J. Stalans and S. S. Diamond, "Formation and Change in Lay Evaluations of Criminal Sentencing: Misperception and Discontent," *Law and Human Behavior* 14 (1990): 199–214.

29. Ibid., p. 201.

30. D. Kahneman and A. Tversky, "The Simulation Heuristic," in D. Kahneman and A. Tversky, eds., *Judgment under Uncertainty: Heuristics and Biases* (Cambridge: Cambridge University Press, 1982), pp. 201–208.

31. Fox et al., "Death Penalty Opinion," p. 509.

32. Ibid., p. 513.

33. N. Vidmar and P. Ellsworth, "Public Opinion and the Death Penalty," *Stanford Law Review* 26 (1974): 1263.

34. N. J. Finkel, "De Facto Departures from Insanity Instructions: Toward the Remaking of Common Law," *Law and Human Behavior* 14 (1990): 105–122.

35. O. W. Holmes, *The Common Law,* ed. M. D. Howe (Cambridge, Mass.: Harvard University Press, 1963; orig. pub. 1881), p. 36. I omitted four words from the end of the quote, which are significant. Holmes added, "whether right or wrong." A discussion of this addendum will have to wait.

36. *Roe v. Wade,* 410 U.S. 113 (1973).

37. "Excerpts from the Court's Decision on Rejecting Jurors on the Basis of Race," *New York Times,* June 19, 1992, p. A22.

38. *Batson v. Kentucky,* 476 U.S. 79 (1986).

39. "'Our Obligation Is to Define the Liberty of All,'" *Washington Post,* June 30, 1992, p. A8.

40. E. J. Dionne Jr., "Justices' Abortion Ruling Mirrors Public Opinion,"

Washington Post, July 1, 1992, p. A4. The article cites both a national random sample by the *Washington Post* and results from a CBS–*New York Times* poll. Interestingly enough, the article makes a point that I made earlier, when it states that "abortion is controversial among pollsters, because the public's qualms on the subject mean that the results of polls depend to an unusual degree on how questions are framed."

41. Holmes, *The Common Law,* p. xxii.

42. H. Kalven Jr. and H. Zeisel, *The American Jury* (Chicago: University of Chicago Press, 1971), p. 498.

43. S. Jacoby, *Wild Justice: The Evolution of Revenge* (New York: Harper and Row, 1983).

44. M. Kinsley, "Ask a Silly Question," *Washington Post,* June 18, 1992, p. A23.

45. R. Dworkin, *Law's Empire* (Cambridge, Mass.: Harvard University Press, 1986), p. 164.

46. Ibid.

47. Ibid., p. 165.

48. Ibid., p. 164.

49. C. Haney, "The Fourteenth Amendment and Symbolic Legality: Let Them Eat Due Process," *Law and Human Behavior* 15 (1991): 185.

50. A. Hamilton, J. Madison, and J. Jay, *The Federalist Papers* (New York: Mentor, 1961), no. 78 (Hamilton).

51. Ibid., p. 467.

52. Ibid., p. 469.

53. "Excerpts from the Court's Decision on Rejecting Jurors."

54. "'Our Obligation Is to Define the Liberty of All.'"

55. T. R. Tyler, *Why People Obey the Law* (New Haven: Yale University Press, 1990).

56. T. R. Tyler and K. Rasinski, "Procedural Justice, Institutional Legitimacy, and the Acceptance of Unpopular U.S. Supreme Court Decisions: A Reply to Gibson," *Law and Society Review* 25 (1991): 621–630.

57. J. L. Gibson, "Institutional Legitimacy, Procedural Justice, and Compliance with Supreme Court Decisions: A Question of Causality," *Law and Society Review* 25 (1991): 631–635.

2. UNDERSTANDING NULLIFICATION

1. The opening discussion here is based on D. N. Robinson, "Antigone's Defense: A Critical Study of *Natural Law Theory: Contemporary Essays,*" *Review of Metaphysics* 45 (1991): 363–392.

2. Sophocles, *Antigone,* in D. Grene and R. L. Lattimore, eds., *Greek Tragedies* (Chicago: University of Chicago Press, 1954), vol. 1, p. 196.

3. T. A. Green, *Verdicts According to Conscience: Perspectives on the En-*

glish Criminal Trial Jury, 1200–1800 (Chicago: University of Chicago Press, 1985), p. 153.

4. Ibid., p. 154.
5. Ibid., p. 159.
6. Ibid., p. 163.
7. Ibid.
8. Ibid., p. 163.
9. V. P. Hans and N. Vidmar, *Judging the Jury* (New York: Plenum, 1986).
10. Green, *Verdicts According to Conscience*, p. 170.
11. Ibid., p. 174.
12. Ibid., p. 174.
13. Ibid., p. 175.
14. Ibid., pp. 184–185.
15. Ibid., p. 185.
16. Ibid., p. 203.
17. Ibid., p. 222.
18. Ibid.
19. Ibid., p. 223.
20. Ibid.
21. Ibid.
22. Hans and Vidmar, *Judging the Jury*, p. 21.
23. Green, *Verdicts According to Conscience*, p. 225.
24. Hans and Vidmar, *Judging the Jury*, p. 33.
25. Ibid., p. 34.
26. Ibid.
27. Ibid., p. 35.
28. *Georgia v. Brailsford*, 3 U.S. (3 Dall.) 1 (1794).
29. Hans and Vidmar, *Judging the Jury*, p. 38.
30. I. A. Horowitz and T. E. Willging, "Changing Views of Jury Power: The Nullification Debate, 1787–1988," *Law and Human Behavior* 15 (1991): 165–182.
31. *United States v. Battiste*, 24 F. Cas. 1042 (C.C.D. Mass.), no. 14,545 (1835).
32. *United States v. Morris*, 26 F. Cas 1323 (C.C.D. Mass.), no. 15,815 (1851).
33. Horowitz and Willging, "Changing Views," p. 169.
34. *Sparf and Hansen v. United States*, 156 U.S. 51 (1895).
35. Horowitz and Willging, "Changing Views," p. 170.
36. Ibid.
37. M. R. Kadish and S. H. Kadish, "The Institutionalization of Conflict: Jury Acquittals," in J. L. Tapp and F. L. Levine, eds., *Law, Justice, and the Individual in Society: Psychological and Legal Issues* (New York: Holt, Rinehart and Winston, 1977), p. 318.

38. *Duncan v. Louisiana,* 391 U.S. 145 (1968).

39. Hans and Vidmar, *Judging the Jury,* p. 42.

40. *United States v. Dougherty,* 475 F. 2d 1113 (D.C. Cir. 1972).

41. Horowitz and Willging, "Changing Views," p. 171.

42. Ibid.

43. Ibid., p. 165.

44. G. P. Fletcher, *A Crime of Self-Defense: Bernhard Goetz and the Law on Trial* (Chicago: University of Chicago Press, 1988), p. 154.

45. Ibid.

46. Green, *Verdicts According to Conscience.*

47. Horowitz and Willging, "Changing Views," p. 174.

48. Hans and Vidmar, *Judging the Jury,* p. 149.

49. L. M. Friedman, *A History of American Law,* 2nd ed. (New York: Simon and Schuster, 1985).

50. L. Parker, "Charges against Father Dismissed in Babyseat Case," *Washington Post,* May 4, 1991, p. A6.

51. Ibid.

52. Ibid.

53. Ibid.

54. Ibid.

55. Ibid.

56. F. Cope, "U-Va. Student Gets 13 Months in Drug Case: Judge Says Mandatory Sentencing 'Tears Up the Court's Conscience,'" *Washington Post,* June 4, 1991, pp. A1, A6.

57. Ibid.

58. Ibid.

59. P. Duggan, "P.G. Slayer of Father Spared Jail," *Washington Post,* August 28, 1991, pp. B1, B2.

60. Ibid.

61. Ibid.

62. P. Duggan, "Abused Son Escapes Murder Rap," *Washington Post,* March 29, 1991, pp. C1, C6.

63. Ibid.

64. D. Edwards, "Congress Swamped the Courts," *Washington Post,* July 7, 1993, p. A21; Editorial, "Mandatory Madness," *Washington Post,* July 7, 1993, p. A20; Editorial, "Swamping the Courts," *Washington Post,* June 22, 1992, p. A16.

65. R. Goldfarb, "Mindless Sentencing: What's the Point of Taking Away Judges' Power to Use Their Judgment?" *Washington Post,* May 31, 1993, p. A19.

66. M. York, "Judge Rejects Federal Sentencing Guidelines," *Washington Post,* April 30, 1993, p. D5.

67. Ibid.

68. Editorial, "Clemency in Annapolis," *Washington Post,* March 11, 1991,

p. A10. "Following the lead of former Ohio governor Richard Celeste, Maryland Gov. William Donald Schaefer has used his powers of executive clemency to free seven women convicted of killing, and one of assaulting, their husbands or boyfriends."

69. K. D. Moore, *Pardons: Justice, Mercy, and the Public Interest* (New York: Oxford University Press, 1989), p. 4.

70. Ibid., p. 16.

71. Ibid.

72. L. Cannon, "Justice Dept. to Review King Beating Case," *Washington Post,* April 30, 1992, p. A1.

73. A. Kamen and R. Castaneda, "Fires, Looting Spread in Stunned Community," *Washington Post,* April 30, 1992, p. A1.

74. Cannon, "Justice Dept.," p. A26.

75. Editorial, "The Los Angeles Verdict," *Washington Post,* May 1, 1992, p. A26.

76. D. L. Brown and P. Thomas, "In D.C., Some Link Verdict to Racism, Police Power," *Washington Post,* April 30, 1992, p. A25.

77. R. Morin and S. Warden, "Views on the King Verdict," *Washington Post,* May 1, 1992, p. A31.

78. R. Morin, "Polls Uncover Much Common Ground on L.A. Verdict," *Washington Post,* May 11, 1992, p. A15.

79. *Planned Parenthood of Southeastern Pennsylvania v. Casey.* The paraphrase comes from, 'Our obligation is to define the liberty of all,' *Washington Post,* June 30, 1992, p. A8.

80. Indiana, Maryland, and Georgia are the three states that let jurors know they have the right to decide the law.

81. See, for example, *Enmund v. Florida,* 458 U.S. 782 (1982), and *Tison v. Arizona,* 481 U.S. 137 (1987), regarding capital felony-murder; and *Thompson v. Oklahoma,* 487 U.S. 815 (1988), and *Stanford v. Kentucky,* 492 U.S. 361 (1989), regarding the juvenile death penalty.

3. REVEALING JURORS' SENTIMENTS

1. L. Smith, "Jury Was Asked to See Events as Police Did," *Washington Post,* April 30, 1992, p. A25.

2. L. Cannon, "Justice Dept. to Review King Beating Case," *Washington Post,* April 30, 1992, p. A26.

3. L. Deutsch, "Juror Says She Prayed, Argued for at Least 1 Conviction," *Washington Post,* May 6, 1992, p. A8.

4. Smith, "Jury Was Asked."

5. "The Jury's View," *Washington Post,* May 1, 1992, p. A33.

6. G. Fletcher, *Rethinking Criminal Law* (Boston: Little, Brown, 1978).

7. "The Jury's View."

8. Ibid.

9. Ibid.
10. See J. D. Casper, K. Benedict, and J. L. Perry, "Juror Decision Making, Attitudes, and the Hindsight Bias," *Law and Human Behavior* 13 (1989): 291–310; B. Fischhoff, "Hindsight Is Not Equal to Foresight: The Effect of Outcome Knowledge on Judgment under Uncertainty," *Journal of Experimental Psychology: Human Perception and Performance* 1 (1975): 288–299; S. A. Hawkins and R. Hastie, "Hindsight: Biased Judgments of Past Events after the Outcomes Are Known," *Psychological Bulletin* 107 (1990): 311–327; D. K. Kagehiro, R. B. Taylor, W. S. Laufer, and A. T. Harland, "Hindsight Bias and Third-Party Consentors to Warrantless Police Searches," *Law and Human Behavior* 15 (1991): 305–314.
11. "The Jury's View."
12. T. Rohrlich, "From Anger and Tears to Final High-Fives: The King Beating Jury," *Washington Post,* April 25, 1993, p. A22.
13. W. Hamilton and J. Crosby, "L.A. Beating Case Jurors Call Videotape Critical, Deliberations Emotional," *Washington Post,* April 20, 1993, p. A4.
14. G. P. Fletcher, *A Crime of Self-Defense: Bernhard Goetz and the Law on Trial* (Chicago: University of Chicago Press, 1988).
15. Ibid., p. 11.
16. Ibid.
17. Ibid.
18. Ibid., p. 98.
19. Ibid., p. 185.
20. Ibid., p. 186.
21. Ibid.
22. Ibid.
23. Ibid.
24. Ibid., p. 187.
25. Ibid.
26. Ibid., p. 186.
27. Ibid.
28. Ibid., p. 188.
29. R. Dworkin, *Law's Empire* (Cambridge, Mass.: Harvard University Press, 1986).
30. Fletcher, *Bernhard Goetz,* p. 188.
31. H. Kalven Jr. and H. Zeisel, *The American Jury* (Chicago: University of Chicago Press, 1971).
32. Ibid., p. 45.
33. Ibid., table 11, p. 56.
34. Ibid., table 12, p. 58.
35. Ibid., p. 167.
36. Ibid., p. 164.

37. Ibid., p. 165.
38. Ibid., p. 219.
39. Ibid., p. 241. The Holmes epigram comes from *Brown v. United States,* 256 U.S. 335, 343 (1921).
40. Ibid., p. 257.
41. Ibid., p. 285.
42. Ibid., p. 286.
43. T. A. Green, *Verdict According to Conscience: Perspectives on the English Criminal Trial Jury, 1200–1800* (Chicago: University of Chicago Press, 1985).
44. Kalven and Zeisel, *The American Jury,* p. 375.
45. I. A. Horowitz, "The Effect of Jury Nullification Instruction on Verdicts and Jury Functioning in Criminal Trials," *Law and Human Behavior 9* (1985): 25–36.
46. Ibid., p. 29.
47. Ibid., pp. 30–31.
48. Kalven and Zeisel, *The American Jury.*
49. I. A. Horowitz, "Jury Nullification: The Impact of Judicial Instructions, Arguments, and Challenges on Jury Decision Making," *Law and Human Behavior* 12 (1988): 439–453.
50. See, for example, H. S. Feild and N. J. Barnett, "Simulated Jury Trials: Students vs. 'Real' People as Jurors," *Journal of Social Psychology* 104 (1978): 287–293.
51. Ibid., p. 452.
52. Kalven and Zeisel, *The American Jury,* p. 474.

4. HOW JURORS CONSTRUCT REALITY

1. W. Shakespeare, *The Tragedy of Hamlet, Prince of Denmark* (Baltimore: Penguin, 1957), Act V, scene ii, line 277.
2. Ibid., line 324.
3. W. L. Bennett and M. S. Feldman, *Reconstructing Reality in the Courtroom: Justice and Judgment in American Culture* (New Brunswick, N.J.: Rutgers University Press, 1981).
4. Ibid., p. 3.
5. Ibid., p. 7.
6. Ibid.
7. Ibid.
8. Ibid., p. 41.
9. Ibid.
10. Ibid., p. 62.
11. Ibid., p. 65.
12. Ibid., pp. 143–144.

13. T. S. Kuhn, *The Structure of Scientific Revolutions* (Chicago: University of Chicago Press, 1962).

14. For example, P. K. Feyerabend, *Against Method* (New York: Humanities Press, 1976); W. V. O. Quine, *Word and Object* (Cambridge, Mass.: MIT Press, 1960); S. Toulmin, *The Philosophy of Science* (New York: Harper and Row, 1960).

15. W. G. Parrott, "Rhetoric for Realism in Psychology," *Theory and Psychology* 2 (1992): 159.

16. For example, P. L. Berger and T. Luckmann, *The Social Construction of Reality* (New York: Doubleday, 1966); K. J. Gergen, "The Social Constructionist Movement in Modern Psychology," *American Psychologist* 40 (1985): 266–275.

17. For example, J. D. Greenwood, "Realism, Empiricism and Social Constructionism: Psychological Theory and the Social Dimensions of Mind and Action," *Theory and Psychology* 2 (1992): 131–151; R. Harré, *Varieties of Realism* (Oxford: Blackwell, 1986).

18. R. Harré, "Metaphysics and Methodology: Some Prescriptions for Social Psychological Research," *European Journal of Social Psychology* 19 (1992): 439–453.

19. Ibid., p. 440.

20. L. Wittgenstein, *Philosophical Investigations* (Oxford: Blackwell, 1953).

21. L. S. Vygotsky, *Thought and Language* (Cambridge, Mass.: MIT Press, 1962; orig. pub, 1934).

22. Harré, "Metaphysics," p. 451.

23. For example, P. C. Vitz, "The Use of Stories in Moral Development: New Psychological Reasons for an Old Education Method," *American Psychologist* 45 (1990): 709–720.

24. J. Bruner, *Actual Minds, Possible Worlds* (Cambridge, Mass.: Harvard University Press, 1986).

25. Ibid., p. 11.

26. L. Wrightsman, *Psychology and the Legal System,* 2nd ed. (Pacific Grove, Calif.: Brooks/Cole, 1991): p. 284.

27. E. Tulving, *Elements of Episodic Memory* (New York: Oxford University Press, 1983).

28. Ibid., p. 9.

29. For example, M. L. Hoffman, "The Contribution of Empathy to Justice and Moral Development," in N. Eisenberg and J. Strayer, eds., *Empathy and Its Development* (New York: Cambridge University Press, 1987): 47–80.

30. R. Coles, *The Moral Life of Children* (New York: Atlantic Monthly Press, 1986).

31. L. Kohlberg, *Essays on Moral Development,* vol. 1: *The Philosophy of Moral Development* (New York: Harper and Row, 1981); L. Kohlberg,

Essays on Moral Development, vol. 2: *The Psychology of Moral Development* (New York: Harper and Row, 1984).

32. C. Gilligan, *In a Different Voice: Psychological Theory and Women's Development* (Cambridge, Mass.: Harvard University Press, 1982).

33. T. R. Sarbin, "The Narrative as a Root Metaphor for Psychology," in T. R. Sarbin, ed., *Narrative Psychology: The Storied Nature of Human Conduct* (New York: Praeger, 1986), pp. 3–21.

34. Vitz, "The Use of Stories," p. 711.

35. Sarbin, "Narrative as a Root Metaphor," p. 11.

36. K. Scheibe, "Self-Narratives and Adventures," in Sarbin, ed., *Narrative Psychology,* pp. 129–151.

37. G. S. Howard, "Culture Tales: A Narrative Approach to Thinking, Cross-Cultural Psychology, and Psychotherapy," *American Psychologist* 46 (1991): 187–197.

38. Ibid., p. 194.

39. H. L. Ansbacher and R. R. Ansbacher, *The Individual Psychology of Alfred Adler* (New York: Harper and Row, 1956), p. 77.

40. H. Vaihinger, *The Philosophy of "As If": A System of the Theoretical, Practical and Religious Fictions of Mankind* (New York: Harcourt, Brace, 1925).

41. G. A. Kelly, *A Theory of Personality: The Psychology of Personal Constructs* (New York: Norton, 1963).

42. Howard, "Culture Tales," p. 194.

43. Ibid., p. 193.

44. J. Barth, *The End of the Road* (New York: Bantam, 1958), p. 5.

45. J. Barth, *The Friday Book: Essays and Other Nonfiction* (New York: Putnam's, 1984), p. 16.

46. C. A. Visher, "Juror Decision Making: The Importance of Evidence," *Law and Human Behavior* 11 (1987): 1–17.

47. For example, D. C. Baldus, C. Pulaski, and G. Woodworth, "Comparative Review of Death Sentences: An Empirical Study of the Georgia Experience," *Journal of Criminal Law and Criminology* 74 (1983): 661–753.

48. H. Kalven Jr. and H. Zeisel, *The American Jury* (Chicago: University of Chicago Press, 1971). For a review of the effects of prejudice and sympathy on jurors' decisions, see V. P. Hans and N. Vidmar, *Judging the Jury* (New York: Plenum, 1986), pp. 131–148.

49. For example, W. C. Thompson, G. T. Fong, and D. C. Rosenhan, "Inadmissible Evidence and Juror Verdicts," *Journal of Personality and Social Psychology* 40 (1981): 453–463; S. Tanford and M. Cox, "Decision Processes in Civil Cases: The Impact of Impeachment Evidence on Liability and Credibility Judgments," *Social Behavior* 2 (1987): 345–353.

50. V. L. Smith, "Prototypes in the Courtroom: Lay Representations of Legal

Concepts," *Journal of Personality and Social Psychology* 61 (1991): 857–872.

51. L. Stalans, "Citizens' Crime Stereotypes, Biased Recall, and Punishment Preferences in Abstract Cases: The Educative Role of Interpersonal Sources," *Law and Human Behavior* 17 (1993): 451–470.

52. Ibid.

53. V. P. Hans, "Law and the Media: An Overview and Introduction," *Law and Human Behavior* 14 (1990): 399–407.

54. Ibid., p. 399. See also R. Surette, ed., *Justice and the Media: Issues and Research* (Springfield, Ill.: Thomas, 1984).

55. Ibid. See also D. A. Graber, *Crime News and the Public* (New York: Praeger, 1980).

56. Ibid., p. 400.

57. Ibid.

58. J. V. Roberts and A. N. Doob, "News Media Influences on Public Views of Sentencing," *Law and Human Behavior* 14 (1990): 453.

59. Ibid., pp. 453–454.

60. Stalans, "Citizens' Crime Stereotypes."

61. A. Tversky and D. Kahneman, "Judgment under Uncertainty: Heuristics and Biases," *Science* 185 (1974): 1124–1131.

62. G. P. Kramer, N. L. Kerr, and J. S. Carroll, "Pretrial Publicity, Judicial Remedies, and Jury Bias," *Law and Human Behavior* 14 (1990): 409–438.

63. Stalans, "Citizens' Crime Stereotypes."

64. Smith, "Prototypes in the Courtroom."

65. Ibid., p. 867.

66. Ibid., p. 869.

67. N. Pennington and R. Hastie, "Explaining the Evidence: Tests of the Story Model for Juror Decision Making," *Journal of Personality and Social Psychology* 62 (1992): 189–206. See also N. Pennington and R. Hastie, "Evidence Evaluation in Complex Decision Making," *Journal of Personality and Social Psychology* 51 (1986): 242–258; R. Hastie, S. D. Penrod, and N. Pennington, *Inside the Jury* (Cambridge, Mass.: Harvard University Press, 1983).

68. Bennett and Feldman, *Reconstructing Reality*.

69. The law's fictional assumption is akin to a stricture ordering readers of detective fiction not to think about whodunnit until they reach the last chapter. It cannot be done, except, perhaps, by the most incurious of minds, or by a mind so compartmentalized that a psychiatric diagnosis is in order.

70. Pennington and Hastie, "Explaining the Evidence," p. 190.

71. Ibid.

72. Ibid.

73. Ibid.

74. Ibid.
75. Ibid., p. 191.
76. Pennington and Hastie, "Evidence Evaluation."
77. G. Perrin and B. D. Sales, "Artificial Legal Standards in Mental/Emotional Injury Litigation," *Behavioral Sciences and the Law* 11 (1993): 193.
78. Ibid., p. 194.
79. Ibid.
80. Ibid., p. 200.
81. For example, M. Ross and G. J. O. Fletcher, "Attribution and Social Perception," in G. Lindzey and E. Aronson, eds., *Handbook of Social Psychology,* vol. 2 (New York: Random House, 1985), pp. 73–122.
82. M. D. Alicke, "Culpable Causation," *Journal of Personality and Social Psychology* 63 (1992): 368–378.
83. Ibid., p. 369.
84. Smith, "Prototypes in the Courtroom," p. 858.

5. OBJECTIVITY VERSUS SUBJECTIVITY IN THE LAW

1. R. A. Posner, ed., *The Essential Holmes: Selections from the Letters, Speeches, Judicial Opinions, and Other Writings of Oliver Wendell Holmes, Jr.* (Chicago: University of Chicago Press, 1992).
2. O. W. Holmes, *The Common Law,* ed. M. D. Howe (Cambridge, Mass.: Harvard University Press, 1963; orig. pub., 1881).
3. Posner, *The Essential Holmes,* p. x.
4. Holmes, *The Common Law,* p. 88.
5. Ibid.
6. Ibid., p. 43.
7. Ibid., p. 7.
8. "Model Penal Code" (Proposed Official Draft, 1962), sec. 2.01(1).
9. N. Walker, *Crime and Insanity in England: The Historical Perspective,* vol. 1 (Edinburgh: Edinburgh University Press, 1968).
10. H. L. A. Hart, *Punishment and Responsibility: Essays in the Philosophy of Law* (New York: Oxford University Press, 1968), p. 188.
11. B. Wootton, *Crime and Criminal Law* (London: Stevens, 1963).
12. Hart, *Punishment and Responsibility,* p. 203.
13. Holmes, *The Common Law,* p. 37.
14. Ibid., p. 39.
15. Ibid., p. 42.
16. Ibid., p. 36.
17. Ibid., p. 44.
18. Ibid., p. 45.
19. Ibid.
20. Ibid.

21. G. P. Fletcher, *Rethinking Criminal Law* (Boston: Little, Brown, 1978), p. 242.
22. Ibid.
23. Ibid., p. 243.
24. Ibid.
25. *Bedder v. Director of Public Prosecutions,* 2 All E.R. 801 (H.L.) (1954).
26. Fletcher, *Rethinking,* p. 248.
27. Ibid., p. 249.
28. R. M. James, "Jurors' Assessment of Criminal Responsibility," *Social Problems* 7 (1959): 58–67.
29. Walker, *Crime and Insanity in England,* p. 16.
30. Fletcher, *Rethinking,* p. 118.
31. Ibid., p. 117.
32. Ibid.
33. Ibid., p. 142. Quoting from *The King v. Barker,* N.Z.L.R. 865, 874 (Ct. App. 1924).
34. Ibid., p. 138.
35. Ibid.
36. Holmes, *The Common Law,* p. 68.
37. Fletcher, *Rethinking,* p. 144. The two Alabama cases are *Lewis v. State,* 35 Ala. 380 (1860), and *McQuirter v. State,* 36 Ala. App. 707, 63 So. 2d 388 (1953).
38. Ibid., p. 145.
39. Holmes, *The Common Law,* p. 1.
40. Ibid., p. 32.
41. Ibid., p. 1.
42. R. Dworkin, *Law's Empire* (Cambridge, Mass.: Harvard University Press, 1986).
43. J. Biskupic, "Scalia Sees No Justice in Trying to Judge Intent of Congress on a Law," *Washington Post,* May 11, 1993, p. A4.
44. Ibid.
45. Ibid.
46. N. Hentoff, "Sentencing by Sophistry," *Washington Post,* July 17, 1993, p. A17.
47. J. Biskupic, "High Court Rejects Relaxation of Standard for Guilty Verdict," *Washington Post,* June 2, 1993, p. A4.
48. Ibid.
49. Hentoff, "Sophistry."
50. Ibid.
51. R. A. Posner, *The Problems of Jurisprudence* (Cambridge, Mass.: Harvard University Press, 1990), p. 43.
52. Ibid.
53. *Lochner v. New York,* 198 U.S. 45, 75 (1905).
54. R. A. Posner, *Law and Literature: A Misunderstood Relation* (Cambridge, Mass.: Harvard University Press, 1988), p. 285.

55. Dworkin, *Law's Empire*, p. 36.
56. Posner, *Jurisprudence*, p. 10.
57. Ibid., p. 459.
58. Dworkin, *Law's Empire*, p. 229.
59. Ibid., p. 380.
60. Ibid., p. 360.
61. Ibid., p. 369.
62. *Missouri v. Holland*, 252 U.S. 416, 433 (1920).
63. Dworkin, *Law's Empire*, p. 164.
64. Ibid., p. 165.
65. Ibid., p. 225.
66. Ibid., p. 227.
67. Ibid., p. 166.
68. Ibid., p. 219.
69. Posner, *Law and Literature*, p. 258.
70. Ibid., p. 259.
71. Posner, *Jurisprudence*, p. 22.
72. Posner, *Law and Literature*, pp. 258–259.
73. Ibid., p. 259.
74. Ibid.
75. Posner, *Jurisprudence*, p. 22.
76. Ibid., p. 23.
77. Ibid.
78. Ibid., p. 41.
79. Ibid., p. 48.
80. Ibid., p. 130.
81. Ibid., p. 136.
82. C. Stanislavski, *Building a Character*, trans. E. R. Hapgood (London: Max Reinhardt, 1969).
83. Ibid., p. 239.
84. R. Pound, "The Need of a Sociological Jurisprudence," *Green Bag* 19 (1907): 612.
85. L. L. Weinreb, *Natural Law and Justice* (Cambridge, Mass.: Harvard University Press, 1987).
86. Ibid., p. 615; A. J. Tomkins and K. Oursland, "Social and Scientific Interpretations of the Constitution: A Historical View and an Overview," *Law and Human Behavior* 15 (1991): 101–120.

6. THE SACRED PRECINCT OF THE BEDROOM

1. *Griswold v. Connecticut*, 381 U.S. 479, 527 (1965)(Stewart, J., dissenting).
2. *Griswold v. Connecticut*, 381 U.S. 479, 480 (1965).
3. Ibid., p. 479.
4. Ibid., p. 484.

5. Ibid., p. 484.
6. Ibid., p. 486.
7. Ibid., pp. 485–486.
8. Ibid., p. 486.
9. Ibid., p. 530.
10. Ibid., p. 488.
11. Ibid., p. 489.
12. A. Hamilton, J. Madison, and J. Jay, *The Federalist Papers* (New York: Mentor, 1961), No. 37.
13. *Griswold v. Connecticut,* p. 494.
14. Ibid., p. 500.
15. Ibid., p. 508.
16. Ibid., p. 509.
17. Ibid., p. 529.
18. Ibid., p. 509.
19. Ibid., p. 522.
20. Ibid., p. 525.
21. Ibid.
22. Ibid., p. 526.
23. Ibid., pp. 526–527. Citing L. Hand, *The Bill of Rights: The Oliver Wendell Holmes Lectures* (1958), p. 73.
24. R. Dworkin, *Law's Empire* (Cambridge, Mass.: Harvard University Press, 1986).
25. *Griswold v. Connecticut,* 486, 493 (Goldberg, J., concurring). Goldberg cites *Snyder v. Massachusetts,* 291 U.S. 97, 105.
26. Ibid., p. 519, n. 13.
27. *Eisenstadt v. Baird,* 405 U.S. 438 (1971).
28. Ibid., p. 442.
29. Ibid., p. 453.
30. Ibid., p. 453.
31. Ibid., p. 472.
32. *Roe et al. v. Wade,* 410 U.S. 113 (1973).
33. Ibid., p. 112.
34. Ibid., p. 116.
35. Ibid.
36. Ibid., p. 129.
37. Ibid., p. 174.
38. *Roe et al. v. Wade,* p. 117.
39. *Lochner v. New York,* 198 U.S. 45, 76 (1905).
40. Ibid., p. 76.
41. *Roe et al. v. Wade,* p. 174.
42. Ibid.
43. G. F. Will, "Loose Translation," *Washington Post,* July 1, 1992, p. A23.
44. *Griswold v. Connecticut,* pp. 485–486.

45. *Bowers v. Hardwick,* 478 U.S. 186 (1986).
46. Ibid., p. 194.
47. Ibid., p. 197. Citing W. Blackstone, *Commentaries on the Laws of England,* vol. 4 (1769), p. 215.
48. Ibid., pp. 192–193.
49. Ibid., p. 196.
50. *Stanley v. Georgia,* 394 U.S. 557 (1969).
51. *Katz v. United States,* 389 U.S. 347 (1967).
52. *Bowers v. Hardwick,* p. 199. Citing *Olmstead v. United States,* 277 U.S. 438, 478 (1928)(Brandeis, J., dissenting).
53. Ibid., p. 200.
54. Ibid.
55. Ibid.
56. Ibid.
57. Ibid., pp. 203–204.
58. Ibid., p. 206.
59. *Stanley v. Georgia,* p. 565.
60. *Bowers v. Hardwick,* p. 207.
61. Ibid.
62. Ibid., p. 207. Citing *Olmstead v. United States,* 277 U.S. 438, 478 (1928)(Brandeis, J., dissenting).
63. Ibid., p. 208.
64. T. DeAngelis, "Kentucky High Court Repeals Sodomy Law," *APA Monitor* 23 (December 1992): 1, 30.
65. Ibid., p. 1.
66. Ibid.
67. Ibid., p. 30.
68. *Bowers v. Hardwick,* pp. 203–204.
69. *Katz v. United States.*
70. Ibid., p. 361.
71. See D. K. Kagehiro, R. B. Taylor, and A. T. Harland, "*Reasonable Expectation of Privacy* and Third-Party Consent Searches," *Law and Human Behavior* 15 (1991): 121–138.
72. *Rakas v. Illinois,* 439 U.S. 128, 144 (1978).
73. Although *Bowers* still remains in effect, on September 24, 1992, the Supreme Court of Kentucky struck down Kentucky's seventeen-year-old sodomy law in *Commonwealth v. Wasson et al.,* relying on state constitutional grounds. In addition, the Kentucky Supreme Court relied on empirical evidence, citing the American Psychological Association's brief on gay and lesbian sexuality. See DeAngelis, "Kentucky High Court Repeals."
74. C. Slobogin and J. E. Schumacher, "Rating the Intrusiveness of Law Enforcement Searches and Seizures," *Law and Human Behavior* 17 (1993): 183–200.

75. Ibid., p. 183.
76. Ibid., p. 190.
77. R. Pound, "The Need of a Sociological Jurisprudence," *Green Bag* 19 (1907): 615.
78. Slobogin and Schumacher, "Rating the Intrusiveness," pp. 198–199.
79. Pound, "Sociological Jurisprudence," p. 615.
80. Slobogin and Schumacher, "Rating the Intrusiveness," p. 199.
81. Kagehiro et al., "Third-Party Consent Searches."
82. *United States v. Matlock*, 415 U.S. 164 (1974).
83. Ibid., p. 171 and n. 7.
84. Kagehiro et al., "Third-Party Consent Searches."
85. *Griswold v. Connecticut,* pp. 485–486.

7. THE RIGHT TO DIE

1. S. Barr, "Accused of Failing to Protect Data, IRS Says It Will Buttress Safeguards," *Washington Post,* August 5, 1993, p. A6.
2. M. S. Greene, "Appeals Court Bars Media from Juvenile Case," *Washington Post,* July 4, 1991, p. A6.
3. L. S. Wrightsman, *Psychology and the Legal System,* 2nd ed. (Pacific Grove, Calif.: Brooks/Cole, 1991), p. 317.
4. D. A. Kaplan, "Remove That Blue Dot," *Newsweek,* December 16, 1991, p. 26.
5. E. Marcus, "AIDS Patient Sues Hospital over Privacy," *Washington Post,* July 22, 1991, pp. D1, D2.
6. N. Lewis, "D.C. Court Refuses to Stop AIDS Test of Rape Suspect," *Washington Post,* June 19, 1991, p. C3.
7. Ibid.
8. Ibid.
9. Staff, "Doctors and AIDS," *Newsweek,* July 1, 1991, p. 52.
10. *Cheatham v. Rogers,* 824 S.W. 2d 231 (1992); C. P. Ewing, "Judicial Notebook: Do Mental Health Professionals Forfeit Their Right to Privacy When They Testify in Child Custody Litigation?" *APA Monitor* 24 (July 1993): 6.
11. *Tarasoff v. Regents of the University of California,* 118 Cal. Rptr. 129, 529 P. 2d 553 (1974); *Tarasoff v. Regents of the University of California,* 17 Cal. 3d 425, 131 Cal. Rptr. 14, 551 F. 2d 334 (1976); see also J. C. Beck, ed., *The Potentially Violent Patient and the "Tarasoff" Decision in Psychiatric Practice* (Washington, D.C.: American Psychiatric Press, 1985).
12. J. D. Matarazzo, "Behavioral Immunogens and Pathogens in Health and Illness," in B. L. Hammonds and C. J. Scheirer, eds., *Psychology and Health* (Washington, D.C.: American Psychological Association, 1984), pp. 5–43.
13. I. Keilitz, J. C. Bilzor, T. L. Hafemeister, V. Brown, and D. Dudyshyn,

"Decisionmaking in Authorizing and Withholding Life Sustaining Medical Treatment: From *Quinlan* to *Cruzan*," *Mental and Physical Disability Law Reporter* 13 (1989): 5, 482–493.

14. See, for example, A. Meisel, *The Right to Die* (New York: Wiley, 1989).

15. N. J. Finkel, M. L. Hurabiell, and K. C. Hughes, "Right to Die and Euthanasia: Crossing the Public/Private Boundary," *Law and Human Behavior* 17 (1993): 487–506.

16. *In re Quinlan*, 70 N.J. 10, 355 A. 2d 647, cert. denied sub nom., *Garger v. New Jersey*, 429 U.S. 922 (1976).

17. *Cruzan v. Director, Missouri Department of Health*, 110 S. Ct. 2841 (1990).

18. For example, *Superintendent of Belchertown State School v. Sailewicz*, 373 Mass. 728, 370 N.E. 2d 417 (1977); *Severns v. Wilmington Medical Center*, 421 A. 2d 1334 (Del. 1980); *Brophy v. New Eng. Sinai Hosp.*, 398 Mass. 417, 497 N.E. 2d 626 (1986); *Rasmussen v. Fleming*, 154 Ariz. 207, 741 P. 2d 674 (1987); *In re Guardianship of Browning*, 568 So. 2d 4 (Fla. 1990).

19. V. T. Borst, "The Right to Die: An Extension of the Right to Privacy," *John Marshall Law Review* 18 (1985): 895–914; N. L. Cantor, "The Permanently Unconscious Patient, Non-Feeding and Euthanasia," *American Journal of Law and Medicine* 15 (1989): 381–437; S. R. Martyn and H. J. Bourgignon, "Coming to Terms with Death: The Cruzan Case," *Hastings Law Journal* 42 (1991): 817–860.

20. World Medical Organization, "Declaration of Madrid" (1987); but see D. Humphry, *Final Exit* (Eugene, Ore.: Hemlock Society, 1991).

21. Finkel et al., "Right to Die and Euthanasia."

22. H. Kalven Jr. and H. Zeisel, *The American Jury* (Chicago: University of Chicago Press, 1971), p. 375.

23. For example, Committee on Pattern Jury Instructions, District Judges Association, Fifth Circuit, *Pattern Jury Instructions (Criminal Cases) with Case Annotations* (St. Paul, Minn.: West, 1983).

24. G. P. Fletcher, *A Crime of Self-Defense: Bernhard Goetz and the Law on Trial* (Chicago: University of Chicago Press, 1988).

25. N. J. Finkel, M. L. Hurabiell, and K. C. Hughes, "Competency, and Other Constructs, in Right to Die Cases," *Behavioral Sciences and the Law* 11 (1993): 135–150.

26. B. J. Winick, "On Autonomy: Legal and Psychological Perspectives," *Villanova Law Review* 37 (1992): 1705–1777.

27. *Planned Parenthood v. Casey*, 112 S. Ct. 2791, 2807 (1992)(plurality opinion).

28. E. Walsh, "Kevorkian Acquittal Leaves Painful Issues Unresolved," *Washington Post*, May 4, 1994, p. A2.

29. E. Walsh, "Kevorkian Acquitted in Suicide," *Washington Post*, May 3, 1994, pp. A1, A12.

30. Ibid., A12.

31. Walsh, "Issues Unresolved."

32. Walsh, "Acquitted in Suicide."

33. Ibid.

34. Editorial, "The Kevorkian Solution," *Washington Post*, May 7, 1994, p. A18.

35. C. Krauthammer, "Judicially Assisted Suicide," *Washington Post,* May 13, 1994, p. A23.

36. Ibid.

37. Winick, "On Autonomy," pp. 1707–1712.

38. R. A. Posner, *Law and Literature: A Misunderstood Relation* (Cambridge, Mass.: Harvard University Press, 1988).

8. CRUEL AND UNUSUAL PUNISHMENT

1. Many, however, have questioned the root of that right. See, for example, H. L. A. Hart, *The Concept of Law* (Oxford: Clarendon, 1961).

2. H. L. A. Hart, *Punishment and Responsibility: Essays in the Philosophy of Law* (New York: Oxford University Press, 1968).

3. G. Fletcher, *Rethinking Criminal Law* (Boston: Little, Brown, 1978).

4. R. Singer, "The Resurgence of Mens Rea, II: Honest but Unreasonable Mistake of Fact in Self Defense," *Boston College Law Review* 28 (1987): 459–519.

5. Fletcher, *Rethinking,* p. 487.

6. Ibid.

7. Ibid.

8. N. J. Finkel, S. T. Maloney, M. Z. Valbuena, and J. L. Groscup, "Lay Perspectives on Legal Conundrums: Impossible and Mistaken Act Cases," *Law and Human Behavior* (1995), forthcoming.

9. Fletcher, *Rethinking,* p. 388.

10. Editorial, "Singapore's Shame," *Washington Post,* May 7, 1994, p. A18.

11. L. S. Stepp, "The Crackdown on Juvenile Crime," *Washington Post,* October 15, 1994, pp. A1, A12.

12. *O'Neil v. Vermont,* 144 U.S. 323, 331 (1892).

13. *O'Neil v. Vermont,* 144 U.S. 323, 339–340 (1892)(Field, J., dissenting).

14. *Weems v. United States,* 217 U.S. 349 (1910).

15. Ibid.

16. Ibid., p. 350.

17. Ibid.

18. Ibid., p. 380.

19. Ibid.

20. *Weems v. United States,* 217 U.S. 349, 382 (1910)(White, J., dissenting).

21. *Graham v. West Virginia,* 224 U.S. 616 (1912).

22. *Badders v. United States,* 240 U.S. 391 (1916).

23. *Francis v. Resweber,* 329 U.S. 459 (1947).

24. *Trop v. Dulles,* 356 U.S. 86 (1958).

25. Ibid., p. 99.

26. Ibid.
27. Ibid., p. 102.
28. Ibid.
29. Ibid., p. 101.
30. *Stanford v. Kentucky,* 492 U.S. 361, 379 (1989).
31. *Coker v. Georgia,* 433 U.S. 584 (1977).
32. Ibid.
33. J. Dressler, "The Jurisprudence of Death by Another: Accessories and Capital Punishment," *University of Colorado Law Review* 51 (1979): 17, 39–40.
34. *Solem v. Helm,* 463 U.S. 277 (1983).
35. Ibid., pp. 279–280.
36. Ibid., p. 285. Citing Earl of Devon's Case, 11 State Tr. 133, 136 (1689).
37. Ibid., p. 290.
38. Ibid., p. 292.
39. Ibid.
40. Ibid., p. 293.
41. Ibid., p. 296.
42. Ibid.
43. Ibid., p. 298.
44. Ibid., pp. 296–297.
45. Ibid., p. 299.
46. Ibid., p. 303.
47. *Solem v. Helm,* 463 U.S. 277, 304, 314 (1983)(Burger, C.J., dissenting).
48. *Rummel v. Estelle,* 445 U.S. 263 (1980).
49. Ibid., pp. 269–271.
50. Ibid., p. 279.
51. Ibid., p. 280.
52. Ibid., p. 281–282.
53. *Rummel v. Estelle,* 445 U.S. 263, 285, 296 (1980)(Powell, J., dissenting).
54. Ibid., p. 298.
55. Ibid., p. 300.
56. N. J. Finkel, S. T. Maloney, M. Z. Valbuena, and J. L. Groscup, "Recidivism, Proportionalism, and Individualized Punishment," Paper presented at the Law and Society Association's annual conference, Phoenix, Arizona, June 16, 1994.
57. M. M. Cuomo, speech before the National Press Club, Washington, D.C., December 16, 1994.
58. W. Claiborne, "Tough Sentencing Law Sparks Legal Debate," *Washington Post,* December 31, 1994, p. A3.

9. MURTHER MOST FOUL

1. N. J. Finkel and K. B. Duff, "Felony-Murder and Community Sentiment: Testing the Supreme Court's Assertions," *Law and Human Behavior* 15 (1991): 405–429.

2. Something akin to this hypothetical case occurs in *People v. Stamp,* 2 Cal. App. 3d 203, 82 Cal. Rptr. 598 (1969).

3. N. J. Finkel, "Capital Felony-Murder, Objective Indicia, and Community Sentiment," *Arizona Law Review* 32 (1990): 819–913.

4. H. L. A. Hart, *Punishment and Responsibility: Essays in the Philosophy of Law* (New York: Oxford University Press, 1958), p. 20.

5. G. Fletcher, *Rethinking Criminal Law* (Boston: Little, Brown, 1978), p. 303.

6. N. E. Roth and S. E. Sundby, "The Felony-Murder Rule: A Doctrine at Constitutional Crossroads," *Cornell Law Review* 70 (1985): 446–492.

7. R. M. Perkins and R. N. Boyce, *Criminal Law* (Mineola, N.Y.: Foundation Press, 1982), p. 921.

8. Various cases in different states have attempted to limit the felony-murder rule's applicative reach when a third party kills. See, for example, *People v. Washington,* 62 Cal. 2d 777, 402 P. 2d 130, 44 Cal. Rptr. 4422 (1965); *Commonwealth v. Redline,* 391 Pa. 486, 137 A. 2d 472 (1958). But see, for example, *People v. Taylor,* 12 Cal. 3d 686, 477 P. 2d 131, 91 Cal. Rptr. 275 (1970).

9. *People v. Aaron,* 299 N.W. 2d 304 (1980).

10. H. D. Bracton, *De Legibus et Consuetudinibus Angliae,* [On the Laws and Customs of England], ed. Woodbine (New Haven: Yale University Press, 1915).

11. *People v. Aaron,* p. 310.

12. "Criminal Law: Felony-Murder Rule—Felon's Responsibility for Death of Accomplice" (note), *Columbia Law Review* 65 (1965): 1496.

13. J. F. Stephen, *History of the Criminal Law of England* (London: Macmillan, 1883), pp. 57–58.

14. Ibid., p. 57.

15. Ibid., p. 65.

16. See *Regina v. Serne,* 16 Cox. Crim. Cas. 311 (1887).

17. *People v. Phillips,* 64 Cal. 2d 574, 583 n. 6, 414 P. 2d 353, 360 n. 6, 51 Cal. Rptr. 225, 232 n. 6 (1966).

18. *People v. Washington,* 62 Cal. 2d 777, 783, 402 P. 2d 130, 134, 44 Cal. Rptr. 442, 446 (1965).

19. Finkel, "Capital Felony-Murder," p. 819.

20. Ibid., pp. 819–822.

21. *Enmund v. Florida,* 458 U.S. 782 (1982).

22. *Tison v. Arizona,* 481 U.S. 137 (1987).

23. *Tison v. Arizona,* 481 U.S. 137, 159, rehearing denied, 482 U.S. 921 (1987)(Brennan, J., dissenting).

24. F. Heider, *The Psychology of Interpersonal Relations* (New York: Wiley, 1958).

25. M. Ross and G. J. O. Fletcher, "Attribution and Social Perception," in G. Lindzey and E. Aronson, eds., *Handbook of Social Psychology,* vol. 2 (New York: Random House, 1985), p. 74.

26. N. J. Finkel and S. F. Smith, "Principals and Accessories in Capital Felony-Murder: The Proportionality Principle Reigns Supreme," *Law and Society Review* 27 (1993): 129–156.

27. E. E. Jones and K. E. Davis, "From Acts to Dispositions: The Attribution Process in Person Perception," in L. Berkowitz, ed., *Advances in Experimental Social Psychology,* vol. 2 (New York: Academic, 1965).

28. See *Enmund v. Florida.*

29. *Coker v. Georgia,* 433 U.S. 584 (1977).

30. Finkel, "Capital Felony-Murder," p. 825.

31. *Enmund v. Florida,* pp. 788–796.

32. Ibid.

33. Ibid., pp. 822–823 (O'Connor, J., dissenting).

34. Finkel, "Capital Felony-Murder," p. 830.

35. Ibid.

36. Ibid., p. 833.

37. *Tison v. Arizona,* p. 148.

38. Ibid., p. 154.

39. Ibid., pp. 157–158.

40. Ibid., p. 168 (Brennan, J., dissenting).

41. Ibid., p. 155.

42. Ibid., p. 175 (Brennan, J., dissenting).

43. Finkel, "Capital Felony-Murder," pp. 840–841.

44. Ibid., pp. 796.

45. Finkel and Duff, "Supreme Court's Assertions."

46. It was originally designated as ACCIDENT, but STRUGGLE seems more apt.

47. The lesser offense percentages can be gotten by adding the guilty to the not guilty, and subtracting from 100.

48. *D,* the numerator, is the number of death sentences given. *N,* the denominator, is the number of DQ subjects in the capital condition who rendered a judgment for that defendant in that case. Since the non-DQ subjects have substantial qualms against the death penalty and would be eliminated from a capital jury, the DQs are the appropriate sample; in addition, only capital condition DQs have both the inclination and the opportunity to give the death sentence *at the beginning of the case.* For the second percentage, *D/FM,* the denominator, *FM,* is the number of DQ subjects in the capital condition who rendered a guilty verdict on the felony-murder (or first-degree murder) charge. This *FM* denominator represents those subjects who have the inclination and the opportunity *at the sentencing phase* to give the death sentence, since only a guilty verdict can lead to the death sentence.

49. Finkel and Smith, "Proportionality Principle Reigns."

50. N. J. Finkel, M. B. Liss, and V. R. Moran, "Equal or Proportional Justice? Children's Judgments of Accessory Liability," Paper presented at the American Psychological Association's annual convention, Toronto, August 22, 1993.

51. Finkel, "Capital Felony-Murder."

52. G. P. Fletcher, *A Crime of Self-Defense: Bernhard Goetz and the Law on Trial* (Chicago: University of Chicago Press, 1988), p. 154.

53. W. Shakespeare, *The Tragedy of Hamlet, Prince of Denmark* (Baltimore: Penguin, 1957), Act I, scene v, line 27.

54. W. Shakespeare, *The Tragedy of Macbeth* (New York: Simon & Schuster, 1959), Act I, scene i, line 12.

55. Shakespeare, *Hamlet,* Act I, scene v, line 188.

56. Shakespeare, *Macbeth,* Act V, scene ii, lines 24–25.

10. DEATH IS DIFFERENT

1. *Furman v. Georgia,* 408 U.S. 241 (1972).

2. *McGautha v. California,* 402 U.S. 183 (1971).

3. *Furman v. Georgia,* p. 248 (Douglas, J., concurring).

4. *McGautha v. California,* pp. 198–201.

5. *Furman v. Georgia,* pp. 245–247 (Douglas, J., concurring).

6. Ibid., pp. 246–247; *McGautha v. California,* p. 199.

7. *Furman v. Georgia,* p. 200.

8. *Winston v. United States,* 172 U.S. 303, 313 (1899).

9. Ibid., p. 313.

10. *McGautha v. California,* p. 202; quote is from *Witherspoon v. Illinois,* 391 U.S. 510, 519 (1968).

11. Ibid., p. 202.

12. Ibid., pp. 207–208.

13. *Furman v. Georgia,* p. 402.

14. Ibid., pp. 249–251 (Douglas, J., concurring).

15. Ibid., p. 364 (Marshall, J., concurring).

16. Ibid., p. 310 (Stewart, J., concurring).

17. Ibid., p. 313 (White, J., concurring).

18. *Gregg v. Georgia,* 428 U.S. 153 (1976); *Jurek v. Texas,* 428 U.S. 153 (1976); *Proffit v. Florida,* 428 U.S. 242 (1976); *Woodson v. North Carolina,* 428 U.S. 280 (1976).

19. A similar mandatory scheme arose in Louisiana, and was declared unconstitutional in *Roberts v. Lousiana,* 428 U.S. 325 (1976).

20. *Gregg v. Georgia.*

21. Ibid., p. 164, n. 9.

22. Ibid., p. 200.

23. *Furman v. Georgia,* p. 252.

24. But see *Lowenfield v. Phelps,* 484 U.S. 231, 232 (1987). Here, the Court held that the "duplicative nature of the statutory aggravating circumstance did not render petitioner's sentence infirm, since the constitutionally mandated narrowing function was performed at the guilt phase and the Constitution did not require an additional aggravating circumstance

finding at the penalty phase." This response fails to respond, since a finding of at least one aggravating circumstance was required; the double counting problem remains.

25. *Gregg v. Georgia,* p. 188.
26. *Lockett v. Ohio,* 438 U.S. 586 (1978).
27. Ibid., p. 605.
28. Ibid., p. 622 (White, J., concurring in part and dissenting in part).
29. Ibid., p. 631 (Rehnquist, J., concurring in part and dissenting in part).
30. R. Hertz and R. Weisberg, "In Mitigation of the Penalty of Death: *Lockett v. Ohio* and the Capital Defendant's Right to Consideration of Mitigating Circumstances," *California Law Review* 69 (1981): 326.
31. G. Goodpaster, "The Trial for Life: Effective Assistance of Counsel in Death Penalty Cases," *New York University Law Review* 58 (1983): 315.
32. S. Gillers, "Deciding Who Dies," *University of Pennsylvania Law Review* 129 (1980): 31.
33. Ibid., p. 36.
34. *Sumner v. Shuman,* 483 U.S. 66 (1987).
35. *Maynard v. Cartwright,* 486 U.S. 356 (1988).
36. *Clemons v. Mississippi,* no. 88-6873, slip opinion, (1990).
37. *Mills v. Maryland,* 486 U.S. 367 (1988).
38. *McKoy v. North Carolina,* no. 88-5909, slip opinion, (1990).
39. *Jurek v. Texas,* p. 269.
40. *Franklin v. Lynaugh,* 487 U.S. 164 (1988).
41. *Penry v. Lynaugh,* 492 U.S. 302 (1989).
42. *Graham v. Lynaugh,* 492 U.S. 915 (1989).
43. *Satterwhite v. Texas,* 486 U.S. 249, 268 (1988)(Blackmun, J., concurring).
44. R. Rosenbaum, *Travels with Dr. Death* (New York: Penguin, 1991).
45. *Satterwhite v. Texas,* p. 259.
46. *Barefoot v. Estelle,* 463 U.S. 880 (1983).
47. For example, J. Monahan, *The Clinical Prediction of Violent Behavior* (Washington, D.C.: U.S. Government Printing Office, 1981). For a more recent update, which suggests some improvement under some conditions, see J. Monahan, "Mental Disorder and Violent Behavior: Perceptions and Evidence," *American Psychologist* 47 (1992): 511–521.
48. *Barefoot v. Estelle,* p. 901.
49. See, for example, *Penry v. Lynaugh.* Did the jury have the opportunity and vehicle for factoring his mental retardation into the death decision? That was the question.
50. *Witherspoon v. Illinois.*
51. J. B. Kadane, "After *Hovey:* A Note on Taking Account of the Automatic Death Penalty Jurors," *Law and Human Behavior* 8 (1984): 115–120.
52. V. P. Hans, "Death by Jury," in K. C. Haas and J. A. Inciardi, eds.,

Challenging Capital Punishment: Legal and Social Science Approaches (Newbury Park, Calif.: Sage Publications, 1988), p. 151. Hans cites R. Fitzgerald and P. C. Ellsworth, "Due Process vs. Crime Control: Death Qualification and Jury Attitudes," *Law and Human Behavior* 8 (1984): 31–51.

53. P. C. Ellsworth, "Unpleasant Facts: The Supreme Court's Response to Empirical Research on Capital Punishment," in Haas and Inciardi, eds., *Challenging Capital Punishment*, pp. 177–211.

54. Ibid., p. 190.

55. *Witherspoon v. Illinois,* p. 517.

56. See *Hovey v. Superior Court,* 28 Cal. 3d 1 (1980); *Grigsby v. Mabry,* 569 F. Supp. 1273 (E.D. Ark. 1983).

57. *Lockhart v. McCree,* 476 U.S. 162 (1986).

58. Amicus Curiae Brief for the American Psychological Association, "In the Supreme Court of the United States: *Lockhart v. McCree,*" *American Psychologist* 42 (1987): 59–68.

59. Hans, "Death by Jury," p. 151.

60. For some of the specific studies and findings, see *Law and Human Behavior* 8 (1984).

61. H. Packer, *The Limits of the Criminal Sanction* (Stanford: Stanford University Press, 1968).

62. But see R. Elliott, "Social Science Data and the APA: The *Lockhart* Brief as a Case in Point," *Law and Human Behavior* 15 (1991): 59–76. Elliott presents evidence to show that the conviction-proneness finding is not as uniform or robust as earlier findings would have it.

63. Ellsworth, "Unpleasant Facts," p. 193.

64. R. Paternoster and A. Kazyaka, "Racial Considerations in Capital Punishment: The Failure of Evenhanded Justice," in Haas and Inciardi, eds., *Challenging Capital Punishment*, pp. 113–148.

65. *McCleskey v. Kemp,* 481 U.S. 279 (1987).

66. D. C. Baldus, C., Pulaski, and G. Woodworth, "Comparative Review of Death Sentences: An Empirical Study of the Georgia Experience," *Journal of Criminal Law and Criminology* 74 (1983): 661–753; D. C. Baldus, G., Woodworth, and C. A. Pulaski, "Monitoring and Evaluating Contemporary Death Sentencing Systems: Lessons from Georgia," *University of California, Davis* 18 (1985): 1375–1407.

67. Ellsworth, "Unpleasant Facts," p. 188.

68. *McCleskey v. Kemp,* pp. 292–293.

69. Ellsworth, "Unpleasant Facts," p. 189.

70. C. Haney, "The Fourteenth Amendment and Symbolic Legality: Let Them Eat Due Process," *Law and Human Behavior* 15 (1991): 183–204.

71. *McCleskey v. Kemp,* p. 315.

72. Ibid., p. 318.

73. Ibid., p. 339.

74. *Parker v. Dugger,* no. 89-5961, slip opinion (1991).

75. *Lankford v. Idaho,* no. 88-7247, slip opinion (1991).

76. *Yates v. Evatt,* no. 89-7691, slip opinion (1991).

77. *Booth v. Maryland,* 482 U.S. 496 (1987).

78. Ibid., p. 519 (Scalia, J., dissenting).

79. Ibid., p. 520.

80. Ibid.

81. *South Carolina v. Gathers,* 490 U.S. 805 (1989).

82. *Payne v. Tennessee,* no. 90-5721, slip opinion (1991).

83. Ibid., p. 1 (Scalia, J., concurring).

84. Ibid., p. 1 (Marshall, J., dissenting).

85. Ibid., p. 12.

86. Ibid., p. 4 (Stevens, J., dissenting).

87. M. Kaplan, "The Influencing Process in Group Decision Making," in C. Hendrick, ed., *Review of Personality and Social Psychology,* vol. 8 (Beverly Hills: Sage Publications, 1987).

88. M. Costanzo and S. Costanzo, "Jury Decision Making in the Capital Penalty Phase: Legal Assumptions, Empirical Findings, and a Research Agenda," *Law and Human Behavior* 16 (1992): 185–201.

89. W. Geimer and J. Amsterdam, "Why Jurors Vote Life or Death: Operative Factors in Ten Florida Death Penalty Cases," *American Journal of Criminal Law* 15 (1988): 1–54.

90. J. Luginbuhl and K. Middendork, "Death Penalty Beliefs and Jurors' Responses to Aggravating and Mitigating Circumstances in Capital Trials," *Law and Human Behavior* 12 (1988): 263–282; J. Luginbuhl, "Comprehension of Judge's Instructions in the Penalty Phase of a Capital Trial: Focus on Mitigating Circumstances," *Law and Human Behavior* 16 (1992): 203–218.

91. *Brooks v. Kemp,* 762 F. 2d 1383 (1985).

92. J. Platania, G., Moran, and B. Cutler, "Prosecutorial Misconduct during the Penalty Phase of Capital Trials: Harmless Error?" *The Champion* (July 1994): 19–22.

93. P. Ackroyd, *Introduction to Dickens* (New York: Ballantine, 1991), pp. 143–149.

94. C. Dickens, *A Tale of Two Cities* (New York: Books Inc., 1868), p. 1.

95. R. Marcus, "Murder Defendants Can Ask about Death Penalty," *Washington Post,* June 16, 1992, p. A4.

96. R. Marcus, "Death Row Prisoners' Return to Federal Court Is Made More Difficult," *Washington Post,* June 23, 1992, p. A5.

97. Ibid.

98. Ibid.

99. "Execution and Inconsistency," *Washington Post,* January 4, 1995, p. A14.

100. Ibid.

101. "Texas Death Row Appeals Denied Despite Prosecutor's Turnabout," *Washington Post,* January 4, 1995, p. A16.
102. S. Pressley, "Texas Prisoner Executed Despite Questions of Guilt," *Washington Post,* January 5, 1995, p. A4.
103. N. Hentoff, "The Supreme Court Has Diminished Itself," *Washington Post,* January 14, 1995, p. A25.
104. Pressley, "Texas Prisoner Executed."

11. THE JUVENILE DEATH PENALTY

1. "The Young and the Violent," *Wall Street Journal,* September 23, 1992, p. A16.
2. Ibid.
3. Ibid.
4. E. McNamara, "Crime and Punishment: When 15-Year-Old Damien Bynoe Shot Korey Grant and Charles Copney, He Triggered a Political and Judicial Debate—How Do We Punish Children Who Kill?" *Boston Globe,* November 24, 1991, p. 14.
5. Ibid.
6. R. Seven, "15-Year-Old May Face Death Penalty in Trial," *Seattle Times,* October 3, 1992, p. A16.
7. See V. L. Streib, "Death Penalty for Children: The American Experience with Capital Punishment for Crimes Committed While under Age Eighteen," *Oklahoma Law Review* 36 (1983): 613–639; V. L. Streib, "The Eighth Amendment and Capital Punishment of Juveniles," *Cleveland State Law Review* 34 (1986): 363–399; V. L. Streib, "Imposing the Death Penalty on Children," in K. C. Haas and J. A. Inciardi, eds., *Challenging Capital Punishment: Legal and Social Science Approaches* (Newbury Park, Calif.: Sage Publications, 1988), pp. 247–267.
8. For example, *Weems v. United States,* 217 U.S. 349 (1910); *Trop v. Dulles,* 356 U.S. 86 (1958).
9. For example, *Robinson v. California,* 370 U.S. 660 (1962); *Solem v. Helm,* 463 U.S. 277 (1983).
10. *Coker v. Georgia,* 433 U.S. 584 (1977).
11. *Enmund v. Florida,* 458 U.S. 782 (1982).
12. *Ford v. Wainwright,* 477 U.S. 399 (1986).
13. *Thompson v. Oklahoma,* 487 U.S. 815 (1988).
14. *Weems v. United States.*
15. R. Dworkin, *Law's Empire* (Cambridge, Mass.: Harvard University Press, 1986).
16. *Stanford v. Kentucky,* 492 U.S. 361 (1989).
17. Streib, "Imposing the Death Penalty."
18. Southern Coalition on Jails and Prisons, "SCJP Poll Results: Don't Execute Juveniles," *Southern Coalition Report on Jails and Prisons,* 13

(1986): 1; S. E. Skovron, J. E. Scott, and F. T. Cullen, "The Death Penalty for Juveniles: An Assessment of Public Support," *Crime and Delinquency* 35 (1989): 546–561.

19. Skovron et al., "The Death Penalty for Juveniles."
20. *Stanford v. Kentucky.*
21. *Weems v. United States.*
22. *Trop v. Dulles.*
23. *Coker v. Georgia.*
24. Ibid., p. 584.
25. N. J. Finkel, "Socioscientific Evidence and Supreme Court Numerology: When Justices Attempt Social Science," *Behavioral Sciences and the Law* 11 (1993): 67–77.
26. *Stanford v. Kentucky,* p. 378.
27. Ibid.
28. Ibid., p. 379.
29. Ibid.
30. Ibid.
31. *Enmund v. Florida,* p. 797.
32. Ibid., p. 823 (O'Connor, J., dissenting).
33. *Tison v. Arizona,* 481 U.S. 137, 148 (1987).
34. *Thompson v. Oklahoma.*
35. *Stanford v. Kentucky,* p. 383 (Brennan, J., dissenting).
36. Ibid., p. 382 (O'Connor, J., concurring in part and concurring in the judgment).
37. Ibid., p. 370.
38. Ibid., pp. 370–371.
39. Ibid., p. 384.
40. Ibid.
41. Ibid.
42. Ibid.
43. Ibid., p. 370.
44. Ibid.
45. Ibid., p. 385.
46. Ibid.
47. Ibid., p. 371, n. 3.
48. "Thompson," at 868 n.4 (Scalia, J., dissenting).
49. *Stanford v. Kentucky,* p. 374.
50. *Thompson v. Oklahoma,* p. 871 (Scalia, J., dissenting).
51. Ibid.
52. Ibid., p. 870.
53. W. Shakespeare, *The Tragedy of Macbeth* (New York: Washington Square Press, 1959), Act I, scene i.
54. *Stanford v. Kentucky,* p. 378.
55. For an early discussion of the place of certainty or lack of it in science,

see D. Hume, *An Inquiry Concerning Human Understanding* (Indianapolis: Bobbs-Merrill, 1955).

56. S. Toulmin, *The Philosophy of Science* (New York: Harper and Row, 1960), p. 81. "Certainly, every statement in a science should conceivably be *capable* of being called in question, and of being shown empirically to be unjustified; for only so can the science be saved from dogmatism."

57. Ibid.

58. *Stanford v. Kentucky,* p. 371, n. 3.

59. Shakespeare, *Macbeth,* Act V, scene ii, lines 17–18. The full quote is: "He cannot buckle his distempered cause within the belt of rule."

60. P. B. Gerstenfeld and A. J. Tomkins, "Age as a Mitigating Circumstance in Juvenile Homicide Sentencing," Paper presented at the American-Law Society Conference, San Diego, March 1992.

61. N. J. Finkel, K. C. Hughes, S. F. Smith, M. L. Hurabiell, "Killing Kids: The Juvenile Death Penalty and Community Sentiment," *Behavioral Sciences and the Law* 12 (1994): 5–20.

62. *Furman v. Georgia,* 408 U.S. 238 (1972).

63. See for example, S. Gross and R. Mauro, *Death and Discrimination* (Boston: Northeastern University Press, 1989); E. Rapaport, "The Death Penalty and Gender Discrimination," *Law and Society Review* 25 (1991): 367–383.

64. J. R. P. Ogloff, "The Juvenile Death Penalty: A Frustrated Society's Attempt for Control," *Behavioral Sciences and the Law* 5 (1987): 447–455.

65. J. L. Hoffmann, "On the Perils of Line-Drawing: Juveniles and the Death Penalty," *Hastings Law Journal* 40 (1989): 229–284.

66. *Penry v. Lynaugh,* 492 U.S. 302 (1989).

12. ON SELF-DEFENSE JUSTICE

1. R. Singer, "The Resurgence of Mens Rea, II: Honest But Unreasonable Mistake of Fact in Self Defense," *Boston College Law Review* 28 (1987): 472.

2. Ibid.

3. Ibid.

4. C. K. Gillespie, *Justifiable Homicide: Battered Women, Self-Defense, and the Law* (Columbus: Ohio State University Press, 1989), p. 43.

5. Singer, "Resurgence," p. 461. Quoting 1 M. Hale, *Pleas of the Crown,* 42 (1736). Also citing 4 W. Blackstone, *Commentaries on the Laws of England,* 27 (1776).

6. Ibid.

7. *Granger v. State,* 13 Tenn. 459 (1830).

8. Ibid., p. 461.

9. Ibid., p. 462.

10. Ibid., pp. 461–462.

11. Singer, "Resurgence," p. 480.

12. *People v. Shorter,* 2 N.Y. 193 (1849).

13. *Hill v. State,* 94 Miss. 391, 49 So. 145 (1908).

14. Ibid., pp. 394–395, 49 So., p. 146.

15. *State v. Jennings,* 96 Mont. 80, 91, 28 P. 2d 448, 451 (1934).

16. *State v. Wanrow,* 88 Wash. 2d 221, 559 P. 2d 548 (1977).

17. Singer, "Resurgence," p. 498.

18. *State v. Bartlett,* 170 Mo. 658, 71 S.W. 148 (1902).

19. *State v. Dunning,* 8 Wash. App. 340, 342 506 P. 2d 321 322 (1973).

20. *Cook v. State,* 194 Miss. 467, 473, 12 So. 2d 137, 139 (1943).

21. *Lundy v. State,* 59 Tex. Crim. 131, 134, 127 S.W. 1032, 1034 (1910).

22. Singer, "Resurgence," p. 499.

23. G. Fletcher, *Rethinking Criminal Law* (Boston: Little, Brown, 1978), p. 808.

24. Gillespie, "Justifiable Homicide," p. 4.

25. Ibid., p. 182.

26. Ibid., p. 94.

27. For example, A. Browne, *When Battered Women Kill* (New York: Free Press, 1987); C. P. Ewing, *Battered Women Who Kill* (Lexington, Mass.: Lexington Books, 1987).

28. For example, E. M. Schneider, "Equal Rights to Trial for Women: Sex Bias and the Law of Self-Defense," *Harvard Civil Rights Law Review* 15 (1980): 623–647; E. M. Schneider and S. B. Jordan, "Representation of Women Who Defend Themselves in Response to Physical or Sexual Assault," *Women's Rights Law Reporter* 4 (1978): 149–163.

29. Browne, *When Battered Women Kill,* p. 11.

30. E. Rapaport, "The Death Penalty and Gender Discrimination," *Law and Society Review* 25 (1991): 367–383.

31. L. E. Walker, *The Battered Woman* (New York: Harper and Row, 1979); L. E. Walker, *The Battered Woman Syndrome* (New York: Springer, 1984).

32. M. E. Wolfgang, *Patterns in Criminal Homicide* (Philadelphia: University of Pennsylvania Press, 1958).

33. Browne, *When Battered Women Kill.*

34. Ibid.

35. G. W. Barnard, H. Vera, M. I. Vera, and G. Newman, G. (1982). "Till Death Do Us Part: A Study of Spouse Murder," *Bulletin of the American Association of Psychiatry and Law* 10 (1982): 271–280.

36. *State v. Schroeder,* 199 Neb. 822, 261 N.W. 2d 759 (1978).

37. S. J. Schulhofer, "The Gender Question in Criminal Law," *Social Philosophy and Policy* 7 (1990): 105–137.

38. Ibid., p. 106.

39. C. Gilligan, *In a Different Voice: Psychological Theory and Women's Development* (Cambridge, Mass.: Harvard University Press, 1982).

40. Schulhofer, "Gender Question," p. 106.
41. Ibid.
42. Walker, *The Battered Woman,* p. xv.
43. M. E. P. Seligman, *Helplessness: On Depression, Development, and Death* (San Francisco: Freeman, 1975).
44. Schulhofer, "Gender Question," p. 118.
45. Ewing, *Battered Women Who Kill.*
46. Schulhofer, "Gender Question," p. 120.
47. Ibid.
48. American Psychiatric Association, *Diagnostic and Statistical Manual of Mental Disorders,* 3rd rev. ed., DSM-III-R (Washington, D.C.: American Psychiatric Association, 1987).
49. P. L. Crocker, "The Meaning of Equality for Battered Women Who Kill Men in Self-Defense," *Harvard Women's Law Review* 8 (1985): 149.
50. *Brown v. United States,* 256 U.S. 335, 343 (1921).
51. Singer, "Resurgence."
52. G. P. Fletcher, *A Crime of Self-Defense: Bernhard Goetz and the Law on Trial* (Chicago: University of Chicago Press, 1988).
53. W. Shakespeare, *The Tragedy of Hamlet, Prince of Denmark* (Baltimore: Penguin, 1957), act 5, scene 1.

13. THE SELF-DEFENSE DRAMA

1. C. K. Gillespie, *Justifiable Homicide: Battered Women, Self-Defense, and the Law* (Columbus: Ohio State University Press, 1989).
2. F. McNulty, *The Burning Bed* (New York: Harcourt Brace Jovanovich, 1980).
3. R. A. Schuller and N. Vidmar, "Battered Woman Syndrome Evidence in the Courtroom: A Review of the Literature," *Law and Human Behavior* 16 (1992): 273–291.
4. D. R. Follingstad, D. S., Polek, E. S. Hause, L. H. Deaton, M. W. Bulger, and Z. D. Conway, "Factors Predicting Verdicts in Cases Where Battered Women Kill Their Husbands," *Law and Human Behavior* 13 (1989): 253–269.
5. Ibid., p. 259.
6. J. P. Greenwald, A. J. Tomkins, M. Kenning, and D. Zavodny, "Psychological Self-Defense Jury Instructions: Influence on Verdicts for Battered Women Defendants," *Behavioral Sciences and the Law* 8 (1990): 171–180.
7. C. P. Ewing, *Battered Women Who Kill* (Lexington, Mass.: Lexington Books, 1987).
8. Ibid., p. 79.
9. Ibid.
10. K. Kinports, "Defending Battered Women's Self-Defense Claims," *Oregon Law Review* 67 (1988): 393–465.

11. N. J. Finkel, K. H. Meister, and D. M. Lightfoot, "The Self-Defense Defense and Community Sentiment," *Law and Human Behavior* 15 (1991): 585–602.

12. *People v. Jones,* 12 Cal. Rptr. 777 (Cal. App. 1961).

13. Gillespie, *Justifiable Homicide.*

14. E. M. Schneider and S. B. Jordan, "Representation of Women Who Defend Themselves in Response to Physical or Sexual Assault," *Women's Rights Law Reporter* 9 (1978): 195–222.

15. M. Kasian, N. P. Spanos, C. A. Terrance, and S. Peebles, "Battered Women Who Kill: Jury Simulation and Legal Defenses," *Law and Human Behavior* 17 (1993): 289–312.

16. M. J. Brondino, K. J., Kleinfelter, and D. R. Follingstad, "Defendant Variables Affecting Juror Verdicts in Cases Where Battered Women Kill Their Husbands," Paper presented at the American Psychology-Law Society's Mid-Year Conference, San Diego, March, 1992.

17. Kasian et al., "Battered Women Who Kill," p. 308.

18. R. A. Schuller, "The Impact of Battered Woman Syndrome Evidence on Jury Decision Processes," *Law and Human Behavior* 16 (1992): 597–620.

19. W. L. Prosser, *Handbook of the Law of Torts,* 2nd ed. (St. Paul, Minn.: West, 1955).

20. R. Singer, "The Resurgence of Mens Rea, II: Honest but Unreasonable Mistake of Fact in Self Defense," *Boston College Law Review* 28 (1987): 504.

21. Ibid., p. 502.

22. B. McGraw, D. Farthing-Capowich, and I. Keilitz, "The Guilty but Mentally Ill Plea and Verdict: Current State of the Knowledge," *Villanova Law Review* 30 (1985): 117–191.

23. L. A. Callahan, M. A. McGreevy, C. Cirincione, and H. J. Steadman, "Measuring the Effects of the Guilty but Mentally Ill (GBMI) Verdict: Georgia's 1982 GBMI Reform," *Law and Human Behavior* 16 (1992): 447–462.

24. G. P. Fletcher, *A Crime of Self-Defense: Bernhard Goetz and the Law on Trial* (Chicago: University of Chicago Press, 1988).

25. P. Duggan, "P.G. Slayer of Father Spared Jail," *Washington Post,* August 28, 1991, pp. B1, B2.

26. Singer, "Resurgence," pp. 515–516.

14. THE MADDENING CHANGES IN INSANITY LAW

1. N. J. Finkel, *Insanity on Trial* (New York: Plenum, 1988).

2. N. Walker, *Crime and Insanity in England: The Historical Perspective,* vol. 1 (Edinburgh: Edinburgh University Press, 1968), p. 168.

3. R. Moran, *Knowing Right from Wrong: The Insanity Defense of Daniel McNaughtan* (New York: Free Press, 1981), p. 40.

4. L. Caplan, *The Insanity Defense and the Trial of John W. Hinckley, Jr.* (Boston: Godine, 1984).

5. Finkel, *Insanity on Trial.*

6. M. L. Perlin, "Psychodynamics and the Insanity Defense: 'Ordinary Common Sense' and Heuristic Reasoning," *Nebraska Law Review* 69 (1990): 9 (hereafter referred to as "OCS"). See also M. L. Perlin, "Unpacking the Myths: The Symbolism of Insanity Defense Jurisprudence," *Case Western Reserve Law Review* 40 (1989–1990): 599 (hereafter referred to as "Myths"); M. L. Perlin, "Mental Illness, Crime, and the Culture of Punishment", in Perlin, *The Jurisprudence of the Insanity Defense* (Durham, N.C.: Carolina Academic Press, 1994), pp. 13–71.

7. R. Smith, *Trial by Medicine: Insanity and Responsibility in Victorian Trials* (Edinburgh: Edinburgh University Press, 1981).

8. *Northern Sec. Co. v. United States,* 193 U.S. 197, 400 (1904).

9. Ibid.

10. Walker, *Crime and Insanity in England,* p. 16.

11. H. Fingarette and A. F. Hasse, *Mental Disabilities and Criminal Responsibility* (Berkeley: University of California Press, 1979).

12. G. P. Fletcher, *Rethinking Criminal Law* (Boston: Little, Brown, 1978), p. 836; But see B. Wootton, *Crime and Criminal Law* (London: Stevens, 1963). Fletcher's position is quite different from Lady Wootton's, for she would set the question of responsibility aside and go straight to disposition, believing that neither the courts nor the experts can fathom the defendant's mind. Thus, if the question is essentially unanswerable, move on to disposition. Fletcher believes that this tough question must be faced, not begged, for it goes to the heart of our notions of crime and punishment.

13. H. D. Bracton, *De Legibus et Consuetudinibus Angliae* [On the Laws and Customs of England], ed. Woodbine (New Haven: Yale University Press, 1915).

14. Walker, *Crime and Insanity in England,* p. 26.

15. *Rex v. Arnold,* 16 How. St. Tr. 684 (1723).

16. Walker, *Crime and Insanity in England,* p. 56.

17. Finkel, *Insanity on Trial.*

18. *Hadfield's Case,* 27 Howell's State Trials 1281 (1800).

19. D. N. Robinson, *Psychology and Law: Can Justice Survive the Social Sciences?* (New York: Oxford University Press, 1980), p. 42.

20. Walker, *Crime and Insanity in England,* p. 77.

21. Finkel, *Insanity on Trial,* p. 16.

22. Walker, *Crime and Insanity in England,* p. 78.

23. *M'Naghten's Case,* 10 Cl. and Fin. 200, 8 Eng. Rep. 718 (1843).

24. N. J. Finkel, "Maligning and Misconstruing Jurors' Insanity Verdicts: A Rebuttal," *Forensic Reports* 1 (1988): 98. See also Moran, *Knowing Right from Wrong,* p. 13.

25. Finkel, *Insanity on Trial,* p. 21.
26. Ibid., p. 23.
27. Walker, *Crime and Insanity in England,* pp. 86–87.
28. Finkel, *Insanity on Trial.*
29. Perlin, "Myths."
30. F. Winslow, *The Plea of Insanity in Criminal Cases* (New York: Da Capo, 1983; orig. pub. 1843). Forbes Winslow was one of the doctors who testfied for M'Naghten.
31. Smith, *Victorian Trials.*
32. I. Ray, *A Treatise on the Medical Jurisprudence of Insanity* (New York: Da Capo, 1983; orig. pub. 1838).
33. Smith, *Victorian Trials.*
34. For example, *Parsons v. State,* 2 So. 854 (Ala. 1887); *Davis v. United States,* 165 U.S. 373 (1897).
35. See, for example, Sir J. F. Stephen, *History of the Criminal Law of England* (London: Macmillan, 1883); *R. v. Davis,* 14 Cox C.C. 563 (1881); but see *R. v. True,* Cr. App. R. 164 (1922).
36. Sir E. Gowers (Chairman), *Report of the Royal Commission on Capital Punishment, 1949–1953* (London: HMSO, 1953), Cmd. 8932. The testimony is also reported in *United States v. Currens,* 290 F. 2d 751 n. 5 (1961).
37. *Durham v. United States,* 214 F. 2d 862 (1954).
38. A. S. Goldstein, *The Insanity Defense* (New Haven: Yale University Press, 1967), p. 83.
39. D. L. Bazelon, "Veils, Values, and Social Responsibility," *American Psychologist* 37 (1982): 115–121.
40. Goldstein, *Insanity Defense,* p. 82; R. Leifer, "The Psychiatrist and Tests of Criminal Responsibility," *American Psychologist* 19 (1964): 828.
41. Goldstein, *Insanity Defense,* p. 82.
42. Finkel, "Maligning," p. 104.
43. Walker, *Crime and Insanity in England,* p. 139.
44. Ibid.
45. *People v. Gorshen,* 51 Cal. 2d 716, 7200–7221, 336 P. 2d 492, 494–495 (1959); *People v. Wolff,* 61 Cal. 2d 795, 394 P. 2d 959, 40 Cal. Rptr. 271 (1964); *People v. Ray,* 14 Cal. 3d 29, 533 P. 2d 1017, 120 Cal. Rptr. 377 (1975).
46. American Law Institute, "Model Penal Code" (1962), Proposed Official Draft, sec. 4.01.
47. *United States v. Hinckley,* 525 F. Supp. 1342 (D.C. 1982).
48. Committee on the Judiciary, United States Senate, *The Insanity Defense* (Washington, D.C.: U.S. Government Printing Office, 1982); Subcommittee on Criminal Justice of the Committee of the Judiciary, House of Representatives, *Insanity Defense in Federal Courts* (Washington, D.C.: U.S. Government Printing Office, 1983), serial no. 134; Subcommittee

on Criminal Justice of the Committee of the Judiciary, House of Representatives, *Reform of the Federal Insanity Defense* (Washington, D.C.: U.S. Government Printing Office, 1984), serial no. 21; Subcommittee on Criminal Law of the Committee on the Judiciary, United States Senate, *Limiting the Insanity Defense* (Washington, D.C.: U.S. Government Printing Office, 1983), serial no. J-97-122.

49. N. J. Finkel and S. M. Fulero, "Insanity: Making Law in the Absence of Evidence," *International Journal of Medicine and Law* 11, nos. 5–6 (1992): 383–404.

50. P. Arenella, "Reflections on Current Proposals to Abolish or Reform the Insanity Defense," *American Journal of Law and Medicine* 8 (1983): 217–284.

51. Perlin, "Myths,"

52. Perlin, "Mental Illness," p. 18.

53. Ibid.

54. For example, B. J. Ennis and T. R. Litwack, "Psychiatry and the Presumption of Expertise: Flipping Coins in the Courtroom," *California Law Review* 62 (1974): 693–752; J. M. Livermore, C. P. Malmquist, and P. E. Meehl, "On the Justification for Civil Commitment," *University of Pennsylvania Law Review* 117 (1968): 75–96; H. J. Steadman, "Predicting Dangerousness among the Mentally Ill: Art, Magic, and Science," *International Journal of Law and Psychiatry* 129 (1983): 304–310. As for the law's presumption that the mentally ill are dangerous, see N. N. Kittrie, *The Right to Be Different: Deviance and Enforced Therapy* (Baltimore: Johns Hopkins University Press, 1971); T. J. Scheff, "The Societal Reaction to Deviance: Ascriptive Elements in the Psychiatric Screening of Mental Patients in a Midwestern State," in R. H. Price and B. Denner, eds., *The Making of a Mental Patient* (New York: Holt, Rinehart and Winston, 1973).

55. Perlin, "Mental Illness," p. 19.

56. Ibid., p. 20.

57. For example, H. J. Steadman, "Statement," in Hearings before the Subcommittee on Criminal Law of the Committee on the Judiciary, United States Senate, "Limiting the Insanity Defense," pp. 367–373; S. J. Morse, "Statement on Behalf of the Association for the Advancement of Psychology and the American Psychological Association," in Hearings before the Subcommittee on Criminal Justice of the Committee on the Judiciary, House of Representatives, "Reform of the Federal Insanity Defense," pp. 311–402.

58. Finkel and Fulero, "Absence of Evidence," p. 3.

59. Ibid.

60. N. J. Finkel, "The Insanity Defense Reform Act of 1984: Much Ado about Nothing," *Behavioral Sciences and the Law* 7 (1989): 403–419.

61. Senate Subcommittee, "Limiting the Insanity Defense."

62. N. Morris, *Madness and the Criminal Law* (Chicago: University of Chicago Press, 1982), p. 65.

63. R. J. Gerber, *The Insanity Defense* (Port Washington, N.Y.: Associated Faculty Press, 1984).

64. For example, *People v. Grant,* 71 Ill. 2d 551, 377 N.E. 2d 4 (1978).

65. C. Slobogin, "The Guilty but Mentally Ill Verdict: An Idea Whose Time Should Not Have Come," *George Washington Law Review* 53 (1985): 494–527.

66. *Harris v. State,* 499 N.E. 2d 723 (Ind. 1986); *People v. Crews,* 122 Ill. 2d 266, 522 N.E. 2d 1167 (1988).

67. American Psychiatric Association, *Statement on the Insanity Defense* (Washington, D.C.: American Psychiatric Association, 1982), pp. 9–10.

68. L. A. Callahan, M. A. McGreevy, C. Cirincione, H. J. Steadman, "Measuring the Effects of the Guilty but Mentally Ill (GBMI) Verdict: Georgia's 1982 GBMI Reform," *Law and Human Behavior* 16 (1992): 460.

69. R. Rogers, "APA's Position on the Insanity Defense: Empiricism versus Emotionalism," *American Psychologist* 42 (1987): 840–848.

70. But see R. M. Wettstein, E. P. Mulvey, and R. Rogers, "A Prospective Comparison of Four Insanity Defense Standards," *American Journal of Psychiatry* 148 (1991): 21–27. Psychiatrists turn out to be more confident as to whether the defendant met ALI's volitional test than as to whether he or she met ALI's cognitive test.

71. A. A. Stone, *Law, Psychiatry, and Morality: Essays and Analysis* (Washington, D.C.: American Psychiatric Press, 1984).

72. Fletcher, *Rethinking Criminal Law,* p. 835.

73. Perlin, "Mental Illness."

74. Finkel, *Insanity on Trial,* p. 172.

15. HOW JURORS CONSTRUE INSANITY

1. R. M. James, "Jurors' Assessment of Criminal Responsibility," *Social Problems* 7 (1969a): 58–67; see also R. M. James, "Status and Competence of Jurors," *American Journal of Sociology* 64 (1959b): 563–570; R. J. Simon, *The Jury and the Defense of Insanity* (Boston: Little, Brown, 1967).

2. Ibid.

3. Ibid.

4. Ibid., p. 68.

5. N. J. Finkel, R. Shaw, S. Bercaw, and J. Koch, "Insanity Defenses: From the Jurors' Perspective," *Law and Psychology Review* 9 (1985): 77–92.

6. H. Fingarette and A. F. Hasse, *Mental Disabilities and Criminal Responsibility* (Berkeley: University of California Press, 1979).

7. N. J. Finkel, "The Insanity Defense Reform Act of 1984: Much Ado about Nothing," *Behavioral Sciences and the Law* 8 (1989): 403–419.

8. Subcommittee on Criminal Law of the Committee on the Judiciary, United States Senate, *Limiting the Insanity Defense* (Washington, D.C.: U.S. Government Printing Office, 1983), serial no. J-97-122.

9. Finkel, "Much Ado."

10. N. J. Finkel and S. F. Handel, "Jurors and Insanity: Do Test Instructions Instruct?" *Forensic Reports* 1 (1988): 65–79; N. J. Finkel and S. F. Handel, "How Jurors Construe 'Insanity,'" *Law and Human Behavior* 13 (1989): 41–59. See also Finkel, "Much Ado."

11. Insanity Defense Reform Act of 1984, Public Law 98-473, secs. 401, 402, sec. 20(a)(b).

12. J. R. Ciccone and C. Clements, "The Insanity Defense: Asking and Answering the Ultimate Question," *Bulletin of the American Academy of Psychiatry and Law* 15 (1987): 329–338; D. Cohen, "Punishing the Insane: Restriction of Expert Psychiatric Testimony by Federal Rule of Evidence 704(B)," *University of Florida Law Review* 10 (1988): 541–562; but see D. L. Bazelon, *Questioning Authority: Justice and Criminal Law* (New York: Knopf, 1988).

13. C. Slobogin, "The 'Ultimate Issue' Issue," *Behavioral Sciences and the Law* 7 (1989): 259–266.

14. S. M. Fulero and N. J. Finkel, "Barring Ultimate Issue Testimony: An 'Insane' Rule?" *Law and Human Behavior* 15 (1991): 495–507.

15. J. R. P. Ogloff, "A Comparison of Insanity Defense Standards on Juror Decision Making," *Law and Human Behavior* 15 (1991): 509–531.

16. Finkel et al., "Insanity Defenses"; Finkel, "Much Ado."

17. J. T. Lamiell and S. J. Trierweiler, "Personality Measurement and Intuitive Personality Judgments from an Idiothetic Point of View," *Clinical Psychology Review* 6 (1986): 471–491.

18. Finkel and Handel, "Jurors Construe."

19. Simon, *The Jury.*

20. *Durham v. United States*, 214 F. 2d 862 (1954).

21. M. S. Moore, *Law and Psychiatry: Rethinking the Relationship* (Cambridge: Cambridge University Press, 1984).

22. Ibid., p. 244.

23. S. J. Morse, "Statement, and Additional Remarks," in Hearings before the Subcommittee on Criminal Justice of the Committee on the Judiciary, House of Representatives, *Reform of the Federal Insanity Defense* (Washington, D.C.: U.S. Government Printing Office, 1984), serial no. 21, pp. 311–402; S. J. Morse, "Excusing the Crazy: The Insanity Defense Reconsidered," *Southern California Law Review* 58 (1985): 780–836.

24. Morse, "Statement," p. 390.

25. Ibid.

26. N. J. Finkel, "De Facto Departures from Insanity Instructions: Toward the Remaking of Common Law," *Law and Human Behavior* 14 (1990): 110.

27. Fingarette and Hasse, *Mental Disabilities,* p. 218.
28. Ibid.
29. Ibid.
30. Finkel, "De Facto," p. 110.
31. Bazelon, *Questioning Authority,* p. 45.
32. Ibid., pp. 50–51.
33. Ibid., p. 51.
34. Ibid., p. 45.
35. Finkel, "De Facto," p. 110.
36. Finkel and Handel, "Test Instructions"; Finkel and Handel, "Jurors Construe."
37. Finkel, "De Facto," p. 114.
38. Finkel, "Much Ado."
39. M. S. Aldenderfer and R. K. Blashfield, *Cluster Analysis* (Beverly Hills, Calif.: Sage Publications, 1984).
40. N. J. Finkel and K. Duff, "The Insanity Defense: Giving Jurors a Third Option," *Forensic Reports* 2 (1989): 235–263.
41. P. H. Robinson, "Causing the Conditions of One's Own Defense: A Study in the Limits of Theory in Criminal Law Doctrine," *Virginia Law Review* 71 (1985): 2.
42. M. D. Alicke and T. L. Davis, "Capacity Responsibility in Social Evaluation," *Personality and Social Psychology Bulletin* 16 (1990): 465–474.
43. G. P. Fletcher, *Rethinking Criminal Law* (Boston: Little, Brown, 1978), p. 589.
44. American Psychiatric Association, *Statement on the Insanity Defense* (Washington, D.C.: American Psychiatric Association, 1982), p. 9.
45. B. D. McGraw, D. Farthing-Capowich, and I. Keilitz, "The 'Guilty but Mentally Ill' Plea and Verdict: Current State of the Knowledge," *Villanova Law Review* 30 (1985): 117–191.
46. C. F. Roberts, S. L. Golding, and F. D. Fincham, "Implicit Theories of Criminal Responsibility: Decision Making and the Insanity Defense," *Law and Human Behavior* 11 (1987): 207–232.
47. Ibid., p. 207.
48. Ibid., p. 218.
49. Finkel and Duff, "Third Option."
50. N. J. Finkel, "The Insanity Defense: A Comparison of Verdict Schemas," *Law and Human Behavior* 15 (1991): 533–555.
51. C. F. Roberts, E. L. Sargent, and A. S. Chan, "Verdict Selection Processes in Insanity Cases: Juror Construals and the Effects of Guilty but Mentally Ill Instructions," *Law and Human Behavior* 17 (1993): 261–275.
52. Ibid., p. 270.
53. Ibid., p. 273.
54. N. J. Finkel, *Insanity on Trial* (New York: Plenum, 1988).
55. N. J. Finkel and S. M. Fulero, "Insanity: Making Law in the Absence of

Evidence," *International Journal of Medicine and Law* 11 (1992): 383–404.

56. G. E. Dix, "Psychological Abnormality as a Factor in Grading Criminal Liability: Diminished Capacity, Diminished Responsibility, and the Like," *Journal of Criminal Law and Criminology* 62 (1971): 332–333.

16. MURDEROUS PASSIONS, MITIGATING SENTIMENTS

1. Homer, *Iliad,* trans. A. H. Chase and W. G. Perry Jr. (New York: Bantam, 1950).
2. R. A. Posner, *Law and Literature: A Misunderstood Relation* (Cambridge, Mass.: Harvard University Press, 1988).
3. H. Selye, *The Stress of Life* (New York: McGraw-Hill, 1956).
4. Ibid.
5. T. H. Holmes and R. H. Rahe, "The Social Readjustment Ratings Scale," *Journal of Psychosomatic Research* 11 (1967): 213–218; see also American Psychiatric Association, *Diagnostic and Statistical Manual of Mental Disorders,* 3rd rev. ed., DSM-III-R (Washington, D.C.: American Psychiatric Association, 1987). Axis IV deals with psychosocial stressors.
6. R. Singer, "The Resurgence of Mens Rea, I: Provocation, Emotional Disturbance, and the Model Penal Code," *Boston Law Review* 27 (1986): 253.
7. *Watts v. Byrnes,* Noy 171, 74 Eng. Rep. 1129. The case is undated, but one scholar puts it at about 1580; Singer, "Resurgence."
8. Singer, "Resurgence."
9. *Williams, Jones,* W. 432, 82 Eng. Rep. 227.
10. *Royley's Case,* 2 Cro. Jac. 296, 79 Eng. Rep. 254 (1666).
11. Singer, "Resurgence," p. 255.
12. *Maddy's Case,* 1 Vent. 158, 86 Eng. Rep. 108 (1672).
13. Singer, "Resurgence," p. 255.
14. Ibid., p. 256.
15. Ibid.
16. Ibid., pp. 262–263.
17. Ibid., p. 276.
18. 88 Wash. 304, 153 P. 9 (1915).
19. Singer, "Resurgence," p. 279.
20. *State v. Gounagias,* 88 Wash. 304, 153 P. 9, 14 (1915).
21. Singer, "Resurgence," p. 280.
22. Ibid.
23. Ibid.
24. G. Williams, "Provocation and the Reasonable Man," *Criminal Law Review* (1954): 740, 742.
25. G. Fletcher, *Rethinking Criminal Law* (Boston: Little, Brown, 1978), p. 247.

26. Singer, "Resurgence," p. 262.
27. 10 Mich. 212 (1863).
28. Ibid., p. 219.
29. Singer, "Resurgence," p. 283.
30. 121 Pa. 586, 592–592, 15 A. 465, 466 (1888).
31. 1 W.L.R. 1119 (1954).
32. Singer, "Resurgence," p. 289.
33. Fletcher, *Rethinking,* p. 248.
34. Singer, "Resurgence," p. 289.
35. In DSM-III-R, Axis IV categorizes the severity of psychosocial stressors that an individual experiences in the last year on a 1-to-6 scale, from "none" to "catastrophic."
36. Holmes and Rahe, "Social Readjustment Rating Scale," quantifies various stressors (that is, life events), such that "death of a spouse" earns 100 points, on the top end of the scale, and "minor violations of the law" earns 11 points, on the bottom end.
37. *State v. Gounagias,* p. 14.
38. For example, R. B. Zajonc, "On the Primacy of Affect," *American Psychologist* 39 (1984): 117–123.
39. Ibid., p. 117.
40. Ibid.
41. R. B. Zajonc, "Feeling and Thinking: Preferences Need No Inferences," *American Psychologist* 35 (1980): 151–175.
42. R. S. Lazarus, "On the Primacy of Cognition," *American Psychologist* 39 (1984): 124–129.
43. R. S. Lazarus, "Cognition and Motivation in Emotion," *American Psychologist* 46 (1991): 353.
44. Ibid., p. 361.
45. Zajonc, "Primacy of Affect," p. 117.
46. W. G. Parrott and J. Schulkin, "Neuropsychology and the Cognitive Nature of the Emotions," *Cognition and Emotion* 7 (1993): 43–59.
47. Ibid., p. 48.
48. Ibid., p. 50.
49. J. R. Averill, *Anger and Aggression: An Essay on Emotion* (New York: Springer, 1982).
50. Ibid., p. 115.
51. Ibid.
52. Ibid., p. 116.
53. Ibid., p. 115.
54. Ibid.
55. W. G. Parrott, "On the Scientific Study of Angry Organisms," in R. S. Wyer Jr. and T. K. Srull, eds., *Perspectives on Anger and Emotion: Advances in Social Cognition,* vol. 6 (Hillsdale, N.J.: Erlbaum, 1993), pp. 167–177.

56. Ibid., p. 171.
57. R. Pound, "The Need of a Sociological Jurisprudence," *Green Bag* 19 (1907): 615.
58. Singer, "Resurgence," p. 310.
59. Ibid.
60. Ibid., p. 322.
61. Ibid.
62. 182 Conn. 388, 391–97, 438 A.2d 696, 698–701 (1980).
63. 177 Conn. 1, 411 A.2d 3 (1979).
64. Singer, "Resurgence," p. 295.
65. *State v. Elliot,* p. 8.
66. Singer, "Resurgence," p. 322.

17. THE PATH OF COMMONSENSE JUSTICE

1. *Director of Public Prosecutions v. Bedder,* 1 W.L.R. 1119 (1954).
2. *State v. Gounagias,* 88 Wash. 304, 153 P. 9 (1915).
3. R. Singer, "The Resurgence of Mens Rea, I: Provocation, Emotional Disturbance, and the Model Penal Code," *Boston College Law Review* 27 (1986): 243–322.
4. J. Barth, *Lost in the Funhouse* (New York: Bantam, 1969), p. 91.
5. H. Kalven Jr. and H. Zeisel, *The American Jury* (Chicago: University of Chicago Press, 1971).
6. See R. Dworkin, *Law's Empire* (Cambridge, Mass.: Harvard University Press, 1986); R. A. Posner, *The Problems of Jurisprudence* (Cambridge, Mass.: Harvard University Press, 1990).
7. W. L. Bennett and M. S. Feldman, *Reconstructing Reality in the Courtroom: Justice and Judgment in American Culture* (New Brunswick, N.J.: Rutgers University Press, 1981).
8. G. P. Fletcher, *Rethinking Criminal Law* (Boston: Little, Brown, 1978).
9. Ibid.
10. Ibid., p. 388.
11. Ibid., p. 389.
12. Ibid., p. 388.
13. Ibid., p. 119.
14. O. W. Holmes, *The Common Law* (Cambridge, Mass.: Harvard University Press, 1963; orig. pub., 1881).
15. Ibid., p. 88.
16. R. Pound, "The Need of a Sociological Jurisprudence," *Green Bag* 19 (1907): 612.
17. Holmes, *Common Law,* p. 88.
18. Ibid., p. 108.
19. Singer, "Resurgence," p. 243.

20. G. P. Fletcher, *A Crime of Self-Defense: Bernhard Goetz and the Law on Trial* (Chicago: University of Chicago Press, 1988), p. 186.
21. Ibid.
22. Ibid., p. 187.
23. R. Cohen, "Balkan Justice in LA," *Washington Post,* October 26, 1993, p. A17.
24. Ibid.
25. Ibid.
26. J. Crosby, "Juror Says Doubt, Not Fear, Produced Denny Verdicts," *Washington Post,* October 27, 1993, pp. A1, A22.
27. C. Krauthammer, ". . . Or Crime and Therapy?" *Washington Post,* October 29, 1993, p. A27.
28. Ibid.
29. Editorial, "The Denny Trial Polemics," *Washington Post,* November 1, 1993, p. A16.
30. Ibid.
31. Ibid.
32. Ibid.
33. Crosby, "Doubt, Not Fear," p. A1.
34. Singer, "Resurgence."
35. P. Gramm, "Crime and Punishment . . .," *Washington Post,* October 29, 1993, p. A27.
36. Ibid.
37. Ibid.

Index

young daughter that he was dying. The loss of privacy was a loss of control. This is also the case when private citizens "out" someone who is gay—that is, inform the world of an individual's homosexuality without that individual's permission. Under some circumstances, as in trials involving juveniles, the courts may bar the press from releasing the juvenile's name and may impose punishments if the press fails to comply. Once, when the *Wall Street Journal* published the name of a young alleged offender, the judge excluded the *Journal's* reporter from the legal proceedings, while granting access to other media that had not revealed the name.[2]

The individual's right to privacy, the right of a free press to publish trial facts, and the defendant's right to present the best defense all come into conflict in cases of alleged rape, particularly when the defense claims consent on the part of the plaintiff. The highly publicized case of William Kennedy Smith in 1991 is an example. "Rape shield" laws, and the Privacy Protection for Rape Victims Act of 1978,[3] often keep the plaintiff's name and sexual history out of the trial. In the Smith trial, which was broadcast on television, the alleged victim appeared on camera with an electronically generated blue dot obscuring her face, and although most newspapers and news organizations honored the anonymity, NBC broadcast her name.[4] NBC's action generated considerable controversy, which nearly overwhelmed discussion of the defendant's right to privacy. It may be a legally naïve question, or just a question of balance—but why wasn't the defendant given a blue dot as well? After all, he was only an *alleged* rapist and was innocent until proven guilty. As it turned out, Smith was acquitted, but one could argue that his life has been affected negatively by having his face and identity exposed daily during the trial.

As these incidents and cases reveal, there are times when we want our facts, faces, and history to stay off the front pages. More than just wanting privacy, many of us clearly believe it is our right; we do not want to lose control over a zone we consider ours. But as these incidents and cases also reveal, we are not sure how many people would allege a privacy *right* in these circumstances. In which situations would the claim to privacy garner the greatest support? With conflicts rife between one citizen and another, between the press and the citizen, between business and the citizen, and, of course, between government and the citizen, how does community sentiment delimit the zone of privacy in such various instances? The questions may change from conceptual and constitutional to empirical, but we still await answers.

One area in which there are strong and unmistakable expectations of privacy concerns our own health. We expect that when we see a doctor our health records will remain private, and the Hippocratic Oath has long affirmed the doctor's duty to protect our right to confidentiality. That was certainly the expectation of a twenty-four-year-old man who, in 1991, lay in the intensive care unit of a hospital in Rockville, Maryland; but when the fact that he had AIDS became generally known, he "filed a $4.5 million lawsuit against Shady Grove Adventist Hospital and two respiratory therapists who worked there, saying one of the therapists—a high school acquaintance not involved in his care—obtained his hospital record from the other and called his friends and relatives, telling them that he had AIDS."[5] This case seems straightforward: the patient's right to privacy had been violated. Yet other sides to the issue are a good deal more complex, as the next two cases reveal.

"The D.C. Court of Appeals . . . refused to block a test to determine the presence of HIV antibodies in the blood of a rape suspect who allegedly told his victim during the assault that he was infected with the AIDS virus."[6] Although the suspect's lawyer said it was an "extraordinary invasion of Mr. Brown's most valued and important rights," the government prosecutors countered that Brown had given up his privacy rights, since he had "placed the issue of his infection with the AIDS virus in the public domain when he made that frightening statement" during the rape.[7] The judge overruled the defendant's privacy claim and came down on the side of the alleged victim: "There are some things which to me are so right, just so absolutely right and humane, . . . that it really just strikes me as absolutely appropriate to order that it be done."[8] Yet few things seem "absolutely right" and "absolutely appropriate" when it comes to privacy.

Unlike the accused rapist Brown, who may have forfeited his privacy rights, Dr. David Acer, a dentist, committed no crime. Acer, too, wanted his AIDS condition kept private, and it was kept private by the Florida health officials who regulate health workers. Yet his patient Kimberly Bergalis—who had never had sexual relations with anyone, had never used intravenous drugs, and had never had a blood transfusion (three facts quite germane to her case)—nonetheless became infected with the AIDS virus. And she had become infected, as it turned out, during dental treatments by Dr. Acer. Kimberly Bergalis died, but before she did she raised the issue of her right to know in a letter to Florida health officials— officials she blamed for knowing about the risk Dr. Acer posed and doing not "a damn thing about it."[9]

Bergalis' case is heartrending. But if her right to know were regarded as taking precedence over Dr. Acer's right to privacy, then wouldn't all patients have a similar right to see the private records of their doctors and "positive thinking." It was a transformational, permanent change, a change that came about because of the process outlined by the intervention of Marley and the order of Scrooge's three visitors.

You—and only you—have the power to determine the course of your future. Regardless of your past, regardless of where you may have been headed, you have the power to change; but to do so, you must act—often in ways that are unfamiliar, new and challenging.

**You must act, or do something differently,
to change your future.**

With your whole future before you, what will you change? What will you do differently? How will you use the information that you've learned to modify your destructive money scripts so you can achieve your life's dreams? We can find guidance by seeing what Scrooge does with his new wisdom.

Because of the visit from the Ghost of Christmas Past, Scrooge was able to access long dormant emotions that he had buried for years. Because Scrooge had looked honestly at his past, the Ghost of Christmas Present was able to show him reality. Scrooge was able to see what normal was and to begin modifying his destructive money scripts. He had good intentions to change after the visit of the Ghost of Christmas Present, but having good intentions wasn't enough. It took a visit from the Ghost of Christmas Future to get Scrooge to act on his good intentions.

There is great wisdom here. It applies to you as well as to Scrooge. Too often, people congratulate themselves in seeing the error of their ways. They have good intentions to change— later. But somewhere they interrupt the process, perhaps after visiting their past or viewing their present. As a result, they spend years in therapy or rationalize their old behaviors just a little longer.

> **Action is the antidote to despair.**
>
> —Joan Baez

Scrooge's New Behaviors

Upon awakening, Scrooge acts immediately to change his old behaviors. His new behaviors are a radical departure from the old Scrooge. Undoubtedly, they feel unfamiliar to Ebenezer. He seems as surprised by them as everyone else. Here are a few of Scrooge's new behaviors along with the modified money scripts that made the new behaviors possible:

- He sends a turkey to the Cratchit family for Christmas dinner.
  - Modified money script: "It's okay to spend money on others."
- He dresses in all his best. He goes out and walks the streets. He greets everyone he sees with a delighted smile.
  - Modified money script: "Happiness is not about having money."

- He meets the churchwardens who had previously asked for a donation to charity. Scrooge makes a generous contribution.
  - Modified money script: "Giving to the poor does not necessarily encourage laziness."
- He drops in on his nephew, Fred, for Christmas dinner.
  - Modified money script: "Some people want you for yourself, and not because you have money."
- The following day, he increases Bob Cratchit's pay.
  - Modified money script: "I have enough money."
- He provides financial assistance to Cratchit to help Tiny Tim.
  - Modified money script: "Money is a tool that can add meaning to my life and help others."
- He directs the surprised Crachit to add another shovelful of coal to the fire, a clear sign that Scrooge has changed his miserly ways.
  - Modified money script: "It's okay to spend money on myself and others."
- He becomes a second father to Tiny Tim.
  - Modified money script: "Relationships can give life meaning and are worth the investment of my time and money."

Henceforth, I ask not good fortune,
I myself am good fortune.

—Walt Whitman

Some Present-Day Christmas Carols

A traumatic childhood caused Scrooge to develop distorted beliefs about money. Those money scripts brought Scrooge significant pain, loneliness and isolation. By revisiting his past, Scrooge discovered that these beliefs were only partial truths. This knowledge gave Scrooge the opportunity to modify his beliefs and change his behavior. With new clarity and presence, he discovered who he really was and who he could become. He discovered—as we hope all readers of this book will discover—that money was not the real issue. It never was.

Remember, it's not about money.

A Christmas Carol, despite its genius, might be dismissed as just a fanciful story; yet we've witnessed many workshop participants and private clients who have had transformational experiences similar to Scrooge's.

• Christine and Don cut their spending by 30 percent after just three days of intensive work with their money scripts. Their managers and accountants had been unsuccessful in similar attempts for seven years. They changed one of their money scripts from "God will provide, so why worry?" to "God is already providing, and we are charged with the responsibility to be good stewards of what God provides us."

- James fulfilled a life-long dream of owning a home on the lake. His money script changed from "Only rich people can live where they want" to "My remodeling skills are an asset, and I can use them to fix up a home on the lake."

- Richard reduced his unsecured debt by $70,000 in less than twelve months. His money script changed from "I work hard, I should be able to do whatever I want" to "Spending more than I have is a form of cheating. I want to live in integrity, and this means living within my means."

- William, a husband and father of a young child, was finally able to create a will and get a life insurance policy after years of procrastination. His script changed from "I am too young and can't understand all of this" to "I am a college graduate, and if I want to, I can apply myself to this subject, too. This is part of being a responsible dad and partner to my wife."

- Donna realized that she had always wanted to be a teacher. Her script changed from "You were given a good education, now you must use it" to "It is okay to change your mind about what you want to do."

We were with Donna when she fearfully contacted her husband with whom she was in business and told him of her newly realized dream. Much to her surprise, he told her, "I knew there had been something wrong; you have seemed very unhappy working with me. I thought it was me. I am relieved that it is only that you want to do something different. How can I help?"

She began school two months later.

These people changed their financial lives and futures in different ways. However, all of them would agree on one thing: the most important change took place on an even bigger stage. The money, while significant, was secondary to the greater understanding they gained about themselves, who they really are, what they really want, and what excites them and gives them energy and enthusiasm for life.

We have included two more very special stories that perhaps will give you hope to begin your own journey. The first is from one of our clients, whose circumstances have been changed to protect his confidentiality. The last story belongs to one of this book's coauthors.

Angels Dancing

As I approached my thirty-first birthday, though parts of my life had never been better, in other ways it seemed as if my life might be in free fall. One of the most serious problems was that though I made what most people would consider a lot of money each year, at the rate I was spending it, I and my family would be destitute and broke within a few years if something didn't change. A group of caring friends helped me see the truth about my out-of-control financial behavior. The truth was, I was spending three times the amount each month that I could afford to be spending. As I look back, I realize that the overspending had seldom been self-indulgent, but it had been motivated by a desire to "help others." I agreed to get some help to address this issue.

This led to attending a workshop, led by the authors of this book, designed to help people address out-of-control money behaviors. My wife and I learned that in addition to the typical external factors of money behavior, such as income, spending plans, cost cutting and the like, there were also internal factors, such as our mostly unconscious feelings, dreams, beliefs and goals, that were just as important. One thing we realized was that I had been trying to make up for my childhood lack of family by trying to "buy" family. In this attempt to take care of others, I had, for years, ignored my own family and myself.

At one point in the workshop, one of the topics being discussed was ways to cut expenses, both personally and professionally. Since I began in show business, more than a decade ago, I have always performed with a wonderful and talented group of musicians. I have always thought of and treated them as "family." As I sat there that afternoon, I contemplated seriously, albeit very briefly, for the first time what it might be like to appear on stage with just one or two musicians. The thought frightened me terribly. I wasn't sure that I would ever be able to do that. Though I had been performing for years, all over the world, before millions of people, I had been told more than once that I had no talent and that whatever success I had been able to achieve had to do with luck and the people around me rather than any skills I might have. Though I wanted to believe they were wrong, I carried the secret fear that perhaps they were right.

As fate would have it, a few months later I was challenged by some producers of a TV special I was doing to perform without my usual entourage. From somewhere inside, a voice said "sure," sounding much more convincing than I felt. I chose to perform a song with a message that has been a theme for my life—wanting to love and to be loved. As I stood and approached the microphone, all the faces, voices and messages of those people over the years who had shared their doubts about my abilities suddenly came rushing toward me like a tidal wave.

I have never been one to duck a challenge, and I decided there was no time or place like the present to go toe-to-toe once and for all with this nemesis that had shadowed me all my life. I found it ironic that it just happened to be in one of the most visible public settings imaginable, with millions of people watching, rather than some small concert or club setting as I had ever so briefly envisioned just months before.

As I stood up to sing, instead of fear and doubt, I suddenly felt a sense of incredible peace come over me. I later described to others that it felt as if God's spirit somehow washed over me, moved through and blessed me. I don't believe that I ever sang any better. By the last note, everyone—the audience, my wife and family, and even the host of the show—was moved to tears. People who knew nothing of what a challenge my performing alone meant to me have since told me that even watching from thousands of miles away, they felt like they were witnessing a miracle. If they had only known! As has often happened in my life, I had done my job of showing up and God had used me in a very special way. Little did I know just how special.

Two of the people watching that TV show were a mom and her daughter. While I was singing the song, the little girl exclaimed to her mom, "Look mommy, I see angels dancing all around him." Though the mother was not able to see what her daughter was seeing, she was stunned by her daughter's comment.

Incredibly, a few weeks later this girl's mother learned that I was performing a concert near their hometown. She decided to get tickets and bring her daughter to the show. During the show, the little girl's mom sent a note to me and told me that her daughter said she had seen angels dancing all around me during the TV special. Knowing that I had felt God's blessing and energy bathe me during that performance and how powerful a moment it had been for me, I wanted to meet this special little girl and invited them to join me backstage after the show.

As the little girl sat beside me, she could hardly hold still. I said to her, "You seem scared and nervous," and she replied, "I am." There was a long moment of silence between us and then she began talking a mile a minute; it was like taking a finger out of a dike. At one point in the conversation she said, "You know, I saw angels all around you the day you sang on TV." I was awestruck. There was no doubt in her mind about what she saw, and there was no doubt in my mind that she was telling me her truth. Profoundly moved, I thanked her for telling me that and told her of my belief in God and angels and their power in our lives.

As they were leaving, the little girl's mom leaned over to me and whispered in my ear, "You know, my daughter is autistic. The words she spoke the day she saw you sing on TV were the first words I have ever heard her speak. Tonight is the second time. Her connection with you and your music is a miracle for us." I sat there stunned, speechless and in awe. We hugged as I choked back my tears, and as they left, I once again felt fully blessed.

How am I doing with the money issues? In the year following the workshop, my wife and I have been able to reduce our monthly expenditures by 51 percent. Because I've overcome my fear of performing alone, the profitability of my performances has increased by two to four times. My net income has doubled while I have cut my appearances by two-thirds. And while I am astounded at such amazing results in such a short period of time, I am far from finished. I have a long way to go.

I have learned that this is a process, not an event. Perhaps the bigger message here is that when we have the courage to do the work we need to do to get our lives in order, whatever the presenting issue, we make way for God to do His miracles through us, in ways we can never imagine. Money issues led me to seek help. The help I received was not really about money.

Here is another story, a real-life example of the power of the exercise we asked you to do at the end of chapter 5.

Twenty-Four Hours to Live
BY TED KLONTZ, PH.D.

First of all, you have learned a bit of my story already. I am the dad that Brad talked about in his story about "doing it differently" that he shared earlier in this book. I remember asking him a few years ago, when he was in his twenties, where he had gotten the idea that planning for retirement, investing while you were young and paying off all your debts as quickly as possible was a good strategy for living. His answer was "by watching you, Dad." For a moment I started to swell up a bit, as fathers are prone to do, beginning to feel proud of myself for the lessons I had taught my son, but then just as quickly became a little perplexed.

So I asked, "What do you mean? I never did any of those things." He replied, "I know, Dad, that's the point, I've watched you and the mistakes you have made and have decided I don't want to be in the place you are when I am your age." Touché, ouch, point well taken. I also was reminded of the old adage, "Don't ask, if you don't want to know."

It has been said that "our message" to the world has its roots in "our mess." For me, this is absolutely true. My relationship with money had always been one filled with a good bit of mystery and intrigue in the sense that in the realm of finances, I seldom knew what was going to happen until it happened. Throughout my life, I had always carried the belief that if I worked hard (perhaps harder than anyone else), if I had good intentions and was a good person, the money stuff would take care of itself. I had taken the law of Karma, twisted it a bit for my own purposes and organized my life that way. I figured that there was no real need to initiate financial planning for myself; the universe would provide. In terms of my relationship with money, I played the role of "reactor" rather than taking personal responsibility, stumbling from one situation to another without much of a sense of purpose or plan. After all, if God takes care of the sparrow, what was there to worry about?

I now jokingly call this "Ted's Perverted Law of Karma." Olivia Mellon calls it becoming a money "monk." You know, don't worry about the worldly stuff like money and focus on the "important stuff." A supporting factor was that I worked for a governmental system that reinforced my doing nothing. "Do your job, stay out of trouble and we will take care of you for life." And I practiced a religion that reenforced not worrying about something as insignificant as money.

Though I had nearly twenty years of therapy under my belt and had seen my relationship with my children, wife, friends and myself heal, grow, flower and mature in ways that I could never have imagined, I just couldn't seem to wrap my head around how this money thing worked and so just tried not to worry about it.

My Marley first intervened one day when an eighty-two-year-old wise woman asked me if my wife and I were taking care of ourselves financially. She had just been the beneficiary of a gift of a workshop that we had given her and several other ladies who had recently lost their husbands. I casually said, "Sure we are, at least we are doing the best we know how. I figure if we do the right things for the right reasons, everything will be okay." She pondered that answer for a moment and said, "For your children's sake, I hope you are right." What she was saying, I now understand, is that if we weren't taking care of ourselves, the burden might very well fall to our children to take care of us in our later years. At the moment, however, I was stunned by her comment. I had never thought of that.

She followed that left jab of a comment with an uppercut that nearly floored me. She said, "I know what your problem is. You don't believe that you deserve more than what you need at any given moment." It was one of those moments where you know that someone has told one of your absolute truths before even you are aware of it. I stood speechless before her. As if to finish me off, as I was going down for the count, she had one final comment. She said, "I have more than I need, and I feel comfortable with that. I am comfortable knowing that no matter what happens to me, my children will not have the financial burden of caring for me. You and your wife are very generous people, but because you have limited means, you may be able to help fifteen to twenty people a year. Because I have more than I need, I get to help thousands each year and upon my death those thousands will continue to have the opportunity to be supported through the foundations that I have endowed." Talk about a clarifying moment! I wasn't sure what to do with this information, but I knew it was important.

Shortly after that, a gentleman approached my wife and me and essentially said, "I have been watching you over the last decade and you work hard. You are generous and giving to a fault and I want to make your life complete. My wife and I want to endow your retirement right now, so you can live the rest of your lives exactly the way you want to."

Ah, that law of Karma, I thought. *It really works.* Though we were initially suspicious, over the next few months, after many conversations with him, his therapist, his CPA and his financial advisors, we grew to understand that he really wanted to do this and that he could afford to do this. Who were we to disallow this good thing to come into our lives? After all, isn't this the way I thought, and actually told other people, it would work? Isn't this the law of Karma in action?

On Thanksgiving afternoon, three days before the check was to be written, my wife and I received a phone call from the gentleman simply saying, "My wife and I have changed our minds. We are sorry, but we don't want to do this." I hung up the phone in shock. My wife asked, "Who was that?" I said, "It was Fred, The trip to New York is off, and he doesn't want to do it."

My wife began gently weeping on the couch in our living room, and I said out loud to no one in particular, "I don't know what I mean or how to fix it, but there is something really, really wrong with my thinking around money and how it works that keeps getting me into situations like this."

What I meant was I had always been at the mercy of someone else's behavior in terms of what happened with my financial life. For the first time, that day I realized there might be something basically wrong with my belief system regarding how money works. I now call that "poor" thinking; in other words, thinking small and being unaware of the multitude of possibilities or opportunities. I had hit my financial bottom. I had learned enough from other elements of my recovery process to know that in every painful situation, each party brings about 50 percent of the responsibility to the event, and I was determined to find out what my part of the equation was.

I eventually discovered that one of my most basic and influential money scripts came from growing up on my grandfather's farm, working for him. One day, when I was about ten, I had finally mustered up the courage to ask him if he would be willing to pay me a dollar a day to help bale, pick up and store the hay we were putting up. At the time, he had hired other boys my age, many of them friends of mine, and was paying them a dollar an hour to do the same work I was doing. I knew he would never pay me a dollar an hour, but I thought maybe a dollar a day would work. I will never forget the words he spoke. They became the guiding principle of my life for the next thirty years.

"I will decide whether or not I think you are worth anything, and if I do, I will pay you," he replied. "Furthermore, you should feel lucky that you have something to eat, a place to sleep and clothes to wear."

End of conversation. I never got a cent. Every job I worked at for the next thirty-five years was one where other people decided what I was worth and paid me that. Those jobs were union-type jobs where you were paid by years of service, not whether or not you did a good job or a bad one, put in extra effort or not. My monetary value was decided by others saying essentially the same things my grandfather had: "We'll decide what you are worth; you should feel lucky to have a job afford a place to live and clothes to wear."

Following the pattern that had worked in other parts of my recovery, I began reading all that I could about the psychology of money, talked to everyone that I could about the subject, began seeking therapeutic support and contacted our CPA. I told him that we were determined to take control of our own financial future and that we wanted to beginning preparing for retirement. We came up with a pretty simple plan. We were to send him a check each month, and we could reach our goal in a reasonable amount of time.

Unfortunately, my journey with money was not going to be that simple. Though I had the money, I could not bring myself to actually send him the check. He would call and badger, cajole, plead and beg me to send him the money. I would write the check out, address the envelope and put it on my desk. I just couldn't send it. I had lots of excuses, but the fact was I just couldn't do it, and I didn't really understand why. My journey to understanding was to take two more years of this seemingly illogical behavior.

In what I have come to understand as God's timing, one day I received a note from an acquaintance that I had not heard from in twelve years. He is a financial planner and in recovery. He told me about his work with people around their money issues and wanted me to let him know if I knew of anyone who might be interested in what he was doing. Did I know of someone? It was me! In talking with him about the quest I was on and the problems I had in taking care of myself, even though I knew what to do, he very quickly helped me get to the core of my dilemma. Along with Brad, we ended up writing this book and creating coaching and workshop services designed to help others discover what we have learned.

Rick first asked me to envision what retirement would look like to me. My mind went blank. I really had no immediate picture come to mind, but gradually one began to emerge of me sitting looking out the window in a nice warm place doing nothing. I realized that what retirement meant to me was, "I quit." That vision was quickly followed by the thought; "I don't want to quit." Suddenly it was perfectly clear to me why I wasn't able to send in the retirement checks. If quitting was what retirement represented, I didn't want to do it. By not sending the checks in I was guaranteeing that I never would be able to quit. I would be one of those people who, in their sixties, would be complaining about not being able to quit working, as if someone else had made that happen.

This was followed by a growing awareness that maybe I could make my retirement mean anything I wanted it to. The picture of how my retirement could look then began to emerge, and in it I was imagining what it would be and feel like to do only what I wanted to do, when I wanted to do it, with the people that I wanted to do it with. I really liked that picture. Then I had the thought, "Why wait until then to begin living and working that way?"

The second set of exercises involved discovering what my deepest loves and needs were. One part of the process was to imagine that I had only twenty-four hours to live. Instead of figuring out how I would spend my last day, I was to consider what I would regret never having accomplished. I felt good about the fact that, because of my recovery, I could not think of very many regrets. But that very simple exercise motivated me to begin immediately taking care of those few regrets that I did have. These issues were really about making sure that the three most important people in my life, my wife and two children, knew unequivocally how much I love them, how thankful I am that they are a part of my life and how grateful I am for the healing our family has enjoyed.

As a result of that work, I began sending checks in for my retirement at four times the rate that I had suggested I was capable of doing. In addition, I immediately began sorting out the things about my work that I could let go of, so that I could begin living my vision of what retirement is, years before I actually retire.

I was born with hemophilia, a rare bleeding disorder that has resulted in my receiving the equivalent of as many as a half-million blood transfusions. A consequence of that was contracting Hepatitis C, which went undiagnosed and untreated for fifteen years. In the late 1980s I began a series of chemotherapy treatments to try to manage the virus. Last April during my annual health check up at the Mayo clinic, my doctor said, "We will need to start monitoring your health much more closely because it seems your liver disease has progressed to stage IV, the last stage before liver failure. We don't believe you have liver cancer yet, but we need to keep a close watch." He said a few other things that I didn't quite catch. We said our good-byes and I left the office.

I was stunned by the news. I had never felt better in my life. In one brief moment it seemed that everything had changed. I thought about my plans for retirement, wondering if I would live to see that day. I called my wife and told her the news. As I was talking to her, I suddenly remembered the no longer hypothetical twenty-four-hours-to-live exercise I had done several years earlier in my quest to understand my relationship with money. I heard myself saying, "Remember that exercise, the one that asked you to consider what regrets you might have if you had only twenty-four hours to live? Well, I can't think of any regrets I have. All of the people that I love know I love them. I know that they love and honor me. There is no unfinished business with any of them. I can't tell you how grateful I feel." As ironic as it may sound, tears of joy began to run down my cheeks. Who would have thought that my journey to understanding my irrational money behaviors would pay off with such dividends?

At this moment I am doing well. I am grateful to have found a way to make peace with myself and my family. Exploring and attempting to understand my relationship with money has given me a serenity that money cannot buy. I believe that until we know and truly understand that we, in our humanness, are in fact enough, that there will never be enough—not enough fame, money, fortune, things, etc. I am grateful for the healing that tells me that I am enough.

What Will Be the Ending of Your Christmas Carol?

In previous chapters, you were given the opportunity to identify your money scripts. By now, you may know what past events triggered those money scripts. You may have taken a journey into your past and begun to heal old emotional wounds. You may have new clarity and be viewing the world differently. Thinking about the future consequences of your old behaviors may have motivated you to change. Whether you have completed these stages of transformation or are still somewhere on the path, you are ready to begin formulating a plan of action.

Before we go there, we would love to hear from you if you have had your own Scrooge-like experience in resolving and making peace with your relationship with money. Contact us at *www.wisdomofscrooge.com*.

You Need a Plan

Just acting on your newfound insights isn't enough. You must have a plan, and part of your plan needs to be clear goals that support your core values and aspirations.

We know that destructive money behaviors are not about the money, but that doesn't mean that money isn't important. Scrooge always knew that money was important. His problem was that he saw money as an end itself, not as a resource.

After his transformation, Scrooge realized he could use his money to achieve a goal that was suddenly very important to him: helping others. His actions matched his goal:

- He bought a turkey for the Cratchits' Christmas dinner.
- He made a generous contribution to the churchwardens.
- He increased Bob Cratchit's pay.
- He provided financial assistance to Cratchit to help Tiny Tim.

Bringing healing, joy and ease into the lives of others is a goal that many people use money to achieve. Other goals that money can help us achieve include the following:

- Educating ourselves and our children
- Protecting ourselves and our loved ones against a premature death, disability or sickness
- Providing for our support and independence in our later years
- Creating nurturing environments in which to live, work and play
- Housing, feeding and healing our physical bodies

Money is a resource, just as time, energy, faith, friends, relationships and health are resources.

What are your dreams and desires? The following exercises will help you uncover your life aspirations and authentic lifetime goals, as well as identify the tasks you need to achieve them.

Exercise 7

IDENTIFYING YOUR LIFE ASPIRATIONS

1. Pretend you have a fairy godmother who can give you all the money, time and talent that you want. What have you always dreamed of doing or becoming—physically, mentally, emotionally and spiritually? Write down whatever comes to mind or has ever come to mind. Dream big, be outrageous; reality is not important in this exercise. You have complete freedom. What you put down can be complete fantasy and can have nothing to do with the reality of your current situation. The more daring, the better.

   The list may include items like building a new home on the beach, swimming with the stingrays, writing a best-selling book, going to the moon, becoming a world-class skater, directing a movie, singing with Garth Brooks, becoming President of the United States, living in Europe or raising award-winning roses.

2. Life aspirations can be described as broad, important dreams that you hope to achieve over your lifetime. Most of us have several of them. Look at each item in the preceding step and ask yourself, "Why do I want to do this? What desire will it satisfy?" When you figure out the underlying reason for each item on your

list, write that underlying reason down on a separate piece of paper that we'll call your life aspirations worksheet. Start each one with the words, "to be . . . ." For example, if you want to take your kids to Sea World, this may satisfy your desire to be a good parent, so you would write, "to be a good parent." You may want to travel to remote places or to the moon, so you might write down "to be an adventurer."

3. After a long and full life, you have passed away. Your funeral or memorial service is today. Imagine all your family members, friends and coworkers at that memorial service. Each of them has prepared an acknowledgment of you, describing all you did or became in your life. They are about to read what they have written. You will be taking notes on what they say.

    One by one, the most important people in your life take the podium and speak about you. What do you hope each would say about you and your life, what you did, and what you became? Be specific and write several paragraphs that summarize what you would want them to say.

4. Boil down what the people at your gathering said about you to brief phrases describing your characteristics. Again, on your life aspirations worksheet, write these phrases beginning with "to be. . . ." For example, if someone said, "She was always so

supportive of her coworkers," you might write, "to be a mentor." Some of these phrases may already exist from the previous exercise, so you don't need to write them down again.

5. Now go to your life aspirations worksheet and look at all your "to be" statements. Which ones really reflect your intentions in life? Leave every statement that is true, whether you feel you have accomplished it or not. Cross out any that don't resonate with you. Add any additional ones that come to mind. You should now have a complete list of your life aspirations. You may feel free to modify this list as often as you need. In fact, we recommend that you do this exercise annually. Although it may change over time, this list will become the foundation or the touchstone of every goal you set out to achieve.

It is not uncommon to struggle a bit with this exercise your first time through. You may be like Laura, who uncovered lifetime goals of becoming a missionary and going into nursing, but initially had trouble finding the common life aspiration "to be a healer." Don't worry. It takes time to reduce lifetime desires, goals and intentions down to a simple, but broad, life aspiration.

Doing this exercise will help you become more conscious of your life purposes and what you are doing to achieve them. Once you have a set of conscious life aspirations, you can use them to generate and test your goals. Goals are specific objectives that will help accomplish or fulfill at least one life aspiration. Some goals will satisfy several life aspirations.

For example, some of coauthor Rick's life aspirations are to be authentic, to be wise, to be a student, to be a seeker, to be a healer and to be a teacher. These aspirations are supported by many goals he has had, including obtaining his master's degree in personal financial planning, cocreating the Financial Integration Workshop and writing this book.

Now you are ready to begin to develop your authentic goals, followed by the tasks that will be necessary to move you toward realizing your life aspirations.

Exercise 8

DEVELOPING YOUR AUTHENTIC GOALS

1. Label a piece of paper your "authentic goals worksheet." Now, review your life aspirations worksheet. On your authentic goals worksheet, we want you to list some actions or things you might want to do, be or have that would move you closer to fulfilling your life aspirations. Don't worry about how much these things may cost or how much time they might take to get. Let the items come spontaneously from within you. Quickly write down whatever comes up, no matter how silly or frivolous it sounds. Again,

this is no time to censor yourself. Try to list twenty to thirty specific goals. Here is a sample list:

- Learn to fly an airplane
- Take the kids on a vacation
- Buy a new house
- Remodel the kitchen
- Start a new business
- Buy a new car
- Learn to rock climb
- Buy a laptop computer
- Write a novel
- Take a class in marketing
- Buy a vacation home
- Join a quilting club
- Volunteer at the hospital
- Visit the grandkids more often
- Go dancing

2. Look at the goals on your authentic goals worksheet. Do these goals fill you with enthusiasm? Or do some of them leave you with heaviness or dullness? Cross off the goals that don't excite you, that feel heavy. That doesn't necessarily mean these are things you won't do. But these may be tasks, not goals, such as getting rid of credit card debt, making a will, fixing the roof, getting health insurance, etc. Notice how different tasks feel from authentic or heartfelt goals. One key for determining whether

you have a task or a goal before you is to ask yourself: "Will I feel relieved when it is done?" If the answer is yes, chances are the item is a task.

3. Now, pick the goal that excites you the most, put the number one beside it and circle the number. Look at your list again, pick the next goal that energizes you, put the number two beside it and circle the number. Continue until you have prioritized all of your goals. Now, go back and assign a dollar cost to each goal, if any.

4. Now you are going to look at your prioritized goals on your authentic goals worksheet and test them for their authenticity and attainability. Select the goal that you marked as number one. Check it with the acronym TEST:

   - Is it **True**? Make sure the goal fulfills at least one life aspiration on your worksheet. Then, on a scale of 1 (low) to 10 (high), rate how much you want to see the action item completed in an attainable amount of time. If it is a seven or less, cross it off the list.

   - Is it **Exact**, explicit, precise? Being vague about what you want keeps you in a cycle of financial unconsciousness. You will accomplish this goal or you won't. Leave no escape routes; nail down your goal. Make sure your goal is not another life aspiration. Those are broad rather than exact. Authentic goals are exact and specific.

- Is it **Sensible**? A goal needs to be a stretch, but not impossible. Make the goal worth the challenge, but something that is attainable. If this goal will require money, you will want to work out a financial plan to assure that achieving it is possible.

- Is it **Time-based**? Pick a specific date by which you will obtain or start this action item: the next few months, year, five years or ten years.

- Now select the goal that you numbered as your second priority and go through this same process until all of your goals have been TEST-ed.

5. The next step is to look at all your goals that have been successfully TEST-ed and assign any tasks that will help you reach them. Write each of the surviving goals at the top of a separate sheet of paper. On each goal sheet, make a list of tasks to support the goal. Include the date by which you will complete each of them. You may want to put these in a folder or binder so you can conveniently refer back to them. It may be helpful to put them in order of priority.

For example, you may have a life aspiration to be a traveler. Supporting that life aspiration, you may have a goal to take a Baltic cruise by August 1 of next year. Now you need a list of tasks that will move you toward that goal. You will need to select a cruise line, pick an itinerary, determine how much you will spend on the trip, create a plan to accumulate the money, get a passport, employ someone to feed the dog, ask your employer for the time off, and so on. Now you will have an action plan to reach the goal.

6. This is for couples. Once you have each listed and prioritized your individual TEST goals, take your top five goals and compare them with your partner's top five goals. Are some of them the same? Are some of them different? The assignment now is for both of you to combine your top five goals into "our goals." While you may have some similar goals, you may not have them in the same priority. Work on combining similar goals and then on prioritizing all of your similar and individual goals.

This doesn't mean all of your individual goals need to be combined with your spouse's individual goals. It is important, however, to be able to work together toward mutual goals and also to support one another's individual goals. This may require some compromise and creativity.

For example, you may have a goal of retiring in London to support a life aspiration of living abroad. Your spouse may have a goal of retiring in Omaha, close to the grandchildren, to support a life aspiration of being closely involved with family members. Additionally, you may both have as part of your goals the desire to buy a $300,000 retirement home. The problem may be that it is not realistic to buy two retirement homes, especially if you want to maintain the resources to travel between the two locations. How will you resolve this issue? Sometimes these resolutions come easily. Other times many difficult emotions may arise, sending you back to uncovering new money scripts and applying our exercises to reach clarity. Sometimes it requires the assistance of a counselor and financial planner to fully resolve the issues.

The preceding exercises are used with permission from *Conscious Finance: Uncover Your Hidden Money Beliefs and Transform the Role of Money in Your Life*, by Rick Kahler, CFP® and Kathleen Fox (Foxcraft, 2005).

Used wisely, money can help us achieve many worthwhile goals. Money is also a resource to help handle difficult situations that might arise. Without planning, such situations could become financial disasters, resulting in stress, bankruptcies, relationship problems or even divorce. Living within your income, using your money for what is important to you, and saving for known and unknown needs is the key to a happier, more fulfilling, less stressful life.

"Annual income twenty pounds,
annual expenditure nineteen six, result
happiness. Annual income twenty pounds,
annual expenditure twenty pound
ought and six, result misery."

—*Charles Dickens,* David Copperfield

Finding Your Own Ghosts to Facilitate Your Transformation

We've said it before and Scrooge modeled it: part of your plan is asking for and getting the help you need to facilitate your transformation. Finding facilitators who have experienced their own transformation and who model authenticity, abundance and integrity may be essential to your success.

In *A Christmas Carol,* everyone lives happily ever after. In real life, we cannot realistically live "upon the total abstinence principle," as did the transformed Scrooge:

> *He had no further intercourse with spirits, but lived upon the total abstinence principle, ever afterwards; and it was always said of him that he knew how to keep Christmas well, if any man alive possessed the knowledge."*

Dickens invokes a popular phrase whereby teetotalers abstained from all alcoholic spirits, implying that Scrooge needed no further assistance from the spirits.

While he may not have needed further intervention from the ghosts, Scrooge was a savvy businessman. We can assume that he knew the importance of having a support team. Otherwise, the old Scrooge would never have formed a business partnership with Jacob Marley.

Similarly, you don't have to do it alone. It's true that only you can be the general contractor of your financial affairs, but you don't have to build your financial house alone. A variety of resources and professionals are available to assist you.

Asking for help is a new concept for many of us. It certainly was for Scrooge with his "trust no one" script. Also, it's hard to talk about money because money scripts—such as, "I should know about money" or "I can't know about money because I'm not good at math"—hinder discussion.

Curiously, we don't have the same script when it comes to performing a major operation. We recognize that an expert surgeon who has done a procedure many times could do a far better job than we could do. It's the same with money. Don't let your fear that advice might be too expensive or that your assets aren't big enough to interest an advisor stop you.

One advisor you should consider is a financial planner. Here is a list of questions taken from *Conscious Finance* that you may want to ask a financial planner. This is not meant to be an all-inclusive list, just a place to start.

1. What are the characteristics of your typical client?
2. What is your education?

3. What is the process you use? How long does it take? What should I expect?

4. What is your own relationship with money? What are your primary money scripts?

5. What are the terms of your engagement agreement?

6. Can you give me the names of three clients I can call as references?

7. How will you deliver information?

8. Will you describe what you consider a fully diversified portfolio?

9. Will I be a customer or a client?

10. How do you charge for your services?

Some financial planners are commission-only, which means they do not charge fees to clients but earn their money solely through commissions on products they sell. Others are fee-based, which means they operate on a combination of commissions and fees. Others are fee-only, meaning they sell no products for commission but charge clients directly for the services they provide.

Our bias is toward fee-only advisors who also have the Certified Financial Planner™ (CFP®) designation. There are three reasons for this. First, a CFP® has the basic education needed to practice financial planning. Also, be aware that not all CFPs® are engaged in the practice of financial planning. You want a CFP® who is a practicing financial planner.

The second is that commission-only planners, no matter

how pure their intentions, require you to buy something from them to be compensated for their time. Commission-only planners are essentially salespeople. Many of them can only sell products from just a limited number of companies, when what might be best for you is a product found in a company that they cannot or do not represent.

For example, a General Motors car dealer cannot sell you a Toyota, even if a Toyota would be in your best interest. No matter how honorable a commission-only planner might be, they are paid only when they sell a product. That fact cannot help but influence their judgment. It's a bit like asking for advice from a doctor who isn't going to be paid unless you have surgery.

The third reason we prefer fee-only financial planners is that very few commission-only planners will be doing extensive financial planning, such as working on your money relationships, cash flow, life aspirations or legacy planning. The reason is that commission-only planners aren't compensated for that work.

At some point, you may believe that you or a loved one could benefit from the assistance of a counselor trained in financial therapy. Unfortunately, we find that most counselors lack specific training in this area, and in fact, many have not explored their own unresolved issues and self-destructive behaviors around money.

We recognize that for a variety of reasons, you might not be able to work directly with a well-trained financial counselor. As such, here are some questions you can use to interview prospective therapists near you:

1. What are the characteristics of your typical client?
2. What is your education?
3. What are the therapeutic processes you use? What might a typical session look like?
4. Have you been through your own counseling? Why or why not?
5. Have you ever explored your own issues around money? What is your relationship with money like? What are your primary money scripts or beliefs about money?
6. Do you have a therapist-patient service agreement and treatment plan?
7. How do you charge for your services?
8. How will I/you determine when I am finished with this phase of my personal growth?

If you're already working with a CFP®, ask him or her to recommend a counselor. Our experience is that it is incredibly helpful, if not critical, for the counselor and financial planner to be on the same page when it comes to applying the five principles of financial prosperity.

At *www.wisdomofscrooge.com*, you'll find a free assessment to evaluate your level of financial well-being and other useful tools and resources to help you on your journey.

Whatever questions you ask, do your research and trust

your feelings. It is important that you feel comfortable, safe and respected. If you feel uncomfortable after a few sessions, it could be that you and the therapist are simply not a good fit. Ask him/her for a recommendation. It is not unusual to try out several counselors before you find a good match.

Today, many CFPs® and psychotherapists are exploring their own relationships with money and are receiving formal training in this area. Still, it may be many years before it becomes standard practice for financial planners and counselors to have both money knowledge and counseling skills. Until then, a collaborative approach is most likely the best option for most clients.

> **A certified financial planner and counselor**
> **working together are exponentially more capable**
> **of facilitating a transformational experience**
> **around your relationship with money**
> **than either one is individually.**

This is not just a theory. We routinely do this type of facilitation and have done so for a number of years. We have seen the life-changing outcomes that surpass anything that either the counselor or financial planner could have achieved independently.

In our work with clients, when finances are being discussed, we observe quietly to make sure the client "gets it." If we see any nonverbal signs of confusion, fear or resistance, we give clients the opportunity to work through any obstacles that might be keeping them stuck in painful patterns.

One well-known international business management firm that we consult with is so sold on this approach that their clients who are having trouble modifying destructive financial behaviors must go through this process or the firm will no longer work with them.

Living happily ever after doesn't just happen. It requires maintenance, planning and the support of a professional team. For some, this book may provide all the support you need. For others, you'll need to build a professional supporting staff to assist you in reaching your life aspirations.

Money as a Tool

After traveling from one extreme to the other with Scrooge, we finally learn the truth about money: it's a tool to help us achieve authenticity and our most important life aspirations. Like any tool, it's important to learn how to use it wisely.

> Men have become the tools of their tools.
>
> —*Henry David Thoreau*

To the Future

And so we have reached the end of the journey with Scrooge. His was a difficult journey, and one he was hesitant to embark on. He was living life exactly as he thought he should, blind to the destructiveness of his behavior, content in his misery. At first terrified to even look at his past, he learned to embrace the lessons the spirits had for him and became a new man.

Scrooge was transformed. There is no doubt whatever about that.

A similar transformation is possible for you, and perhaps has already begun.

In the words of Tiny Tim,

"God bless us all, every one."